ITALIAN AMERICANS
IN THE '80s
A SOCIODEMOGRAPHIC
PROFILE

ITALIAN AMERICANS
IN THE '80s
A SOCIODEMOGRAPHIC
PROFILE

Edited by
Graziano Battistella

1989
Center for Migration Studies
New York

**Italian Americans in the '80s
A Sociodemographic Profile**

First Edition
Copyright 1989 by
The Center for Migration Studies
All rights reserved. No part of this book may be reproduced
without permission from the publisher.

CENTER FOR MIGRATION STUDIES
209 Flagg Place, Staten Island, New York 10304-1199

Library of Congress Cataloging-in-Publication Data

Italian Americans in the '80s:
a sociodemographic profile

edited by Graziano Battistella

p. xii - 207 cm. 27.5 x 21.5

ISBN - 0934733-41-4

1. Italian Americans -- Social conditions.

I. Battistella, Graziano

E184.I8I74 1989   305.8'51'073--dc19   88-29932

TABLE OF CONTENTS

FOREWORD

The Italian ethnic group, whose immigration to the United began over one hundred years ago, is now considered to be in the final phase of the immigration process. The era of massive arrivals to this side of the Atlantic Ocean, with each new wave of immigration subverting the societal equilibrium reached by the previous one has now become memories. Also behind Italian Americans, are the struggles of the early generations fighting for their opportunities behind the "golden door". Even though their struggle for recognition is not entirely over, Italian Americans now feel they belong to the mainstream.

The final phase of Italian immigration has been posing some questions to scholars and sociologists: how is ethnic identity being maintained among Italian Americans? Are Italian Americans simply blending into the mainstream, or is a new identity emerging, compatible with advanced integration into American society? Richard Alba's volume, "Twilight of Ethnicity", has initiated debate and even been considered as being a premature death sentence of ethnic Italian distinctiveness. The recent approach of Lieberson and Waters is more balanced; analyzing ethnic groups emerging from the 1980 census, the authors concluded that the most evident dissimilarities lie between Europeans and recent immigrants, such as Hispanics and Asians and that differences still exist among Europeans, but in certain aspects only. Economic achievements of European ancestry groups are not significantly different. However, immigrants from Southern and Eastern Europe show a higher level of endogamy and remain longer in geographical locations established by their early ancestors. Nevertheless, as people move toward the fourth generation, they tend to join a group simply called "unhyphenated whites". Only a portion of Italians have reached the fourth generation. Will they follow the same pattern?

The primary objective of this study is not to address the theory of ethnicity, but to present a set of unpublished data on Italian Americans which was prepared by the United States Bureau of the Census, specifically for the Center for Migration Studies. A collection of twelve data sets were compiled, each set comprises 248 tables regarding the entire nation and the following eleven states which have high concentrations of Italian Americans: California, Connecticut, Florida, Illinois, Massachusetts, Michigan, New Jersey, New York, Ohio, Pennsylvania and Rhode Island. The tables—the design of which was derived from a previous project of the Census Bureau in an effort to contain processing costs—will basically follow the model laid out in official Bureau of the Census publications. Each set of data displays eight tables of demographic, cultural and economic characteristics. The eight-set tables are crossed with such variables as type of household, place of birth, age, language, education, labor force, occupation, earnings and citizenship. In addition, the same characteristics are tabulated by educational achievements and age for the whole population, single ancestry, multiple ancestry and the population born in Italy.

The vast amount of tabulated data released by the Census, compared to the microdata files used by other researchers, have the shortcomings of all aggregated data. Possibilities for additional analysis are limited; in particular, data on intermarriage are missing. However, the data allow the advantage of being derived from the master file of the United States Census Bureau and thus, allow comparability with previous publications of the Census Bureau. Data also permit, and to the best of our knowledged, for the first time to such an extent, a detailed comparison between the single and multiple ancestry portions of an ethnic group. However, some cautiousness should be exercised in such a comparison. The 1980 data reveal that Italians of multiple ancestry are a young group, still in the early stages of formation. Many social indicators will reflect the influence of age more than the influence of mixed ethnicity.

With so much to examine and relatively limited time available, a decision was reached to provide the scientific community with a collection of data on Italian Americans intended to serve as a practical point of reference. For this reason a series of appendices accompany the text that are intended to provide a cursory overview of the data. For further analysis, the original tabulations provided by the Census are available at the Center for Migration Studies library.

The second part of this volume is comprised of six appendices:

Appendix A comprises data concerning immigration from Italy to the U.S. and derived from the Statistical Yearbook of the Immigration and Naturalization Service.

Appendix B collates tables concerning population born in six European countries and derived from data on the foreign born population released by the Bureau of the Census in microfiche format. The reason this particular source was utilized was due to the fact that it created the opportunity to compare Italian born with other foreign born persons. The choice of the five European groups to which Italians are compared was dictated to maintain parallelism with the major ancestry groups that the Census Bureau had selected in its publications when presenting data on population of single ancestry.

Appendix C summarizes data on major European-origin groups of single ancestry that the Census Bureau has previously presented. However, since these data were already published, we thought it useful to offer only percentage values only in Appendix C.

Appendices D, E and F are derived from unpublished special tabulations compiled by the Bureau of the Census on Italian Americans: Appendix D compares Italian Americans by type of ancestry and place of birth; persons born in the United States are subdivided into single and multiple ancestry. This subdivision was not maintained for persons born in Italy or born abroad because the multiple ancestry group would have been too small; Appendix E displays the characteristics of Italian Americans in eleven selected states and; Appendix F is an aggregation of data by education and sex for the total Italian American population, also the single and multiple ancestry groups born in the United States and persons born in Italy. In this Appendix, Tables Nine to Sixteen, concerning single ancestry Italian Americans, regardless of the place of birth, reports on the same group of tables contained in Appendix C; therefore, these tables are totally comparable.

Throughout this volume, where reference is made to tables not contained within the text, it refers to a table found in one of the appendices. Also, all graphs are derived from the tables located in the appendices.

A special note of thanks goes to the staff at the Center for Migration

Studies who offered considerable assistance throughout the project and also to the Agnelli Foundation for their generous grant, without which this volume would not have been possible.

Graziano Battistella
Center for Migration Studies

INTRODUCTION

Four years ago, the Giovanni Agnelli Foundation, in cooperation with the Center for Migration Studies, published the first Directory of Italian American Organizations. In 1988, a new edition of this text was published with the assistance of the National Italian American Foundation, and lists more than 1500 organizations whose common goal is the preservation of Italian culture and civilization and the Italian American heritage.

One significant result of these studies was that approximately half of the existing institutions were established after 1970, indicating Italian American awareness of and sensitivity toward the new ethnic consciousness.

These associations, however, are only the visible representations of a vast group comprised of children, grandchildren and great grandchildren of those Italians who, from the second half of the nineteenth century undertook the initial immigration. True, another wave of Italians has arrived in the United States more recently. However, this group is still far smaller in number than those early migrations. Indeed, the flow of Italians towards America may have abated somewhat, but has never altogether ceased.

Today, the people of Italy emigrate more from choice than from economic necessity or desperation. In fact, over this past century, Italy has advanced considerably in economy and technology, boasting a high standard of living and a phenomenon of net immigration as opposed to net emigration.

Yet, it is important to note, that as Italy was becoming the fifth most industrialized country in the world, the emigrants and their children were involved in what Braudel has termed 'the renewal of the human substance', in the Americas. Not only in the United States, but in Brazil, Argentina, Uruguay and Venezuela, Italian emigrants were becoming the agents for multinational social change and renewal. These migrants brought with them a host of qualifications, but the mainstay of their luggage was, invariably, a system of values where the work ethic was central and perceived as the principal means of social advance.

The past century has witnessed their full assimilitation into American society, with all of its consequences: both positive and negative. So, while a distinct level of well-being, higher education, greater political infuence, and scientific and cultural excellence have attended the assimilation process, so has a marked loss of the Italian language and the fixed existence of certain stereotypes of the Italian American, and Italy in general.

Responsibility for the loss of the Italian language in the United States rests solely with the Italian Government, which has failed to offer the educational structures in the United States which would have permitted the preservation and the teaching of Italian.

As for the persistence of stereotypes, certain clarifications must be made.

Italians in Italy can only applaud and take pleasure in the American success. This is, no doubt at least to some extent, a result of the well-known success stories of Mario Cuomo, Antonin Scalia, Rudolph Giuliani, Lee Iacocca and Robert Gallo, only a few among a lengthy list also including numerous directors and actors. Fascinating though they may be, success stories are rarely indicative of the norm: they are, by definition, exceptional, as real success in any circumstance and country is exceptional.

There is, therefore, a need to describe Italian experiences in America more fully, using scientific means, for only by using the tools of social research is it possible to embrace the entire reality of a group numbering, in the United States alone, more than twelve million; spread over four generations and multiple social groups; and scattered over the whole of the American continents. Historical, economic, sociological, demographic and anthropological surveys are indispensable for this clarification and to see beyond the success stories of the exceptional personalities to the history and the contemporary enigma of those twelve million Americans of Italian origin.

The Giovanni Agnelli Foundation has deployed various of these analytical tools to delineate the social, economic and cultural realities of Italy and to redress the stereotypes and preconceptions which so often cloud relations between countries and societies.

This need for clarification is also present in the relations between Americans of Italian origin and Italians. The former often have notions of Italy filtered through family experiences and recollections. These concepts are nearly always linked to a poor, agricultural and culturally backward Italy. Coupled with these memories is the superficial news coverage by the international press, which largely presents the pathological aspects of Italian life: government crises; the mafia; and natural disasters. However, with these aspects of Italian life exists also the richness of the cultural life, the economic wealth, the high living standards, and the achievements in social organization.

Even the positive stereotypes – excellence in the arts, cuisine, fashion, although true, are not enough. One must look behind the shadow of the stereotypes to discover the vitality of a population whose collective action has permitted these achievements of excellence.

To achieve these goals the Giovanni Agnelli Foundation has already taken various steps. The travelling exhibition "Italy. A Country Shaped by Man" is the most comprehensive and spectacular example. The Foundation has continued this program and is presently preparing a series of historical texts on modern Italian society to be published in English. The Foundation has also provided for the placing of Italian books and scholarly journals in university and public libraries. The donation of the videodisc encyclopedia "de Italia" (which comprises over 20,000 annotated images and 15,000 texts in English) to over 100 universities, museums and libraries is also a means to the same end.

Ten years ago, the Giovanni Agnelli Foundation decided to work towards a clarification among the American Italians in the belief that, apart from being useful, it would also be a start in explaining, in Italy, who were, and who are, the Americans of Italian origin.

From this decision there grew many happy relations with important American institutions.

Out of the many I would like to mention two: the excellent rapport with the NIAF (National Italian American Foundation), and the fruitful scientific cooperation with CMS.

The research which comprises this volume is proof of the latter, and of the common goal of clarifying the social reality of the Italian ethnic group. Since there is also evidence in Italy of widespread interest in citizens of Italian origin, not just in the United States, but also Brazil, Argentina, Australia and other countries, the research will be translated into Italian and published in this country.

It is important that such interest be satisfied with scientific information, other than fantastic or unreal tales. Social research is useful here as it bases information on important and objective data, interpreted, wherever humanly possible, without bias.

This volume is thus another step in the clarification of the concept and culture of the Italian peoples around the world. Other initiatives are in progress, in the American countries and in Australia. One example is the publication of an international journal dedicated to the worldwide study of Italian ethnicity.

This is a scientific undertaking, destined for scholars, but it is also of great cultural and political significance as it proposes to highlight the existence of an Italian ethnic group outside Italy. Thus, there is a need to circulate these data, to compare research methods and to promote the comparison of results.

Rediscovering the bonds between the various Italian groups means conducting not only scientific research but also a cultural action. Wherever they went, the Italians took with them the same system of values: an idea of the family and the memory of a tradition. The rediscovery of these links, weak or strong, is a significant contribution to mutual understanding between these countries and between them and Italy, and thus, Europe.

Social research also means making a valid point. If cultural roots are important, then the influences exerted on arrival are equally so: the experiences and education undergone through the successive generation in the American countries. There are, now, many different ways of being part of Italian culture and Italy. This variety must be underlined and studied to give an historical foundation to being and "feeling" Italian.

This research concentrates on the subject of immigrants in the last twenty years without ignoring the hundred year history of Italians in the USA. It should, therefore, be seen as a further contribution towards the conceptual clarification and cultural evaluation of a people and of a social and civil experience.

Marcello Pacini
Director, The Giovanni Agnelli Foundation

ITALIAN IMMIGRANTS TO THE UNITED STATES: THE LAST TWENTY YEARS

Graziano Battistella
Center for Migration Studies

The Immigration Reform and Control Act of 1986 is a controversial piece of legislation. It is also the major legislative effort on U.S. immigration since the 1952 Walter-McCarren Act. However, while the 1986 Act tries to tackle the most problematic issue of contemporary immigration—that of illegal immigration—through a legalization program and employer sanctions, it does not modify the key underlying principles of U.S. immigration policy as established in 1952 and amended in 1965: *i.e.*, those of the preference system and family reunification.

Unlike the 1986 Act, the Kennedy-Simpson Immigration Bill of 1987 lacked controversy and was approved quickly and overwhelmingly by the U.S. Senate on March 8, l988. Submitted without fanfare, it caused no public outcry, but if also approved by the House, as submitted by Representative Charles E. Shumer (D-N.Y.), it will constitute a major policy change in immigration, particularly for migrants originating in Europe. This Bill proposes an overall ceiling on legal immigration and would allow the entry of a higher percentage of immigrants on the basis of skills and abilities that are in short supply in the U.S. The two measures combined aim to facilitate immigration from Western Europe, while containing immigration growth from Central America and Southeast Asia.

If passed, the 1987 Bill could also influence Italian immigration to the U.S. In 1986, Italian immigration to the U.S. reached its lowest level in 50 years. However, a backlog of requests for visas exists in Italy, as well as other European countries. Judging from approvals, the majority of immigrants on the waiting list is comprised of brothers and sisters of naturalized Italians. Yet, the proposed Bill would curtail eligibility for married brothers and sisters, in-laws, and nieces and nephews of U.S. citizens. Consequently, certain questions need to be posed. That is, with the passage of this legislation, would we witness an increase in the number of independent immigrants from Italy who would consequently form substitutes to those currently admitted under the relative preferences? Or, would we witness a further decrease in immigration from Italy once the family preferences were limited?

Before attempting some answers, an analysis of recent Italian immigration is necessary. This chapter presents an overview of Italian migration to the United States from the year 1966. The choice of that date is not arbitrary. Public Law 89-236, signed by President Lyndon B. Johnson on October 3, l965, shifted U.S. immigration policy from a quota system to a preference system. Immigrants from the Eastern Hemisphere were given equal access to the U.S., under a ceiling of 170,000 and, for the first time, immigrants from the Western Hemisphere were limited to 120,000 per year. A maximum

> *Unlike the 1986 Act, the Kennedy-Simpson Immigration Bill of 1987 lacked controversy and was approved quickly and overwhelmingly.*

number of 20,000 immigrants per country was applied to all countries. No limit was imposed on family reunification for close relatives.

The effects of the law on Italian immigration were immediate. The number of Italian immigrants admitted to the U.S. jumped from 10,821 in 1965 to 25,154 in 1966. The increase was largely a result of immigrants admitted under the relative preferences. The effect of Public Law 89-236 lasted about ten years. In 1974, Italian immigration to the U.S. started a trend to decline which continues to the present. However, from 1966 to 1986, over 290 thousand Italians immigrated to the U.S. Who were they? How did they enter the U.S.? And, what bearing do their current characteristics have upon contemporary and future migration from Italy?

SOURCE AND QUALITY OF DATA

The principal sources of data for this analysis are the statistical yearbooks of the Immigration and Naturalization Service (INS). INS collects data on new arrivals through immigrant visas and applications for adjustment of status. After the immigrant is admitted, information is forwarded to the INS Immigrant Data Capture (IMDAC) facility for processing. IMDAC generates statistical records which are published annually.

Data provided by INS have some limitations. "The number of immigrants admitted for legal permanent residence in a year is not the same as the number of net immigrants who enter the United States in the year" (United States Department of Justice, 1987). The reasons for this difference in counts are adjustments of status, which are not reported in the year of entry, and lack of data on all emigration and illegal immigration.

The majority of adjustments occur within two years of entry. Over 80 percent of adjustments concern persons exempt from numerical limitations. This category is largely comprised of refugees who must wait one year before applying for permanent residence status. The next largest category of entrants seeking adjustments is that of tourists (32% in 1986).

Currently, the U.S. has no acceptable method for counting illegal immigrants. For this reason it is necessary to revert to statistical estimates.

Currently, the U.S. has no acceptable method for counting illegal immigrants. For this reason it is necessary to revert to statistical estimates. "The Census Bureau uses an estimate of 200,000 net growth due to illegal immigration in its annual population estimates" (United States Department of Justice, 1987).

While the lack of data concerning illegal aliens is inevitable, it is more difficult to explain the lack of data concerning emigration. Until 1957, when the process was arbitrarily discontinued, these data had been regularly collected. Consequently, from the year 1957, once again we must rely on estimates. Since the turn of the century the ratio of immigration to emigration has been three to one (Warren, R. and E.P. Kraly, 1985). The same authors indicate that an average of 2,700 U.S. citizens per year have emigrated to Italy during the years 1960-1976. These data are confirmed by other sources, for at least one country, as Italy provides figures on repatriation (Rosoli, G., 1979).

Data comparison also takes us into another issue: the difference in migration statistics between Italy and the U.S. For the period 1966-1976, 201,816 Italians were admitted to the U.S. according to INS; however, only 163,782 emigrated from Italy to the U.S. according to Italian statistics. We already explained how immigration data are collected in the U.S. In Italy, where the methodology to collect migration data has been changed several times, data collection is equally problematic. In Italy, information is gathered through change of residence which monitors the movement of population within and to and from Italy. A file concerning immigrants and emigrants is kept in each town and updated once a year. The results are forwarded to ISTAT (Central Institute of Statistics). Since change of residence is not always communicated, or not communicated in the same year of emigration, discrepancies between statistics provided by Italy and by the United States may be expected.

Even though accuracy and reliability of INS data on migration are flawed and requests for improvements are frequent (Tomasi, S.M. and C.B. Keely, 1975), they are still the only available data and they do shed some light on the phenomenon. While the following observations do not give an exact picture of Italian immigration, they do offer an adequate sketch of at least the major trends in population movements between these two countries.

Observations in this chapter will focus on Italian immigrants during the last twenty years, but will expand on the whole Italian-born population present in the U.S. in 1980. Data for this latest aspect will be taken from the 1980 census of the U.S. population (United States Bureau of the Census, 1985).

Traditionally, Italian immigrants have been compared with immigrants from Eastern and Southern Europe. Various reasons support this choice. Geographically, Italy is located in the southern part of Europe. Historically, Italian immigration to the U.S. has developed at the same time as immigration from Eastern Europe. The laws regulating immigration have included Italians in the Eastern Hemisphere and, thus, similarly affected Italians. Nevertheless, traditionally and culturally Italy belongs to the west, and it has developed economic, political and cultural ties with the Germans and the French more than with the Czecks, Slovaks and Poles. For these reasons, this study will present a synopsis of the foreign born population of the five ethnic groups that, together with the Italians, contribute the most numerous European groups in the United States.

Number of Entrants

In 1986, the U.S. admitted more immigrants than in any single year over the past 50 years. This pattern of increase in the total number of immigrants admitted has held since the end of World War II. Legislative interventions over the past 60 years regulated, but did not stop immigration to the U.S. which appears, basically, to be driven by the gap in economic development between the U.S. and other areas of the world. Regulation aside, immigration policy and economic development have determined certain shifts in the source areas for immigration. Immigration from Italy has also been affected by a variety of legislative and economic factors. An important source country of immigration twenty years ago, Italy is now the fifth industrialized country in the world and an irrelevant source of immigration to the U.S. While the U.S. reached the highest number of immigrants admitted since the end of World War II, Italy reached the lowest number of emigrants sent to America.

Two major events determined the size of the flow of immigrants from Italy to the U.S. over the past twenty years. The first, of course, was the Immigration Act of 1965. This piece of legislation opened the door to relatives of U.S. immigrant citizens. For eight years the number of Italian immigrants rose over 20,000. Then, in two years (1974-1975), it dropped under 10,000 per year (Table 1.2).

The second event affecting the number of entrants from Italy occurred in 1974. This was the oil crisis and the world-wide recession that followed.

Two major events determined the size of the flow of immigrants from Italy to the U.S. over the past twenty years.

Fig. 1 - Italians Admitted to the U. S. by Year of Entry: 1966-1986

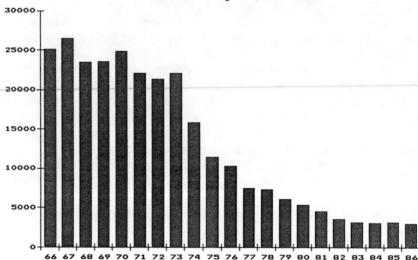

Migration decreased as a world-wide phenomenon. Countries of employment modified their immigration policy, favoring integration of immigrants already in the territory, discouraging new entries and encouraging repatriation. Emigration from Italy decreased in general and for the first time repatriation edged emigration (Rosoli, 1979). The movement of the Italian population toward the U.S. remained in favor of emigration but continued in a steady decline in numbers. From a prior eight percent share of total immigration to the U.S., over the past seven years immigration from Italy has supplied less than one percent of the U.S. inflow.

The change in percentage points, besides in absolute numbers, is further motivated by the general increase of immigration to the U.S. The 1965 Immigration Act not only allowed a large number of European immigrants into the U.S., but opened the way for an expansion of immigration from Central America and South East Asia. While European economies thrived, providing employment for their own people and also becoming countries of immigration, and their population growth stabilized, Asian and Latin American countries provided a larger quantity of potential emigrants, since their population growth remained much higher than that of the Western countries, while their economies developed at a slower pace. After an initial wave of immigrants from Eastern and Southern Europe, the beneficiaries of the 1965 Immigration Act were the recent immigrants from Central America and Asia with large families in the country of origin waiting to be reunited in the U.S.

The decrease of Italian immigration to the U.S. for the general reasons mentioned above does not indicate a lack of demand for entry. According to the U.S. Department of State, Bureau of Consular Affairs, there were 1.9 million active registrants awaiting numerically limited immigrant visas at consular offices abroad (United States Department of Justice, 1986). About twelve thousand of these were Italians. Since visas are grouped on a first-come/ first-serve basis, an Italian applying for immigration to the U.S. must wait four to five years before receiving a decision.

When considering Italian immigration in the context of selected European countries some differences may be noted. Countries such as France, Germany, Great Britain and Ireland were not subject to the same restrictions as the Southern and Eastern European countries under the Walter-McCarren Act. Therefore, when the 1965 Public Law was fully enacted in 1969, it produced a different effect marking a substantial decrease in immigration among those European nations. The decrease continued until the mid 1970s, reflecting the world-wide consequences of the economic recession. Since then, however, the number of immigrants from Western Europe has returned to the levels experienced during the early 1970's, indicating that some population movement between industrialized countries is functional to the capitalist system (Table 1.3).

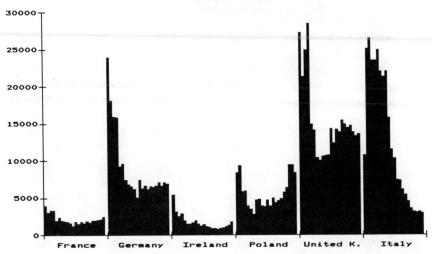

**Fig. 2 - Immigrants to the U.S.
from Selected European Countries:
1965-1986**

The case of Poland, whose immigration dated slightly earlier than Italy, is quite different. Among immigrants from Poland there is a substantial number of refugees who came to the U.S. through other countries and who adjusted their status. In fact, contrary to the other nations, immigrants who had Poland as their country of last residence are less numerous than immigrants who had Poland as country of birth. The unique trend of immigration from Italy among the selected European nations, not only determines that Italy should not be considered a country of emigration any longer, but indicates that population movement between Italy and the U.S. has not reached its final balance, and it will find some adjustment in the future.

Types of Entrants

Public Law 89-236 established two major categories of admissible immigrants; those subject to universal limitations (a maximum of 20,000 per year from Italy within the overall ceiling of 270,000 per year) and those exempt from universal limitations. For the first ten years approximately 80 percent of Italian immigrants were subject to universal limitation while twenty percent were exempt. When total immigration from Italy decreased to fewer than twenty thousand individuals per year, the percentage distribution also changed. In 1986 Italian immigrants subject to numerical limitations reached the lowest level, 43 percent, while exempt Italians comprised almost 57 percent of the total Italian immigrants (Table 1.4).

Immigrants exempt from numerical limitation include three major categories of immigrants; parents, spouses and children of U.S. citizens.

When total immigration from Italy decreased to fewer than twenty thousand individuals per year, the percentage distribution also changed.

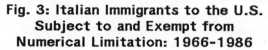

Fig. 3: Italian Immigrants to the U.S. Subject to and Exempt from Numerical Limitation: 1966-1986

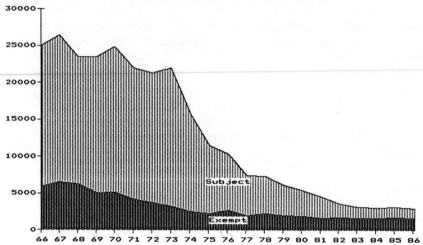

Following the decline of total Italian immigration, parents and children also decreased accordingly. While in the late 1960s these two categories comprised half of the number of exempt Italians, in 1985 they contributed only 25 percent to this category. Spouses of U.S. citizens have increased their share in this category of immigrants and for the past ten years have remained at a steady level in absolute numbers. Since 1980 the INS Statistical Yearbook has discontinued giving separate accounts for husbands and wives. For the period prior to that date, where those figures were released, married females were more numerous than married males.

The category of immigrants subject to numerical limitation includes immigrants admitted under the relative preferences and immigrants admitted under the occupational preference (Table 1.5). Relative preferences include four categories of relatives of which the most commonly used categories are the second (spouses and unmarried children of permanent resident aliens), and the fifth (brothers and sisters of U.S. citizens). In fact, in 1986, the second preference accounted for 41 percent while the fifth preference accounted for 26 percent of all immigrants subject to numerical limitation. However, among Italian immigrants brothers and sisters of U.S. citizens (30%) are more numerous than spouses and unmarried children of permanent residents.

Relatives of Italian immigrants permanently established in the U.S. were the major benefactors of Public Law 89-236. However, the depletion over ten years of the backlog of relatives of Italian immigrants waiting to be admitted was one of the major factors for the decrease in Italian immigration, since they were not replaced by other categories of immigrants. In fact, immigrants admitted under the occupational preference were always a small number, subject to sharp variations, although these numbers had stabilized over the past six/ seven years at approximately four hundred individuals per year.

Age and Sex

The format of INS statistical yearbooks varies through the years, owing to the improved processing capabilities ushered in with the computer age. Variations, however, create gaps and make it difficult to follow some trends. Other times, data are lost and some records are missing. Nevertheless, the pool of social variables provided are sufficient to extract a profile of Italian immigrants in the last twenty years. Since Italians, upon immigration, usually join a community of already established immigrants, we will not limit our analysis to the immigrants, but we will consider also the population born in Italy and present in the U.S. in 1980. Data for this enlarged profile will, as noted, be taken from the 1980 census.

Immigration and Naturalization Service Yearbooks limit the age brackets to ten-year brackets, starting at age twenty. To present a uniform tabulation in this report, age cohorts have been combined into three major categories. The cohorts under twenty and over 60 will indicate dependent population.

Overall, Italian immigration in l985 has a higher median age than in l966. Immigrants under twenty years of age have decreased from 37 to nineteen percent of the total immigration. Consequently, the other categories have increased, particularly that group from twenty to 59 years of age (Table 1.6). The aging of the Italian immigration, however, is not dramatic. Median age was 25.9 in 1966 and 28.8 in 1985. Among the reasons for the aging of the Italian immigrant group are the following:

1. The median age of the population in Italy has increased.
2. Families are less numerous and, therefore, the pool of children available for family reunification is smaller.
3. The number of years of school completed by individuals in Italy has also increased and has resulted in a delayed decision to emigrate.

In 1966, Italians were found to have the second highest median age (immigrants from Poland had the highest median age), among European immigrants to the U.S. Twenty years later the ranking of age groups has not changed, with the sole exception of the Irish.

In 1966, Italians were found to have the second highest median age among European immigrants to the U.S.

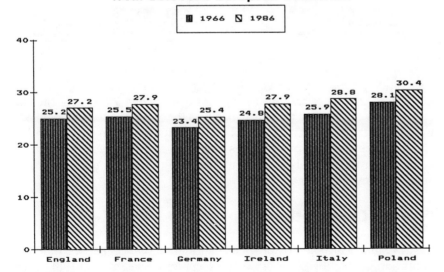

Fig. 4: Median Age of Immigrants from Selected European Countries

■ 1966 ▨ 1986

	England	France	Germany	Ireland	Italy	Poland
1966	25.2	25.5	23.4	24.8	25.9	28.1
1986	27.2	27.9	25.4	27.9	28.8	30.4

Variations over the twenty year period indicate that the average immigrant from Europe—particularly those from Ireland and Italy—has a higher median age than their countrymen of twenty years ago as well as than other immigrants to the U.S. Also interesting to note is the increased age of male immigrants. This group is now older than female immigrants from all countries of origin.

Throughout the past twenty years, Italian male immigrants were a numerically larger group than females. While that difference was never so pronounced, it is currently increasing (Table 1.6). The reason for this trend can be found in the greater proportional relevance that immigrants admitted by occupational preference (usually male immigrants) have toward immigrants admitted under family preference. In fact, in the under-twenty and over-60 age cohorts, females still outnumber males.

The trend in sex proportion among other European immigrants over the past twenty years deserves further attention. In fact, except for Polish immigrants, whose pattern is similar to the Italian pattern, immigrants from France, Ireland and the United Kingdom reduced the proportion of females by many points.

The decrease in the proportion of female immigrants is a phenomenon affecting all European countries under examination here.

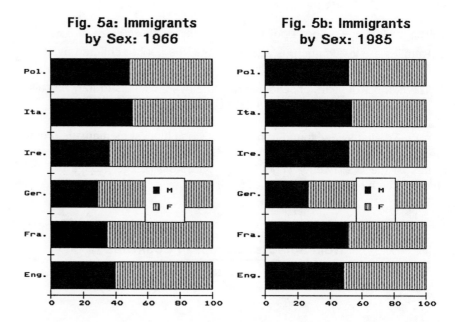

Fig. 5a: Immigrants by Sex: 1966

Fig. 5b: Immigrants by Sex: 1985

The principal exception is West Germany, a country with a highly imbalanced immigration. Here, females represent more than 70 percent of total immigration. In the past, the imbalance was the consequence of World War II. Now, it is the result of a lack of job opportunities in Germany for females with the same qualifications as males. Note, however, that there is also some impact upon these numbers from marriages between U.S. males based in West Germany and German females.

Type of Occupation

The INS Statistical Yearbook provides information on occupations of immigrants admitted to the U.S. every year, except for the years 1980-1981, when data were lost. If caution is in order when considering immigration data, special care is required for the analysis of occupational data. INS tabulations frequently lump information from different sources (labor certification forms and INS forms) and given for different reasons. It is not clear whether occupation refers to the intended first occupation in the U.S. or the occupation at the time of applying for a visa or if it is just a rough indicator of skill level (Tomasi, S.M. and C.B. Keely, 1975).

Bearing in mind these caveats, available data still provide some insight into the immigration phenomenon, particularly if one considers that the same bias applies throughout the twenty year period we are considering. The first observation concerns the high percentage (58.4) of immigrants without occupation, or occupied as housewives (Table 1.10). Even though it is typical of the immigrant to migrate because of a lack of job opportunities in the country of origin, and it is typical of the immigrant wives to work in the house, it should not be forgotten that an immigrant tends to declare no occupation if he is to receive benefits from the main applicant. Consequently, the percentage of persons with no occupation remained practically unchanged since 1966. All other occupation categories went through a significant variation, attesting primarily to the changes that occurred in the Italian economy. Craftsmen, laborers and farmers are now less numerous, while professionals, managers and persons employed by the service industry have more than doubled. Thus, Italian immigrants are entering the U.S. labor market with better qualifications and experience and a greater balance in the occupational distributions.

This pattern, however, is not unique to Italian immigrants (Table 1.11). For all European countries, clerical work and crafts, general labor and farmwork have decreased, as the international economic system has moved from agriculture and manufacturing to the service and information industries. Particularly dramatic, is the decrease of Polish farmers entering the U.S. Proportionally, Italy remains the country with the lowest number of professional, technical, managerial, and administrative support personnel entering the U.S. It is also interesting to note that the occupation of entrepreneurial vending—a standard of the older Italian migration—is not an occupational category under which Italians enter the U.S., rather, it is an occupation acquired subsequent to U.S. entry.

State of Intended Residence

From the time of the large immigrations from Italy, Italians coming from rural areas tended to settle in urban areas. This apparent paradox would be difficult to explain were it not for some obvious factors. Principal among these factors are: the nature of American agriculture; the shortage of cash for travel beyond the point of debarkation; the lack of time and funds for long-term investments; and the intention of changing life-style and amassing quick savings to return to Italy (Alba, R.D., 1985). Thus, the history of Italian migration developed as the history of major urban areas, in which "Little Italies" became both the focal points for the life of the community as well as the centers of first arrival for new immigrants. By no means do we intend to say that the urban experience was the only one known by Italian immigrants. "The big cities did not exhaust the categories of environment in which the Italians lived and worked" (Vecoli, R.J., 1987). However, the clustering of Italians in urban areas determined and fixed the selection of states in which the majority of Italians settled. Ten states comprised almost 90 percent of the total Italian immigration and still account for 90 percent of Italians living in the U.S.

During the 1960s—a period of much higher Italian migration to the U.S.—

For all European countries, clerical work and crafts, general labor and farmwork have decreased, as the international economic system has moved from agriculture and manifacturing to the service industries.

immigration followed the established rural-urban, seaboard, pattern and individuals were reunited with their families in the traditional states of Italian settlings. However, twenty years later, with a much reduced immigration flow, the states of residence for Italian immigrants have changed considerably. The states of the Midwest have lost attractiveness for recent Italian immigrants, who seem to prefer the states of the sunbelt. In fact, California now ranks in second place and Florida and Texas appear among the top ten states of intended residence (Table 1.12). Despite the fact that we are speaking of small numbers, the significance of the trend remains in the sense that it confirms the national trend favoring population growth precisely in the southern and western region of the U.S.

Naturalization

Naturalization numbers increased again during the 60s, spurred by the new ethnicity movement and the pressure from Italian American Organizations as part of a general move to acquire greater political power.

Application for naturalization is the moment when immigration acquires the character of permanence. In fact, even when immigration to the U.S. was a far lengthier and more costly trip, returns were not infrequent (Boyd Caroli, B., 1973), defeating the widespread assumption that immigration to the U.S. was always permanent. The naturalization pattern in the history of Italian immigration to the U.S. evolved in four stages. In the early migrations, the rate of naturalization of Italian immigrants remained low. On average, the Italian immigrant remained twenty years before applying for citizenship (Vecoli, R.J., 1987). However, between 1920 and 1940 naturalized Italians increased in number from 30 to 60 percent of the Italian population in the U.S. (Archdeacon J. Thomas, 1983). The troubled years of the Fascist regime did not supply new flows of immigrants to be naturalized and advised the residents against a return to Italy.

Naturalization numbers increased again during the 60s, spurred by the new ethnicity movement and the pressure Italian American Organizations and their affiliates placed upon members to acquire citizenship as part of a general move to acquire greater political power. However, this trend in naturalizations seems to have reversed again. In 1966, Italians contributed ten percent to total number of naturalizations, but less than two percent in 1986 (Table 1.13). This decrease was due not only to the fact that the total number of naturalizations more than doubled while Italian immigration decreased, but it is also a result of the fact that, traditionally, the time for applications for naturalization among Italians is deferred. For the more than two hundred thousand Italian immigrants who entered the U.S. from 1966 to 1975, there are only 90,000 naturalizations. Even considering that some returned to Italy and that applications are entered over a longer period of time after admission into the country, still the rate is lower than before. In fact, the INS Statistical Yearbook, providing the breakdown of applications by year of entry, shows that Italians who applied for naturalization within twelve years of entry represented more than 90 percent of those who naturalized in 1966. Instead, only 35 percent of Italians who became American citizens in 1985 entered the U.S. within the previous twelve years; all others had been admitted prior to that date (Table 1.15).

This trend is not peculiar to the Italian immigrants. The percent of naturalizations within twelve years of entry decreased for all European countries, albeit at different paces. Germans tend to procrastinate naturalization as Italians do, while Poles are still becoming citizens almost as fast as they had. Of course, the decreased number of admitted immigrants within the twelve years prior to natuaralization accounts for the general decrease in percentage of recent immigrants among naturalizing persons. That is, fewer recent immigrants are available to be part of the stock of persons who become citizens every year. Moreover, Europe is now only a few hours from the United States and the possibility for return is far easier to consider practical. In fact, when economic and political conditions remain difficult in countries of emigration—such as in Poland—the naturalization rate remains high.

An analysis of the ways in which naturalization is obtained by Italians provides additional insights into the reasons for changing patterns in this area. Persons seeking naturalization through marriage to a U.S. citizen represented more than fourteen percent in 1966, but accounted for fewer than three percent in 1985 (Table 1.17). Since the number of spouses admitted to the U.S. has remained steady for the past ten years (Table 1.4), or, rather, the number of spouses in relation to total immigration has increased, one can only conclude that the prevailing trend is to have families in which the spouses maintain different citizenship to preserve the wider range of possibilities offered by both countries.

The trend to procrastinate naturalization, or not to seek it at all, appears less dramatic when considered in terms of the inflow of admitted immigrants. In fact, while immigration decreased by 87 percent from 1966 to 1986, naturalizations decreased by 71 percent; moreover, while in the first decade there were fewer than 50 naturalized immigrants to every 100 who entered, since 1976, Italians who acquired American citizenship have been more numerous than the total number of Italian immigrants for each year. The decrease in immigration that singles Italy out from other European nations, is matched by its distinction in the proportions of naturalizations to immigration.

Fig. 6 - Italian Immigration and Naturalization: 1966-1986

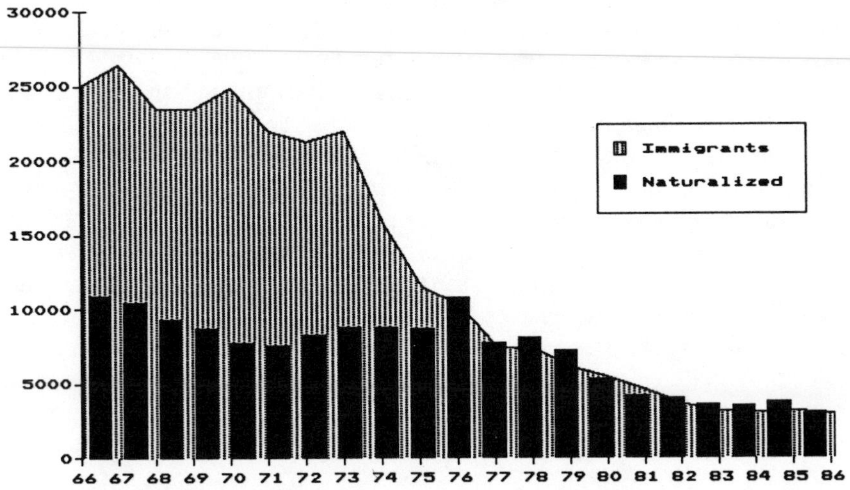

After recalling some caveats in reference to occupational data provided by the INS, it could appear a futile exercise to compare occupation of admitted immigrants with that of naturalized citizens. However, provided that the two groups represent a similar universe, that comparison is revealing. That is, over a relatively short period of time, a distinct change in employment pattens may also be noted. As expected, the category most affected during the period between admission and naturalization is that of persons who entered without occupation. This category has practically halved, and is decreasing. The obvious explanation for this trend is the number of dependent children who become part of the labor market after ten years. In addition, over the past ten years, housewives and persons working at home have found jobs in the labor market. Indeed, one apparently can conclude that immigration does provide the job opportunity that was sought.

The new jobs taken by these groups are mostly in the clerical field and the service industry; others found employment in crafts and manual labor. The percentage of naturalized professionals, however, appears to be lower than that of immigrants admitted as professionals. Of the two conclusions (Italians do not find jobs as professionals in the U.S. and/ or Italians of professional occupations do not naturalize at the same rate as other categories of employment) the second one seems preferable.

ITALIANS LIVING IN THE UNITED STATES

Of the many terms used to indicate non-native Americans, that of foreign born seems the most comprehensive for a presentation on Italians living in the U.S. In fact, "immigrant", defined as an alien admitted to the United States as a lawful permanent resident, seems to limit its semantics to the process of admission. Persons who have been residing in the U.S. for an extended period of time resent being called immigrants. "Alien" simply indicates any person who is a not a citizen or a national of the U.S.; all Italians who acquired U.S. citizenship would be excluded if this term were selected for the present analysis. Conversely, a naturalized person refers only to the immigrant who, after a minimum of five years as permanent resident, acquired U.S. citizenship. Aliens and naturalized citizens are mutually exclusive; however, combined, they comprise all the foreign born who settled in the U.S.

For many years the U.S. census of the population provided an additional category of people: foreign stock, which was inclusive of foreign born and native born of foreign or mixed parentage. This group (also identified as first and second generation) was discontinued in 1980, when the question on place of birth of parents was substituted by the question on ancestry. Ancestry data, while providing the possibility of identifying an entire ethnic group, do not differentiate among generations. The question on place of birth, which allows the identification of foreign born population, remains the source of information on immigrants living in the U.S. However, a person could be born in a foreign country, but not be a citizen or national of that country. Therefore, even the foreign born population deserves further specification. There are persons living in the U.S. who were born in Italy, but are not and do not consider themselves Italians. Concomitantly, there are persons born in foreign countries other than Italy who are and consider themselves Italians.[1] The difference between persons born in Italy and persons born in Italy of Italian ancestry was 28,289 or, 3.4 percent of the Italian born population; a share that does not overly affect the major social descriptors of the population we are considering.

The Italian born population in the U.S. was most numerous in 1930 and has decreased in number since.

Size and Geographical Distribution of the Population

The Italian born population in the U.S. was most numerous in 1930 and has decreased in number since. The rate of decrease (12% from 1950 to 1960, 20% from 1960 to 1970, 18% from 1970 to 1980) is of such magnitude that Italians in the 90s will be one third the number of the 1930s (Table 2.1).

Deaths, returns and the decrease of immigration flows are the factors responsible for the decrease of Italian-born population. A simple subtraction of persons present in the U.S. in 1980 who declared they arrived between 1965 and 1980 from the total number of persons who were admitted to the U.S. in the same period according to INS shows a loss of 30 percent.[2]

Immigration patterns have an obvious impact on the size of the resident foreign born population. People born in Ireland and Poland decreased in number to an even larger extent than did the Italians; the high levels of immigration from Germany and the United Kingdom however maintained the decrease of those foreign born at a more limited level.

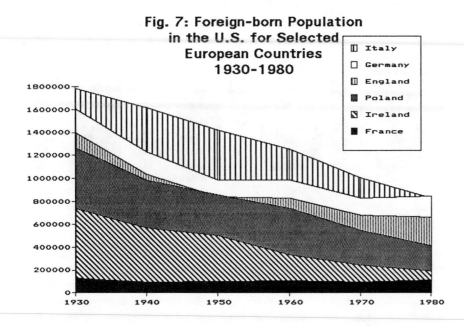

Fig. 7: Foreign-born Population in the U.S. for Selected European Countries 1930-1980

Italy
Germany
England
Poland
Ireland
France

The internal mobility of Italians is a limited phenomenon. Basically, they participated in the post-war exodus to the suburbs, or were evicted from the neighborhoods whose buildings were "prime targets for the urban renewal movement of the 1950s and early 1960s" (Archdeacon J. Thomas, 1983). They also participated, but in a limited form, in the movement of the 1970s from the Northeast and Midwest toward the South and the West. Nevertheless, two Italians out of three still live in the Northeast region, which is the area most populated by European-born immigrants.

Over two thirds of the Italian population arrived before 1960 (Table 2.3). The implications of this simple notation are manifold. General social characteristics of Italians depict a population with high median age, many retired persons and therefore a low percentage of population in the labor force. Even more important, the great majority of Italians is comprised of persons who spent more time in the U.S. than in Italy. Their level of integration is expected to be high. On the other hand, the image they preserve of Italy is so outdated that it does not correspond to the present reality. Even if some updating has been brought about by vacations and brief visits, they did not participate in key events that occurred after 1960, which shaped contemporary Italian politics, ideology, and mentality. For these reasons, in this chapter, Italians will be subdivided in two groups, when pertinent, taking the year of 1960 as discriminatory. Yet it is important to remember that, sometimes, differences are not so accentuated as expected; moreover, available data do not measure such characteristics as degree of attachment to the country of origin or knowledge of political, social and cultural events occurring in Italy.

Fig. 8 - Immigrants by Region of Residence: 1980

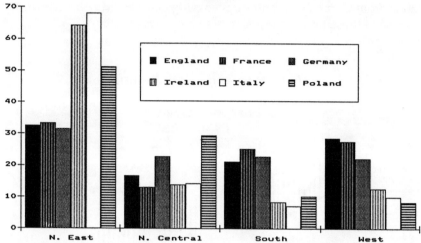

Age, Sex and Citizenship

The average Italian living in the U.S. in 1980 was 60 years old. As stated before, the Italians are an aging group of immigrants. However, it could be misleading not to mention that next to the immigrants who arrived before 1960 and have a median age of 65, there is a group of approximately 250 thousand Italians who arrived after 1960 and have a median age of 36. Italians are not the oldest group, but find themselves close to the Poles and Irish, more than the Germans or the French.

Year of immigration and age also affect sex distribution. Since life expectancy is higher for women than men, the sex distribution in favor of women is higher for those who immigrated before 1960 and declines in the recent immigration periods. As previously noted, when speaking of immigrants, the other European countries have a much higher proportion of women than Italy does. This is the result of an immigration that has long since become motivated by family reunification.

Confirming the naturalization trend previously discussed, 78 percent of Italians are American citizens. Of the 22 percent who still maintain alien status, one quarter arrived before 1960. Percentage wise this is not a significant number of people (8% of the early immigrants); but the absolute number is more indicative of the strong attachment to the country of origin felt by a significant group of persons.

78 percent of Italians are American citizens. Of the 22 percent who still maintain alien status, one quarter arrived before 1960.

The naturalization rate obviously decreases for the recent immigration. Among the older immigrants, however, Italians maintain the highest percentage of naturalized persons (Table 2.6). Apparently, it was not so desirable for those people to return to Italy as it was for immigrants from other countries. However, this same result does not obtain in recent years as Italians aligned themselves with other Europeans in the decision to procrastinate the time to apply for American citizenship.

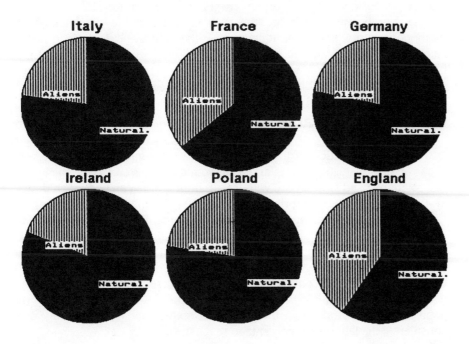

**Fig. 9: Citizenship
of Selected Foreign-born Groups: 1980**

Family

The relevance of family among Italian immigrants and the role of the family in forging the personal and social ethos and providing identity to Italians have been long investigated. From the idea of immigration as a destructive factor on the family (Handlin, O., 1951) to the idea of immigration as a phenomenon strengthening the extended family (Yans-McLaughlin, V., 1977); from the concept of "amoral familism" (Banfield, E.C., 1958) to the concept of "peer group society" (Gans, H., 1962), social theories have been developed to explain the distinctive behavior of Italian Americans as a group. The underlying assumption has been that much of the adjustment of this ethnic group can be understood by the continuities and discontinuities they demonstrate with their past. However, Italy is not a country immobilized in its past, nor has family life-style and social behavior remained unchanged. Traditional interpretations of Italians in America will have to be adjusted. As indicators relevant to family adjustment, we will consider fertility and divorce rate.

Data from the 1980 census confirm the findings by Andrew Greely in the 1960s that Italian Americans present a very low divorce rate—the lowest among the European nations reported on Table 2.7. Considering that divorce was introduced in Italy only in 1974, there is no possibility of measuring its impact on the immigrants. In fact, those who immigrated after 1965 have a lower divorce rate than those who have been in the United States for a longer period of time. However, the lower median age and, therefore, the more brief the marital period, must also be considered in this case. Instead, the percentage of divorces among Italians between fifteen and 44 years of age who immigrated before 1959 is relatively high, indicating that those who were raised predominantly in the American value system absorbed the American mentality also in regard to family life.

The fertility rate among Italian women was the highest of all other European nations (Table 2.8). Since we are considering the first generation of immigrants, this behavior is totally predictable. However, the difference is not particularly significant. Italian families have been aligning themselves with the average European family, and migrants are no exception (Table 2.9).

More significant instead are the data concerning the percentages of mothers among women. The Italians have the highest percentage in every category (married, widowed, divorce and separated women). However, they have the second to lowest percentage of single mothers, somehow suggesting that family control is still enforced in regard to single girls.

Economic Characteristics

In the end, immigration is driven primarily by economic reasons. However, age is an obviously important variable affecting labor force.

In the end, immigration is driven primarily by economic reasons. However, age is an obviously important variable affecting labor force. In fact, the European nations used to compare with Italian immigrants can be broken down in two groups: one comprises France, West Germany and the United Kingdom, with a median age under 50 and 50 percent or more of the population in the labor force; the other group includes Ireland, Italy and Poland, whose foreign born population has a median age in the sixties and, therefore, the labor force percentage is reduced to 40 percent. However, if only those who immigrated in the past ten years are considered, labor force participation among Italians (68.4) is higher than both the U.S. (62) and foreign born population (64.4). And, if only those between sixteen and 64 years of age are considered, the labor force percentage reaches 70.

The year of immigration is not significant, except for the recent immigrants, because it shows that it takes more than five years to reach the level of participation in the labor market that older immigrants have. Of some interest is the observation on labor force participation of the population between sixteen and nineteen years of age. Since more than 50 percent of this group is working, a high percentage has not completed high school. The difference between former an recent immigrants is non-existent in this trend, demonstrating that the attitude toward school or job or necessities of life remains the same for those educated in the U.S. and those educated in Italy.

Unemployment among Italians was high in 1980; higher than other European immigrants and higher than the national rate. Immigrants who arrived after 1970 were affected by unemployment more than were the former immigrants.

Participation of Italian women in the labor force was particularly low in 1980—the lowest among European immigrants and lower than the national average. Social change in Italy did not affect this trend; there is no significant difference between immigrant women who arrived before and after 1960. A difference, however, is seen at the level of age cohorts. Women who are under 45 years of age and have been in the U.S. for a long time demonstrate a higher degree of participation in the labor force. This concept of female employment is also very much a part of the American mentality. Instead, for women who are over 45 years of age the trend goes in the opposite direction, indicating that family-support takes priority for recent immigrants.

Although all nations have a higher percentage of female population, the Italy, Ireland and Poland labor force is largely comprised of men. The main reason for this lies in the fact that a higher percentage of the female population is over 65 years of age. However, cultural reasons (the value these countries place on the role of the woman in the family) should not be dismissed (Table 2.10).

Italians had the highest percentage of full time workers in 1979. However, they also had the highest experience of unemployment (Table 2.11), which, unsurprisingly, affected women more than men.

Construction has been a traditional industry for Italians abroad and it has also become a specific category of migration, particularly to the Arab countries which are heavily involved in construction projects resulting from the oil production cash flow. The Italians in the U.S.A. confirm this trend; in fact, they have the highest percentage working in construction jobs (Table 2.12). The tradition of early immigrants building railroads and subways has continued with Italian contractors.

The type of industry Italians are predominantly employed in is manufacturing; only Poles have a higher percentage of employees in this category. However, while male Poles are particularly involved with manufacturing, it is the Italian women who found employment in this industry. Manufacturing and trading occupy half of the Italian labor force (Table 2.13).

Personal services, such as garment, beauty, barber, and dressmaking, remain a favorite occupation among male Italians (only French born have a higher percentage of employees in this category, but with a significantly lower percentage of males). In the category of professional services, instead, Italians rank in the last place. While more than a quarter of the number of women from European countries are employed as teachers and in the legal and health services, only sixteen percent of Italian women work in those fields.

From the above observations it appears that immigrants from Poland bear the greatest similarity to the immigrants from Italy. This is further confirmed by the percentage of persons working in public administration. Apparently, the local political machines require some time before substantiating ethnic support in terms of jobs.

Almost 50 percent of Italian immigrants are employed in crafts and labor. With the exception of Poles, all other groups have only one quarter or less of the immigrant population holding those kinds of occupations. Even the total U.S. population and the entire immigrant population have a lower percentage of mechanics, repairers and machine operators. Generally speaking, Italians are not employed as technicians or sales representatives or in the administrative branch. The blue collar type of occupations reflect the generally inferior preparation of Italians in terms of education and knowledge of the English language. The importance of women in the overall picture should not be forgotten. Italian women, who hold unskilled jobs, mainly as laborers, seek employment to help meet the family budget requirements.

Perhaps because the security of Government employment is not so accessible or perhaps entrepreneurial pursuits are more attractive, Italians have the highest percentage of self-employed workers (Table 2.14).

The general profile of Italian labor force and occupational characteristics explains the statistical indicators concerning salary. Italians have the lowest salary of all European groups, and this ranking remains unchanged in every measure by which salary is considered: median, mean, or per capita. The high percentage of retired persons, the low percentage of population in the labor force, particularly of women, the high percentage of unemployment and the type of industry and occupation are variables that explain the reason for the low salary among Italians, who once again compare with those nations having similar immigration experiences: Ireland and Poland. However, recent immigrants do have higher median incomes than the U.S. population as a whole as well as the total immigrant population. This salary is still not to the level of other European immigrants.

Fig. 10: Median Household and Family Income of Foreign Born Population in 1979

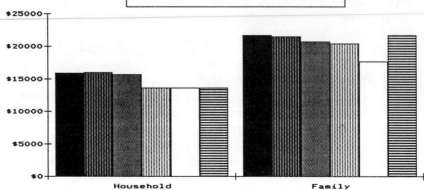

Education and Language

Various countries have various educational curricula. As such, the only way to compare educational attainment among immigrant groups is by years of schooling completed.

Until 1963, at which time it was increased to eighth grade, a completion level of fifth grade was the minimum legal requirement for all Italian citizens. Consequently, it is not at all remarkable that educational levels of Italian born persons are generally low. One in every five Italians, twenty years of age or over, has not attended school beyond the fifth grade. Indeed, only 30 percent of all Italians have graduated high school. Yet, other Western European countries maintain a high school graduate level of more than 50 percent among their population. College graduates among Italians are equally less numerous.

Indices concerning the educational levels of immigrants do depend upon the year of immigration. However, despite the significant rise in educational levels among the more recent emigrants from Italy, these figures remain proportionally low in relation to other Western European countries.

Statistically, foreign born women have more years of schooling than do immigrant men up until the high school graduate level. There, however, the female numerical superiority ceases and male college graduates far outnumber female college graduates among immigrant groups. However, among Italians, it is interesting to note that, men have more years of schooling even at the high school level.

Frequency of usage of mother toungue is also indicative of attachment to country of origin and the endurance of ethnic characteristics. Italian immigrants manifested the highest percentage of foreign language usage, of all immigrant groups, where a language other than English was in use in the home. Fewer than twenty percent of the immigrant group simply lacked extended exposure and had either never actually learned the Italian language, or had forgotten their limited exposure.

Considering the same aspect from a different angle, three quarters of those who arrived before 1960 retained the Italian language, despite extended residence in the U.S.; and, of those who arrived after 1960 more than 90 percent

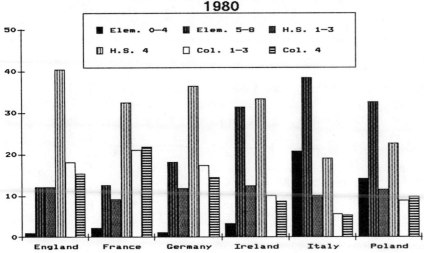

Fig. 11 - Years of School Completed
of Foreign Born 20 Years Old and Over:
1980

■ Elem. 0—4   ■ Elem. 5—8   ▨ H.S. 1—3
▥ H.S. 4   □ Col. 1—3   ▤ Col. 4

*Legislative interventions,
when properly enforced,
have exercised a decisive
control on population
movements.*

still speak Italian. Permanent residence in the country of immigration takes its toll on conservation of the mother tongue; but it appears to be a slow moving factor.

CONCLUDING REMARKS

The twenty years between the 1965 Amendments to the Immigration and Nationality Act (Hart-Celler Act) and the 1986 Immigration Reform and Control Act (Simpson-Rodino Bill) constitute the latest of several phases for Italian immigration to the U.S. Legislative interventions, when properly enforced, have exercised a decisive control on population movements. Thus, the 1924 Permanent National Origin Quota Act brought to a minimum the massive exodus of population from Italy that had begun in the 1880s. The 1952 Immigration and Nationality Act (Walter-McCarran Act) prolonged the limitation and discrimination toward Southern European immigrants. The 1965 liberalization favored 291,885 Italians. At the same time it created a spiral effect process by which countries of recent immigration increased their chances for the share of available admissions. However, American legislation should not be considered the agent principally responsible for the shrinking of the immigration flow from Italy. This flow was drying out at the source, as the decrease of emigration from Italy in general demonstrates.

Immigration is not the only type of population movement between countries. In fact, "non-immigrants" is a complex category that includes a variety of persons reaching the United States under different entitlements. A couple of categories are related to our topic. "Visitors for business", functions as a thermometer of the economic relations between the two countries. This category of people increased by 700 percent in the last twenty years, emphasizing the changes that have taken place in Italy. Formerly, Italy sent people who sought a job in the United States; it is now sending people who participate in the process of creating jobs.

Even more related to our topic is the category of temporary workers, which includes three types of alien workers: "Aliens of distinguished merit and ability...; aliens coming to the United States to perform temporary services or labor, if unemployed persons capable of performing the service cannot be found in the United States; and aliens coming temporarily to the

United States as trainees". (United States Department of Justice, 1986).

This last category increased considerably in the 1980s. Now, for every two immigrants, one temporary worker is admitted. Because of the nature of admissions and the different lengths of stay in the U.S., it is difficult to assess the types of involvement these persons maintain in the local society and among the local Italian community.

Adjustment of status has become a popular way of being admitted as an immigrant.

Some visitors for business and some temporary workers eventually adjust their status to become permanent residents. Adjustment of status has become a popular way of being admitted as an immigrant. In 1986, 37 percent of all admitted immigrants to the U.S. were already in the country and adjusted their status. Usually, this is possible because those persons are not subject to numerical limitation (only 17% of the 1986 adjustments belonged to the categories subjects to limitation). The most common types of entries are those of refugees (44%) and tourists (32%). Italians follow the same route at a higher rate. However, among Italians 70 percent of those who adjusted their status entered as tourists. Overstaying after the tourist visa expired is one of the most common routes to becoming an illegal alien. Therefore, it is quite probable that Italy also has its share in the mass of illegals in the U.S. who did not qualify for the amnesty.

Trends in Italian immigration (small numbers of persons who intend to join relatives and take their chances in America; who are better qualified and better prepared to enter the U.S. labor market and less determined to settle permanently in the United States) lead to some indications for the future of the Italian community in America.

- The low supply of new immigrants will leave the Italian-born a much reduced group in the United States, with less influence on the Italian-American group in general. Knowledge of Italian language, Italian customs and traditions, survival of Italian culture will become increasingly less common among the group.

- Immigrants will have a weakened role in the relationships between the two countries. However, if immigration from Italy becomes an exchange of increasingly more qualified personnel, immigrants, even though reduced in number, will have a greater impact in the dialogue between the two nations.

- Temporary visitors and workers will have a more important role to play, especially if the community creates infrastructures to communicate and easily integrate them.

- Immigrants, reflecting the mentality of contemporary Italy, will require less assistance and more participation. The increasingly temporary type of immigration will demand a more institutionalized type of link with the country of origin.

- The decrease of first, and soon also second generation, requires a different strategy in conveying the image of Italy to the general American public.

- The network of Italian organizations and associations will weaken, leaving room for a different type of ethnic aggregation. The recently constituted "Comitati dell'Emigrazione Italiana" (CO.EM.IT.) intend to acquire a central role in the organization of the Italian community. However, because they are limited to the Italians who remained aliens and because they are an institution of the Italian state they will hardly achieve the participation of a dispersed and fractioned community.

FOOTNOTES

[1] The set of Tables 4.1 through 4.8 provides information on persons who consider themselves of Italian descent and are born in Italy. That information should be the focus of our overview in the following pages. However, since these data do not have direct comparability with any other foreign country, we will instead refer to Tables 2.1 through 2.15 for this profile of Italians in the U.S.

[2] However, the same calculation performed on immigrants from other European nations shows inconsistencies, reaffirming the problematic nature of available data on migration.

REFERENCES

Alba, R.D.
1985 *Italian Americans. Into the Twilight of Ethnicity.* Englewood Cliffs, NJ: Prentice-Hall, p.47.

Archdeacon J. Thomas
1983 *Becoming American. An Ethnic History.* New York: The Free Press. p.157.

Banfield, E.C.
1958 *The Moral Basis of a Backward Society.* New York: The Free Press.

Boyd Caroli, B.
1973 *Italian Repatriation from the United States, 1900-1914.* Staten Island, NY: The Center for Migration Studies, Pp.25-50.

Gans, H.
1962 *The Urban Villagers: Group and Class in the Life of Italian Americans.* New York: The Free Press, Pp.74-75.

Handlin, O.
1951 *The Uprooted: The Epic Story of the Great Migrations that Made the American People.* New York: Grossett, Pp.227-258.

Rosoli, G., Ed.
1979 *Un secolo di emigrazione italiana, 1876-1976.* Roma: CSER, p.371.

Tomasi, S. and C.B. Keely
1975 *Whom Have We Welcomed?.* Staten Island, NY: The Center for Migration Studies, Pp.57-72.

United States Bureau of the Census
1985 *Census of Population, 1980: Foreign-born Population in the United States*, Microfiche (microform), Washington, D.C. It should be remembered that data are taken from a sample of the population and, therefore, are subject to sampling errors. The choice of data distributed by the U.S. Census in microfiche format instead of the special tabulations prepared by the Census on population of Italian ancestry is dictated by the possibility of comparing Italians with other groups.

United States Department of Justice, Immigration and Naturalization Service
1987 *1986 Statistical Yearbook of the Immigration and Naturalization Service*, October. Pp.XXI.

Vecoli, R.J., Ed.
1987 *Italian Immigrants in Rural and Small Town America.* AIHA, p.1.

Warren, R. and E.P. Kraly
1985 *The Elusive Exodus: Emigration from the United States.* Population Trends and Public Policy, Occasional Paper No. 8, March. Washington, D.C.: Population Reference Bureau. p.13.

Yans-McLaughlin, V.
1977 *Family and Community: Italian Immigrants in Buffalo, 1880-1930.* Ithaca, NY: Cornell University Press, Pp.117-118.

Demographic and Cultural Aspects of Italian Americans

Joseph Velikonja
Department of Geography, University of Washingtion

The Italians are a significant demographic component (5.4`) of the U.S. population.

For the first time in U.S. census-taking history, the 1980 Census asked Americans to declare ancestry: over 12 million (12,183,692) respondents stated to be Italian. Although the 1979 Pre-Census estimate gave almost the same figure of 11.7 million (United States Bureau of the Census, 1979), the total caught many researchers by surprise. Most revealing was the size of the third and later generation of Italian-Americans. The Census previously neglected this ethnic component by limiting the assessment of the "foreign stock" to the first and second generation. The figures indicate that:

a) the Italians are a significant demographic component (5.37%) of the U.S. population;

b) the contribution and relative influence of Italians in the American social, political and cultural life is inadequately recognized.

The numerical magnitude alone demonstrates an awareness in the respondents that one or both of their ancestral lines have some Italian connection. It does not state that this ancestry is excusively Italian, nor that the Italian ancestry prevails. Among the 12.2 million who stated their Italian ancestry, 6,883,320 or 56.5 percent reported Italian as their only ancestry (single ancestry) and 5,300,372 or 43.5 percent listed some other ancestry in addition to the Italian, making their italianitá somewhat diluted. The pre-Census estimate of 1979 was very close to the 1980 figure for the total, but the estimate for single ancestry was 800,000 below the 6.9 million of the 1980.

The ancestry data therefore include also the 5.3 million "Italians" who are also conscious of their non-Italian identity.

Since persons who reported multiple ancestries were included in more than one group, the sum of persons reporting at least one ancestry or a multiple ancestry for all ancestry responses is greater than the population of the United States (McKenney, N.R., *et al.*, 1985).

Allen and Turner resolved the issue by estimating that each ancestry group consisted of: a) single ancestry; and b) one third of multiple ancestry (Allen, J.P. and E.J. Turner, 1988). Their estimated figures were used for the construction of the U.S. map of the Italian Ancestry, 1980.

ANCESTRY DATA

The data available for the study of the contemporary scene of the Italian Americans consist of an enormous volume of national data, and some regional and locational data, all provided by the U.S. Census Bureau. The 1980 data are derived from the Census sample and provide the general characteristics of the Italian-ancestry or the Italian born population; these data are not directly comparable to earlier sets and must be used with considerable caution.

Because the fundamental ethnic issue in the United States today is not the position of the "ethnics of European descent", the aim of U.S. Census statistics is to focus on those "ethnic groups" that are numerically more prominent, or are targeted for special policies and implementations. The information set is, therefore, geared to their needs and special interests and often misses the significant aspects of "ethnicity" that are equally or more relevant for other groups.

One valuable source of information was lost when, in 1980, the Alien Address Program was discontinued. The assurance that more reliable information will be made available have not been met. Those who have used the data were aware of the reliability factor, but even poor data are better than none.

GENERAL COMPOSITION

In 1980, the 930,201 foreign born Italians (Table 4.3) included 803,633 people of Italian ancestry born in Italy and 126,568 born elsewhere abroad. This includes the Italians from the Mediterranean lands as well as the increasing number of Italian born in Germany and France, the offspring of the Italians in Western Europe.

The second group, which is not identified in the 1980 Census are the people born in the United States from Italian born parents. This category was included in the 1970 Census, but omitted in 1980. Using the ratio of 1:4 as the ratio between the first and the second generation, the number of the second generation amounts to approximately 3.2 million people (Lieberson, S. and L. Santi, 1985).

TABLE A

COMPOSITION OF POPULATION OF ITALIAN ANCESTRY, 1980

SINGLE ANCESTRY		
Born in the U.S.		6,008,966
Foreign born (Italy and elsewhere)		874,354
	Subtotal	6,883,320
MULTIPLE ANCESTRY		
Born in the U.S.		5,244,525
Foreign born (Italy and elsewhere)		55,847
	Subtotal	5,300,372
Total single and multiple ancestry		12,183,692

The balance belongs to the third and subsequent generations. The present composition of the people of Italian ancestry therefore consists of:

Population of Italian Ancestry	Estimates	Percentage
a) Born in Italy	803,633	6.6
b) Born abroad, not in Italy	126,568	1.0
c) Born in the U. S. of Italian born parents	3,200,000	26.3
d) Born in the United States of U.S. born parents	8,053,500	66.1
Total	12,183,200	100.0

(The figures do not match Lieberson's estimates exactly).

When we speak of Italians in the United States we could use any figure between that of the 831,900 people born in Italy to the 12.2 million who identified their total or partial Italian ancestry. The demographics of these composites are directly affected by more than one century of continuous immigration and by the events that occurred after the arrival of the immigrants in the United States. The survivors of these migrants received an expanded addition by the post-1965 migration when the abolition of the nationality quota permitted a significant number of Italians to enter the United States. This trend lasted until 1980 and has since subsided.

In this light, the figure of 12.2 million people of Italian ancestry (5.4% of the U.S. population), must be approached with caution. A more appropriate figure would be 6.9 million [single ancestry], since 5.3 million also claimed non-Italian ancestry and there is no indication which identity dominates.

Foreign born Italians (7.6 of the total Italian ancestry), as a group, demonstrate the age and sex structure of old migration.

DEMOGRAPHIC STRUCTURE

The age structure of the total population of Italian ancestry corresponds closely to the U.S. population (Tables 6.1, 6.9, 6.17, 6.33), although the median age of the Italians (27.9) is 2.1 years lower than that for the U.S. population; however, for the single ancestry group, the median age is 42 contrasted by the median age of 18 for the multiple ancestry group. The median age of foreign born Italians is exceptionally high: 60.1. A fundamental difference is evident between the structure of the total Italian ancestry group and its single ancestry component. In the total, the single ancestry group accounts for 56.5 percent of those of Italian ancestry, the proportion of the single ancestry subgroup amounts to 89.4 percent in the ages 45 and above and only 30.8 percent for the age groups under twenty. This declining dominance of single ancestry in younger age groups indicates the transition from the earlier prevalence of in-group marriage. Among the post-World War II-born (ages 35 and lower), the multiple ancestry or children of ethnically mixed marriages dominates. Among those younger than ten years of age, multiple ancestry represents 73.7 percent of the total.

Foreign born Italians (7.6% of the total Italian ancestry), as a group, demonstrate the age and sex structure of old migration. As noted, the median age is 60.1, compared to the median age of 30.0 for the U.S. population. Foreign born Italians have been in the U.S. for many years and the small recent migration is not sufficient in number to rejuvenate the group.

Analysis of the age structures also reveals the coexistence of three generations of Italian ancestry. The oldest generation consists of those born in Italy, as well as those born in the United States early in this century. Few survivors remain. Subsequent generations are American born, marrying outside the ethnic group, and spreading territorially from the original clusters.

The age structure of natives of various regions demonstrates the young median age of Italian ancestry group in the South and West (22.5 and 21.6 respectively), with higher median ages in the Northeast (28.4). The stages of migration are evident in the fact that 76.2 percent of those of Italian ancestry who are older than 85, are Italian born.

The share of the Italian born in the total population of Italian ancestry amounts to 6.6 percent. The proportion of the Italian born increases with the age of the cohort: It represents 0.12 percent for the zero to four age group and increases progressively to 9.2 percent for the 45 to 54 age group, passing fifty percent for the 75 and over. This structure has been, in part, a product of small postwar immigration—and the absence of U.S. born people of Italian ancestry, age 80 and above (*i.e.,* born before the turn of the century).

POPULATION PYRAMIDS

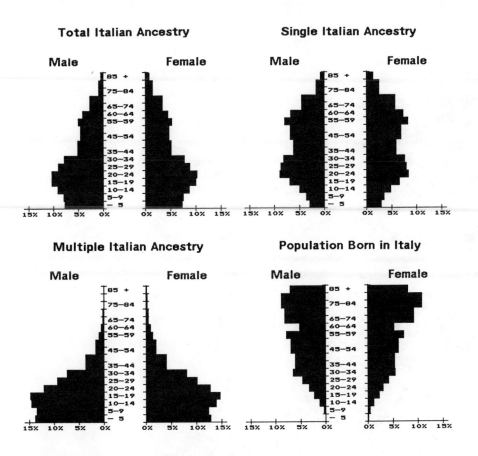

TERRITORIAL PATTERNS

The preference of Italians to live in urban areas is greater than for the U.S. population: only 12.8 percent of people of Italian ancestry (1,557,696) live in rural areas as compared to 26.3 percent for the U.S. population. Furthermore, only 57,983 or 0.47 percent are classified among farm population. This urban prominence is even more evident among people born in Italy: only 5.1 percent live in rural areas and 0.23 percent is classified as farm population.

The 1980 territorial distribution differs from the patterns of earlier studies. The areas and centers of older migration dominate the Atlantic Seaboard with an extension toward Chicago and the Midwest. Two other older areas are still noticeable on the U.S. map: Louisiana with an extension along the Texas coastal region; and the San Francisco Bay area.

Two new regions appear with greater prominence that they did in previous decades: Florida in the Southeast; and Arizona and Southern California. The Sunbelt regions are receiving their share of the Italians. The difference between the regions of older settlement is in the concentration of the Italians in selected city neighborhoods, while in the newly settled region, the spatial concentration in Italian neighborhoods and communities is less evident. The significant component of these Italian clusterings are older people, many of them joining the general migration trend toward warmer zones. The regional dispersal is similar to the general trend of the U.S. population. In the area between the Mississippi River and the Rockies only three counties have more than 10,000 people of Italian single ancestry. These include those coun-

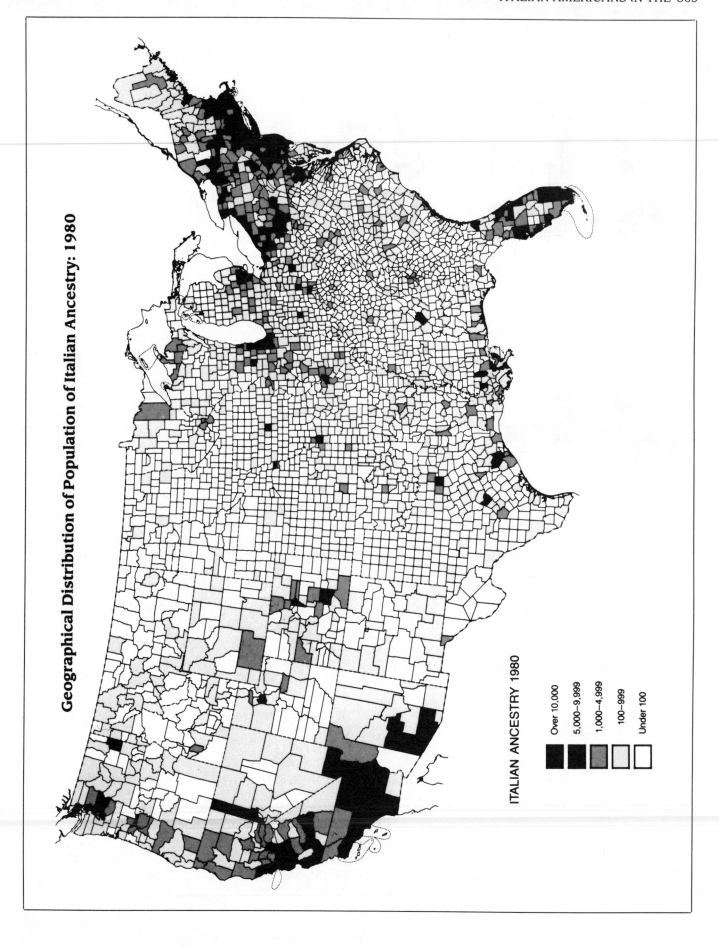

Geographical Distribution of Population of Italian Ancestry: 1980

ITALIAN ANCESTRY 1980

Over 10,000

5,000–9,999

1,000–4,999

100–999

Under 100

ties containing the cities of Houston, Texas, Kansas City and St. Louis in Missouri. New Orleans in the South and King County with Seattle in the Pacific Northwest are the only other western counties outside California and the Southwest to be in the same category.

The territorial spread of the Italian ancestry group reflects more than a century of migration. The present pattern is a product of direct migration of the Italian immigrants to various regions of the country and of the intensive secondary migration of the U.S. born Italians. The internal migration among the group consists of city-ward migration from small towns and villages, evident in the high urbanization rates, and interregional migration. There is some evidence that these relocations involve older populations directed toward the "Sunbelt" and, very recently, the migration of younger generations.

The clustering in major cities of the Atlantic seaboard continues to characterize the Italian ancestry group. Nevertheless, the dilution of the once cohesive Little Italies and the consistent decline of ethnic communities from both an aging population as well as secondary migration, continues. Observations in New York, Chicago, Detroit and San Fransisco point to the fact that the behavior of the Italians is similar to the rest of the U.S. population. After three generations, the traditional Italian neighborhoods retain their italianità in the gentrified atmosphere of ethnic restaurants and luxury shops, and much less in the once prevailing form of community halls, ethnic parishes and street markets. Jerre Krase reviewed these transformations in his presentation for the 1987 Chicago meetings of the American Italian Historical Association (AIHA).

The composite picture reveals that of the total of 12.2 million people, 58 percent were born in the Northeastern region and almost the same number (56.9) still reside there.

The composite picture reveals that of the total of 12.2 million people, 58 percent were born in the Northeastern region and almost the same number (56.9%) still reside there. The loss of 142,032 amounts to a two percent decline. The change in the Midwestern part of the country was minimal: from 1,961,008 born in Midwest to 1,995,424 now residing there, an absolute increase of 34,316 or 1.75 percent; significant increases—as expected, are evident in the Western and Southern region: In the South the increase is from 1,017,075 born in the region to 1,555,340 now residing there, an absolute increase of 558,381 amounts to a percentage growth of 48.8. The two gaining regions increased by over one million (1,096,646) while the total loss of the Northeast amounts to 142,032. The balance is covered by new immigrants.

McKenny and associates (McKenney, N.R., *et al.,* 1985) examined the regional breakdown of single and multiple ancestry data and observed that while the single ancestry is most prominent (more than 50% of the total Italian ancestry) in the states of Massachusetts, Rhode Island, Connecticut, New York, New Jersey, Pennsylvania and West Virginia, a contiguous area of significant Italian presence may be noted; not in isolated cities and villages but in the area in general. The only isolated states with a high percentage are Illinois, Florida and Nevada, where only Illinois counts among the prominent states of the Italian presence. Nevada and Florida show the presence of older, relocated single ancestry Italians. In aggregated figures, the Northeastern region harbors 4,372,070 of the 6,883,320 single-ancestry Italians (63.5% of the national total).

The analysis of the cities with the largest populations of Italian ancestry reveals two types of cities: a) centers of old Italian settlements, most prominently present in the U.S. core area from the East coast to Chicago, which embraces sixteen of the 23 cities with more than 25,000 people of Italian ancestry; to these, the New Orleans and the San Francisco clusters are to be added, to make it eighteen. The second set are cities of new prominence, San

Diego, San Jose, Houston and Phoenix, where the large clustering of persons of Italian ancestry is the result of relocational migration of the 1970s.

ASPECTS OF MIGRATION PROCESS

The new fact that is significant although not evident in recent migration figures is also the presence of the "Italians temporarily abroad". These are primarily professionals, counted in the foreign born population, but with limited association with the Italian American population and rarely seeking closer assocation. While the population could—and in rare instances does—provide the cultural and social link with Italy of today, it often remains separated from the Italian American reality. The Italians of Harvard have limited if any contacts with the Italian American community of North Boston or Boston's surroundings. The Italians, faculty or students at Yale do not associate with the New Haven Italians. It should be pointed out that the political refugees of 1930s often lived away from Italian American communities, but cultivated ties with them; otherwise they would have remained powerless in the political and social struggle of the period.

It does make a great deal of difference, however, for the social and cultural attitude of individuals and of the groups to distinguish between those who came to the United States to stay and those who came temporarily. At the present stage of technology it is more common that the migrants consider themselves to be in the United States temporarily and that the temporary nature of their migration could eventually become permanent.

The macro-data that are provided by the Census do not permit us even to begin an investigation of these aspects of Italian migration.

The Italians born outside Italy and outside the United States are part and parcel of the "nomadic" migration. Once uprooted, migration becomes easier.

Among them are the Italians in Germany or France. They are the source of three migration streams:

a) those that stay and change from temporary to permanent residents in Germany;

b) those who return to Italy, either to their home area or to some other part of Italy (return migration);

c) those who move forward to the next country of immigration which, according to some preliminary data, consists primarily of Argentina, Canada and the United States. The Canadian statistics identify this group because of their regular reporting of "country of birth" and also the "country of last permanent residence". It is assumed that the major portion of the 100,000 foreign born of Italian ancestry in the U.S. and not born in Italy, originates from this stream.

No matter which of the groups we examine, the population of Italian ancestry is constantly changing its composition, based on, as John de Vries (deVries, J., 1987) states in his study of linguistic minorities:

a) entries of new members
b) exits of existing members
where the entries consist of:
(i) births
(ii) immigration
(iii) language shift;
and where the exits are represented by:

(iv) deaths
(v) emigration
(vi) language shifts

The "language shift" component should be replaced here with the "ethnic awareness" that is, the undefined and unstable property of individuals, affected by both internal motivations and external constraints. In the demographic analysis of change, the entries and exits are reduced to births, deaths and in- and out-migration, although the variations of each component produces a significantly different composite even when the demographic balance sheet appears to be in equilibrium: the deaths of foreign born are often balanced by the births of native born, leaving the total aggregate (Italian ancestry) numerically unchanged. The fact of the matter, however, is that the Italian ancestry group still demonstrates noticeable growth: the number of births exceeds the replacement demand. We witness, nevertheless, a decline of the "foreign born cohort" concurrently with the growth of the Italian ancestry group. To a social analyst, it becomes relevant to recognize the transition from the dominance of the Italian born group to the prevailing of the American born group, from the dominance of the first generation to that of the second and by now the third and subsequent generations. The italianità of the group is greatly changed and carries with it major social, cultural and political consequences.

We can study these changes even further, by examing the transformation of individual participants: the acquistion of skills and experiences of individuals and cumulatively of Italian American society. The Italian person of 1960, Italian born or U.S. born, is twenty years older in 1980. He or she moved into a different age category and maybe replaced somebody else with equal, similar or different characteristics. The same individual in the longitudinal process maybe changed objectively and subjectively, maybe changed his household characteristics, and maybe the command of the Italian language. The further complication in this assessment is that the aggregate data provided by the Census do not permit us to analyze these modifications. They depend on the individual's declaration, based on his or her memory. Personal recollections, however, cannot replace the documented evidence of events.

The comparative analysis of the three generations, based largely on estimates, confirms that while the distinctiveness of the ethnic group is pronounced in the first generation (foreign born), it generally "disappears by the third generation" (Farley, R. and J. Noldert, 1984). This aspect becomes evident in the use of language where the use of the Italian language becomes less prominent from the first to the second and to the third generation and is also revealed in the language use data by age groups.

It would be most revealing to compare the demographic characteristics, longevity, educational achievement *etc.* of the Italian ancestry group with the demographic data on the Italian population in Italy. The speculation would be that the environmental circumstances are not the same, nor is the population of Italian ancestry in the United States a representative equivalent of the Italian population.

Of the 831,900 Italian born counted in 1980, almost 70 percent (69.6) came to the United States before 1960 and are, therefore, included in the 1960 Census; it is also interesting that 80.6 percent of all the Italian born acquired U.S. citizenship; 50,149 however, who came to the United States prior to 1960, are not yet citizens. The recent arrivals (1975-80) amount to four percent of the Italian born; because of residency requirements, they did not yet have the chance to obtain citizenship.

The comparative analysis of the three generations, based largely on estimates, confirms that while the distinctiveness of the ethnic group is pronounced in the first generation, it generally disappears by the third generation.

CULTURAL CHARACTERISTICS

It is much more difficult to assess the cultural characteristics of the Italians in the United States. Except for the educational level and literacy, we depend on information that is compiled through samples and often for other purposes. Even when objectively verifiable, it often depends on "soft" and vaguely formulated definitions.

In general, the "alien" Italian aspects, by which the Italians are distinct from other populations in the United States is less alien in 1980 than it was in 1880. The modernization of contemporary Italy has reduced the level of difference between the two countries and has also greatly reduced the regional differences within Italy. Keeping this in mind, the immigrants, Italian born of the 1980s, though placed under the same label (born in Italy), are a different group than those who arrived in the U.S. one hundred years ago.

The second consideration is that, in 1880, most U.S. Italians were foreign born, one century later, in 1980, only 6.6 percent consists of the Italian born. The third generation dominates. The overall image of the Italians as a distinct cultural group is receding and is becoming more aligned with the general American culture. The Italian ancestry group is not particularly dissimilar to other U.S. white populations be it by the educational achievement, by literacy, or by social and cultural properties.

The overall image of the Italians as a distinct cultural group is receding and is becoming more aligned with the general American culture.

Literacy

The "illiterate Italians" of the turn of the century are now followed by recent immigrants from Italy, where illiteracy has been greatly reduced. The 1981 figures of the Italian Census indicate an almost total elimination of illiteracy in the North (1.0%) and the Center (2.3%), and significant decline in the South (6.3 in 1981, as compared to 10.7 in 1971). The 1979 survey discovered that the illiteracy rate among the people of Italian ancestry is 0.54 percent, for the population over 24 years of age. Simply put, the Italians of 1900 are not the Italians of 1980.

Italian Language

> When language groups share an environment, some form of linguistic adaptation is necessary to allow communication... The two processes, mother-tongue shift versus intergenerational language retention, have numerous implications for the continued cohesion of minority groups, for processes of group assimilation and for inter- and intragroup relations (Stevens, G., 1985).

Morris Janowitz (Janowitz, M., 1978) states that "the intergenerational retention of minority languages [is] the key measure of ethnic solidarity and self-conception". It is evident—as expected that the most likely Italian speaking household consist of an adult population where both parents are of Italian ancestry; the percentage is reduced to half for the children ages five to seventeen.

The Italian-speaking group consists primarily of the people born in Italy: 77.9 percent of Italian born speak Italian at home; they form 45.5 percent of all the Italian ancestry group that speaks Italian at home. The percentage of Italian speakers (at home) increases proportionately with the age of the population, from 3.9 percent at age group five to thirteen to 15.1 for the 65-74 age group and reaches 17.1 percent of the 75 and older. For the young generation, the percentage figures are low, which indicates the progressive Americanization of their Italian ancestry group, with the English language as the language of communication. This observation has some consequences for the Italian language activities in the United States.

TABLE B

PERSONS OF ITALIAN ANCESTRY SPEAKING ITALIAN AT HOME
BY PLACE OF BIRTH

	Percentages		
	Age 5-17	Age 18 and over	Total
Born in Italy	92.0	80.4	648.411
Born in the U.S. — Multiple Ancestry	0.9	1.3	51,324
Born in the U.S. — Single Ancestry	9.8	13.8	771,971
Total Ancestry	4.5	16.2	1,499,149

Source: *Appendix E,* Tables 6.3, 6.19, 6.27, 6.35

TABLE C

ALL PERSONS OF ITALIAN ANCESTRY SPEAKING ITALIAN AT HOME
BY HOUSEHOLD COMPOSITION

	Households Total	Householder and Spouse Italian		
		Both	One	Neither
ages 5-17	4.4	14.1	1.2	0.9
ages 18 and over	16.2	28.6	6.5	4.3

Source: U.S. Bureau of the Census: *Special Tabulations on Italian Population.* 1987. The United States, Table 3. (Unpublished data).

Of the 80,085 people of age 85 and above, 2,600 or 3.3 percent do not speak Italian, while the younger generation has a higher proportion of English speakers. The median age of those who speak only English (27.7), is contrasted by the median age of those who do not speak it at all (median age 65.0).

TABLE D

ITALIAN LANGUAGE SPOKEN AT HOME, REGIONAL DIFFERENCES

	Total	Italy	U.S. Total	Northeast	Midwest	South
age 5-17	4.4	92.0	3.5	4.5	2.9	0.9
age 18 and over	16.2	80.4	9.4	10.8	7.4	5.4

Source: U.S. Bureau of the Census: *Special Tabulations on Italian Population.* 1987. The United States, Table 11. (Unpublished Data).

Ancestry and Nativity

Stanley Lieberson and Lawrence Santi (Lieberson, S. and L. Santi, 1985), analyzing the ancestry and nativity data, and comparing the Italians with other ethnic groups (1979 information), rank them sixth (after German, Irish, British, Scottish, French) by size, and thirteenth by percentage in the third and later generations. Italians are, therefore, among the older immigrants, but not quite so old as the West and Northern Europeans; they are aligned with the Central and Southern European group; and much older than the more recent immigrants from Latin America and Asia. The historical analysis of the Italian data, as shown by Lieberson and Santi, gives a high degree of correspondence between ancestry and nativity data, while for some other groups, the discrepancies are more pronounced.

Anna Maria Birindelli (Birindelli, A.M., 1986), in her recent study of permanent features and changing aspects of Italian migration abroad identified the change of direction and the change of composition of the Italian migration: in the pre-1956 period the largest flow was directed overseas; in the post-1956 it is oriented toward countries of Western Europe. Western Europe was the primary destination of the Italian manual workers; the Extra-European areas became the preferred destination of "white collar workers" in 1970s. It is therefore not only the country of destination, but also the composition of the migration flows that differ.

Numerous issues raised by McKenney and Seggar (Tomasi, L.F., 1985) at the Columbia University conference in 1983 and published in Tomasi's volume of 1985, including the comments of William D'Antonio (D'Antonio, W.V., n.d.), expressed as promising avenues of future research, remained mostly unfulfilled. We may ask why?

First and foremost is the difficulty of obtaining cross-tabulation, with the consistent data needed for research.

An example is the need to study the relationship between the first, second, third and subsequent generations of the Italians. Firm data exist for the first generation (foreign born), although even here the consistency is not total. The numerical magnitude of single ancestry for second, third and subsequent generations is not available in the same reliable form. They are only approximate estimates. These figures are obtained through interpolation, based in part on the 1970 data, in part on the sample surveys. The conclusions, therefore, on the third and subsequent generations are less a result of actual counts and more products of estimates. It should also be understood that the proportion of single ancestry toward multiple ancestry changes with generations. It is high in the first, but is less and less consistent in subsequent generations. While the progressive expansion of the magnitude of Italian ancestry increases with generations, their italianitá progressively declines to become one half, one fourth, one eighth or even less of the original italianitá.

FUTURE RESEARCH AND POLICY AGENDA

The 1990 Census will again collect information on ancestry, on place of birth, citizenship and year of entry in the United States. Because of consistency with the 1980 Census, a comparative analysis will be possible. It is generally known that the ancestry question was introduced for the first time in 1980 and therefore has no U.S. precedents, although it has been used by the Canadian Census for decades.

In a short presentation it is not possible to enumerate the components that

> *There is a major need to investigate the process by which individuals make their choices and how these are integrated (or not) with the societal choices.*

are relevant for a proper assessment of the Italians and for future investigation.

While on one hand the availability of data on tapes from the Census Bureau enables an easier access to some types of information, the reduction of printed versions makes the same information unavailable to many—and those public agencies that are not endowed with the hardware for data processing. The consequence is that while the information is being compiled, the access is not significantly improved, in fact it is often more restricted.

The future research, be it discipline-specific or interdisciplinary, has some major tasks ahead. The recent consultations of the National Science Foundation (not published) indicate some directions for future research for the social sciences. My colleague Richard Morrill (Morril, R.L., *n.d.*), summarized them in four categories; they are presented here as they could be applied to the study of Italians.

a) *Individual Decision Making* There is a major need to investigate the process by which individuals make their choices and how these are integrated (or not) with the societal choices. For the Italians in the United States, we do not know much about their decision making choices. Why did they decide to migrate, why did they decide to migrate to the United States, why to specific locations in the United States? We do have studies of information, available to potential immigrants. We do have some investigations regarding their choices between the United States and other potential destinations. However, we have little tangible information about their reasons to move to specific locations in the United States. The general theory of chain migration introduced by John MacDonald is often applied to the Italians; many local studies aim to verify the process. Yet, the integration of individual choices with the societal decisions is still open to further review and investigation.

This particular aspect of relationships between micro and macro studies is only at the beginning. The availability of Census track data for Single and Multiple Ancestry for the Italians is a treasure of information, which, however, requires extensive analyses (U.S. Bureau of the Census, 1980). This is the smallest unit of recording that is uniform for the census tracks of the U.S. Standard Metropolitan Statistical Areas—not quite the level of individuals but, nevertheless, in small aggregations. Such a national study has not been done. It would enable us to draw some historical perspectives on the present status and the results of over one hundred years of immigrant development.

b) *The Study of Collective Choices* How does the society choose between the alternatives? We do know something about the political decision making process, but in specific cases of the Italians within their formally constituted or not institutionalized communities: how do they choose their alternative? How important is it to identify the nature of the Italian American society, be it on the national as well as on the regional and local level, and then pursue the research about their collective choices? This is associated with the realization that of the twelve million people of Italian ancestry, only a fraction is in any way linked to the Italian American organized communities while the vast majority is a full partner to the otherwise not differentiated American society.

c) *Internationalization of Life and Institutions* While we are concerned with the specific territorial and organizational frames, within which the society operates, and we recognize the specificity of their characteristics, we are also aware of the persistent process through which the international barriers, be they political, social or cultural, are subsiding and linking the

> *The structures, often perceived as facilitators, obviously also restrict the flexibility of individual actions.*

"world" into an integrated and interdependent system.

The Italians in the United States are in this framework carriers of italianità far beyond the borders of Italy or of Europe and are, therefore, contributing to the internationalization of the world society.

At the Chicago meetings of the American Italian Historical Association in November 1987, the Italian consul general of Chicago stressed the presence of Olivetti and Fiat and the recognition of Columbus and Pavarotti, as evidence of transatlantic linkages. The internationalization, however, transcends these commercial and artistic interactions and links all the people of Italian descent into a "world agency", where the specificity of location and country becomes less prominent. We are, in fact, participants in this system.

d) *The Role of Institutions and Structures* Do they stimulate or hinder societal processes? What is the role of institutional inertia? How rigid or flexible are these structures?

The structures, often perceived as facilitators, obviously also restrict the flexibility of individual actions. Migration research has, for a long time, focused on these regulatory restraints, be it in dealing with migration as a process or with migrants as actors in this process.

Here, again, the data are scarce and difficult to obtain. The official data of the Census are of little use, since the institutions that we deal with are not recorded and counted. We do not have comprehensive information about the newspapers and their circulations. We do not have the mailing lists and the reviews of their spatial and temporal fluctuations. Even when these data exist locally, they are not accessible with ease and they are seldom comparable to other sets of data.

The fundamental issues directly related to the demographic and cultural aspects of the Americans of Italian descent, is that they are anything but a homogeneous group, that they are anything but an integral part of the American society with various levels of integration and adjustment.

What remains are two levels of further investigation:

1) The micro analyses, from individual behavioral research to micro-territorial investigation. For individual behavioral research, field work is needed. For micro-territorial research, the Census provided census track information for the Italian ancestry group for Standard Metropolitan Statistical Areas. The availability of microcomputer programs makes the automatic plotting feasible and further research opportunities at hand.

2) Further studies on the macro-level, with disaggregation of data into sub-categories. The Italians in the United States are not so homogeneous and uniform a group as many researchers imply.

Most of all, we need many more people of good will and dedication to pursue these research tasks. Every small step is an addition to the painstaking investigative effort—which is far from being completed.

REFERENCES

Allen, J.P., E.J. Turner
1988 *We The People. An Atlas of America's Ethnic Diversity.* New York: MacMillan Publishing Company, reference on p.224.

Birindelli, A.M.
1986 "Stable Features and Changing Aspects of Italian Migration Abroad in Recent Times", *Genus.* Vol. 42, No. 3-4. Luglio-Dicembre:141-163.

D'Antonio, W.V.
n.d. "Comments on Papers...", Pp. 57-60.

de Vries, J.
1987 "Problems of Measurement in the Study of Linguistic Minorities", *Journal of Multilingual and Multicultural Development No. 8.* 1-2:23-31.

Farley, R. and L.J. Neidert
1984 "How Effective Was the Melting Pot? An Analysis of Current Ethnic Differences in the United States", *Population Center Research Report*, No. 84-68, December. Ann Arbor, MI: University of Michigan, Population Studies Center, reference on p.23.

Janowitz, M.
1978 *The Last Half-Century: Societal Change and Politics in America*. Chicago, IL: Chicago University Press, p.308.

Lieberson, S. and L. Santi
1985 "The Use of Nativity Data to Estimate Ethnic Characteristics and Patterns", *Social Science Research*. 14:31-56.

McKenney, N.R., M.J. Levin and A.J. Tella
1985 "A Sociodemographic Profile of Italian Americans". In *Italian Americans. New Perspectives in Italian Emigration and Ethnicity*. Edited by L.F. Tomasi. Staten Island, NY: Center for Migration Studies, Pp.3-31, Reference on p.28.

n.d. "A Sociodemographic Profile of Italian Americans", Pp.3-31; Seggar, J., "Italian Migration to the U.S., 1966-1978: The Transition Period and a Decade Beyond Public Law 89-236", Pp.32-56.

Morrill, R.L.
n.d. personal communication.

Stevens, G.
1985 "Nativity, Intermarriage, and Mother Tongue Shift", *American Sociological Review*. Vol. 50, February:74-83. Quote on p.74.

Tomasi, L.F., Ed.
1985 *Italian Americans. New Perspectives in Italian Immigration and Ethnicity*. Staten Island, NY: Center for Migration Studies.

United States Bureau of the Census
1987 *Data User News*. May, Vol. 22, No. 5, p.1-3.

1983 *Ancestry of the Population by States: 1980*. 1980 Census of Population. PC80-S1-10. U.S. Government Printing Office, Washington, D.C.

1983 *1980 Census of Population and Housing. Census Tracts*. PHC80-2 Series. U.S. Government Printing Office, Washington, D.C.

1982 *Ancestry and Language in the United States: November 1979*. Current Population Reports, Series P-23, No. 116. U.S. Government Printing Office, Washington, D.C.

ITALIAN AMERICANS AND EDUCATION

Francis X. Femminella
Department of Educational Theory and Practice
State University of New York at Albany

Almost two centuries have passed since Benjamin Franklin wrote of his burning desire to see a system of pedagogy developed in the new nation he helped to forge. He proposed and advocated the establishment of schools that would achieve more than what schools were doing then. Franklin's ideas centered around the needs he perceived, especially in his home state of Pennsylvania, for schools that would teach, not only the skills of reading and writing to those who chose to attend, but the meaning of the *Office of Citizen* which was a prized status newly attained by the inhabitants of the colonies, and acquired at the price of blood, sweat and tears. Too many of Pennsylvania's people seemed to Franklin not to appreciate the import of their transformation from Subject to Citizen. Many, he asserted pointedly, either out of ignorance or, like refractory pieces of metal which are difficult to fuse or work, obstinately refused to speak the English language, and mulishly retained their German tongue.

During the half century that followed Franklin's writings, the cry was taken up by Horace Mann who also perceived a need for schools to reach the meaning of America, its language, its values and its ways. Mann was surrounded by the Irish throughout the Commonwealth of Massachusetts, whose foreignness offended. Schools, to his mind, would be the common experience drawing Americans to each other to eliminate differences while creating the fullness of the new nation. Mann's influence on schooling in America was stronger than Franklin's and he is credited with founding the public school system in the United States. Ethnic and religious schools did not disappear, but a new social structure began to develop, whose purpose ultimately was the cultural homogenization of the inhabitants of the land.

> *Another fifty or sixty years, and the subtle, hidden agenda of Americanization becomes a matter of public record and even demand.*

Another fifty or sixty years, and the subtle, hidden agenda of Americanization becomes a matter of public record and even demand. Ellwood O. Cubberley and Henry Pratt Fairchild, persons of high moral character and motivation, called for the "breaking up" of the immigrant communities and the eradication of ancestral heritage. The Jeffersonian notion that America as a democracy was a vital and ongoing experiment was narrowly interpreted by them; and they joined those who asserted that the American culture was now permanently established and all newcomers had to change their ways in order to fit into it. Clearly, as Tassone has so well put it, what was demanded was not Americanization but "Anglo-Saxonization".

Three score years more, and a new revolution was engendered in America, a revolution against white exploitation of blacks. The engaging impressiveness of this social movement inspired others and eventually it grew to include all those who rejected Anglo imposition. Fifteen years ago, in the halls of Congress a Bill was passed that sought to insure that all American school children should have the opportunity to learn about their's and their classmates' ethnic heritage; and the President signed it into law. Feeling themselves to be American, and having righteous claims based upon, among other things, their own and/or their relatives patriotic sacrifices in wars, those who participated in that revolution and those who lobbied for the passage of that bill call themselves Americans and they demand their rights, as citizens, to the full participation in the American heritage. The Italians in the United States are among these Americans (*See*, Figure I).

Fig. I: Foreign Born Population: 1980

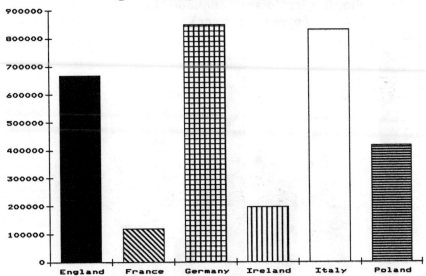

II

From the earliest times that Italians came to this country there were always at least some that participated in the educational system that was available to them. And there were some who made education available to others and these include the Waldensians, the early colonial Italians, and later, Father Giovanni, S.J., the first president of Georgetown University, and Father Anthony Maraschi who founded the University of San Francisco, and Father Joseph Cataldo who started Gonzaga University of Spokane, Washington, and Orazio De Attellis, the Molisano who began the Italian American periodical press in 1836, and others. In the migration of Italians from the Mezzogiorno, the educational background of most was poor or totally lacking. Participation in American education was for them a two edged sword.

In the value system of the Southern Italian, education was a high ideal, a privileged state, something not available to *contadini*, except in the case of one chosen for the priesthood. Practical, realistic people do not waste time on the unattainable. The educated person was viewed from two aspects: the good educated person was to be accorded the highest deference; the rest were thought of as probably being part of, or in cahoots with, the exploiting rich, and so were not to be trusted. In the United States, the statistics show clearly that the number of immigrants from Italy that went to school was small. Of course those who could, did go on to be educated; but more often they sent their children. In any case, what is clear is that education was not

From the earliest times that Italians came to this country there were always at least some that participated in the educational system that was available to them.

the main line to "success" for the Italians of the first or second generation. And make no mistake about it, the Italians who came to the United States came here for the most part to be relieved of their poverty. They learned quickly the workings of the American industrial machine; they saw lacunae in it and filled the need whatever it took. Hard work, risk taking and a lot of self respect were not unusual descriptors of these immigrants. Even the disadvantage of their limited literacy and their foreign tongue did not prevent them from moving up (*See,* Figure II).

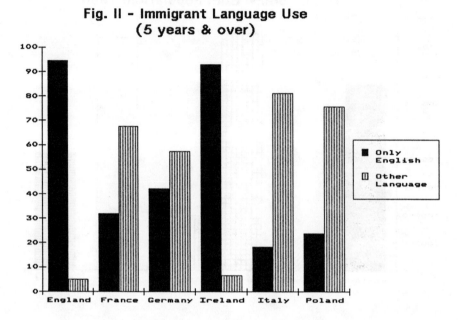

Fig. II - Immigrant Language Use (5 years & over)

Today's Italian immigrants are better advantaged than their earlier compatriots, but relative to competing immigrants they remain somewhat behind (*See,* Figure III).

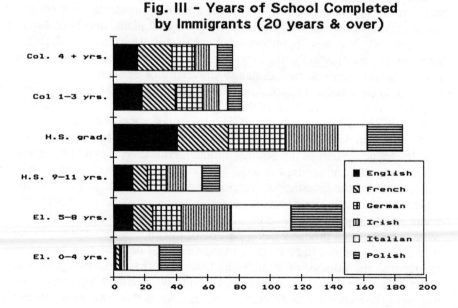

Fig. III - Years of School Completed by Immigrants (20 years & over)

Italian participation in education today, or at least as of 1980, is lower over all than that of certain other European ethnic groups with whom they have been contrasted if one takes the raw scores without measuring proportionality (*See,* Figure IV, Table 3.3).

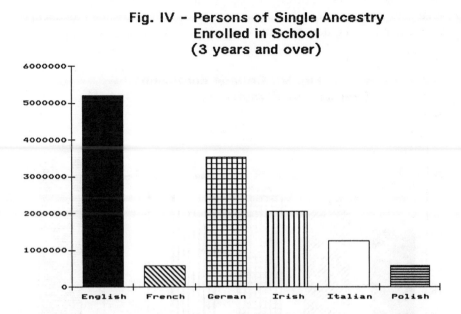

Fig. IV - Persons of Single Ancestry Enrolled in School (3 years and over)

But there are other ways of measuring these things. Third generation Italians and those beyond are heavily involved in education (*See,* Figures IV and V).

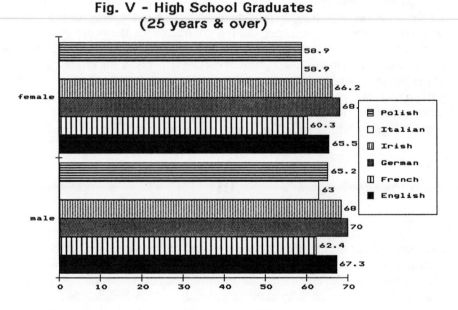

Fig. V - High School Graduates (25 years & over)

Of those over 25 years of age, 67.8 percent are high school graduates, not significantly different from the rest of the nation.

Of the total of 3,331 institutions of higher education in the United States in 1984, Sammartino listed 40 Italian American Presidents, or 1.2 percent of the total. Incidentally, in the SUNY system of some 64 campuses, less than one percent of the administration was Italian, there were two Presidents. In 1979, on the other hand, the American Italian Historical Association gave its attention to the Italian Americans in the professions in its annual conference coordinated by Professor Pane. Clearly, by then, Italians were using education for upward mobility and success. Of the population 25 years and over, 12.3 percent are college graduates. Enrollment in college is growing dramatically; and the number of graduates can be expected to increase (*See*, Figure VI).

One of the most important issues that has to be dealt with relates to our understanding of the significance of single and multiple ancestry.

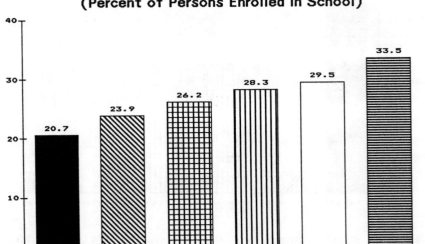

**Fig. VI: College Enrollment
(Percent of Persons Enrolled in School)**

While the census data can not be expected to provide us with explanations for these happenings, they do provide us with the basis for interesting speculations; and these conjectures and the contrasts that they illuminate may be provocatively persuasive. The statistics, when analyzed with caution, may contribute to a verifiable description of certain aspects of the changing lives of the Italian Americans. Sensitive interpretations must accompany the analysis so that they may contribute to our understanding of the salient dimensions and directions of the movement of the people. Important questions will remain, dealing with a variety of issues, requiring other kinds of research.

III

One of the most important issues that has to be dealt with relates to our understanding of the significance of single and multiple ancestry. In the past, certain dimensions of Italian American behavior has been explained by reference to this variable. The theory, for example, that Southern Italians placed relatively little value on education in general, and on higher education in particular, and that the immigrants carried this value to the U.S., seemed to be supported by the data collected in 1979 and 1980 (*See*, Figure VII).

The 1979 data included all Italians of single or multiple ancestry without regard to place of birth. Comparable data for 1980 reveals that the percent of

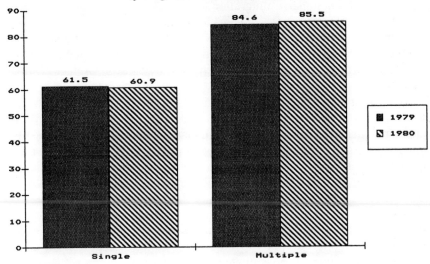

**Fig. VII: High School Graduates
(25 years & over)**

high school graduates among the over 25 age group is essentially unchanged, and, as before, it is not significantly different from the wider population (*See*, Figure. VIII).

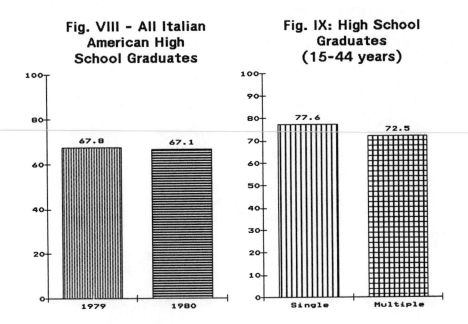

Fig. VIII - All Italian American High School Graduates

**Fig. IX: High School Graduates
(15-44 years)**

The new tabulation of 1980 data permits more intensive scrutiny and allows the presentation of a few different pictures. The result is that questions have to be raised about the type and nature of the data and the theory regarding single and multiple ancestry may have to be reassessed. The decision to look at the educational achievement of all persons 25 years and over may have produced misleading interpretations of Italian ethnicity.

To test the viability of the new tabulation, an alternate approach to the data was suggested. Instead of the 25 years and over cohort, the fifteen to 44 years cohort of persons of single or multiple ancestry born in the U.S. were analyzed. The choice, seemingly somewhat simplistic, was not entirely without logical foundation.

The great mass of Italian immigration to the U.S. took place between 1880 and 1920. Assuming twenty to 22 years for a generation, by the World War II period, native born Italian Americans clearly outnumbererd the foreign born. The Italian American new born were far more likely to be third generation or beyond than to be second generation. Many would be the children of multiple ancestry.

Students of Italian American census data have pointed out that these data reveal that as generations passed and outmarriage increased, the level of educational achievement rose; and a causal relationship is implied. By comparing persons of single and multiple ancestry in the fifteen to 44 age cohort it was felt that there would be less chance of error or the derivation of spurious meaning. The inclusion of the fifteen to 24 years cohort allows for the inclusion of more high school graduates than are eliminated by the exclusion of the 45 and over cohort which contains so many foreign born and children of foreign born. The more homogeneous and younger population of the fifteen to 44 age cohort may be expected to reflect more accurately the direction in which that population is moving (*See*, Figure IX).

Similarly, use of the 25 and over cohort tends to yield spurious interpretations when analyzing college graduates. There appears to be a large and significant difference between single and multiple ancestry achievement. However, what is being reflected is the survival of large numbers of individuals, many the children of the immigrants, and others the children of working class families enduring the "great depression" of the 1930s for whom higher education was unattainable.

In 1980, the percent of all persons of Italian ancestry, 65 years of age and over, in the United States was 9.3, relatively young, as compared to 11.3 percent for the total U.S. population. Of all single ancestry Italian Americans, 15.6 percent were 65 years of age and over, whereas only 1.1 percent of multiple ancestry Italian Americans were 65 and over. The Figure for single ancestry Italian Americans, born in the United States, was 13.8 percent; and for those of multiple ancestry born in the U.S. the Figure was one percent; and this is reflected in the 25 and over cohort (*See*, Figure X).

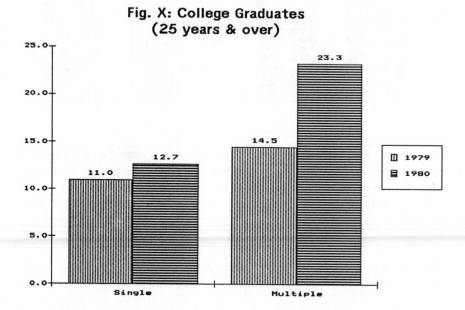

Fig. X: College Graduates (25 years & over)

This divergence in levels of attainment tends to fade when a more realistic birth cohort is used. The twenty to 44 age cohort was chosen, reflecting the ages that might be expected for completion of college graduation by type of ancestry (*See,* Figure XI).

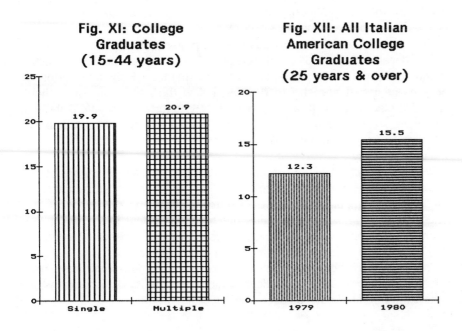

Fig. XI: College Graduates (15-44 years)

Fig. XII: All Italian American College Graduates (25 years & over)

Finally, when the total numbers of Italian Americans born in the U.S. of single and multiple ancestry are compared, the outmarriage of Italian Americans is clear; 51.1 percent are of multiple ancestry, 48.9 percent are of single ancestry (*See,* Chart 1).

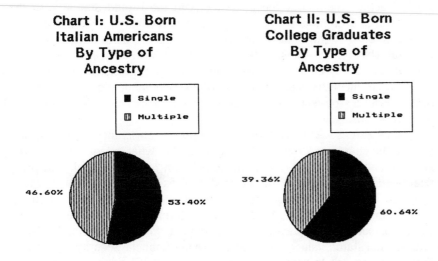

Chart I: U.S. Born Italian Americans By Type of Ancestry

Chart II: U.S. Born College Graduates By Type of Ancestry

But of all those born in the United States who have graduated from college, 59 percent are of single ancestry and 41 percent are of multiple ancestry (*See,* Chart 2).

Regularity within these groups is high as seen from the fact that 11.1 percent of all Italian Americans of single ancestry born in the U.S. have graduated from college and while 8.8 percent of those of multiple ancestry did as well. When the data is reviewed this way, the significance for education of type of ancestry is not very clear; certainly it cannot be said that single ancestry impedes educational achievement or that multiple ancestry is a predictor of higher achievement.

Since, of all U.S. born Italian Americans, 6.9 percent are of single ancestry and below the age of fifteen, while 19.2 percent are of multiple ancestry and below the age of fifteen, what is becoming increasingly evident is that longitudinal studies are required. To illustrate the problem, during the second half of the decade of the 1950s, children born in the U.S. of multiple ancestry outnumbered those of single ancestry for the first time. Even considering all persons of Italian ancestry in the U.S., below the age of fifteen, without regard to place of birth, (that is born in the U.S., in Italy, or elsewhere abroad) the Figure stays essentially the same. The less than 6.9 percent noted above, changes to 6.6 percent being of single ancestry, and 17.8 percent being of multiple ancestry.

Relative to each other, 74 percent of all U.S. born Italian Americans below the age of 15 are of multiple ancestry and 26 percent are of single ancestry (and, disregarding place of birth, the Figures are 73% and 27% respectively). The increasing ancestry population difference is evident in the under five years of age cohort where the single ancestry group reduces to 22.5 percent and the multiple ancestry group increases to 77.5 percent.

This much seems quite certain on the basis of those data we do have: irrespective of type of ancestry, college achievement by Italian Americans, as others have pointed out, has been rising (*See*, Figure XII).

IV

Educational achievement among Italian Americans follows upon their general achievement over the generations in the United States. With the acquisiton of even modest financial ability, and a willingness to make sacrifices, schooling, highly valued but generally denied to them in Italy, became an attainable reality. Census data seem to confirm this. But these data cannot tell us why education was sought. The ancient dichotomy between education to meet the needs of society on the one hand, and on the other, to help individuals perfect their nature provides the perspective for possible interpretations.

To what extent was education looked upon as enrichment of the person beyond the character formed in the family; and to what extent was it viewed pragmatically as a means of material enrichment? At least initially, the practical needs of making a living dictated choices. Primary education, which provided skills in reading and writing and arithmetic, was useful in enhancing employment or job advancement. If one could afford higher, especially postsecondary education one sought it so that one could acquire professional status, valued more for the greater financial security it promised than anything else. In time, as income levels improved, educational achievement rose. By then, the prestige one might accrue from education had become a motivating feature. For many, too, the intrinsic value of self enlightenment and creativity was impelling.

Perhaps a clue to understanding this can be found in another significant area of analysis, the relationship of gender and education, and the changing values in all industrial societies with respect to this important variable. Traditionally, higher levels of education were reserved for males; and women were discouraged from and even denied access to them. This was true in the U.S. as well as in Italy. With increased consciousness and the demand by women for recognition of their rights, schooling began to be more equally available to them.

In the total United States population, male and female high school graduates during the period from 1950—1980 divided as follows: male—49 percent, females—51 percent. The comparable age cohort of Italian Americans, once again, is the fifteen to 44 years, in which 47 percent of the high school graduates are male and 53 percent are female. There appears little difference between the Italian American and total U.S. population.

When comparing college graduates, the similarity between the two populations (total and Italian American) continues but a difference within these populations, based on gender, appears. For those same years, 58 percent of the total U.S. (college graduate) population was male and 42 percent female. Italian American college grads in the 20 to 44 age cohort were 50 percent male and 40 percent female (*See*, Figure XIII).

What is seen here is that in earlier days, education was either simply not affordable, or perceived only in its utilitarian value for increased material gain.

Fig. XIII: School Achievement By Gender

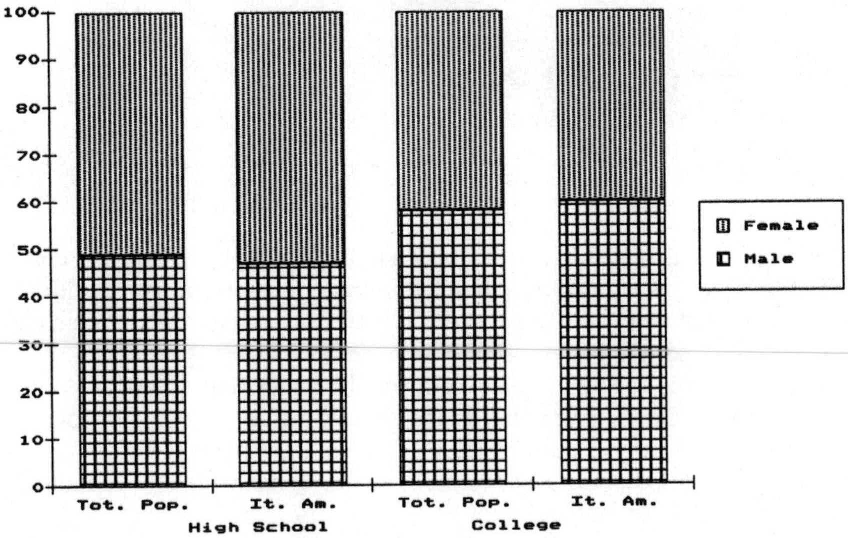

What is seen here is that in earlier days, education was either simply not affordable, or perceived only in its utilitarian value for increased material gain. Since earning a livelihood was thought mainly to be a male function, higher education for women was either not greatly valued or in many cases, genuinely devalued. At the same time, young women might be expected to be well spoken and able to read, so, secondary education, which might have interfered with a young mans employment, was permitted to girls. This is reflected in the 44 and over high school graduates (of total Italian ancestry) where females outnumbered males, 55 percent to 45 percent.

These were not only the Italian traditions found in Italy, they were the values of Americans in the U.S. as well. Female high school graduates of multiple Italian ancestry, 44 and over, born in the U.S., outnumber males 58 percent to 42 percent. In recent decades higher education has become increasingly available to women in the U.S., in Italy and in other industrial societies as well.

The census data show these relationships and confirm the similarity between both the Italian American and the wider total population. When the data pertaining to type of ancestry, whether single or multiple, and college graduation, is examined, the relationships change significantly. Here it appears that the traditional emphasis on male responsibility for livelihood continues in single ancestry homes as evidenced by higher rates of educational achievement (*See*, Figure XIV).

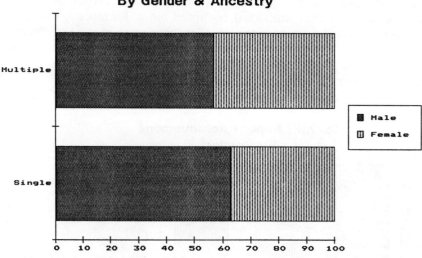

Fig. XIV: Italian American College Graduates By Gender & Ancestry

Among persons of Italian ancestry born in Italy in the twenty to 44 cohort, more than twice as many males than females are college graduates.

Among persons of Italian ancestry born in Italy in the twenty to 44 cohort, more than twice as many males than females are college graduates. With the changing enrollment rates at southern Italian Universities, these ratios can be expected to soften.

In the meantime, the relationship of schooling and Italian Americans continues to perplex. On the one hand, Italian Americans are enrolling in colleges in proportionately higher numbers than all other ethnic groups except Polish, on the other hand, dropout rates remain unconscionably high if education is valued for more than material gain.

Dropout figures are not directly available for the Italian American population either nationally nor even in the states with high Italian populations. Figures are now available, however, that describe persons having "less than twelve years of school". The figures for both the total and the white American population may be compared to the Italian Americans of the twenty to 24 year cohort. Little difference is seen when compared by type of ancestry, but once again gender makes a difference; females drop out in lesser numbers (*See*, Table 1).

Once again the question of meaning arises. What do these drop out figures signify, to us, and to those who leave school? Obviously, there may be a great waste of talent and a pitiful exposure to future failure as a result of being unprepared for life either with practical knowledge or with the personal discipline that study teaches us. Drop outs mean that teachers have not reached our young, the social milieu has not motivated them and, in time, both the drop out and all of society will, in many different ways, have to pay for this.

TABLE 1

PERSONS WHO DID NOT GRADUATE FROM HIGH SCHOOL
(Age 20-24)

| | Total | ITALIAN AMERICANS | | | | | US POPULAT. | |
| | | Single | Multip. | Single | Multip. | Born in | White | Total |
				US born	US born	Italy		
Percent of Total Population:								
Male	5.9	6.5	5.4	6.1	5.4	15.2	---	---
Female	4.7	4.9	4.5	4.5	4.5	13.0	---	---
Total	10.6	11.3	10.0	10.5	9.9	28.1	14.0	15.2
Percent of population with less than 12 years of school:								
Male	56.0	56.9	54.4	57.4	54.4	54.0	---	---
Female	44.0	43.1	45.6	42.6	45.6	46.0	---	---

Source: U.S. Bureau of the Census. *Statistical Abstract of the United States: 1987* (107th edition.) Washington, DC, 1986, and *Appendix F,* Tables 6.1, 6.9, 6.17, 6.25, 6.33 and derivatives.

Relative to the wider population for persons 25 years and over Italian Americans are not different.

Little or no institutional support is given by Italian Americans to combatting the problem of high school drop outs. Perhaps, the success of so many Italians over the generations of their presence in the United States leads to the belief that education is of no importance. There is no polemic about this once definitions are established. The meanings and aims of education are not the subject of this study, neither is the metaphoric use of the term by Italian Americans.

Among Italian Americans, education was not, as was asserted earlier, the major means of upward mobility. The median income of $21,960 for Italian American families compares favorably with the $20,439 for white American families. Of all Italian American families with income exceeding $25,000, more than 21 percent have less than twelve years of school, and 27 percent are college graduates. Of those earning $50,000 or more, 16.3 percent have less than twelve years of school, and less than 42 percent are college graduates. Relative to the wider population for persons 25 years and over Italian Americans are not different.

The integration of Italian Americans into American society is evident in all aspects of their lives and is also apparent in the lives of other Americans. While the statistics show that the younger members of the group are "succeeding" in higher proportions than the average for white American society, the census data also indicate that even the 25 years and over group has lower rates of incompletion of school, and higher rates of high school and college graduation.

One hundred years ago, when the enormous transmigration of people from the villages of Italy to all parts of this country and especially to the cities began, they were handicapped by too much illiteracy and an inadequate knowledge of English. Today, "English only" is spoken by 85 percent of Americans of Italian ancestry, including eighteen percent of those born in Italy (*See,* Figure 15, Tables 3, 11, 19, 27, 35).

This language distribution further demonstrates the Italian American cultural convergence with the wider Anglo American society. At the same time, the increase in higher education enrollments in Italian language and

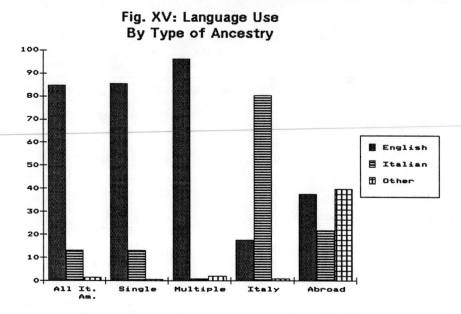

**Fig. XV: Language Use
By Type of Ancestry**

culture as noted in the *ADFL Bulletin* of the Assocation of Departments of Foreign Languages, and in courses on the Italian American experience was unexpected and is in contrast to the declining enrollments in French and German, the traditionally required courses.

This inquiry into the unique history and the age-long values and ideals of one's people may represent an attempt on the part of young Americans of Italian descent to establish a link with their heritage that may have been denied them by the American schools. This may be seen as part of their maturation and what E.H. Erikson calls identity formation. Young adults, making up their own minds, have to have knowledge, and need to feel the connectedness between themselves and the important others in their lives, that teach them who they are and how they came to be. Census data are like good photographs, they reveal much, even things hidden from the naked eye; but they are not the real thing.

ITALIAN AMERICAN FAMILY LIFE

Francis X. Femminella
Department of Educational Theory and Practice
State University of New York at Albany

I

In 1983, when Lydio Tomasi organized the International Conference on the Italian Experience in the United States, a lot of attention was again focused on questions concerning the nature of Italian American identity. Questions were asked about who the Italians were, where they lived, how they perceived themselves and how they related to the American social environment. A sociodemographic profile based upon census data was presented which concluded that, overall, the Italian population is similar to the rest of the population of this country. Whether this finding was surprising or not, a further conclusion was startling, namely that, "The overall figures for Italians mask vast differences between the Italians who reported solely as Italian (largely first- and second generation) and those reported as multiples (almost entirely third- and subsequent generations) in the 1980 census".[1]

The purpose of this chapter is to analyze the newly released data related to these populations of Italian Americans (single versus multiple ancestry, American versus Italian or other foreign place born, *etc.,*) which were not previously presented from the 1980 census. The "vast differences" noted in that earlier study were shown to exist mainly in residential patterns, and in educational achievement. Regarding the family, they quoted what we had said more than a decade ago. "Marriage was essential for the southern Italian as a source of social identity, and family stability still seems to be relatively intact" (Femminella and Quadagno, 1975:73). They went on to say that "information from the 1980 census provides support for the hypothesis that family relationships are very strong among the Italian population".[2]

Among the most critical family questions that could be asked today are those that inquire about the stability of the family. As an institution, in a society that is itself in a state of continuous change and emergence, it is not unrealistic to expect that the family structure might also change, and indeed, as we will point out, it has. Whether the changes that occur are to be thought of as good or bad is, of course, purely a value judgement. But when we characterize changes as being integrative, disintegrative or neutral, based upon whether the change contributes to the organization and its functioning or not, we clarify and measure rather than just moralize. Some changes are neutral in this respect, and others reflect the change in functions that are thought to be needed in the society.

For the most part, family stability traditionally was defined more in terms of what it was not, rather than what it was. It was not dissolution or disorganization. Strong, stable families are those whose members stayed together, performing the reproductive, educational, recreational, religious, protective

> *Among the most critical family questions that could be asked today are those that inquire about the stability of the family.*

and affectional functions thought to be the essential works of the family. Stable families may be upset and disturbed by conflict, sickness, death, poverty, or other obstacles to effective functioning, but they are not actually disintegrated, however burdensome these problems may be. On the other hand, disorganized families are those whose members, experiencing profound crises, simply find it impossible to cope and therefore breakup under the pressure of the disintegrative forces, whether they be physical, psychological or social.

In the next pages we will contrast these new data with some of those which were available, and look at Italian American family life as it is evolving within the different Italian American populations. Although the data were not set up to relate specifically to the relative stability or disorganization of the different groups of Italian American families, (*i.e.* single versus multiple ancestry, *etc.,*) clues were found from which inferences could be made. These judgements by necessity have been made cautiously; and conclusions drawn from them must be recognized as tentative.

II

The first and most obvious finding is that generally speaking, like other Americans, Italian Americans live in families or in non-family households. That is, the number living in group quarters is not significantly different from other Americans. Table I shows the similarity in this respect across ethnic lines and within the Italian American population. "Across ethnic lines" refers to comparison with the five largest white American ethnic groups; "within the Italian American population" refers to comparison with all those 1) who claimed in any way to be all or partly of Italian descent, with those 2) born here or abroad who were of only Italian descent, with those 3) born in the U.S.A. of Single Italian ancestry, or those 4) born in the U.S.A. of multiple ancestry (part Italian), with those 5) of single or multiple Italian ancestry born in Italy. Data for the "across ethnic lines" was previously published; within the Italian population data are unpublished.

Reading down the column, it is clear that there is little difference among the ancestry groups in the percentage of persons living in families. While slightly more Irish and Italians live in families,, fewer Poles do. Within the Italian American population, those of multiple ancestry born in the United States (group 4) stand out in that a slightly larger percentage of them (93%) live in families; but as we look across the column, we see that their families and households have the largest number of persons (5.01 and 5.09). This is in sharp contrast to the Italy born (group 5) 84% of whom live in families, which are, more significantly, the smallest, with 2.06 persons per family and 1.08 per household, which is much smaller even than the average in Italy where the number of persons per family is 3.0. (*See*, Table I).[3]

At first flush it may appear that traditional values are operating in reverse, but a closer scrutiny of the available data shows that other variables are influencing the numbers. Specifically, it must be pointed out that 45 percent of persons of Italian ancestry in the United States born in Italy (group 5) are 65 years of age or older, and 1.9 percent are below the age of fifteen. Italians of multiple ancestry in the U.S. (group 4), on the other hand, have only one percent over the age of 65, and 41 percent aged fourteen or below. The Index of Aging (defined as the number of persons under fifteen multiplied by 100)

The first and most obvious finding is that generally speaking, like other Americans, Italian Americans live in families or in non-family households.

TABLE 1

FAMILY AND HOUSEHOLD COMPOSITION
FOR SELECTED ANCESTRY GROUPS

	PERCENT OF PERSONS LIVING in Families in Households (including non-relatives)		NUMBER OF PERSONS per Family per Household Non-relatives: excluded included	
	in Families	in Households	per Family excluded	per Household included
TOTAL US POPUL.	88	97	3.27	2.74
SELECTED ANCESTRY GROUPS:				
English	87	98	2.82	2.41
French	86	97	2.72	2.35
German	86	97	2.58	2.24
Irish	88	97	2.73	2.32
Italian	88	98	2.60	2.28
Polish	83	98	2.48	2.13
ITALIAN ANCESTRY IN THE U.S.:				
Total Ancestry	90	98	3.52	2.99
Single ancestry	88	98	2.60	2.28
Single anc., U.S. born	89	98	2.70	2.37
Mult. anc., U.S. born	93	98	5.01	5.09
Italy born	84	98	2.06	1.80

Source: *Appendix C,* Table 3.5; *Appendix D,* Table 4.1.

for these multiple ancestry, U.S. born Italians is a remarkably low 2.4 (group 4), while for those born in Italy it is an extremely high 2409 (group 5) (*See,* Table II). Contrast this with what the Italians feel is an aging population in Italy, 44.2 in 1981 and projected to more than double by the year 2001 to about 94.2.[4]

TABLE 2

INDEX OF AGING

Selected Ancestry Groups		Italian Ancestry Groups:	
ENGLISH	86.3	TOTAL ITALIAN	38.2
FRENCH	97.9	SING ANCES ITAL	134.5
GERMAN	207.5	SING BORN IN US	88.8
IRISH	116.0	MULT BORN IN US	2.43
ITALIAN	134.5	ITALY BORN	2409
POLISH	192.9		

Source: *Appendix C,* Table 3.1; *Appendix D,* Table 4.1.

Thus, while Group 4, the multiple ancestry Italians born in the U.S., have larger families, one reason the statistics turn up this way is that so many of these Group 4 persons are still children living with their parents, not independent adults living on their own. Conversely, the older, Italy born group 5), inde-pendently occupying their own households, has a larger number of small families. This finding is supported by the data which show that there is little or no difference in the proportion of family and non-family households in these two groups (*See*, Table III).

On the other hand, the data reveal a larger difference between these two groups in certain household sizes. Of the multiple born in U.S. (group 4) households, 47.3 percent contain one or two persons, while a much larger percent—58.5—of the Italy born group (group 5) households contain one or two persons. But, in the number of three and four person households an obverse relation is exhibited. Of the multiple born in U.S. (group 4) house-holds, 38.6 percent compared to the smaller 28.4 percent of the Italy born (group 5) have three and four persons, which reflects again the different age structures of these families.

Another important way that Italian Americans are like other Americans is that they marry and get divorced, although, in fact, they do marry a little less and divorce quite a bit less.

TABLE 3

PROPORTION OF FAMILY TO NON-FAMILY HOUSEHOLDS
(per 1000 households)

Selected Ancestry Groups:			Italian Ancestry Groups:		
ENGLISH	745 : 255		TOTAL ANCESTRY	762 : 238	
FRENCH	737 : 263		SINGLE ANCESTRY	770 : 230	
GERMAN	747 : 253		SINGLE U.S. BORN	775 : 225	
IRISH	724 : 276		MULT U.S. BORN	739 : 261	
ITALIAN	770 : 230		ITALY BORN	747 : 253	
POLISH	730 : 270				

Source: *See* Table 2

Another important way that Italian Americans are like other Americans is that they marry and get divorced, although, in fact, they do marry a little less and divorce quite a bit less. Obviously, marriage rates are influenced by the sex ratio, defined here as the number of males in the population divided by the number of females, multiplied by 1000 (m/ f * 1000), that prevails in any given society. In the United States in 1980, the sex ratio for Americans of all ages in 1980 was 945. That is to say, there were 945 males in the population for every 1000 females of all ages.

Since women tend to outlive men, the sex ratio declines as the population ages. For Americans 65 years of age and older, the sex ratio in 1980 was 676.[5] In Italy, both ratios seems to be higher, 968 for all ages and 718 for the over 65 population. This difference may in part be explained by differences in the life-expectancies of both countries. For Italy, male life expectancy is 70.6 and female is 77.2 as compared to the U.S. life expectancies in 1980 of 70.7 for white males and 78.1 for white females.[6] Table IV shows the ratio of males to females within the selected white ethnic groups and the Italian ancestry groups (*See*, Table IV).

Age and sex constitute the most basic biological class of demographic characteristics needed to analyze family life. The Tables above will be used as we look at the patterns that emerge in the description of the various groups' marital status. For the sake of discussion, marital statistics will be presented

TABLE 4

RATIO OF MALES TO FEMALES BY AGE AND ETHNICITY

Selected Ancestry Groups:	all ages	65 and ov.	Italian Ancestry Groups:	all ages	65 and ov.
ENGLISH	969	676	TOT ITALIAN	987	785
FRENCH	917	620	SING ANCES ITAL	993	790
GERMAN	1017	735	SING BORN IN U.S.	999	778
IRISH	916	628	MULT BORN IN U.S.	980	668
ITALIAN	993	790	ITALY BORN	957	816
POLISH	944				

Source: *Appendix C,* Table 3.1; *Appendix D,* Table 4.1

in both percentages and rates.

To contrast the marriage rates of the five Italian American groups, the data were analyzed first by computing the percent of persons aged fifteen and over who, at the time of the census, were married (the now married group), and then by computing the percent of all persons fifteen and over who were not single, which includes separated, widowed and divorced persons. This manipulation of the data may permit some contrast with the already published data on marriage rates within the six white ethnic groups we have been looking at.

To use these two different statistical universes, it should be noted that in the selected ancestry groups, the population is those aged fifteen to 54. In the Italian ancestry groups the population consists of those aged fifteen and over. A point of cross-reference is the Italian ancestry group which contains the same universe but different age cohorts as the Single Ancestry Italian (group 2). By way of example, the rates of marriage and divorce for the Italian ancestry group are 400 and 66.8, respectively, which are the functional equivalents of the 689 and 42.1 rates of the Single Ancestry Italians. Comparison of the ranking of all other ratings is facilitated by this cross-reference (*See*, Table V).

While the French ancestry group has the highest rate of marriage and is tied for second place for percent of those married, it is first both in rate and percent of those divorced. The sex ratio seems to have played very little part in this phenomenon; the French are almost tied with the Irish in having a preponderance of females over males in their population. The French also rank fifth in aging; only the English have a younger population. At the same time, the Italians rank fifth in marriage rate and sixth in percent of population married; they rank fifth in both percent and rate of divorce. Only the Polish have lower rates of marriage and divorce. The Italian group is an aging group, second only to the Polish; but it is the group that comes closest to having equal numbers of males and females in the populaton. For what it's worth, a perfect negative correlation exists between the rankings of the percent of population divorced and the means and medians of family income for each of these groups, the Polish having the highest income, the French having the lowest.

Looking now at the "within the Italian ancestry" groups, the Italy born (group 5) is the most aged group and the one with the lowest sex ratio. It is the first both in percent and in rate of marriage and it is last both in percent

TABLE 5

MARITAL STATUS OF SELECTED ANCESTRIY
AND ITALIAN ANCESTRY GROUPS

	Married	Rate*		Divorced	Rate*
SELECTED SINGLE ANCESTRIES: (Percent of those aged 15-54)					
ENGLISH	73	406		11.50	94.7
FRENCH	74	450		11.85	101.6
GERMAN	74	432		10.10	86.4
IRISH	71	416		11.00	95.3
ITALIAN	69	400		7.56	66.8
POLISH	71	384		6.89	62.4

	Not Single	Rate*	Married	Divorced	Rate*
ITALIAN ANCETRY: (Percent of those aged 15 and over)					
TOTAL ANCESTRY	70	527	59	4.93	37.3
SINGLE ANCESTRY	90	689	65	4.77	42.1
SINGLE U.S. BORN	76	660	64	5.14	44.8
MULTIPLE U.S. BORN	53	314	47	5.23	30.8
ITALY BORN	91	894	66	2.30	22.7

*Rate = per 1000 of the groups' total population

Source: *Appendix C,* Table 3.5; *Appendix D,* Table 4.2.

The single ancestry born in U.S. group comes closest of all groups to having equal numbers of male and female members.

and rate of divorce. The multiple born in U.S. group (group 4) is by far the youngest group; it has the fourth lowest sex ratio just above the Italy born group; and while it is last in both percent and rate of marriage, it is first in percent of divorces, but fourth in rate of divorce, just above the Italy born.

The Single born in U.S. group (group 3) comes closest of all groups to having equal numbers of male and female members. It ranks third on the index of aging, third in both percent and in rate of marriage, second in percent of divorce and first in rate of divorce, just slightly higher than the single ancestry Italian group (group 2). Although it has the highest rate of divorce of all Italian groups, it remains below all of the other non-Italian ancestry groups except the Polish.

The age and sex structure of the family enables us to understand the workings of population dynamics. Natural increase is limited in an aging society; and may be in need of check in a young society. Two measures which reflect the age and sex structures of the groups we are studying will be used to describe and compare their reproduction. Both measures deal with actual reproduction rather than fecundity or potential reproduction, but they describe different aspects of the phenomenon. One without the other may be misleading. Together, they provide clues as to what is going on, as it were, within the study populations.

The fertility ratio (F.R.) is defined as the number of children under five years of age in a population in relation to [that population of] the women of childbearing age of that population, *viz.,* fifteen to 44 years of age, multiplied by the constant 1000 (# child < 5 / # of women 15-44 * 1000). This figure may be misleading. A population with a high percentage of women of child-bearing age, if they are having children, may have a higher F.R. than an older population whose fewer, relative to the total population, childbearing age women are having more children. The crude birth rate (B.R.), therefore is used, since it is defined as the number of children ever born of women fifteen to 44 years of age in relation to the total population (# child ever born/ total population * 1000). Together, the F.R. and B.R. give a somewhat more meaningful picture of the actual reproduction activity of a society (*See*, Table VI).

TABLE 6
FERTILITY RATIO AND CRUDE BIRTH RATES

Selected Ancestry Groups:			Italian Ancestry Groups:		
	F.R.	B.R.		F.R.	B.R.
ENGLISH	254	296	TOTAL ANCESTRY	320	240
FRENCH	173	353	SINGLE ANCESTRY	142	249
GERMAN	200	301	SINGLE U.S. BORN	154	252
IRISH	163	315	MULTIPLE U.S. BORN	506	228
ITALIAN	142	249	ITALY BORN	11	227
POLISH	123	253			

Source: *Appendix C,* Table 3.5 and 3.1; *Appendix D,* Table 4.1 and 4.2.

It is clear that Italians and Poles have the lowest fertility ratios and birth rates.

In reviewing the data given for the selected white ancestry groups, it is clear that Italians and Poles have the lowest fertility ratios and birth rates. As we have already seen, these two groups rank highest (oldest) on the aging index, have the lowest percent of persons aged fifteen to 54 married, and have the lowest marriage rates. The English, with the highest fertility ratio are the last (youngest) on the aging index. The French, with the highest birth rate are next to last on the aging index and have the highest marriage rate. The Germans, next to the French on the aging index, have the second highest fertility ratio, the second highest marriage rate and are tied with the French for percent of persons aged fifteen to 54 married. Interestingly, the German also have the highest proportion of males to females, 1017 males to each 1000 females.

Within the Italian ancestry group, the Italy born group with its very high aging index has the lowest fertility ratio and birth rate even though it has the highest percent married and highest marriage rate. This is the group with the smallest household size, and least number of persons living in families. The multiple born in U.S. group with the largest number of persons in families and households, the lowest aging index, lowest percent of persons married, and lowest marriage rate, has the highest fertility ratio. In spite of that it has the second lowest birth rate, almost exactly as low as the Italy born group. Here again values seem to be a less important variable than age, although changing values must not be discounted.

An important reality of modern family life, not only in the United States but in all industrialized societies, is the rising number of children being raised by one parent. Whether this situation is caused by death, divorce or desertion may have value considerations, but is irrelevant to the child's care and welfare needs. Again, given the caution about interpreting in terms of values when other variables may be operating, it appears that the multiple born in the U.S. group and the Italy born group stand apart and at completly opposite poles from all other groups, Italian and otherwise, with respect to the percent of families having a female without spouse with children under age six and under age eighteen (*See*, Table VII).

TABLE 7

PERCENT OF FAMILIES WITH FEMALE HOUSEHOLDER,
WITHOUT SPOUSE, WITH CHILDREN

SELECTED ANCESTRY GROUPS	Under 6	Under 18	ITALIAN ANCESTRY GROUPS	Under 6	Under 18
ENGLISH	2.1	6.08	TOTAL ANCESTRY	1.9	6.15
FRENCH	2.4	7.03	SINGLE ANCESTRY	1.3	4.87
GERMAN	1.5	4.73	SINGLE U.S. BORN	1.5	5.31
IRISH	2.1	6.59	MULT. U.S. BORN	3.7	9.99
ITALIAN	1.3	4.87	ITALY BORN	0.5	2.30
POLISH	1.2	4.48			

Source: *Appendix C*, Table 3.15; *Appendix D*, Table 4.8.

Just under two percent of Italian Americans do not reside in families or in households.

Although we usually think of families residing together, in Table 1 we saw that just under two percent of Italian Americans do not reside in families or in households. These persons reside in various group quarters, including different kinds of hospitals, college dormitories, military quarters, homes for the aged, homes for dependent and neglected children, correctional institutions, rooming and boarding houses, *etc.* By far the predominant form of group living is residence either in Homes for the Aged or in college dormitories.

One difficulty in comparing these data is that different reporting agencies use different and overlapping categories. When talking about group quarters for aged persons unable to maintain their own household, for example, "Old Age Homes", "Homes for the Aged", "Home for the Elderly", "Nursing Homes", "Housing for the Aged and Dependent", "Senior (or Senior Citizen) Housing", are all used and each requires a definition which often is not available. "Aged" is variously defined as chronological age 55, 60, 62 or 65.

Of the six white ethnic groups of our study, Italians have the smallest percent residing in group homes. Table VIII shows the percent of each group's total population residing in all group quarters, and the rate per 100,000 of population residing in homes for the aged and in college dormitories.

Clearly, Italians more than any other group tend not to live their lives in group quarters. In particular, although as we have seen they are an aging population, they tend least of all groups to utilize homes for the aged. Within the Italian ancestry group, the age cohort effect on population statistics is patently evident; the youthful, multiple ancestry, U.S. born, (group 4) exhibits a rate of college dormitory living almost 50 times higher than its rate of residence in homes for the aged. Conversely, the older, Italy born, (group 5) exhibits a rate of college dormitory living less than one 15th the rate of placement in homes for the aged. As a percent of the age cohort of these groups,

TABLE 8

GROUP RESIDENCE

SELECTED ANCESTRY GROUPS			ITALIAN ANCESTRY GROUPS		
Percent	Hom. for Aged*	College Dorm.*		Percent	Hom. for Aged*	College Dorm.*
ENGLISH	2.36	763	744	TOTAL ANC.	1.88	219	1050
FRENCH	2.68	775	852	SINGLE ANC.	1.76	363	747
GERMAN	2.67	783	1078	SING. U.S. BORN	1.74	227	834
IRISH	2.91	767	1088	MULT. US. BORN	2.02	30	1437
ITALIAN	1.76	363	747	ITALY BORN	1.88	1335	87
POLISH	2.18	643	751				

* Per 100,000 of the groups total population

Source: *Appendix C,* Table 3.2; *Appendix D,* Table 4.2.

while 3.8 percent of group 4's college age poplulation (defined here as age 20—44) live in dormitories, only 0.4 percent of those in group 5 do. On the other hand, an equal percentage (*viz.,* 3.0%) of each group's older population (defined here as 65 and over) reside in homes for the aged (*See,* Table IX).

TABLE 9

PERCENT OF AGE COHORTS IN GROUP QUARTERS*

SELECTED ANCESTRY GROUPS			ITALIAN ANCESTRY GROUPS		
	Homes for aged	College dorm.		Homes for aged	College dorm.
ENGLISH	5.1	2.2	TOTAL ANCESTRY	2.4	2.8
FRENCH	5.5	2.1	SINGLE ANCESTRY	2.3	2.0
GERMAN	5.0	2.7	SINGLE U.S. BORN	2.0	2.2
IRISH	4.9	2.8	MULTIPLE U.S. BORN	3.0	3.8
ITALIAN	2.3	2.0	ITALY BORN	3.0	0.4
POLISH	3.6	2.1			

* 65 and over in Homes for the Aged; 22-44 in College Dormitories

Source: *See* Table 8.

By any measure, Italian Americans have not been usisng homes for the aged in any way comparable to the other ancestry groups. The implications of this for pressing for legislation for home care for the aged, for help for families that care for their aged *etc.,* seem quite clear. Until now the Italian groups' response to the crises of old age has been to rally support from within the family. In Italy, as well as in the United States, this response does not seem to fit the values and requirements of the modern, industrial, physically and socially mobile societies. Therefore, we can not expect that the four generation household which we find more and more in evidence among Italian Americans will long obtain.

The contrast in college dormitory usage between the Italy born and all other Italian ancestry groups must not be seen merely as a function of age or college attendance. The Italian educational view that character formation and maturation is a function of family and not the university, is systemic and ancient. It is in deep contrast to the English education system which saw the university as the place for preparation for life as a gentleman and participant in the court. As a result, the English developed a national university system while the Italians developed a network of universities tied to the diverse urban locales in which they were located.[7] Most Italian universities do not have dormitories; and life away from home is not the norm in Italy. When a student does go away to school, he finds residence in the home of a relative or family friend, or sets up a new household. Peer pressure and the very real value of dormitory life in the American school system are influencing this behavior. Thus, of all U.S. born students that are enrolled in college, 16.5 percent live in dormitories while 4.9 percent of the Italy born college students live in dorms.

Although, historically, females outnumbered males in mental hospitals, the situation is now changing.

Among those living in group quarters, a very small number are patients in mental hospitals. Their numbers may well signify trends and certainly should raise questions. Although, historically, females outnumbered males in mental hospitals, the situation is now changing and that is reflected in the Italian ancestry groups. In the born in Italy group the high rate of more than thirteen per 100,000 with 45 percent being female is an exception and probably reflects the incidence of "immigrant psychosis" which refers, in general, to a maladjustment to the new society. Women, who ususally were required to change more than men often exhibited this reaction in larger numbers than men. In the multiple born in U.S. group a relatively low rate is accompanied by the highest male female ratio (*See*, Table X).

TABLE 10

ITALIAN AMERICAN RESIDENTS OF MENTAL HOSPITALS

	M / M+F	Per 100,000 of Pop.
TOTAL ITALIAN ANCESTRY	59	6.9
SINGLE ITALIAN ANCESTRY	58	9.8
SINGLE ANCESTRY BORN IN U.S.	60	9.4
MULTIPLE ANCESTRY BORN IN U.S.	65	3.1
ITALY BORN	45	13.1

Source: *See* Table 8.

In spite of the emphasis that Americans place on the individual, the family continues to be thought of as the basic institution of society, and for Italians, in the United States as in Italy, no matter how individualistic they may be, the family is society. Mario Cuomo, for example, has made the notion of family not only a hallmark of his New York gubernatorial administration, "The Family of New York"; but also, in political speeches around the nation, he has extended the idea to encompass global political relations.[8]

Italian Americans respond warmly to this, first, because it strikes a chord of recognition and rings true, and second, because it is an idea that pleases and uplifts. It is no wonder that Italian Americans are shocked and offended when the concept of "family" is twisted and turned against them, as when it is used to describe crime organizations, whether of Italian ancestry or not, or when it is meant to stand for chauvinistic ethnocentrism.

The identification of "Italians" and "Family" originated, as anyone who has read Vico knows, in ancient times;[9] and in modern times, it is rooted in scholarly understanding based on empirical observation of Italian and Italian American social structures, informed by historical analysis and literary description dating from the Italian classical period to the present. American scholarship on Italian Americans and the Italian American family may be said to have been given its most important impetus by the sociologist, Paul Campisi, whose syndetic work of forty years ago remains a classic in the field.[10] Most, although by no means all, Italian Americanists today reject the "straight line" assimilationist perspective of the early sociologists that underlies Campisi's work; but aside from that, his was the first and most complete systematic analysis of the patterns and variations of Italian family life in the United States.

During the past twenty years, a number of books, articles and chapters have appeared that describe the historical backgrounds and basic structure of the Italian American family, its culture, value system, authority patterns, roles, *etc.*, and more recently, there have been new investigations into the gender roles and relationships that exist in Italian and Italian American families.[11] A plethora of studies of families in crisis have also appeared in recent years, indicating that in many different quarters of our society, family life is still highly valued, and/ or, seen as having great import once for a variety of reasons.

We began this conclusion by asserting that, for Italians and for Italian Americans as well, no matter how individualistic they may be, the family is society. Looked at from the point of view of this new aggregation of census data, there seems, overall, to be little reason to say that this situation is changed. Once again, it may be said that the family is still a central organizing element in the Italian American personality system. The differences we found did not change the fundamental reality that we asserted so long ago, that families are the primary sources of our love, affection and security. They are the origins of our aspirations, the fountains of our values, and the bases of our identities. They provide us with a home, which is, as Geno Baroni has put it, "...the place where they've got to take you in when no one else does".[12]

At the same time, however, the cohesiveness of the American family system is diminishing, as evidenced by a variety of measures. The changes in American society are both a source of and a product of changes in ethnic family. Insofar as Italians are integrated into United States society and culture, 1) they retard this disintegration of family life; but 2) they, as a group, fall prey to the malaise themselves.
fall prey to the malaise themselves.

To call the breakdown of the family a malaise is, of course, a value judgement. But anyone who has lived through the pain and sorrow of a divorce, whether their own or their parents' or any clinician or counsellor who has been called upon to give therapy to marriage partners whose family is in crisis knows the deleterious effects of this disease on society, to say nothing of its effects on the partners and their children themselves. Marriage has always been considered a social behavior affecting society; divorce is no less societal.

The Italian American family is responding to two sets of forces: 1) an internal need, to use Murray's term, springing from certain weaknesses in the Italian family which existed over historical time but which were kept in

At the same time, however, the cohesiveness of the American family system is diminishing, as evidenced by a variety of measures.

check by the pragmatic requirements of peasant society; and 2) an external press of the changing American value system.[13]

But what exactly is being changed in the Italian American family, and why? The census data tell us that young Italian Americans are "marrying out" of the ethnic group, but the data do not explain why. To say that this is assimilation is to beg the question. Ethnographic interviews net us a different kind of data.

The younger generations seem to want to reject, more than anything else, the inexorability of behavior in a "tribalistic" environment. The children of immigrants turned away from their heritage so often when all they wanted to discard were the social constraints and the social requirements that they felt belonged to another place and time. Every generation of adolescents goes through this rebellion against the anachronism of their parents, but in the case of the children of immigrants, confusion accompanied this rebellion and it went much deeper and cost more. These immigrants' children were supported in their repudiation of their parents' way by the host society, and in particular by the schools, and by their recognition of the requirement that to succeed in the United States they would do well to be like other Americans. In effect, they traded what they perceived to be relentless inflexibility of the old world for the conformity of the new.

In the third generation and beyond, Americans of Italian ancestry are no longer under the constraints and pressures of the earlier generations either to over-identify with or to reject their heritage. Many, nevertheless, find the traditional stabiity of the family inviting. Like most Americans they still consider divorce, for example, as a "failed" marriage, and they think of a long and successful marriage as ideal, though not necessarily an ideal that they must achieve. Just as the immigrants sought economic and political freedom for themselvevs and their children, their grandchildren are demanding freedom of choice in many aspects of family life. As useful and interesting as census data are, new studies that look into the hearts and minds of people are needed if we are to understand what the behavior described by the data really mean.

FOOTNOTES

[1] Lydio F. Tomasi Ed., *New Perspectives in Italian Immigration and Ethnicity*. Staten Island: NY: Center for Migration Studies, 1985. Pp.27.

[2] N.R. McKenney, M. Levin and A.J. Tella, "A Sociodemographic Profile of Italian Americans". In *Italian Americans: New Perspectives in Italian Immigration and Ethnicity*. Edited by L.F. Tomasi. Pp.23.

[3] Ministero Affari Esteri, *Italia*. Novara: Istituto Geografico de Agostini, 1987. Pp.58.

[4] Ministero Affari Esteri, *Italia*. Approximations derived from age-sex pyramid, Pp.53.

[5] U.S. Bureau of the Census, *Statistical Abstract of the United States: l987 107th Edition*. Washington, DC: 1986. Pp.17.

[6] Istituto Centrale di Statistica, *Le Regione in Cifre: 1984*. Moncalieri, Torino: Pozzo Bros Monti S.p.A. 1984. Tav. 8. Pp.22.

[7] For a discussion of this and of the aural/oral tradition and the derivations of types of language in Italy and in England, *See*, F.X. Feminella, "Education, and Ethnicity: Euro-Ethnics in Anglo-Ethnic Schools". In Commission on Civil Rights, *Civil Rights Issues of Euro-Ethnic Americans*. Washington, DC: 1990.

[8] Maria Laurino, "Mario, Italian Style: Learning the Uses of an Ethnic Past", *The Village Voice*. 33:18, May 3, 1988. Pp.22 ff.

[9] F.X. Feminella, "Patriarchy, Matriarchy or Something Else Again!: Authority Patterns in the Italian American Family". Revised and reprinted in *Marriage and the Family*, by M. Barash and A.

Scourby. New York, NY: Random House, 1970.

10 P.J. Campisi, "Ethnic Family Patterns: The Italian Family in the United States", *American Journal of Sociology*. May, 1948:443-449. One must also recognize the important earlier contributions of I.L. Child, E. Corsi, L. Covello, R.F. Foerster, J.H. Mariano, L.F. Pisani,G.C. Speranza, C.F. Ware, W.H. Whyte, and H. Zorbaugh.

11 Vaneeta-Marie D'Andrea, "The Social Role Identity of Italian-American Women: An Analysis and Comparison of Families and REligious Expectations". In *The Family and Community Life of Italian Americans*. Edited by R.N. Juliani. New York, NY: The American Historical Association, 1983. Pp.61-68; Vaneeta-Marie D'Andrea, "The Life of Rosa Cavalleri: An Application of Abromson's Model of Rootedness/ Rootlessness". In *The Italians Through the Generations*. Edited by R. Caporale. New York: The American Italian Historical Association, 1986. Pp.112-124; *See also*, Donna Gabaccia, "Kinship, Culture, and Migration: A Sicilian Example", *Journal of American Ethnic History*. 3:2 Spring, 1984. Pp.39-53; Elizabeth Vezzosi, "The Dilemma of the Ethnic Community: The Italian Immigrant Woman Between 'Preservation' and 'Americanization' in America of the Early Twentieth Century", and Cynthia R. Daniels, "No Place Like Home: A Pictoral (sic) Essay on Italian-American Homeworkers in New York: 1910-1913". In *Support and Struggle: Italians and Italian Americans in a Comparative Perspective*. Edited by J.L. Tropea, J.E. Miller and C. Beattie-Repetti. New York: The American Itaian Historical Association, 1986. Earlier seminal work in this area includes: *The Italian Immigrant Woman in North America*. Edited by B.B. Caroli, R.F. Harney and L.F. Tomasi. New York: The American Italian Historical Association, 1978 and: Yans-McLaughlin, *Family and Community: Italian Immigrants in Buffalo, 1880-1930*. Ithaca, New York: Cornell University Press, 1977.

12 Geno Baroni, "An Address". In *Italians and Irish in America*. Edited by F.X. Femminella. New York: The Ameriacan Italian Historical Association, 1985. Pp.20.

13 Dino Cinel, *From Italy to San Francisco: The Immigrant Experiencew*. Stanford, CA: Standord University Press, 1982. Pp.189 ff.

ECONOMIC CHARACTERISTICS OF ITALIAN AMERICANS

Karl Bonutti
Department of Economics
Cleveland State University

The great migration of Eastern and Southern Europeans from 1880 to 1920 brought to the United States about five million Italian immigrants. With few exceptions they came here for economic reasons. Mostly peasants, they had limited skills and little or no formal education, almost all were penniless. In fact, surveys from that period show that immigrants from Italy brought with them an average of $8 to $13 per person,[1] a lot less than Anglo-Saxon, German or Scandinavian immigrants.

1910 ECONOMIC STATUS OF ITALIAN IMMIGRANTS

If the economic status of the 1910 Italian immigrants is compared to that of their 1980 descendants, one can only be amazed by the great economic strides achieved during a period of less than two or three generations. The period around 1910 represents the peak of Italian immigration. It was described by the social economist Thomas Sowell as "the greatest migration ever recorded from one single nation".

Income

Even though existing data are frequently fragmentary, it seems that while Italian male immigrants were among the lowest paid workers, Italian women enjoyed higher than average wages. Based on U.S. 1910 census data, while the average weekly income of white American workers was $14.37, Italian immigrants earned only $10.50, which was less than the average income of American blacks at $10.66. Actually these substantial differences existed even among northern Italians who earned $11.28 a week while southern Italians earned only $9.61. These wages were strikingly lower than the earnings of Russian Jewish immigrants at $12.71 or Norwegians at $13.28. Average weekly wages for women were at $7.00 while Italian women earned $9.00, almost at par with the southern Italian males.[2]

As heads of households, Italian workers were averaging $613 a year, well below the national average ($865) or Scottish immigrants earnings ($1,147). Obviously, 1910 Italian Americans were at the bottom or near the bottom of the economic scale.

Occupation

Initially, most Italian immigrants found jobs as common laborers hired on a daily basis. They did not object to this system of employment because most of them worked under a similar contract system prior to emigration as practiced by the "padrones". Besides, many did not plan to settle here permanently and were not looking for permanent positions. On the other hand, those who were able to find permanent jobs were better off. These workers were employed on road construction projects as canal diggers on railroads, as sewer construction workers or as stone masons. Even better earnings were available in high risk areas of iron, coal and copper mines and steel mills. Only in California one finds them in farming, growing crops and grapes. By 1910 it was too early to detect any type of generational mobility since most Italian Americans were either immigrants or first generation Americans. At that time, mobility was limited to job improvements within the same industry or the same job classification. The most fortunate found opportunities in stable jobs, in the telephone/telegraph system, in sales or as clerical employees.

Poverty

Even though poverty data for the 1910 period are general, one can safely surmise that during the early period of settlement, most Italian immigrants like most other ethnic groups were either at or near the poverty level. However, for most economists, the term poverty can no longer be treated in absolute terms by using physical subsistence as a guideline. Today, poverty is treated in the context of the prevailing standards of living. Therefore, it can be just as much financial as psychological. In this context, practically all Italian immigrants were living in poverty or near poverty as their income was well below the national average. On the other hand, from a psychological point of view, based on their own "feelings" many did not believe themselves to be poor because in their upbringing they were trained to be thrifty. Besides, coming from the most impoverished regions of Italy, they were accustomed to much lower standards of living than the ones prevailing among the poor of the 1910 United States. As long as they were able to spend less than what they earned, they did not "feel" poor.

ECONOMIC PROFILE FROM THE 1980 CENSUS

The picture of the 1980 Italian Americans, whether of single, multiple or total Italian parentage is quite different from the 1910 counterparts. While we might find differences in some areas between single, multiple and total Italian parentage—overall, one finds an ethnic group which is consistently well above average, not only when comparing it with the total U.S. population but also in relation to the white population. An attempt is made in the following pages to analyze the economic data from the 1980 census as related to the labor force, occupation, industry, income and poverty states by analyzing these components in relation to the total U.S. populace as well as the white population only. In addition, differences are analyzed as emerging by comparing Italian Americans of single, multiple and total parentage.

With the exclusion of the Jewish American community, no other major ethnic group has achieved a higher level of upward mobility than the Italian Americans. Moreover available data clearly refute the prevailing stereotyp-

The picture of the 1980 Italian Americans, whether of single, multiple or total Italian parentage, is quite different from the 1910 counterparts.

ical perceptions of the Italian Americans that have been prevailing for so many years in the United States.

Labor Force

The participation rate in the labor force by Italian Americans is somewhat higher than the national average. On the other hand, when compared to the white population only, the difference is less than one percentage point. A similar conclusion was reached by the researchers of the U.S. Civil Rights Commission in a study of major Eastern and Southern European groups. Actually, it shows that the overall labor force participation rate of Eastern Europeans is even higher—94.8 percent for Italians; 95.5 percent for Eastern Europeans.[3]

Similarly, the unemployment rates among Italian Americans are lower than the national average (4.3 *vs.* 7.1). Yet, when compared with other white ethnic groups the difference is insignificant. However, if we take into account the states with the highest concentration of Italian immigrants we find that in these states the unemployment rates are high due to structural changes of their regional industrial economies. The only exceptions are Massachusetts and California.

The participation rate in the labor force by Italian Americans is somewhat higher than the national average.

An interesting aspect of the working age population which is often neglected by researchers is the number of prison inmates from specific ethnic groups. From the available census data, the perception that Italian Americans are heavily involved in crime (one should remember former President Nixon's comment: "...the trouble is, you can't find one that is honest") is not confirmed by census data. In fact, the number of prison inmates of Italian extraction is about 50 percent below the national average (1.4 national *vs.* 0.8 for Italian Americans). On the other hand, the representation of Italian Americans in the Armed Forces is well below the national average (.95 national *vs.* .69 for Italians, *See*, Table 1.

Apparently, the rate of assimilation of Italian women into the mainstream American labor market is greater than among other ethnic groups. The strong values that the Italian culture is placing on the role of the mother-housewife devoting full time to the family is disappearing. With the exception of primary child-rearing age—from 25 to 45—during which we find fewer Italian women in the labor force, at any other age level there are at least ten percent more Italian women employed than would be the national average. Even with the youngest age group, sixteen to nineteen, nationally about 40 percent of teenage girls are employed, while among Italian females the ratio is over 45 percent.

When comparing labor force data of single, multiple and total Italian parentage, one finds no discernible differences. The ratio of employed to unemployed is by a fraction of one percent the same as the general data for Italian Americans.

Almost 65 percent of all college graduates, whether of single, multiple or total ancestry, are employed in the private sector, while twenty percent hold public service positions; only six percent are self-employed (*See,* Figure I).

Of the high school graduates, over 80 percent are employed in the private sector and five percent are self-employed, while the rest hold public service positions (*See,* Figure II).

Occupations

Based on 1980 census data, Italian Americans have clearly shown upward

TABLE 1

LABOR FORCE CHARACTERISTICS

Population		U.S. Total	Italian Single Anc.
Total, 16 years and over		171,214,258	6,003,613
Labor force (Percent of persons 16 years and over)		62.0	61.2
Armed Forces (Percent of persons 16 years and over)		1.0	0.5
Civilian Labor Force (Percent of persons 16 years and over)		61.0	60.7
Unemployed (Percent of civilian labor force)		6.5	5.7
Inmates of Institutions (Percent of persons 16 years and over)		1.4	0.7
Female, 16 years and over		89,482,168	3,026,496
Labor force (Percent of females 16 years and over)		49.9	47.6
Armed Forces (Percent of females 16 years and over)		0.2	0.1
Civilian Labor Force (Percent of females 16 years and over)		49.8	47.6
Unemployed (Percent of females in civilian labor force)		6.5	5.9
Inmate of Institution (Percent of females 16 years and over)		1.4	0.7
Male, 16 to 19 years	employed	42.2	43.0
	unemployed	7.7	6.8
	not in labor f.	47.6	47.6
Male, 20 to 24 years	employed	68.9	71.3
	unemployed	8.8	8.0
	not in labor f.	17.3	17.4
Male, 25 to 54 years	employed	86.2	89.2
	unemployed	4.6	4.1
	not in labor f.	7.5	5.9
Male, 55 to 64 years	employed	68.3	71.2
	unemployed	2.9	3.3
	not in labor f.	28.7	25.5
Male, 65 years and older	employed	18.3	18.0
	not in labor f.	80.7	80.7
Female, 16 to 19 years	employed	39.4	45.2
	unemployed	6.1	5.2
	not in labor f.	54.2	49.4
Female, 20 to 24 years	employed	61.4	68.8
	unemployed	5.8	4.4
	not in labor f.	32.2	26.4
Female, 25 to 54 years	employed	59.6	57.1
	unemployed	3.4	3.1
	not in labor f.	36.8	39.7
Female, 55 to 64 years	employed	39.8	40.9
	unemployed	1.8	2.5
	not in labor f.	58.4	56.7
Female, 65 years and over	employed	7.7	7.5
	not in labor f.	91.8	91.7

Source: U.S. Bureau of the Census. *1980 Census of Population. General Social and Economic Characteristics.*

mobility from lower paying blue collar and craft positions to middle and upper class occupations: managerial and professional. In general, their preference is for well-paying jobs rather than prestigious positions.[4]

As compared to previous census reports, there is a declining participation rate of Italian workers in lower paying jobs with limited or no skills or prestige like laborers, machine operators, assemblers and private household positions. On the other hand, increasing numbers of Italians are found in upper level, well-paying professions: attorneys, doctors, engineers and accountants. The largest increases are in technical fields, among the self-employed and owners of businesses. Business ownership is almost 70 percent higher

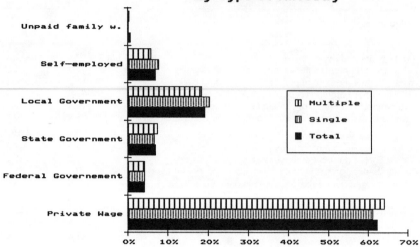

Fig. 1 - Class of Worker of College
Graduates
by Type of Ancestry

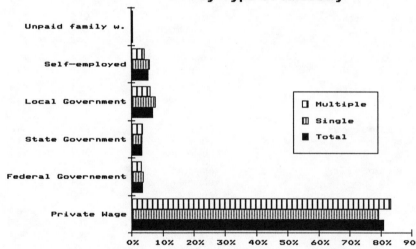

Fig. 2 - Class of Worker
of High School Graduates
by Type of Ancestry

*Some have even reached
the highest positions
within the corporate world
even though this field is
still largely dominated by
Anglo-Saxon Americans.*

among Italian Americans than the rest of the nation (2.1% nationally *vs.* 3.5 among Italian Americans). Some have even reached the highest positions within the corporate world even though this field is still largely dominated by Anglo-Saxon Americans (*See*, Table 2).

For many years the construction industry was viewed as one of the strongholds of Italian Americans. Now, contrary to these stereotyped perceptions, relatively few Italian craftsmen are found in construction (with the exception of stone masons). By now most Italians who are active in the construction industry hold important technical administrative and executive positions. Similarly, there are relatively few employees of Italian extraction in Federal and State government employment. Only at the local level, their presence is still strong (8.7% nationally *vs.* 9.4% among Italian Americans). As has been observed by other researchers (Sowell and Greeley) even though most Italian immigrants came from impoverished rural areas, few are listed as farmers or

TABLE 2

SELECTED OCCUPATIONS

(percentage values)

	U.S. Total	Italian Single Anc.
TOTAL POPULATION		
Managerial and professional specialty occupations	22.7	23.2
Professional occupations	12.3	11.2
Technical, sales, and administrative occupations	30.3	33.5
Sales occupations	10.00	11.4
Administrative support occupations, including clerical	17.3	19.5
Private household occupations	0.6	0.2
Police - Firefighters	0.6	0.9
Operators, fabricators, laborers	12.9	15.9
Farming, fishing, forestry	2.9	1.0
Farm operators and managers	1.4	0.3
Farm workers and related occupations	1.4	0.6
FEMALES ONLY		
Managerial and professional specialty occupations	21.5	19.1
Technical, sales and administrative support	45.6	51.8
Administrative support occupations	31.2	36.9
Secretaries, stenographers, typists	11.0	14.3
Private household occupations	1.4	0.4
Service occupations, except protective	16.1	14.2
Cleaning and building services	2.3	1.3

Source: U. S. Bureau of the Census. *1980 Census of Population. General Social and Economic Characteristics.*

farm workers (1/3 of the national average: 1.3% nationally *vs.* 0.4% Italian). This can be explained by the fact that as immigrants they did not bring with them sufficient funds to buy land and equipment as did the better off settlers from Germany and Scandinavian countries.

About 70 percent of Italian Americans with college degrees selected managerial and professional fields while only 22 percent are found in technical areas (*See,* Figure III). Quite different are the selections of occupations by

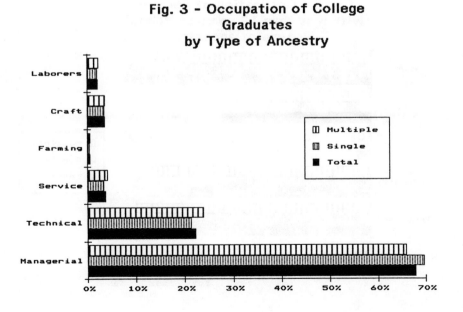

Fig. 3 - Occupation of College Graduates by Type of Ancestry

Italian Americans with high school diplomas only. Almost 43 percent are in technical fields, in precision crafts, repair shops and operator fabricators. Again in this category one does not find much difference between single and multiple Italian ancestry (*See,* Figure IV).

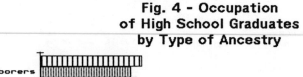

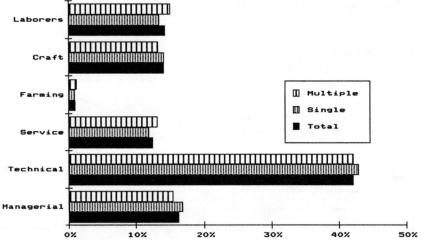

Fig. 4 - Occupation of High School Graduates by Type of Ancestry

Not surprisingly, the largest percentage of Italian Americans without a high school diploma is found among operators, fabricators and laborers (29%) but also a large percentage are in technical roles and supervisory positions (23%), in service occupations (21%) and in precision production, in craft and repair shops (18%—*See,* Figure V). Somewhat different, however, are the ratios for the population of multiple Italian ancestry, which concentrates more heavily in technical, sales and administrative positions.

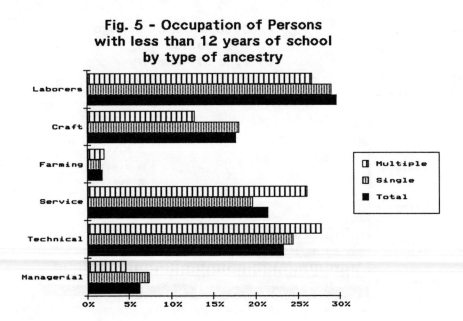

Fig. 5 - Occupation of Persons with less than 12 years of school by type of ancestry

Only among Italians with less than twelve years of schooling one finds a reasonable number in farming (about 2%). Occupational preferences of Italian American women seem to be influenced by their cultural background. Only recently, they enrolled in college in large numbers. Consequently an unusually large percentage of them (51%) selected support type of occupations in technical, administrative and sales positions. This percentage is well above the average for white women in general (46%). Also a relatively large number is found in managerial and professional specialties (19%) and service occupations (16%).

Because of the changing women's role in the labor force, these job preferences are slowly shifting to new more diversified occupations (legal, accounting and medical).

INDUSTRY

Of the 3.5 million Italian Americans who are employed in eleven major industries, the largest percentage is found in service occupations. This percentage is lower than the national average (28.6% national *vs.* 26.7% Italian), because few Italian Americans are now found in low paying service jobs. For instance, few Italians are employed in household services: domestics, servants, *etc.*, representing not more than 1/3 of the national average (2.5% national *vs.* 0.8% Italian). On the other hand, over ten percent more than the national average are found in various business fields (9.7% national *vs.* 11.0% Italian) in personal services (8.5% national *vs.* 11.7% Italian), entertainment and recreation (3.6% national *vs.* 4.7% Italian) and repair services (4.8% national *vs.* 5.3% Italian). Even higher is their representation in the higher paid professional fields, especially legal and engineering, where their participation is twenty percent higher than the national average (10.4% national *vs.* 12.2% Italian). In education, their participation is higher than the national average but not by a significant percent (40.4% national *vs.* 43.0% Italian). In the lower paid professions their participation is below the national averages. For instance, in social service and religious fields they are all well below the national averages (10.7% national *vs.* 9.0% Italian); in hospital jobs they are ten percent lower (22.3% national *vs.* 20.1% Italian). The only exception is in the medical profession where their participation ratio is close to the national average.

Another good indication of the Italian upward mobility is found in the declining industries (which seventy years ago were the most prosperous and promising employment fields), where Italian participation rates are lower than the national averages. In mining their participation is at 35 percent of the national average, in forestry 50 percent of the national average. Additional comparisons in lumber and furniture (9.1% national *vs.* 4.3% Italian), in transportation equipment (18% national *vs.* 15% Italian) in railroads (8.1% national *vs.* 6.6% Italian) confirm the same trends. Equally interesting is their lower than average participation in sanitary services (19.4% national *vs.* 15.4% Italian) where, incidentally, many Italians hold supervisory positions. In the retail trade, the only areas with greater than average participation rates for Italian Americans are in the food, bakery and dairy products and especially in grocery stores with a fifteen percent *vs.* nineteen percent participation rate (*See,* Table 3).

When comparing the single, multiple and total Italian ancestry with the eleven industries listed by the Census Bureau, one does not find major differences within these three ancestry classifications. All seem to prefer manufacturing, retail trade and professional services to other industries. With college

Of the 3.5 million Italian Americans who are employed in eleven major industries, the largest percentage is found in service occupations.

TABLE 3

INDUSTRY OF EMPLOYED PERSONS 16 YEARS AND OVER

(Percentage Values)

Industry	U.S. Total			Italian Single Anc.		
TOTAL LABOR FORCE EMPLOYED	97,639,355			3,435,377		
Agriculture	2.8			0.9		
Forestry	0.2			0.1		
Mining	1.1			0.4		
Construction	5.9			6.1		
Manufacturing	22.4	100.0		22.1	100.0	
Nondurable goods		38.5	100.0		39.3	100.0
Food Products			18.2			15.7
Textile mills and finished products			26.6			29.3
Printing, publishing			18.2			22.2
Chemicals, etc.			15.1			16.3
Durable goods		61.5	100.0		60.7	100.0
Furniture, lumber and wood products			9.1			4.1
Primary metals			9.7			10.1
Fabricated metals			10.6			11.1
Machinery, except electrical			20.5			20.6
Transportation equipment			18.1			15.7
Transportation, communication and public ut.	7.3	100.0		7.8	100.0	
Railroads		8.2			6.6	
Trucking and Warehousing		21.8			19.6	
Other Transportation		30.3			38.1	
Communications		20.3			17.7	
Utilities, sanitary services		19.4			15.4	
Wholesale trade	4.3			4.7		
Retail trade	16.1	100.0		18.3	100.0	
General Merchandise Stores		13.3			13.1	
Food, bakery, dairy stores		15.1			19.1	
Automotive dealers, gas stations		12.1			10.3	
Eating, drinking		26.6			25.9	
Finance (banking insurance), real estate	6.0			7.5		
Services	28.7	100.0		26.9	100.0	
Business services		9.7			11.0	
Repair services		4.9			5.4	
Private households		2.5			0.8	
Other personal services		8.5			11.7	
Entertainment and recreation		3.6			4.7	
Professional and related services		70.1	100.0		66.5	100.0
Hospitals			22.3			20.1
Other health services			14.3			13.9
Schools and colleges			40.5			43.0
Other educational services			1.8			1.8
Social services and religious			10.7			9.0
Legal, engineering and other			10.4			12.3
Public administration	5.3	100.0		5.4	100.0	

Source: U. S. Bureau of the Census. *1980 Census of Population. General Social and Economic Characteristics.*

degrees about 45 percent selected professional services for their careers including business, eight percent went into retail business, seven percent in finance, insurance and real estate, and six percent in public administration. Few college graduates are found in the construction industry (*See,* Figure VI).

A similar picture develops when comparing high school graduates. There are no differences among these three Italian ancestry groups. Over twenty percent selected manufacturing industries for their full time employment and a similar percentage went into retail trade while fifteen percent have chosen service fields. Invariably, few are found in farming and construction, despite strong historical ties to these industries (*See,,* Figure VII).

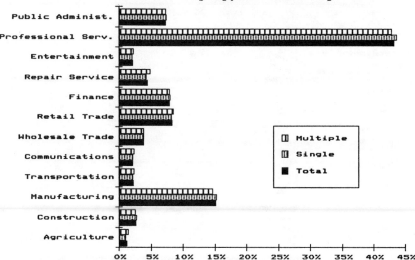

Fig. 6 - Industry of College Graduates by Type of Ancestry

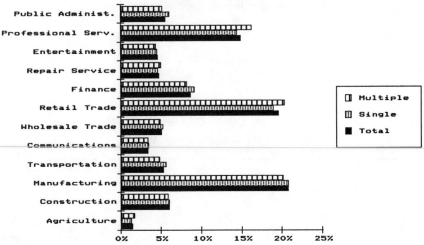

Fig. 7 - Industry of High School Graduates by Type of Ancestry

Somewhat different are the percentages for Italians without high school diplomas. Of people of single ancestry, many more are found in manufacturing (28%), while of those of multiple ancestry almost 40 percent are employed in the retail businesses and only eighteen percent in manufacturing (*See,* Figure VIII).

Income

The most convincing evidence of successful upward mobility by Italian Americans can be observed by their income levels.

In the past seventy years, the average income of Italian immigrants and their descendents have progressed from one of the lowest levels in the country, once below that of black Americans, to income levels which are well above the national average. Whether one compares the household or family

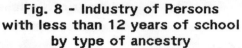

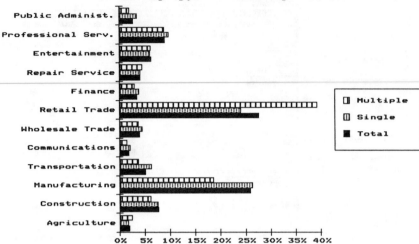

Fig. 8 - Industry of Persons
with less than 12 years of school
by type of ancestry

*Italian Americans' income
is approximately 25
percent higher than the
national average.*

income, the income of unrelated individuals or the median income by age of the United States population to that of Italian Americans, the conclusions are always the same: the income of Italian Americans is almost fifteen percent above the national average. However, if we compare per capita income of Americans with that of Italian Americans, we find Italian Americans' income to be approximately 25 percent higher than the national average (*See*, Table 4).

TABLE 4

SELECTED INCOME CHARACTERISTICS

(Median income when not specified)

Population	U.S. Total	U.S. White	Italian Single Anc.
Families	$19,917	$20,835	$21,842
Families with children under 18	$20,337	$21,475	$23,091
Families with children under 6	$17,757	$18,879	$20,461
Families without children under 18	$19,380	$20,055	$20,679
Married-couple families	$21,635	$22,042	$22,907
Married couple with children under 18	$22,569	$23,147	$24,567
Married couple with children under 6	$19,630	$20,057	$21,161
Female householder, no husband present	$9,960	$11,384	$13,239
With own children under 18	$8,002	$9,138	$9,323
With own children under 6	$5,229	$5,805	$5,428
Households	80,467,427	68,991,307	2,960,756
Percent with earnings	81.3	77.7	80.7
Mean earnings	$20,727	$21,428	$22,752
Mean wage or salary income	$19,796	$20,430	$21,592
Percent with Social Security income	25.9	26.8	29.9
Mean Social Security income	$4,094	$4,187	$4,386
Percent with Public Assistance income	7.9	5.9	5.7
Mean Public Assistance income	$2,518	$2,421	$2,629
Per capita income	$7,298	$7,808	$9,126

Source: U.S. Bureau of the Census. *1980 Census of Population. General Social and Economic Characteristics.*

Equally revealing is the comparison of the income level of the United States white population with that of the Italian American of single ancestry. Generally speaking Italian Americans have a higher income than white Americans and this is quite significant if one remembers that, in this case, single ancestry includes also the portion of the population born in Italy, whose income level is substantially lower than that of individuals born in the United States. However, white Americans maintain the edge in upper class income levels ($50,000 and above). Evidently, one hundred years of presence in America has not been sufficient enough to produce a competitively large upper class among Italian Americans (*See*, Figures IX through XII).

Fig. 9 - Household Income

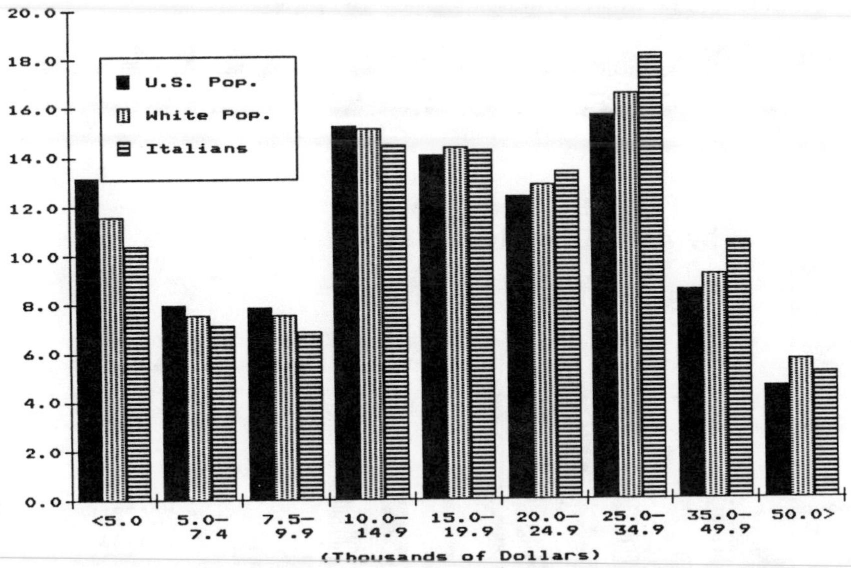

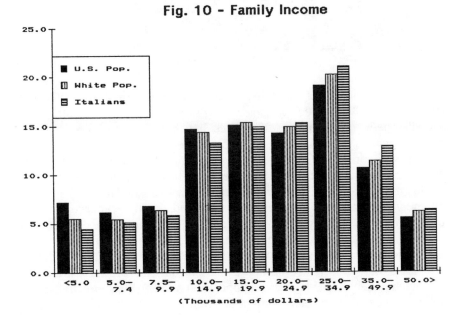

Fig. 10 - Family Income

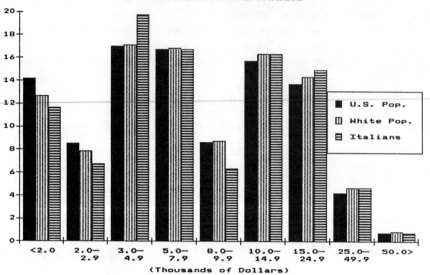

**Fig. 11 - Income Characteristics
of Unrelated Individuals**

(Thousands of Dollars)

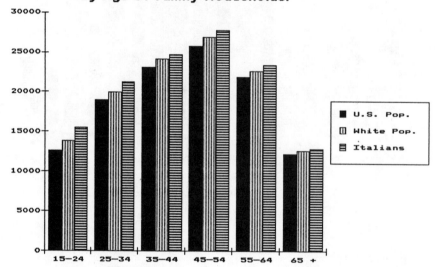

**Fig. 12 - Median Income
by Age of Family Householder**

*Multiple ancestry Italian
Americans show slightly
better achievements than
single ancestry Italian
Americans.*

Comparisons inside of the Italian American group reveal a multifaceted situation originated by such variables as age, education and occupation and we will briefly consider the differences between persons of single and multiple ancestry. Even though inappropriately so, persons of multiple ancestry are considered to represent a more mature phase of assimilation. Thus, the comparison could allure the promise of revealing whether the ethnic group's economic attainments improve with assimilation.

If median household incomes are compared, multiple ancestry Italian Americans show slightly better achievements than single ancestry Italian Americans. However, in all other types of measurement, single ancestry persons have a better income than their counterparts of multiple ancestry (*See,* Table 4.7). Family income and per capita income are measurements very much in debt to the family and population age and structure. Italians of multiple ancestry are a very young population with a large portion in it that

Fig. 13 - Median Household, Family and Individual Income of Italians by Type of Ancestry

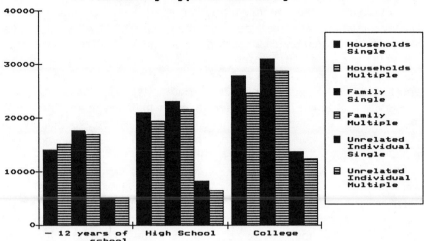

did not reach the earning age yet. Thus, their per capita income is substantially lower. Household income, on the other hand, is less influenced by family members and reflects more the earning capabilities of the householders. However, instead of coming to the conclusion that exogamy produces better economic achievements we like to consider first the educational achievements of householder (*See,* Figure XIV). A brief examination reveals that householders of multiple ancestry have more years of schooling than those of single ancestry. In particular, the larger and less income producing segment of the population of single ancestry lowers the average of the whole group, giving the small overall edge to the population of multiple ancestry. In

Fig. 14 - Educational Achievements of Householders

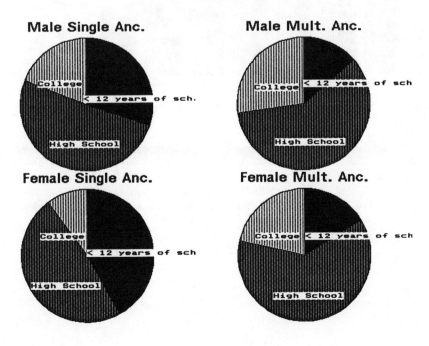

fact, high school and college graduates of single ancestry have a higher income than those of multiple ancestry.

Women's income is generally less than half the income of men. For every $1,000 of income of the American man the American woman gets $432. The disparity increases with the increase of the group's median income. Thus, considering the United States white population only, women receive $415 for every $1,000 received by men. Among the European groups compared in this publication, the gender gap is highest among the Poles who are also the highest paid; the Italians immediately follow the Poles in this comparison. For every $1,000 earned by an Italian man, an Italian woman's income is $395. However, the gap narrows when multiple ancestry population is considered. The income of Italian households with a female householder of the multiple ancestry group is higher than that of the single ancestry group. Different levels of schooling becomes an important factor in this comparison. The majority of female householder's are concentrated in the section of high school graduates (62 percent *vs.* 48 percent of women of single ancestry). Instead, a great number of women of single ancestry attended high school for less than twelve years and are earning a correspondingly lower income (*See,* Figure XV). However, as mentioned before, households

The income of Italian households with a female householder of the multiple ancestry group is higher than that of the single ancestry group.

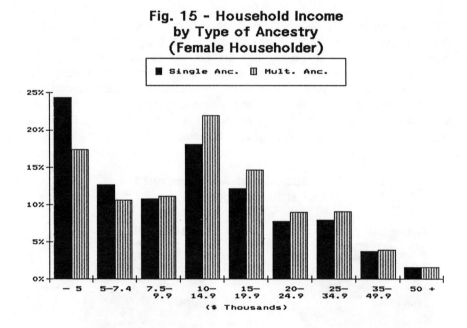

Fig. 15 - Household Income by Type of Ancestry (Female Householder)

■ Single Anc. ▥ Mult. Anc.

($ Thousands)

with a female householder of single ancestry, graduating high school as well as college, show better income levels than their counterparts of multiple ancestry. Age and work experience become the decisive factor in this case. In fact, the highest income producing age bracket is that composed of individuals 45 to 50 years of age (*See,* Figure XII). However, relatively few persons of multiple ancestry had reached this age in 1980.

An analysis of the income distribution of households with a male householder requires similar observations, since the same general pattern is followed, although there are some differences (*See,* Figure XVI). The total group of male householders maintain a level of income similar to that of male householders of multiple ancestry. While the difference in male distribution by education for single and multiple ancestry is even more

Fig. 16 - Household Income by Type of Ancestry (Male Householder)

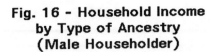

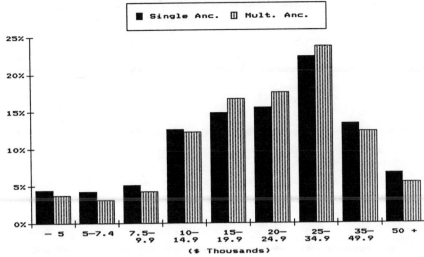

pronounced, the difference in income is less dramatic. Acquisition of a high school diploma makes a significant difference for female householders, a less incisive difference, instead, in the case of male householders, particularly those of multiple ancestry.

Poverty

The poverty level of Italian Americans is well below the national average. In fact, at the rate that it has been decreasing over the previous decade, one can expect that in the near future, poverty among Italian Americans may be below 50 percent of the national average. The national average for all persons was 12.4 in 1980, 9.4 among whites and 7.8 among Italian Americans of single ancestry. Different values but similar proportions are provided by data on the poverty level of families. Nationwide, 9.6 percent of American families were below the poverty level; among Italian Americans the percentage was 5.4.

Considerations on poverty status are obviously parallel to those on income, since the poverty threshold consists of an income cutoff, revised annually (in 1979 it was $7,412). However, a closer analysis reveals some peculiarities that must be considered, in particular, the datum that identifies families with female householders and no husband as primary candidates for falling below the poverty level. In fact, seventeen percent of Italian families headed by females had incomes falling below the poverty level in 1980, 94 percent of these women did not have a husband present and 81 percent supported children under eighteen years of age. Comparatively, less than four percent of families headed by men in 1980 fell below the poverty level (*See*, Table 6.8).

A second aspect concerns the Italian elderly (65 years of age and over). They are nine percent of the population for whom poverty is established, but over twelve percent of those below poverty level. The Italian elderly constitute one quarter of the persons who do not live with their families and are below poverty level (83 percent of whom are women). However, households with a householder 65 years of age or older do not show a lower income than

The poverty level of Italian Americans is well below the national average.

TABLE 5

POVERTY STATUS IN 1979

Population	U.S. Total	U.S. White	Italian Single Anc.
Total Population*	220,845,766	184,466,900	6,766,498
Persons below poverty level	12.4	7.0	5.4
Persons 65 years and over	13.1	16.0	21.1
Total Families	59,190,133	50,644,862	2,280,202
Families below poverty level	9.6	7.0	5.4
with Social Security income	20.8	22.4	24.6
with public assistance income	32.5	24.7	21.1
Female householder, no husband present	43.8	34.4	34.5
Householder 65 years and over	13.8	15.7	19.2
Total Unrelated Individuals	27,383,584	23,191,117	177,019
Unrelated individuals below poverty level	25.1	22.6	21.3
with Social Security income	33.4	35.0	36.4
with public assistance income	16.1	12.5	13.4
Unrelated individual 65 years and over	32.8	34.4	36.0

* Poverty status is determined for all persons except inmates of institutions, persons in military group quarters and in college dormitories, and unrelated individuals under 15 years old.

Source: U. S. Bureau of the Census. *1980 Census of Population. General Social and Economic Characteristics.*

> *For the most part socio-economic inequalities among white ethnic groups are both relatively minor and unrelated to patterns of ethnic inequalities found earlier in the century.*

the rest of the population.

Finally, poverty is concentrated within the population with less education. Half of the Italian Americans did not graduate from high school, however, two thirds of those with an income below poverty level did not obtain a high school diploma.

Summary

In their recent volume on ethnic and social groups in contemporary America, based on 1980 census figures, Lieberson and Waters have concluded that "for the most part socioeconomic inequalities among white ethnic groups are both relatively minor and unrelated to patterns of ethnic inequalities found earlier in the century".[5] Our analysis of the Italian American group has led to the same conclusion. We have determined that, Italian Americans do not lag behind other major ethnic groups, they fare even better, exceeded only by the Poles. Differences are of minor entity. Education has certainly played an important role in raising Italian Americans to a more affluential place in American society. Nevertheless, the economic attainments of Italian Americans far exceed their educational achievements. This pattern of social mobility is shared by the other groups of European-origin as substantiated by Lieberson and Waters who concluded that "all sixteen of the specific European-origin groups have higher income distributions than would be expected on the basis of combined influence of their education and occupation".[6]

Based upon their economic success, one would conclude that the assimilation process for Italian Americans has been completed. Although, we further suggest, economic assimilation is but one aspect of a complex process and that the cultural and social assimilation processes advance at a different pace.

FOOTNOTES

[1] Report of the *U.S. Immigration Commission* of 1912; also "Italian Americans and Their Communities of Cleveland" by Gene Veronese, 1977, pp.110 and also; Thomas Sowell, 1973 and 1981.

[2] "Historical Statistics of the United States from Colonial Times to 1970", *United States Bureau of the Census*, Vol.1, 1975.

[3] United States Commission on Civil Rights, *The Economic Status of Americans of Southern and Eastern European Ancestry*. Clearinghouse Publication No. 89, 1986.

[4] Gastaldo, P., "Gli Americani di Origine Italiana, chi sono, dove sono, quanti sono" in *Euroamericani la popolazione di origine italiana*. Torino, Foundazione Giovanni Agnelli, 1987.

[5] Lieberson, S. and M.C. Waters, *From Many Strands. Ethnic and Racial Groups in Contemporary America*. New York: Russel Foundation, 1987. Pp. 155.

[6] *Ibid.*, p.152.

ITALIAN AMERICANS IN SELECTED STATES: A COMPARISON

Graziano Battistella
Center for Migration Studies

In the special issue of April 1988 of *New York* magazine the cover feature was dedicated to the most important persons in New York. Out of the top 20, two were Italian Americans: Mario Cuomo "because he's persuaded so many—if not himself—that he'll be president some day" and Rudolph Giuliani "because he has made the mob, pols and Wall Street quake as never before". The list is necessarily subjective; but it is indicative not only of personal achievements of outstanding persons, but of ethnic achievement as well. Only two Italian Americans were chosen by the magazine. The selection does not reflect the ethnic proportion of the population, since one out of five New Yorkers is an Italian American. However, it does confirm that the Italian American group is on its way up in the American society, at the local level even more prominently than on the national scenario.

The attention of the majority of scholars to Italian Americans has been circumscribed to a few traditional areas of settlement: the Northeast, the Midwest and California. In fact, the preponderant number of studies has focused on the Italian Americans of the East Coast. Italian Americans, however, are spread in many other areas of this nation. Fortunately, the number of essays on Italian American settlements of recently neglected regions has increased, giving the opportunity to appreciate the variety of Italian communities in America.[1] Often, case studies highlight specific characteristics of communities inherited from the different regions or towns of origin in Italy. However, the national profile of the Italian Americans melts the differences into a commonplace portrait, leaving the impression of an indifferentiated group throughout the country. The relative youth of the group, still marked by a strong percentage of second and third generation quotas, while explaining the preservation of ethnic characteristics, motivates also the apparent uniformity of Italian Americans in all the areas of settlement.

> **The most general level of geographical distribution of population in the country is that of the four census regions: Northeast, Northcentral, South and West.**

The most general level of geographical distribution of population in the country is that of the four census regions: Northeast, Northcentral, South and West. Some typical features emerge when Italian Americans in the four regions are compared. The Northeast, port of entry for the vast majority of Italian immigrants, remains the area of settlement for approximately 60 percent. The West is the region with the youngest and best educated of the Italian American population. The Northcentral region presents Italian Americans with the highest income; and The South is the place for resettlement. Such general observations lead to the conclusion that Italian Americans simply follow the stereotypical characteristics of the white population in the area of residence.

With scholars still polarized on the debate about the vitality of Italian American ethnicity or its inevitable twilight, much less attention has been given to dissimilar facets of Italian Americans in the various states. It would also be arguable whether a state is the appropriate geographic boundary for an attempt to let the differences among Italian Americans surface. Since Italian Americans are so heavily an urban type of population, metropolitan areas could be preferred for such study. However, data availability has forced our choice in favor of state comparison.

As the source for the following observations we will use the unpublished special tabulations of the 1980 Census. Only the aggregated data for the entire ethnic group will be examined, since social and economic characteristics of Americans of single Italian ancestry—and sometimes of multiple ancestry —were already published by the Bureau of the Census. This choice permits a cursory overview of the entire population claiming some ties with Italian roots, without measuring degree of ethnic identity. Italian Americans in eleven states will be compared; the top ten states in size of Italian American population plus Rhode Island, the state with the highest density of Italian Americans. These eleven states account for 80 percent of the Italian American population in the U.S.A.

As Alba pointed out "it is essential to have a standard against which to compare Italian Americans in order to delineate clearly their social position. A comparison of Italians with the amorphus category of all other Americans, a composite of many ethnic strands, would leave the true situation of the group uncertain".[2] Consequently, he chose as a comparison group the "American core", the population of British ancestry. In other chapters of this publication Italian Americans are contrasted with other ethnic groups and the appendices are provided to compare Italian Americans with population of selected European ancestries. However, in this chapter we contrast Italian Americans with the white population of each state. Since data on Italian Americans refer to the whole ethnic group both of single and multiple ancestry and data for other ancestries were not available at this aggregated level, the choice of the white population as term of comparison was the most meaningful.

The geographical distribution of Italian Americans is the result of two shifts: immigration and change of residence.

RESIDENCE AND AGE

The geographical distribution of Italian Americans is the result of two shifts: immigration and change of residence. The major states of residence of Italian Americans have been the states of first immigration at the turn of the century. The type of economic activities and development, together with other reasons such as the clustering of people from the same town or region in the same area, dictated the place for settlement. The percentage of Italian Americans within the state population is a relevant descriptor to determine the influence Italian Americans had or will have on one particular state. In some states, the Italian American population was supported by a continuous flow of new arrivals. However, despite the recent change in migration flows, and the considerable abatement in the over-all numbers, the ranking of Italian communities by state was not altered.

The State of New York ranks number one in total Italian American population, in population of single and multiple Italian ancestry, as well as in population born in Italy, or born abroad of Italian descent. Approximately, one Italian American in four lives in the State of New York. The States of New Jersey and Pennsylvania rank second and third; California is fourth, but second in population of mixed Italian ancestry. These four states combined

TABLE I

POPULATION OF ITALIAN ANCESTRY IN SELECTED STATES: 1980

	Total Population	Italian Ancestry	Percentage
California	23,667,902	1,144,102	4.8
Connecticut	3,107,576	561,542	18.1
Florida	9,746,324	461,757	4.7
Illinois	11,426,518	640,304	5.6
Massachusetts	5,737,037	749,583	13.1
Michigan	9,262,078	344,402	3.7
New Jersey	7,364,823	1,315,632	17.9
New York	17,558,072	2,811,911	16.0
Ohio	10,797,630	520,171	4.8
Pennsylvania	11,863,895	1,205,823	10.2
Rhode Island	947,154	185,080	19.5

Source: U.S. Bureau of the Census, *Census of Population 1980. Ancestry of the Population by State: 1980.*

account for more than half of the Italian Americans in the U.S.

Since the state of New York has been and still is the state of intended residence for one Italian immigrant out of three, its percentage of population of mixed ancestry is the lowest. On the contrary, in the states of the Midwest and California multiple ancestry population surpasses that of single ancestry. The highest rate of intermarriage usually couples with generations after the second and testifies to a group well ahead in the assimilation process.

TABLE II

DISTRIBUTION OF POPULATION OF SINGLE AND MULTIPLE ITALIAN ANCESTRY IN SELECTED STATES: 1980

	Italian Ancestry	Single Ancestry	Percentage	Multiple Ancestry	Percentage
California	1,144,102	567,351	49.6	576,751	50.4
Connecticut	561,542	346,053	61.6	215,489	38.4
Florida	461,757	274,202	59.4	187,555	40.6
Illinois	640,304	322,914	50.4	317,390	49.6
Massachusetts	749,583	430,412	57.4	319,171	42.6
Michigan	344,402	170,740	49.6	173,662	50.4
New Jersey	1,315,632	835,277	63.5	480,355	36.5
New York	2,811,911	1,937,791	68.9	874,120	31.1
Ohio	520,171	258,482	49.7	261,689	50.3
Pennsylvania	1,205,823	663,083	55.0	542,740	45.0
Rhode Island	185,080	118,966	64.3	66,114	35.7

Source: U.S. Bureau of the Census, *Census of Population 1980. Ancestry of the Population by State: 1980.*

Internal mobility among Italian Americans is lower than the mobility of the white population in general. However, mobility varies according to regions and states. Close to 90 percent of Italian Americans living in one of the states of the Northeast were born in the same region (Table 5.9). That percentage is lower for the Italian Americans of the Midwest, and even lower for those living in California, where only 61 percent of the Italian Americans are native westerners. Florida is a case apart. Over half of the Italian Americans of that state were born in the Northeast, and a quarter in the South. California and Florida, along with Texas, have been the states more selected for relocation by Americans in the 1970s. The Italians have followed the same pattern, at a lower rate.

Trends are more pronounced when mobility between states is considered. Even though at the national level the percentage of native Italian Americans born in the state of residence (69%) is close to the same national percentage of white population (68%), differences at the state level are pronounced (except for states such as Pennsylvania, Michigan and Rhode Island). On average, Italian Americans were born in greater numbers in the state of their current residence than were white Americans (Table 5.3). Florida is once again the exception. Here, the largest number of current residents are the result of resettlement and internal migration patterns. Change of residence over a five year period is delineated in Table 5.4.

Geographic mobility is a descriptor linked to the evolution of the ethnic group from arrival as immigrants to the first relocation in the suburbs, to the breaking with territorial ties when links to the ethnic group are loosened and mingling with other groups is fostered by mixed marriages. In fact, five years before the census was taken, 71 percent of Italians born in Italy were living in the same house, versus 62 percent of Americans of single Italian ancestry and only 49 percent of Americans of multiple Italian ancestry. Furthermore, the radius of mobility increases with the generations. The Italian-born who moved, tended to remain in the same county or the same state, while people of multiple ancestry change county and state at a higher percentage. The growing of Italian Americans into the third and fourth generation predicts a higher level of mobility during the 1980s.

The observation that Italian Americans are an urban of population is frequently noted and has been variously commented upon in this publication. The degree of urbanization depends on the history of immigration and the state in which Italians reside. It is highest in Illinois and California, and lowest in Pennsylvania. However, it is always above the averages of the white population in each state. Italian Americans residing in rural areas are rarely living on farms; the only two noticeable exceptions among the states under consideration are California and Illinois.

In the total Italian American population, females outnumber males— although not by so much as in the total American population. Comparison of sex ratios in the different states reveal interesting differences.

The only three states where males outnumber females are California, Florida and Michigan. However, while in California and Michigan males outnumber females in the cohorts of young population under fifteen years of age, in Florida the difference is confined to the age bracket of persons 65 years of age and over, indicating that male Italian Americans retire in that state more than females.

The median age of Italian Americans is consistently lower than that of the white population, both at the national as well as the state level. Generally, Italian Americans are more than three years younger than white Americans. The area with the youngest white American population, the Midwest, is also

Italian Americans residing in rural areas are rarely living on farms; the only two noticeable exceptions among the states under consideration are California and Illinois.

TABLE III

RATIO OF ITALIAN AMERICAN MALES TO FEMALES IN SELECTED STATES

	All ages	65 and over
California	1,004	797
Connecticut	968	763
Florida	1,024	1,053
Illinois	993	736
Massachusetts	970	970
Michigan	1,010	873
New Jersey	965	749
New York	965	744
Ohio	993	794
Pennsylvania	975	793
Rhode Island	950	727
United States	988	785

Source: *Appendix E,* Table 5.1.

the area with the youngest Italian Americans. Median age is highest in Florida. The index of aging (obtained by dividing the number of persons 65 and over by the number of persons under fifteen multiplied by 100) confirms the previous observations:

TABLE IV

INDEX OF AGING

California	40.5
New Jersey	43.0
Connecticut	45.1
New York	49.5
Florida	71.0
Ohio	25.9
Illinois	33.1
Pennsylvania	38.4
Massachusetts	39.7
Rhode Island	49.8
Michigan	26.4
United States	38.2

Source: *Appendix E,* Table 5.1

The extreme variation in median age shown for the different types of ancestry (Table 4.1) has some implications for the age of the Italian American population in a single state. Since persons of single Italian ancestry show a median age of 37 while those of multiple ancestry average around eighteen years, the proportion of multiple versus single ancestry in one state influences the median age of the whole population. In fact, Michigan, Ohio and Illinois have half of the Italian American population belonging to the multiple type of ancestry. California is the only state that departs from this pattern. Multiple ancestry in California developed before other states. Multiple ancestry indicates also detachement from the original period of immigration. Therefore, a state with low median age Italian American population is a sign of a state with Italian Americans already settled into the context of the American population in general.

THE ITALIAN AMERICAN FAMILY

The household composition of Italian Americans does not differ significantly from that of white Americans, except for one aspect: Italian households are larger (2.99 *vs.* 2.68 persons per household). The difference stems from the higher number of relatives in family households (43.4 *vs.* 33.1), almost 90 percent of whom are children. However, the real agent for this difference is the portion of Italian Americans of multiple ancestry and the abnormal age distribution of that population (Chart 1 &2). Only 6.6 percent of the population of multiple ancestry is over 45 years of age. Consequently, the larger size of Italian American households seems to be a result of the low median age of a large part of the group—*i.e.,* the population of multiple ancestry. In fact one can readily note that the states of the Midwest, with the highest percentage of population of multiple ancestry also have the largest households and families.

Data on persons living in group quarters are not large enough to allow extensive considerations, except perhaps for students in college dormitories, where, Massachusetts ranks number one, followed by Pennsylvania, Ohio, Rhode Island, Michigan and Connecticut. This datum is influenced mainly by the higher percentage of young in those states. Residents of homes for the

The household composition of Italian Americans does not differ significantly from that of white Americans.

TABLE V

MARITAL STATUS OF ITALIAN AMERICANS IN SELECTED STATES
(Percent of those aged 15 and over)

	Not single	Rate	Now Married	Divorced	Rate
California	69	534	54	7.9	61
Connecticut	70	540	58	4.8	37
Florida	76	599	61	7.0	56
Illinois	69	515	57	5.1	38
Massachusetts	67	505	55	4.2	32
Michigan	68	496	57	5.0	36
New Jersey	71	542	59	3.7	28
New York	70	542	57	3.6	28
Ohio	69	503	58	5.5	40
Pennsylvania	69	522	57	3.9	30
Rhode Island	70	542	56	5.0	39
United States	70	527	57	4.9	37

Rate = per 1,000 of the total population

Source: *Appendix E,* Table 5.2

aged differ also according to the availability of such homes and the type of environment available for the elderly. Thus, Florida, with the highest median age, has the lowest rate of inmates in homes for the aged because the elderly population in Florida is comprised of recent settlers who purchased private houses.

Marital status of Italian Americans follows similar patterns in all states. Only some values stand out as decidedly departing from the common trend. The first is the percentage of non-single population in Florida (decidedly above average) which, however, does not indicate a similarly higher percentage of married people. The high rate of widowed and divorced persons in Florida is responsible for the high percentage of non-single population. At the bottom side of this ranking we expect the states of the Midwest, because of their younger not yet married population of multiple ancestry. Comparing Italians with white Americans, however, we notice that the percentage of single Italians is higher. Instead of concluding that Italians marry at a lower rate than white Americans, we notice that the larger percentage of single Italians is to be found among the youngsters (those younger than 25 years of age). The conclusion should then be that Italian Americans marry later.

The higher percentage of divorces among Italian Americans in California and Florida is in line with the trend of the general population in those states. Higher rates for states such as Ohio and Michigan depend instead once again on the higher share of population of multiple ancestry in those states. In fact, divorce rates increase with the eloignment from the original Italian family ethos and with the increase of exogamy within the group.[3]

TABLE VI

PERCENTAGE OF DIVORCED PERSONS
AMONG ITALIAN AMERICANS AND WHITE AMERICANS

| | ITALIAN AMERIC. | | WHITE AMERICANS | |
	Male	Female	Male	Female
California	6.8	9.0	7.2	10.0
Connecticut	4.0	5.6	4.5	6.2
Florida	6.2	7.8	6.4	8.3
Illinois	4.4	5.8	4.9	6.4
Massachusetts	3.5	4.8	4.0	5.7
Michigan	4.4	5.6	5.2	6.9
New Jersey	2.9	4.4	3.4	4.9
New York	3.0	4.2	3.8	5.3
Ohio	4.8	6.2	5.3	7.0
Pennsylvania	3.4	4.4	3.7	4.8
Rhode Island	4.1	5.7	4.4	6.2
United States	4.2	5.6	5.2	6.8

Source: *Appendix E,* Table 5.2; U. S. Bureau of the Census: *Census of Population, 1980. General Social and Economic Characteristics.*

The number of females who raise a family without males present is increasing. It used to be the condition of widows; it has become the situation of many divorced women and, recently, the case of females who decide not to marry but still have children.

TABLE VII

PERCENTAGE OF FAMILIES WITH FEMALE HOUSEHOLDER, WITHOUT SPOUSE, WITH CHILDREN

| | Italian Ancestry | | White Population | |
	Under 18	Under 6	Under 18	Under 6
California	7.6	2.4	7.8	2.3
Connecticut	5.8	1.7	5.9	1.6
Florida	5.8	1.6	5.4	1.4
Illinois	5.5	1.6	5.4	1.6
Massachusetts	7.0	2.1	7.5	2.2
Michigan	6.4	2.2	6.7	2.2
New Jersey	5.4	1.5	5.5	1.4
New York	5.6	1.6	6.4	2.0
Ohio	5.9	1.9	5.9	1.9
Pennsylvania	5.6	1.7	5.1	1.4
Rhode Island	7.6	2.2	7.5	2.3
United States	6.2	1.9	6.0	1.8

Source: *Appendix E,* Table 5.8; U. S. Bureau of the Census, *Census of Population, 1980. General Social and Economic Characteristics.*

A rapid analysis of Table VII indicates that nationally Italian women who raise children alone are slightly more numerous than the national average for whites, but the difference is minimal. Also at the state level differences are marginal. Of all Italian American female householders with no spouse present, 35 percent are single, 35 percent widows, twenty percent divorced, six percent separated and four percent actually married. However, of that group family householders are only 28 percent, and data were not available to clarify the marital status of these women raising children alone.

In terms of fertility, Italian Americans have already been described as having a low fertility ratio and birth rate,[4] at least compared to other European groups. This has been attributed mainly to the different age of the groups. The following Table contrasts Italian Americans with the white population in general.

It is a consistent trend that Italians have a lower crude birth rate and lower number of children ever born of women who are in the child bearing age than white Americans. The two descriptors lead to the conclusion that the size of the Italian American family is decreasing and, therefore, the whole ethnic group will be reduced. Since the comparison of the percentage of women in the 15-44 age bracket is higher for Italian Americans than for white Americans, any distortion in the total number of children is excluded. However, the general decrease of fertility among Italian American women, at least compared to those of a generation ago, instead of an indicator of assimilation to the American way of life, should be considered as an adaptation to changed behaviors in the industrial society. In fact, the size of families in Italy has also decreased recently.

Considering the fertility ratio, different conclusions are suggested. Since the highest ratio among Italian Americans cannot be attributed to a lower number of women in child bearing age, we can safely conclude that in the five years prior to the census fecundity among Italian American women

It is a consistent trend that Italians have a lower crude birth rate and lower number of children ever born of women who are in the child bearing age. The higher enrollment of Italian Americans in school is confirmed for all age brackets, except for the elementary school.

increased. It can be considered a signal in the opposite direction of the previous one, of which the multiple ancestry group is responsible. In fact, the ratio is highest in the states of the Midwest, that we already identified as being the ones most influenced by the contingent of multiple ancestry population. Multiple ancestry, however, involves other ethnic groups; other variables come into the picture and make the evaluation of statistical indicators more problematic.

The percentage of non catholic students enrolled in catholic school is rising.

TABLE VIII

FERTILITY RATIOS AND CRUDE BIRTH RATES

| | ITALIAN ANCESTRY | | | WHITE POPULATION | | |
	F.R.	B.R.	Per th. w.	F.R.	B.R.	Per th. w.
California	298	234	948	272	273	1,184
Connecticut	285	230	997	243	253	1,113
Florida	281	220	1,005	250	241	1,185
Illinois	351	249	1,048	294	278	1,224
Massachusetts	287	232	977	241	251	1,073
Michigan	360	261	1,080	300	305	1,301
New Jersey	301	230	1,005	256	251	1,130
New York	294	225	999	260	249	1,115
Ohio	371	259	1,073	305	300	1,306
Pennsylvania	338	230	1,000	276	264	1,202
Rhode Island	272	228	996	254	255	1,128
United States	320	240	1,014	293	286	1,246

F.R. = number of children ‹5 / number of women 15-44 * 1000

B.R. = number of children ever born / total population * 1000

Per th. w. = number of children ever born / number of women 15-44 * 1000

Source: *Appendix E;* U.S.Bureau of the Census, *Census of Population 1980. General Social and Economic Characteristics.*

EDUCATION AND LANGUAGE

Education is a field to which immigrants are very sensitive. Usually unavailable to them because of the country of origin educational system or because of the family economic conditions, the immigrants like to see their children achieve a better education. Motivated by pure necessity or by the desire to improve one's social and economic status, migration constitutes a motivating factor for higher education also. It is only unavoidable that future generations take giant leaps into a better education than the first generation of immigrants did.

Data on school enrollment are not significant, unless contrasted with respective age brackets, not available in our tabulations. To help explain the slightly higher percentage of Italian American students enrolled in nursery school, high school and college we made recourse to national data on population of single ancestry and white race. The higher enrollment of Italian Americans in school is confirmed for all age brackets, except for the elementary school. The most significant observation concerns the enrollment after the end of high school. The percentage of Italian Americans seeking higher education, second only to the Poles, speaks well of future achievements of Italian Americans. A marginal, but revealing aspect of school enrollment is the choice of private over public school.

TABLE IX

SCHOOL ENROLLMENT OF STUDENTS OF SINGLE EUROPEAN ANCESTRY BY AGE

	White	English	French	German	Irish	Italian	Polish
3 and 4	32.0	29.0	28.0	27.1	31.9	36.8	32.8
5 and 6	86.1	83.7	85.6	83.6	86.3	90.7	88.5
7 to 13	99.0	98.8	98.5	99.1	99.0	98.9	99.1
14 and 15	98.1	97.3	97.2	98.2	97.9	98.4	98.6
16 and 17	89.0	85.2	83.6	89.5	86.9	90.5	91.9
18 and 19	52.8	48.0	44.5	52.1	53.2	56.2	56.8
20 and 21	33.3	29.0	25.7	32.2	35.7	37.2	39.3
22 to 24	17.4	15.6	13.6	15.9	17.6	18.1	19.2
25 to 34	8.5	7.2	7.2	7.5	8.6	8.3	9.1

Source: *Appendix C,* Table 3.3

TABLE X

PERCENTAGE OF STUDENTS ENROLLED IN PRIVATE SCHOOLS

	ITALIAN AMERICANS				WHITE POPULATION			
	Nursery	Elem.	High S.	Total	Nursery	Elem.	High S.	Total
California	3.8	8.4	3.0	15.2	3.0	5.9	5.0	13.9
Connecticut	3.5	7.9	4.3	15.7	3.3	6.2	3.8	13.3
Florida	3.9	9.9	3.3	17.1	3.2	8.1	2.6	13.9
Illinois	3.0	12.3	5.4	20.7	2.5	8.4	3.4	14.3
Massachusetts	2.6	5.8	3.3	11.7	2.5	5.2	3.0	10.7
Michigan	2.4	7.8	3.2	13.4	1.9	6.0	2.3	10.2
New Jersey	3.5	9.7	4.1	17.3	3.2	8.6	3.6	15.4
New York	2.7	11.0	4.6	18.3	2.6	9.1	3.6	15.3
Ohio	3.4	13.7	4.4	21.5	2.6	7.4	2.7	12.7
Pennsylvania	2.7	15.4	6.0	24.1	2.4	9.9	3.9	16.2
Rhode Island	2.8	9.6	4.1	16.5	2.4	7.9	3.5	13.8
United States	3.2	10.3	4.1	17.6	2.7	6.5	2.4	11.6

Source: *Appendix E,* Table 5.4; U.S. Bureau of the Census, *Census of Population 1980. General Social and Economic Characteristics.*

The indication from the above Table is clear: Italian Americans enroll their children in private school more than other white Americans. Variations among the several states are consistent, even though the ranking of states between Italian Americans and whites differs. Pennsylvania, Ohio and Illinois are the states with the highest percentage of students in private school. Among the whites in general, instead, Pennsylvania is followed by New Jersey and New York. The choice of a private school stems from a variety of motivations. It has to do with the preoccupation of ensuring a better education to the children, of providing a disciplinary and allegedly safe atmosphere during the formation years, and to supplement the religious education. How the different motivations affect choice of school varies from case to case. However, it is not surprising to discover that when a private school is selected, the religious factor is not necessarily the prevalent one. For instance, the percentage of non catholic students enrolled in catholic schools is rising. Nevertheless, enrollment of children in denominational schools can be considered a clue for some measurement of attachement to church institutions—the only possible through the census. In fact, the U.S. census does not provide any data on religion, "an essential ingredient in the social definition of many American ethnic groups".[5]

Years of school completed is a more useful measure of educational attainment. Italian Americans lag behind white Americans in education, even though the gap has been closing, particularly with the third generation.[6] In some states the distance in high school and college graduates between Italian Americans and white Americans is more pronounced. However, states like New York, New Jersey, Connecticut and Massachusetts suffer the higher proportion of first generation immigrants, who came to the country with less education and less possibilities to improve it. On the contrary, when the proportion of subsequent generations increase, as in Ohio, the Italian Americans reach a higher percentage than white Americans of graduates from high school and college.

The percentage of Italian Americans in the labor force is generally above the national and state average.

TABLE XI

EDUCATIONAL ATTAINMENTS

	ITALIAN AMERICANS High Sch. Graduates	4 or more y. of College	WHITE AMERICANS High Sch. Graduates	4 or more y. of College
California	76.2	18.6	76.6	20.8
Connecticut	63.6	14.6	71.5	21.4
Florida	66.2	13.3	69.5	15.8
Illinois	66.2	14.7	68.7	17.0
Massachusetts	67.7	15.3	72.8	20.2
Michigan	68.9	14.9	69.8	14.9
New Jersey	63.5	14.7	69.0	19.1
New York	61.3	12.5	68.7	19.4
Ohio	70.1	14.9	68.2	14.1
Pennsylvania	63.9	12.8	65.8	14.0
Rhode Island	56.8	13.0	61.3	15.6
United States	67.1	15.5	68.8	17.1

Source: *Appendix E,* Table 5.4.

The language spoken at home is the language in which one was raised. Language is the principal vehicle of cultural transmission; when the language of the country of origin persists in a family, it is a clear sign of attachment to the ethnic group that family belongs to. Among Italian Americans, thirteen percent nationwide continue to speak Italian in the family. This group will decrease, since only four percent of the youth between five and seventeen years of age are part of families where Italian is spoken. The decrease of the Italian born Americans will inevitably mark the loss of the Italian language which was transmitted with difficulty from the first to the following generations. Often rejected by the children, who want to be recognized as Americans, the Italian language was hardly part of a successful policy for the preservation of the Italian cultural heritage. Differences among the several states are a reflex of the percentage of foreign born population in that state.

The portion of population of Italian ancestry that uses neither English nor Italian at home constitutes a particular, even though small, segment of population.

The percentage distribution of Italian Americans by type of occupation does not differ dramatically from that of white Americans in general.

TABLE XII

OTHER LANGUAGE SPOKEN AT HOME
BY POPULATION OF ITALIAN ANCESTRY

	5 to 17	18 and over	Total
Total	100.0	100.0	100.0
Single Italian Ancestry	20.5	46.4	40.6
Multiple Italian Ancestry	79.5	53.6	59.4
Born in Italy	0.6	5.9	4.7
Born in the USA	87.7	62.7	68.3
Born in other place	11.7	31.4	27.0

Source: *Appendix F,* Tables 6.3, 6.11, 6.19, 6.27, 6.35 and derivatives.

The percentage declaring Italian as one of its ancestries can easily be identified as a group of people with Italian background, but in which the language of the non-Italian parent became the language spoken at home. For the 40 percent with single Italian ancestry, the likely situation is that of persons born and raised in a foreign country different from Italy and subsequently immigrated to the U.S.A. The fact that almost half of Italian Americans who speak a language other than English or Italian at home is settled in the states of New York, California and Florida, suggests that this most probable language is Spanish, spoken by Italians born in Argentina or Venezuela or by Italians with a Spanish speaking parent.

ECONOMIC CHARACTERISTICS

The percentage of Italian Americans in the labor force is generally above the national and state average. However, unemployment (except for the states of California and Illinois) is also higher among Italian Americans, as the following Table shows. Yet, even this should be interpreted as a positive sign in favor of Italian Americans. Part of the qualification of an employed person is that he or she be looking for a job or be willing to accept a job. Worries increase when population that should belong to the labor force keeps out of it. In this sense, the low percentage of labor force in the state of New York (60.9, the lowest of our states if the peculiar case of Florida is discarded— Table 5.5) is more worrisome than the higher percentage of unemployment in the state of Ohio.[7]

TABLE XIII

UNEMPLOYMENT RATE

| | ITALIAN AMERICANS | | WHITE AMERICANS | |
	Total	Female	Total	Female
California	5.5	5.5	5.8	5.8
Connecticut	4.6	4.5	4.2	4.3
Florida	4.8	5.4	4.5	5.1
Illinois	5.6	4.7	5.9	5.3
Massachusetts	5.2	4.5	4.8	4.4
Michigan	9.8	8.3	9.5	8.7
New Jersey	6.3	7.0	5.9	6.6
New York	6.4	6.6	6.4	6.4
Ohio	7.4	6.5	7.2	6.7
Pennsylvania	7.4	6.8	6.7	6.3
Rhode Island	7.8	8.0	6.8	6.9
United States	6.1	6.0	5.8	5.7

Source: *Appendix E,* Table 5.5.

Controlling for various characteristics that affect earnings, the result indicates that men of Southern and Eastern European ancestry on the whole fare about as well as non-Euroethnic, non-Hispanic white men... Men of Italian or Polish ancestry consistently earn at least four percent more than non-Euroethnic men.

Immigrants are frequently depicted as hard workers, and rightly so. Does this image concerning also Italian Americans endure through the generations? In a comparison with other European groups, Italians fit into the middle of the pack. For instance, percentage of year-round full time workers among Italian males (54.1) is lower than Germans (56.9) and higher than Irish (53.4). This is of particular interest, however, because it confirms observations of Italian American families. That is the percentage of both husband and wife working is highest for Germans (39.6) and lowest for Italians (31.3). Evidently, Italians still value the role of the mother in the house more than other ethnic groups.

The percentage distribution of Italian Americans by type of occupation does not differ dramatically from that of white Americans in general. At the national level, Italian Americans are employed at a higher rate in technical, sales, administrative and service jobs, while white Americans are employed in higher percentages in precision production, craft, and repair jobs and as operators and laborers in general.

The national trend is substantially followed at the state level, except for one category of occupation. In almost all the states we are considering, white American managers and professionals are significantly more numerous than Italian Americans. The widest gap appears in the state of New York, and it is due to the ancestry composition of the population in that state. Repeatedly we notice that population born in Italy is particularly concentrated in the state of New York. There is almost no variation in type of occupation

TABLE XIV

ITALIAN AMERICANS BY MAJOR OCCUPATIONAL CATEGORIES

	Managerial Professional		Technical Sales Administr.		Service		Precision Craft Repair		Operators Fabricators Laborers	
	I.A.	W.A.	I.A.	W.A.	I.A.	W.A.	I.A.	W.A.	I.A.	W.A.
California	25.7	27.3	35.9	33.4	12.2	11.6	12.4	12.7	11.6	12.8
Connecticut	22.6	27.4	33.0	31.7	12.1	10.7	14.1	12.9	17.7	16.3
Florida	23.2	24.4	35.3	34.4	15.6	12.5	14.3	13.9	10.1	12.3
Illinois	21.7	23.6	35.1	32.0	12.4	11.7	13.2	12.6	17.1	17.7
Massachusetts	23.0	26.5	33.1	31.7	14.2	12.9	12.4	11.5	16.5	16.5
Michigan	22.5	22.0	32.3	29.6	14.3	13.2	13.5	13.8	16.7	19.7
New Jersey	23.5	27.0	35.3	34.0	11.6	10.5	13.0	12.2	15.8	15.5
New York	21.7	27.4	36.3	33.8	12.8	12.1	12.8	11.0	15.6	14.2
Ohio	22.6	21.9	31.8	29.2	13.1	11.8	12.6	13.8	19.1	21.4
Pennsylvania	20.9	21.2	31.9	29.4	13.1	11.8	13.7	13.7	19.6	22.2
Rhode Island	20.5	21.5	31.8	28.9	13.6	13.4	14.7	13.6	18.7	21.7
United States	23.4	23.9	34.4	31.1	12.8	11.6	12.9	13.4	15.4	17.1

Source: *Appendix E,* Table 5.5; U. S. Bureau of the Census, *Census of Population 1980. General Social and Economic Characteristics.*

between population of single and multiple Italian ancestry born in the U.S.A. (Table 4.5). However, the immigrants, holding mostly blue collar jobs, are less employed as managers or professionals and, therefore, they lower the percentage for the whole state.

Examining the ranking of states by percentage of labor force in occupational categories it appears that states could be subdivided in two groups: those with prevalent service economies, like California, Florida, New York, New Jersey and Massachusetts, and states with prevalent manufacturing economies, like Pennsylvania, Michigan, Ohio and Rhode Island. Illinois and Connecticut are states with a relatively more balanced distribution of Italian Americans by occupation. The fact that Italian Americans basically follow state variations of occupation, and the fact that type of ancestry is not a primary factor for this variation has its incidence in other indicators, such as the level of income.

Selecting one type of occupation for a brief sketch, we find that managers and professionals, ten percent of the Italian Americans, but almost a quarter of employed Italian Americans, are two thirds male and one third female. There are fewer single, fewer divorced and widowed and more married persons among them than among the Italian American group in general. Women give birth to a lower number of children. Approximately 95 percent of them are native, only five percent Italian born. Over 50 percent are college graduates, 94 percent have a high school diploma. Half of them exercise a managerial role, the other half is engaged in a professional occupation (health, education and other services). Management is distributed in all industries, but it is more prevalent in the manufacturing, trading and financial industries. In 1979 Italian American managers earned approximately 20 thousand dollars (per capita income), more than twice the salary of an Italian American in general.

If occupation patterns of Italian Americans mirror the patterns of the larger white population, distribution of labor force by industry does is even closer. In two of three major industries of employment (manufacturing, 20.9; and professional services, 18.8), Italian Americans trail white Americans (22.3 and 19.9, respectively), preceding them instead in trading (23.8 *vs.* 21.2). They are also less employed in construction jobs, the trademark of Italian immigrant labor. In all other industries, the percentage of Italian Americans employed is higher. Differences, however, are minimal. States differ considerably in terms of types of industry developed, but Italian Americans do not show any peculiar behavior in this regard. Manufacturing is concentrated in the Midwest, construction and trading in Florida, financial services in New York, entertainment in California. Employment of Italian Americans in the public administration is highest in Rhode Island, as expected, where the density of Italian Americans exceeds that of other states. Italians came to the U.S. from peasant regions, but did not seek employment as farmers. The *New York Times* related recently that, according to a report from the Census Bureau, the farm population in the nation has dropped to two percent.[8] Among Italian Americans, however, the percentage of labor force employed in agriculture is under one percent, and the percentage of rural population living on farms is only half of a percentage point.

Age, sex, education and occupation of Italian Americans are all variables that concur in determining income values. To these, add also the geographical distribution of Italians in the various states. There is an incontrovertible difference of income between Italian Americans and white Americans. Median household and family income of Italian Americans is higher than that of white Americans; per capita income is lower. This anomaly finds an explanation in the larger size of an Italian household or family, with more income earning components. In fact, the percentage of families with no workers is lower among Italian Americans (11.1) than among whites (12.3), while the percentage of families with two or more workers is higher (55.7 *vs.* 54.8). Contributing toward that result is also the portion of Italian born persons, whose income is considerably lower than persons of Italian ancestry born in the U.S. Third, the proportion of populaton that did not reach the productive age yet (persons under fifteen years of age) is higher for Italian Americans (24.3) than white Americans (21.3). Conversely, the percentage of population 65 and over, of which twelve percent is still employed, is higher for white Americans. This portion of unemployed people is included in the denominator employed to establish per capita income and, therefore, lowers the average for all Italians.

Lower per capita income cannot be included among the reasons for lower earnings. In fact, comparison of earnings for groups of single ancestry indicate that Italians fare better than all other groups, except for the Polish (Table 3.10).

The findings of the U.S. Commission on Civil Rights concluded, in its report on the economic status of Americans of Southern and Eastern European ancestry that, "controlling for various characteristics that affect earnings, the result indicates that men of Southern and Eastern European ancestry on the whole fare about as well as non-Euroethnic, non-Hispanic white men... Men of Italian or Polish ancestry consistently earn at least four percent more than non-Euroethnic men".[9]

Undoubtedly, the satisfactory overall economic performance of Italian Americans benefits from the geographical distribution of Italians in the leading states in terms of contribution to the U.S. economy. With the exception of Texas, the ten most productive states in 1986, according to a report by the Departement of Commerce, were the same ten states most populated by

Americans of mixed Italian ancestry do not average a better income than Americans of single Italian ancestry.

TABLE XV

MEDIAN HOUSEHOLD INCOME
OF ITALIAN AMERICANS AND WHITE AMERICANS IN 1979 (Dollars)

	Households		Families		Unrelated Individuals		Per capita	
	I.A.	W.A.	I.A.	W.A.	I.A.	W.A.	I.A.	W.A.
California	20,095	19,170	23,598	22,748	8,893	8,491	8,753	9,109
Connecticut	20,080	20,716	22,380	23,890	7,511	8,080	7,479	8,884
Florida	15,611	15,446	17,595	18,244	7,133	7,000	7,200	7,895
Illinois	22,122	20,384	25,307	23,999	8,633	8,215	8,092	8,742
Massachusetts	18,626	17,968	21,258	21,554	6,238	6,597	6,782	7,632
Michigan	22,060	19,983	24,882	22,841	7,762	7,209	7,766	8,048
New Jersey	20,841	20,890	23,273	24,184	7,877	8,195	7,618	8,702
New York	18,916	18,062	21,564	21,672	6,764	7,240	7,128	8,166
Ohio	20,045	18,386	22,468	21,419	7,121	7,033	7,028	7,540
Pennsylvania	18,091	17,427	20,547	20,507	5,598	6,184	6,618	7,337
Rhode Island	16,801	16,363	19,478	19,745	5,161	5,589	6,586	7,030
United States	19,362	17,680	21,960	20,835	7,179	7,036	7,371	7,808

Source: *Appendix E,* Table 5.7; U.S. Bureau of the Census, *Census of Population 1980. General Social and Economic Characteristics.*

The increase of multiple ancestry brings with it a score of other social behaviors observed in our analysis.

Italian Americans and included in this analysis.[10] They ranked in the following order: California, New York, Texas, Illinois, Pennsylvania, Florida, Ohio, New Jersey, Michigan and Massachusetts. Rhode Island, instead, was ranked 43. However, after regression analysis controlling for geographical distribution, the Civil Rights Commission still concluded that income levels of Italian Americans were higher than those of the rest of the population.

Italians of different states have different income, but that depends, before anything else, on the difference of income of any population in those states. In fact, Italian Americans simply reflect the patterns of the general population, with some variations among the five states with highest income. Instead of New Jersey, Connecticut, Illinois, Michigan and California in this order for the white Americans, the ranking of states by income of Italian Americans is Illinois, Michigan, New Jersey, California and Connecticut. Several factors concur to determine the ranking of the States. For the household and family income the most important one is the number of workers per family. Illinois, the state with the highest income, is also the state with the lowest percentage of families with no workers. Similarly, Florida, the state with the lowest income, is also the state with the highest percentage of families with no workers.

Americans of mixed Italian ancestry do not average a better income than Americans of single Italian ancestry, except for the median household income. One could conclude that breaking away from the ethnic group does not pay, since Americans of single Italian ancestry have a better income also than all other European groups except for the Poles. However, we should be more cautious in our conclusions, particularly after observing that people of single Italian ancestry in the age bracket of 45 to 54 (the cohort with the highest income) are thirteen percent, while people of the same cohort among multiple ancestry Italians are only three percent. All considered, it appears that differences in type of ancestry plays a minor role in deter-

TABLE XVI

MEDIAN HOUSEHOLD INCOME OF ITALIAN AMERICANS
BY STATE AND PLACE OF BIRTH (Dollars)

Place of birth	Total	Italy	United States			All Other	
			N. East	Midwest	South	West	Places
California	20,095	12,764	20,732	20,903	17,562	20,911	17,575
Connecticut	20,080	14,883	20,805	20,644	18,113	20,642	18,010
Florida	15,611	10,205	16,064	16,407	16,846	17,041	15,391
Illinois	22,122	18,002	24,984	22,685	18,762	18,820	20,523
Massachusetts	18,626	12,488	19,527	18,091	19,476	16,386	15,000
Michigan	22,060	17,950	24,158	22,444	21,182	21,068	20,918
New Jersey	20,841	14,943	21,560	22,711	18,551	20,761	18,187
New York	18,916	13,555	19,990	18,323	17,308	18,137	15,482
Ohio	20,045	14,387	21,825	20,336	19,636	17,031	15,148
Pennsylvania	18,091	11,591	18,739	19,245	17,712	18,121	15,141
Rhode Island	16,801	10,686	17,393	17,042	17,111	11,708	12,275
United States	16,362	13,544	19,958	20,953	18,651	20,142	16,672

Source: U. S. Bureau of the Census, *Special Tabulations on Italian Population.* 1987 (Un—
published Data),

mining differences of income among Italian Americans. Major factors are
instead age, sex, geographical location, education, family composition and
type of occupation.

TABLE XVII

PERCENTAGE OF ITALIAN AMERICANS BELOW POVERTY LEVEL IN 1979

	Families		Persons	
	I.A.	W.A.	I.A.	W.A.
California	5.6	6.5	7.5	8.9
Connecticut	4.6	4.4	5.7	6.0
Florida	6.6	6.9	8.8	9.7
Illinois	4.3	5.2	5.5	7.2
Massachusetts	6.6	9.2	8.0	12.4
Michigan	5.0	6.1	6.3	7.9
New Jersey	4.8	4.9	5.7	6.4
New York	6.2	7.0	7.6	9.4
Ohio	4.9	6.3	6.5	8.3
Pennsylvania	6.0	5.9	7.8	8.3
Rhode Island	7.0	6.8	8.8	9.3
United States	5.7	7.0	7.3	9.4

Source: *Appendix E,* Table 5.8; U.S. Bureau of the Census, *Census of Population 1980. General
Social and Economic Characteristics.*

The percentage of population below poverty level is an indicator that completes the overall picture provided by data on income, taking the perspective of the low end portion of the social ladder. Poverty level is determined as three times the cost of the economy food plan, which was established at $7,412 in 1979. Italian Americans had a lower percentage of population below the poverty level. Variations among states do not reserve particular surprises, at least for the states with less poverty. However, somehow surprising is to find Massachusetts at the top of the list of states by poverty. Once again, however, Italian Americans do not reveal particular differences with white Americans, except in Massachusetts, where their percentage of population below poverty level is much less pronounced.

SUMMARY

Geographical distribution of Italian Americans has been attributed to many factors, but, as for all other immigrants, it was the result of "the interaction of three major variables—economy, demography and culture".[11] Employment was the major factor. For this reason Italians did not settle overwhelmingly in the South, where the region had already an abundant supply of unskilled labor. And they did not settle in industrial cities with a high percentage of immigrants from Eastern Europe, competing for the same unskilled labor market. When that happened, Italians concentrated in outside construction work while Eastern Europeans went after iron and steel manufacturing and chemical industries.

The work factor alone, however, is not sufficient to explain geographical distribution. The ethnic factor, by which groups responded differently to similar job opportunities and organized themselves in a different way, must also be weighed. "Regardless of the merits and drawbacks of the institution, the *padrone* is essential for understanding early Italian work distribution and settlement patterns in the U.S."[12]

Also, a major role was played by the ethnic neighborhood, which established and prolonged the chain migration system, and gave some stability to new immigrants anxious for cultural similarities with the country they had left.

Generalizations, the result of major trends and large numbers, often overlook minor, but still important phenomena. Italians were well known for outside construction and railroad work and for avoiding underground mining. However, one finds Italians in the iron mines of Northern Wisconsin and copper mines in Montana. Even though Italians remained a largely urban community, they worked in the sugar cane harvests of Louisiana. Many workers, after the railroad projects were completed, turned into growing fruits and vegetables in Colorado, Utah, Nebraska and upstate New York. The valleys of California were the setting for the largest agricultural developments by Italians.[13]

Italian Americans are proceeding toward an increase in mixed ancestry within the ethnic group. This trend does not advance at the same speed in all states. States such as California, Michigan, Ohio and Illinois will increase the majority of mixed ancestry components by the end of the 1980s. The states of the Northeast region, whose high percentage of Italian Americans makes exogamy less probable, will be the last in this process.

The increase of multiple ancestry brings with it a score of other social behaviors observed in our analysis: increase of geographical mobility, of divorce rate and of higher education; decrease of Italian language spoken at home and changes in the types of industry and occupation. However, further anal-

The marching of Italian Americans toward the middle of the mainstream does not translate into a total disappearance of ethnic discrimination.

ysis is needed to assess whether such changes are a result of the multiple ancestry impact, or to a deeper assimilation into the American way of life. Often we noticed that differences were attributable to the distribution of the population in the age cohorts rather than to the type of ancestry.

In many instances we observed the tendency of the states to split into two or three groups. The Italian American population of California, Illinois, Michigan and Ohio showed similarities in terms of education and economic characteristics. The states of the East Coast formed the other group, with the Italian American population of Connecticut and New Jersey emerging as a bridging element. Changes in economic conditions of various states, as well as the decrease of population born in Italy in each state will produce a more homogeneous picture of Italian Americans when data for the 1990 census is collected.

Our cursory overview did not intend to answer any particular question in the still heated debate concerning the preservation of the Italian American identity. Incidentally, census data, lacking basic sections concerning cultural and religious behavior, are not equipped for such endeavor. However, we did observe the peculiar strength of the Italian American family, the upward mobility achieved in educational and economic fields and the differences that distinguish Italian Americans from the white Americans in general.

The marching of Italian Americans toward the middle of the mainstream does not translate into a total disappearance of ethnic discrimination. "Despite the economic gains Euroethnic groups have made, some argue that access to the highest levels of the corporate ladder remains limited. For instance, in a paper concerning this issue, Barta concludes that Poles and Italians are 'grossly underrepresented in the executive suites of Chicago's major corporations'".[14]

Being Italian American carries a different weight according to the state and region of settlement. However, Italian Americans seem equipped enough to express both the sense of belonging to this nation of nations as well as the unmistakable characteristics of their heritage. Regionally, and regionalism has been so radicated in the Italian history, this has been proven time and again. Perhaps the time has come for Italian Americans to give regional achievements a national dimension.

FOOTNOTES

[1] Velikonja, J. In L.F. Tomasi, Ed., *Italian Americans: New Perspectives in Italian Immigration and Ethnicity.* New York: Center for Migration Studies: 1985. Pp.142-172.

[2] Alba, R.D., *Italian Americans. Into the Twilight of Ethnicity.* Englewood Cliffs, NJ: Prentice-Hall, 1985.

[3] *See,* Femminella, herein.

[4] *See,* Femminella, herein.

[5] Alba, *Ibidem*, p.107.

[6] Neidert, Lisa J. and R. Farley, *Assimilation in the United States: An Analysis of Ethnic and Generation Differences in Status and Achievement.* American Sociological Review, December 1985, Volume 50, No. 6, Pp.840-850. The authors, comparing intergenerational data from the 1979 Current Population Survey, argue that by the third generation ethnic background is no longer an important determinant of socioeconomic achievement.

[7] An article in The New York Times, August 3, 1988 related the same concept commenting on the low unemployment rate for the state of New York (4.5 *vs.* 5.8 for the whole nation) in the first six months of 1988, but also the high percentage of population 16 years and over out of labor force (45.3 *vs.* 34.5 for the whole nation) for the same period.

[8] *The New York Times, July 10, 1988.*

[9] *U.S. Commission on Civil Rights, The Economic Status of Americans of Southern and Eastern European Ancestry.* Clearinghouse Publication No. 89. October 1986, p.38.

[10] *The New York Times,* August 6, 1988.

[11] Golab, C., *Immigrant Destinations.* Temple University Press, 1977. p.159.

[12] Golab, C., *Ibidem,* p.59.

[13] Allen, J.P. and E. J. Turner, *We the People. An Atlas of America's Ethnic Diversity.* New York: Macmillan Publishing Company, 1988. p.125.

[14] United States Commission on Civil Rights, *Ibidem,* p.41.

INDEX OF SOURCES FOR FIGURES AND CHARTS

APPENDIX A

Italian Immigration to the United States
in the Last Twenty Years

Source: *Statistical Yearbook of the Immigration and Naturalization Service: 1965-1986*

TABLE 1.1

IMMIGRANTS TO THE U.S. FROM EUROPE AND ITALY BY DECADES

Year	UNITED STATES		ITALY		EUROPE	
	Total	Percent	Total	Percent	Total	Percent
1820	8,385	100.0	30	0.4	7,690	91.7
1821-1830	143,439	100.0	409	0.3	98,797	68.9
1831-1840	599,125	100.0	2,253	0.4	495,681	82.7
1841-1850	1,713,251	100.0	1,870	0.1	1,597,442	93.2
1851-1860	2,598,214	100.0	9,231	0.4	2,452,577	94.4
1861-1870	2,314,824	100.0	11,725	0.5	2,065,141	89.2
1820-1870	7,377,238	100.0	25,518	0.3	6,717,328	91.1
1871-1880	2,812,191	100.0	55,759	2.0	2,271,925	80.8
1881-1890	5,246,613	100.0	307,309	5.9	4,735,484	90.3
1891-1900	3,687,564	100.0	651,893	17.7	3,555,352	96.4
1901-1910	8,795,386	100.0	2,045,877	23.3	8,056,040	91.6
1911-1920	5,735,811	100.0	1,109,524	19.3	4,321,887	75.3
1871-1920	26,277,565	100.0	4,170,362	15.9	22,940,688	87.3
1921-1930	4,107,209	100.0	455,315	11.1	2,463,194	60.0
1931-1940	528,431	100.0	68,028	12.9	347,552	65.8
1941-1950	1,035,039	100.0	57,661	5.6	621,124	60.0
1921-1950	5,670,679	100.0	581,004	10.2	3,431,870	60.5
1951-1960	2,515,479	100.0	185,491	7.4	1,325,727	52.7
1961-1965	1,450,312	100.0	78,893	5.4	528,543	36.4
1951-1965	3,965,791	100.0	264,384	6.7	1,854,270	46.8
1966-1970	1,871,365	100.0	135,218	7.2	594,949	31.8
1971-1975	1,936,281	100.0	93,506	4.8	422,194	21.8
1966-1975	3,807,646	100.0	228,724	6.0	1,017,143	26.7
1976-1980	2,557,033	100.0	35,862	1.4	378,174	14.8
1981-1986	3,466,114	100.0	29,921	0.9	403,365	11.6
1976-1986	6,023,147	100.0	65,783	1.1	781,539	13.0
1966-1986	9,830,793	100.0	294,507	3.0	1,798,553	18.3
1820-1986	53,122,066	100.0	5,335,775	10.0	36,742,838	69.2
1820-1870	7,377,238	13.9	25,518	0.5	6,717,328	18.3
1871-1920	26,277,565	49.5	4,170,362	78.2	22,940,688	62.4
1921-1950	5,670,679	10.7	581,004	10.9	3,431,870	9.3
1951-1965	3,965,791	7.5	264,384	5.0	1,854,270	5.0
1966-1986	9,830,793	18.5	294,507	5.5	1,798,553	4.9
1820-1986	53,122,066	100.0	5,335,775	100.0	36,742,838	100.0

TABLE 1.2

U.S. AND ITALIAN STATISTICS ON MIGRATION FROM ITALY TO THE U.S. AND RETURN MIGRATION: 1966-1986

Year	U.S. Statistics			Total Emigrants	Italian Statistics				
	Total Imm. to U.S.	Italians Admitted	Percentage		Total Repatr.	Emigr. over Repatr.	Emigr. to U.S.	Repatr. from U.S.	Emigr. over Repatr.
1966	323,040	25,154	7.8	296,494	206,486	90,008	31,238	298	30,940
1967	361,972	26,565	7.3	229,264	169,328	59,936	17,896	790	17,106
1968	454,448	23,593	5.2	215,713	150,027	65,686	21,693	1,203	20,490
1969	358,579	23,617	6.6	182,199	153,298	28,901	15,470	4,172	11,298
1970	373,526	24,973	6.7	151,854	142,503	9,351	15,490	4,422	11,068
1971	370,478	22,137	6.0	167,721	128,572	39,149	14,747	5,033	9,714
1972	384,685	21,427	5.6	141,852	138,246	3,606	13,532	5,845	7,687
1973	400,063	22,151	5.5	123,802	125,168	-1,366	11,358	5,924	5,434
1974	394,861	15,884	4.0	112,020	116,708	-4,688	8,999	5,623	3,376
1975	386,194	11,552	3.0	92,666	122,774	-30,108	6,386	5,699	687
1976	398,613	8,380	2.1	97,247	115,997	-18,750	6,973	5,541	1,432
1976q*	103,676	2,035	2.0	0	0	0	0	0	0
1977	462,315	7,510	1.6	87,655	101,985	-14,330	6,604	5,363	1,241
1978	601,442	7,415	1.2	85,550	89,897	-4,347	5,779	4,997	782
1979	460,348	6,174	1.3	88,950	91,693	-2,743	4,638	5,264	-626
1980	350,639	5,467	1.6	84,877	90,463	-5,586	4,334	5,088	-754
1981	596,600	4,662	0.8	89,221	88,886	335	4,146	4,600	-454
1982	594,131	3,644	0.6	98,241	92,423	5,818	5,022	4,762	260
1983	559,763	3,225	0.6	85,138	87,804	-2,666	4,555	4,408	147
1984	543,903	3,130	0.6	77,318	77,002	316	3,959	3,634	325
1985	570,009	3,214	0.6	66,737	67,277	-540	3,541	3,155	386
1986	601,708	3,089	0.5	57,862	56,006	1,856	3,062	3,044	18
Total	9,650,993	274,998	2.8	2,632,381	2,412,543	219,838	209,422	88,865	120,557

Source for Italian Statistics: Ministero degli Affari Esteri. *Aspetti e problemi dell'emigrazione italiana all'estero. 1967-1987.*

* In 1976 the cutoff date for processing immigration information was moved from June 30 to September 30. Fort this reasons data belonging to the transitional quarter from July 1 to September 30 of 1976 are reported separately.

TABLE 1.3

IMMIGRANTS TO THE U.S. FROM SELECTED EUROPEAN COUNTRIES: 1965-1986

YEAR	FRANCE	GERMANY	IRELAND	ITALY	POLAND	U. K.
1965	4,039	24,045	5,463	10,821	8,465	27,358
1966	3,175	18,239	3,241	25,154	9,404	21,441
1967	3,440	16,041	2,624	26,565	5,976	24,965
1968	3,402	15,920	3,004	23,593	5,995	28,586
1969	2,024	9,289	1,989	23,617	4,052	15,014
1970	2,477	9,684	1,562	24,973	3,585	14,158
1971	2,001	7,519	1,614	22,137	2,883	10,787
1972	1,966	6,848	1,780	21,427	4,784	10,078
1973	1,845	6,600	2,000	22,151	4,914	10,638
1974	1,634	6,320	1,572	15,884	4,033	10,710
1975	1,364	5,154	1,285	11,552	3,941	10,807
1976	1,478	5,836	1,171	8,380	3,805	11,392
1976q	397	1,695	302	2,035	960	3,020
1977	1,618	6,372	1,238	7,510	4,010	12,477
1978	1,844	6,739	1,180	7,415	5,050	14,245
1979	1,705	6,314	982	6,174	4,413	13,907
1980	1,905	6,595	1,006	5,467	4,725	15,485
1981	1,745	6,552	902	4,662	5,014	14,997
1982	1,994	6,726	949	3,644	5,874	14,539
1983	2,061	7,185	1,101	3,225	6,427	14,830
1984	2,135	6,747	1,223	3,130	9,466	13,949
1985	2,187	7,109	1,397	3,214	9,464	13,408
1986	2,518	6,991	1,839	3,089	8,481	13,657
Total	48,954	200,520	39,424	285,819	125,721	340,448

YEAR	FRANCE	GERMANY	IRELAND	ITALY	POLAND	U.K.
1965	8.3	12.0	13.9	3.8	6.7	8.0
1966	6.5	9.1	8.2	8.8	7.5	6.3
1967	7.0	8.0	6.7	9.3	4.8	7.3
1968	6.9	7.9	7.6	8.3	4.8	8.4
1969	4.1	4.6	5.0	8.3	3.2	4.4
1970	5.1	4.8	4.0	8.7	2.9	4.2
1971	4.1	3.7	4.1	7.7	2.3	3.2
1972	4.0	3.4	4.5	7.5	3.8	3.0
1973	3.8	3.3	5.1	7.8	3.9	3.1
1974	3.3	3.2	4.0	5.6	3.2	3.1
1975	2.8	2.6	3.3	4.0	3.1	3.2
1976	3.0	2.9	3.0	2.9	3.0	3.3
1976q	0.8	0.8	0.8	0.7	0.8	0.9
1977	3.3	3.2	3.1	2.6	3.2	3.7
1978	3.8	3.4	3.0	2.6	4.0	4.2
1979	3.5	3.1	2.5	2.2	3.5	4.1
1980	3.9	3.3	2.6	1.9	3.8	4.5
1981	3.6	3.3	2.3	1.6	4.0	4.4
1982	4.1	3.4	2.4	1.3	4.7	4.3
1983	4.2	3.6	2.8	1.1	5.1	4.4
1984	4.4	3.4	3.1	1.1	7.5	4.1
1985	4.5	3.5	3.5	1.1	7.5	3.9
1986	5.1	3.5	4.7	1.1	6.7	4.0
Total	100	100	100	100	100	100

TABLE 1.4

ITALIAN IMMIGRANTS BY CLASSES UNDER THE IMMIGRATION LAWS: 1966-1986

Year	Number Admitted	Subject to Numerical Limitation	Exempt from Numerical Limitation	Parents of U.S. Citizens	Wives of U.S. Citizens	Husbands of U.S. Citizens	Children of U.S. Citizens	Four Familial Prefer.
1966	25,154	19,135	6,019	941	1,840	1,324	997	5,102
1967	26,565	19,970	6,595	2,160	1,611	1,208	984	5,963
1968	23,593	17,248	6,345	2,127	1,524	1,176	1,106	5,933
1969	23,617	18,494	5,123	1,634	1,397	979	916	4,926
1970	24,973	19,739	5,234	1,644	1,388	1,280	775	5,087
1971	22,137	17,827	4,310	1,446	1,069	1,075	496	4,086
1972	21,427	17,620	3,807	1,304	919	947	329	3,499
1973	22,151	18,859	3,292	1,112	830	774	257	2,973
1974	15,884	13,235	2,649	909	684	600	208	2,401
1975	11,552	9,213	2,339	802	606	558	177	2,143
1976	8,380	6,202	2,178	721	566	534	135	1,956
1976q	2,035	1,462	573	158	160	142	43	503
1977	7,510	5,397	2,113	648	587	517	151	1,903
1978	7,415	5,089	2,326	646	784	529	171	2,130
1979	6,174	4,091	2,083	553	652	579	146	1,930
1980	5,467	3,448	2,019	513		1,225	117	1,855
1981	4,662	2,880	1,782	473		1,056	111	1,640
1982	3,644	1,756	1,888	452		1,161	107	1,720
1983	3,225	1,501	1,724	337		1,139	115	1,591
1984	3,130	1,407	1,723	296		1,167	97	1,560
1985	3,214	1,386	1,828	294		1,270	139	1,703
1986	3,089	1,336	1,753	274		1,299	97	1,670

Year	Number Admitted	Subject to Numerical Limitation	Exempt from Numerical Limitation	Parents of U.S. Citizens	Wives of U.S. Citizens	Husbands of U.S. Citizens	Children of U.S. Citizens	Four Familial Prefer.
1966	100	76.1	23.9	3.7	7.3	5.3	4.0	20.3
1967	100	75.2	24.8	8.1	6.1	4.5	3.7	22.4
1968	100	73.1	26.9	9.0	6.5	5.0	4.7	25.1
1969	100	78.3	21.7	6.9	5.9	4.1	3.9	20.9
1970	100	79.0	21.0	6.6	5.6	5.1	3.1	20.4
1971	100	80.5	19.5	6.5	4.8	4.9	2.2	18.5
1972	100	82.2	17.8	6.1	4.3	4.4	1.5	16.3
1973	100	85.1	14.9	5.0	3.7	3.5	1.2	13.4
1974	100	83.3	16.7	5.7	4.3	3.8	1.3	15.1
1975	100	79.8	20.2	6.9	5.2	4.8	1.5	18.6
1976	100	74.0	26.0	8.6	6.8	6.4	1.6	23.3
1976q	100	71.8	28.2	7.8	7.9	7.0	2.1	24.7
1977	100	71.9	28.1	8.6	7.8	6.9	2.0	25.3
1978	100	68.6	31.4	8.7	10.6	7.1	2.3	28.7
1979	100	66.3	33.7	9.0	10.6	9.4	2.4	31.3
1980	100	63.1	36.9	9.4		22.4	2.1	33.9
1981	100	61.8	38.2	10.1		22.7	2.4	35.2
1982	100	48.2	51.8	12.4		31.9	2.9	47.2
1983	100	46.5	53.5	10.4		35.3	3.6	49.3
1984	100	45.0	55.0	9.5		37.3	3.1	49.8
1985	100	43.1	56.9	9.1		39.5	4.3	53.0
1986	100	43.3	56.7	8.9		42.1	3.1	54.1

TABLE 1.5

ITALIAN IMMIGRANTS ADMITTED BY PREFERENCES
UNDER THE WORLWIDE NUMERICAL LIMITATION

Year	Number Admitted	Subject to Numerical Limitation	Percent	Relative Total	Preference Percent	Occupational. Total	Preference Percent
1966	25,154	19,135	100.0	16,680	87.2	2,232	11.7
1967	26,565	19,970	100.0	16,462	82.4	3,305	16.5
1968	23,593	17,248	100.0	15,103	87.6	1,913	11.1
1969	23,617	18,494	100.0	17,990	97.3	179	1.0
1970	24,973	19,739	100.0	19,521	98.9	163	0.8
1971	22,137	17,827	100.0	17,703	99.3	151	0.8
1972	21,427	17,620	100.0	17,500	99.3	132	0.7
1973	22,151	18,859	100.0	18,650	98.9	516	2.7
1974	15,884	13,235	100.0	12,100	91.4	1,451	11.0
1975	11,552	9,213	100.0	8,567	93.0	588	6.4
1976	8,380	6,202	100.0	5,638	90.9	315	5.1
1976q	2,035	1,462	100.0	1,357	92.8	56	3.8
1977	7,510	5,397	100.0	4,863	90.1	199	3.7
1978	7,415	5,089	100.0	4,662	91.6	350	6.9
1979	6,174	4,091	100.0	3,745	91.5	448	11.0
1980	5,467	3,448	100.0	2,920	84.7	562	16.3
1981	4,662	2,880	100.0	2,417	83.9	455	15.8
1982	3,644	1,756	100.0	1,319	75.1	484	27.6
1983	3,225	1,501	100.0	1,072	71.4	457	30.4
1984	3,130	1,407	100.0	1,069	76.0	357	25.4
1985	3,214	1,386	100.0	1,028	74.2	377	27.2
1986	3,089	1,367	100.0	977	71.5	378	27.7

Note: Residual nonpreference immigrants are not reported.

TABLE 1.6

ITALIAN IMMIGRANTS ADMITTED BY AGE AND SEX: 1966-1985

Year	UNDER 20 Male	UNDER 20 Female	20-59 Male	20-59 Female	60 AND OVER Male	60 AND OVER Female	TOTAL Male	TOTAL Female	TOTAL
1966	4,608	4,745	7,384	7,211	538	668	12,530	12,624	25,154
1967	4,629	4,461	8,325	7,577	742	831	13,696	12,869	26,565
1968	4,000	3,942	7,260	6,748	782	861	12,042	11,551	23,593
1969	4,071	4,185	7,181	6,663	721	796	11,973	11,644	23,617
1970	4,417	4,400	7,879	6,862	604	811	12,900	12,073	24,973
1971	3,946	3,794	7,106	6,096	559	636	11,611	10,526	22,137
1972	3,913	3,834	6,694	5,822	534	630	11,141	10,286	21,427
1973	4,115	3,923	6,866	6,097	515	635	11,496	10,655	22,151
1974	2,716	2,842	4,893	4,455	437	541	8,046	7,838	15,884
1975	1,889	1,976	3,609	3,315	339	424	5,837	5,715	11,552
1976	1,277	1,253	2,733	2,377	290	450	4,300	4,080	8,380
1976q	375	308	607	583	62	100	1,044	991	2,035
1977	1,154	1,119	2,465	2,086	284	402	3,903	3,607	7,510
1978	1,069	1,044	2,388	2,271	239	404	3,696	3,719	7,415
1979	955	889	2,014	1,806	199	311	3,168	3,006	6,174
1980*	1,485		3,501		481		5,467		5,467
1981*	1,191		3,041		430		4,662		4,662
1982	368	339	1,288	1,090	169	226	1,825	1,655	3,644
Unknown	24		123		17		164		
1983	310	327	1,138	915	121	216	1,569	1,458	3,225
Unknown	42		138		18		198		
1984	340	325	1,210	969	121	165	1,671	1,459	3,130
1985	306	314	1,300	1,027	106	161	1,712	1,502	3,214

Year	UNDER 20 Male	UNDER 20 Female	20-59 Male	20-59 Female	60 AND OVER Male	60 AND OVER Female	TOTAL Male	TOTAL Female	TOTAL
1966	18.3	18.9	29.4	28.7	2.1	2.7	49.8	50.2	25,154
1967	17.4	16.8	31.3	28.5	2.8	3.1	51.6	48.4	26,565
1968	17.0	16.7	30.8	28.6	3.3	3.6	51.0	49.0	23,593
1969	17.2	17.7	30.4	28.2	3.1	3.4	50.7	49.3	23,617
1970	17.7	17.6	31.6	27.5	2.4	3.2	51.7	48.3	24,973
1971	17.8	17.1	32.1	27.5	2.5	2.9	52.5	47.5	22,137
1972	18.3	17.9	31.2	27.2	2.5	2.9	52.0	48.0	21,427
1973	18.6	17.7	31.0	27.5	2.3	2.9	51.9	48.1	22,151
1974	17.1	17.9	30.8	28.0	2.8	3.4	50.7	49.3	15,884
1975	16.4	17.1	31.2	28.7	2.9	3.7	50.5	49.5	11,552
1976	15.2	15.0	32.6	28.4	3.5	5.4	51.3	48.7	8,380
1976q	18.4	15.1	29.8	28.6	3.0	4.9	51.3	48.7	2,035
1977	15.4	14.9	32.8	27.8	3.8	5.4	52.0	48.0	7,510
1978	14.4	14.1	32.2	30.6	3.2	5.4	49.8	50.2	7,415
1979	15.5	14.4	32.6	29.3	3.2	5.0	51.3	48.7	6,174
1980*	27.2		64.0		8.8		100.0		5,467
1981*	25.5		65.2		9.2		100.0		4,662
1982	10.1	9.3	35.3	29.9	4.6	6.2	52.4	47.6	3,644
1983	9.6	10.1	35.3	28.4	3.8	6.7	51.8	48.2	3,225
1984	10.9	10.4	38.7	31.0	3.9	5.3	53.4	46.6	3,130
1985	9.5	9.8	40.4	32.0	3.3	5.0	53.3	46.7	3,214

* Data not available because of incomplete immigrants statistical file. *1981 Statistical Yearbook of the Immigration and Naturalization Service*, p. vii.

TABLE 1.7

MEDIAN AGE OF IMMIGRANTS FROM SELECTED EUROPEAN COUNTRIES: 1966, 1985

Country	Total Immigrants	Median Age 1966	Median Age 1985	Difference
Italy	25,154	25.9	28.8	2.9
Male	12,530	26.0	29.2	3.2
Female	12,624	25.8	28.3	2.5
France	3,175	25.5	27.9	2.4
Male	1,085	24.1	28.2	4.1
Female	2,090	26.0	27.7	1.7
Germany	18,239	23.4	25.4	2.0
Male	5,218	20.9	26.2	5.3
Female	13,021	24.0	25.3	1.3
Ireland	3,241	24.8	27.9	3.1
Male	1,146	25.6	27.9	2.3
Female	2,095	24.3	27.8	3.5
Poland	9,404	28.1	30.4	2.3
Male	4,509	28.2	30.8	2.6
Female	4,895	28.0	29.9	1.9
United K.	21,441	25.2	27.2	2.0
Male	8,406	25.7	28.5	2.8
Female	13,035	25.0	26.4	1.4

TABLE 1.8

IMMIGRANTS FROM SELECTED EUROPEAN COUNTRIES BY SEX: 1966, 1985

COUNTRY	1966	PERCENT	1985	PERCENT
Italy	25,154	100.0	3,214	100.0
Male	12,530	49.8	1,712	53.3
Female	12,624	50.2	1,502	46.7
France	3,175	100.0	2,187	100.0
Male	1,085	34.2	1,114	50.9
Female	2,090	65.8	1,073	49.1
Germany	18,239	100.0	7,109	100.0
Male	5,218	28.6	1,849	26.0
Female	13,021	71.4	5,260	74.0
Ireland	3,241	100.0	1,397	100.0
Male	1,146	35.4	714	51.1
Female	2,095	64.6	683	48.9
Poland	9,404	100.0	9,464	100.0
Male	4,509	47.9	4,840	51.1
Female	4,895	52.1	4,624	48.9
United K.	21,441	100.0	13,408	100.0
Male	8,406	39.2	6,449	48.1
Female	13,035	60.8	6,959	51.9

TABLE 1.9

IMMIGRANTS FROM SELECTED EUROPEAN COUNTRIES BY AGE: 1966, 1985

1966	Total	Under20	20 to 29	30 to 39	40 to 49	50 to 59	60 to 69	70 to 79	80 over	Median
Italy	25,154	37.2	21.7	18.4	9.2	8.7	3.5	1.1	0.2	25.9
Male	12,530	36.8	22.0	19.3	9.3	8.4	3.2	0.9	0.2	26.0
Female	12,624	37.6	21.5	17.5	9.2	8.9	3.7	1.4	0.2	25.8
France	3,175	27.1	42.0	16.9	5.9	3.7	3.0	1.4	0.2	25.5
Male	1,085	36.3	32.9	16.8	7.3	2.8	2.5	1.3	0.1	24.1
Female	2,090	22.1	46.7	16.9	5.2	4.3	3.2	1.4	0.3	26.0
Germany	18,239	34.3	46.3	10.9	3.4	2.5	1.7	0.6	0.1	23.4
Male	5,218	47.3	31.2	13.1	3.7	2.5	1.7	0.5	0.1	20.9
Female	13,021	29.0	52.4	10.0	3.3	2.5	1.7	0.7	0.1	24.0
Ireland	3,241	29.8	42.5	14.2	6.1	4.4	2.2	0.7	0.1	24.8
Male	1,146	27.0	41.3	17.7	7.3	4.5	1.7	0.4	0.1	25.6
Female	2,095	31.4	43.2	12.3	5.4	4.3	2.5	0.8	0.1	24.3
Poland	9,404	37.0	16.1	18.2	14.0	8.7	4.1	1.6	0.2	28.1
Male	4,509	38.1	14.5	18.4	14.8	9.3	3.7	1.0	0.1	28.2
Female	4,895	36.0	17.5	18.1	13.3	8.1	4.5	2.1	0.4	28.0
United K.	21,441	29.2	40.0	15.2	6.7	4.5	2.9	1.2	0.3	25.2
Male	8,406	30.9	33.4	19.0	8.4	4.1	2.7	1.1	0.3	25.7
Female	13,035	28.2	44.2	12.7	5.6	4.7	2.9	1.3	0.4	25.0

1985	Total	Under20	20 to 29	30 to 39	40 to 49	50 to 59	60 to 69	70 to 79	80 over	Median
Italy	3,214	19.3	34.9	19.3	10.8	7.4	4.0	3.4	0.9	28.8
Male	1,712	17.9	34.8	21.8	11.9	7.5	2.9	2.9	0.5	29.2
Female	1,502	20.9	35.2	16.3	9.6	7.3	5.2	4.1	1.5	28.3
France	2,187	18.6	39.5	25.4	9.5	4.4	1.5	0.8	0.3	27.9
Male	1,114	19.2	37.6	26.8	10.7	3.9	1.3	0.3	0.1	28.2
Female	1,073	18.0	41.5	24.0	8.2	4.8	1.6	1.4	0.6	27.7
Germany	7,109	25.4	45.6	16.7	7.5	2.2	1.1	1.1	0.5	25.4
Male	1,849	36.3	22.0	22.0	12.9	4.2	1.6	0.8	0.3	26.2
Female	5,260	21.6	53.9	14.8	5.6	1.4	1.0	1.2	0.5	25.3
Irealnd	1,397	14.5	45.1	24.5	8.7	3.7	1.9	1.3	0.4	27.9
Male	714	14.3	45.0	25.8	9.0	3.9	0.8	1.1	0.1	27.9
Female	683	14.6	45.2	23.1	8.5	3.4	3.1	1.5	0.6	27.8
Poland	9,464	23.1	25.7	31.1	10.9	6.1	2.2	0.7	0.2	30.4
Male	4,840	22.9	24.5	33.9	11.6	4.8	1.7	0.4	0.2	30.8
Female	4,624	23.2	27.1	28.3	10.2	7.5	2.6	0.9	0.2	29.9
United K	13,408	27.1	31.6	23.9	10.8	3.6	1.7	0.9	0.4	27.2
Male	6,449	27.4	26.5	27.0	12.2	4.4	1.6	0.5	0.2	28.5
Female	6,959	26.9	36.3	21.0	9.4	2.8	1.7	1.3	0.6	26.4

TABLE 1.10

ITALIAN IMMIGRANTS ADMITTED BY MAJOR OCCUPATIONAL GROUP: 1966-1985

Year	Number Admitted	Profess. Technical	Managers Administr.	Sales Workers	Clerical Workers	Craftsmen	Transport Laborers	Farmers	Service	Priv. Hous No Occup.
1966	25,154	520	246	98	222	3,146	3,349	1,473	733	15,407
1967	26,565	690	381	108	290	3,810	3,594	1,531	828	15,433
1968	23,593	499	230	90	261	3,113	3,257	1,638	730	13,775
1969	23,617	501	308	99	245	2,638	3,575	1,523	627	14,201
1970	24,973	595	260	128	308	2,942	3,890	1,564	701	14,585
1971	22,137	570	273	96	227	2,535	3,557	1,407	681	12,791
1972	21,427	489	275	72	259	2,399	3,273	1,241	664	12,756
1973	22,151	474	290	82	259	2,554	3,445	1,099	681	13,267
1974	15,884	460	251	82	196	2,000	2,204	691	576	9,424
1975	11,552	420	240	52	133	1,412	1,283	533	450	7,029
1976	8,380	324	237	44	109	966	922	328	406	5,008
1977	7,510	388	273	51	128	740	810	297	372	4,451
1978	7,415	357	247	65	155	767	828	270	347	4,379
1979	6,174	292	235	63	110	592	603	240	262	3,777
1980*	5,467	---	---	---	---	---	---	---	---	--
1981*	4,662	---	---	---	---	---	---	---	---	--
1982	3,644	271	162	34	75	258	291	82	232	2,239
1983	3,225	237	172	37	71	238	204	56	242	1,968
1984	3,130	216	163	52	63	241	191	55	250	1,899
1985	3,214	234	159	77	63	267	210	38	246	1,920
1986	3,089	242	147	60	58	256	191	43	287	1,805

Year	Number Admitted	Profess. Technical	Managers Administr.	Sales Workers	Clerical Workers	Craftsmen	Transport Laborers	Farmers	Service	Priv. Hous No Occup.
1966	25,154	2.1	1.0	0.4	0.9	12.5	13.3	5.9	2.9	61.3
1967	26,565	2.6	1.4	0.4	1.1	14.3	13.5	5.8	3.1	58.1
1968	23,593	2.1	1.0	0.4	1.1	13.2	13.8	6.9	3.1	58.4
1969	23,617	2.1	1.3	0.4	1.0	11.2	15.1	6.4	2.7	60.1
1970	24,973	2.4	1.0	0.5	1.2	11.8	15.6	6.3	2.8	58.4
1971	22,137	2.6	1.2	0.4	1.0	11.5	16.1	6.4	3.1	57.8
1972	21,427	2.3	1.3	0.3	1.2	11.2	15.3	5.8	3.1	59.5
1973	22,151	2.1	1.3	0.4	1.2	11.5	15.6	5.0	3.1	59.9
1974	15,884	2.9	1.6	0.5	1.2	12.6	13.9	4.4	3.6	59.3
1975	11,552	3.6	2.1	0.5	1.2	12.2	11.1	4.6	3.9	60.8
1976	8,380	3.9	2.8	0.5	1.3	11.5	11.0	3.9	4.8	59.8
1977	7,510	5.2	3.6	0.7	1.7	9.9	10.8	4.0	5.0	59.3
1978	7,415	4.8	3.3	0.9	2.1	10.3	11.2	3.6	4.7	59.1
1979	6,174	4.7	3.8	1.0	1.8	9.6	9.8	3.9	4.2	61.2
1980*	5,467	---	---	---	---	---	---	---	---	--
1981*	4,662	---	---	---	---	---	---	---	---	--
1982	3,644	7.4	4.4	0.9	2.1	7.1	8.0	2.3	6.4	61.4
1983	3,225	7.3	5.3	1.1	2.2	7.4	6.3	1.7	7.5	61.0
1984	3,130	6.9	5.2	1.7	2.0	7.7	6.1	1.8	8.0	60.7
1985	3,214	7.3	4.9	2.4	2.0	8.3	6.5	1.2	7.7	59.7
1986	3,089	7.8	4.8	1.9	1.9	8.3	6.2	1.4	9.3	58.4

* *See* note on Table 1.6.

TABLE 1.11

IMMIGRANTS FROM SELECTED EUROPEAN COUNTRIES BY OCCUPATION: 1966,1986

		Number Admitted	Profess. Technical	Managers Administr.	Sales Workers	Clerical Workers	Craftsmen	Transport Laborers	Farmers	Service	Priv. Hous No Occup.
England:	1966	21,441	3,921	593	481	3,012	1,094	1,025	45	689	10,581
	1986	13,657	2,269	1,228	354	746	456	338	32	814	7,420
	Diff.	-7,784	-1,652	635	-127	-2,266	-638	-687	-13	125	-3,161
France:	1966	3,175	427	62	51	309	107	105	29	183	1,902
	1986	2,518	371	241	63	117	84	33	10	216	1,383
	Diff.	-657	-56	179	12	-192	-23	-72	-19	33	-519
Germany:	1966	18,239	1,465	275	411	2,403	776	713	37	698	11,461
	1986	6,991	763	325	322	574	215	101	10	539	4,142
	Diff.	-11,248	-702	50	-89	-1,829	-561	-612	-27	-159	-7,319
Ireland:	1966	3,241	625	41	87	367	196	316	100	246	1,263
	1986	1,839	300	143	44	93	141	103	26	164	825
	Diff.	-1,402	-325	102	-43	-274	-55	-213	-74	-82	-438
Italy:	1966	25,154	520	246	98	222	3,146	3,349	1,473	733	15,367
	1986	3,089	242	147	60	58	256	191	43	287	1,805
	Diff.	-22,065	-278	-99	-38	-164	-2,890	-3,158	-1,430	-446	-13,562
Poland:	1966	9,404	520	172	84	328	690	832	1,252	126	5,400
	1986	8,481	1,066	126	103	227	918	1,215	160	834	3,832
	Diff.	-923	546	-46	19	-101	228	383	-1,092	708	-1,568

		Number Admitted	Profess. Technical	Managers Administr.	Sales Workers	Clerical Workers	Craftsmen	Transport Laborers	Farmers	Service	Priv. Hous No Occup.
England:	1966	21,441	18.3	2.8	2.2	14.0	5.1	4.8	0.2	3.2	49.3
	1986	13,657	16.6	9.0	2.6	5.5	3.3	2.5	0.2	6.0	54.3
	Diff.	-36.3	-1.7	6.2	0.3	-8.6	-1.8	-2.3	0.0	2.7	5.0
France:	1966	3,175	13.4	2.0	1.6	9.7	3.4	3.3	0.9	5.8	59.9
	1986	2,518	14.7	9.6	2.5	4.6	3.3	1.3	0.4	8.6	54.9
	Diff.	-20.7	1.3	7.6	0.9	-5.1	0.0	-2.0	-0.5	2.8	-5.0
Germany:	1966	18,239	8.0	1.5	2.3	13.2	4.3	3.9	0.2	3.8	62.8
	1986	6,991	10.9	4.6	4.6	8.2	3.1	1.4	0.1	7.7	59.2
	Diff.	-61.7	2.9	3.1	2.4	-5.0	-1.2	-2.5	-0.1	3.9	-3.6
Ireland:	1966	3,241	19.3	1.3	2.7	11.3	6.0	9.8	3.1	7.6	39.0
	1986	1,839	16.3	7.8	2.4	5.1	7.7	5.6	1.4	8.9	44.9
	Diff.	-43.3	-3.0	6.5	-0.3	-6.3	1.6	-4.1	-1.7	1.3	5.9
Italy:	1966	25,154	2.1	1.0	0.4	0.9	12.5	13.3	5.9	2.9	61.1
	1986	3,089	7.8	4.8	1.9	1.9	8.3	6.2	1.4	9.3	58.4
	Diff.	-87.7	5.8	3.8	1.6	1.0	-4.2	-7.1	-4.5	6.4	-2.7
Poland:	1966	9,404	5.5	1.8	0.9	3.5	7.3	8.8	13.3	1.3	57.4
	1986	8,481	12.6	1.5	1.2	2.7	10.8	14.3	1.9	9.8	45.2
	Diff.	-9.8	7.0	-0.3	0.3	-0.8	3.5	5.5	-11.4	8.5	-12.2

TABLE 1.12
ITALIAN IMMIGRANTS BY SELECTED STATES OF INTENDED RESIDENCE: 1966-1979, 1986

	CA	CT	FL	IL	MA	MD	MI	NJ	NY	OH	PA	RI	TX	WI	USA
1966	1,039	1,605	97	2,160	1,815	168	664	3,315	10,635	615	1,759	310	50	143	25,154
1967	1,088	1,882	115	2,201	1,807	221	838	3,252	11,661	649	1,601	220	45	137	26,565
1968	883	1,706	113	2,127	1,713	151	676	3,150	9,747	687	1,516	246	64	128	23,593
1969	824	1,536	160	1,818	1,614	123	756	3,087	10,349	700	1,478	307	57	119	23,617
1970	910	1,812	121	1,873	1,709	160	822	3,378	10,809	630	1,376	396	59	131	24,973
1971	823	1,755	120	1,829	1,808	181	584	3,030	9,214	594	1,137	357	33	84	22,137
1972	846	1,509	195	1,853	1,655	185	574	2,596	9,438	525	962	334	46	112	21,427
1973	727	1,288	197	1,831	1,377	132	614	3,347	10,221	390	917	324	54	135	22,151
1974	792	875	203	1,219	981	155	508	2,425	6,834	291	758	140	54	87	15,884
1975	513	776	185	830	841	84	296	1,461	4,797	222	625	98	32	105	11,552
1976	490	509	175	552	506	64	200	1,108	3,477	205	438	73	64	54	8,380
1976q	128	155	58	158	113	13	65	296	765	31	113	18	11	25	2,035
1977	489	556	233	610	390	103	287	911	2,821	195	398	94	70	45	7,510
1978	583	483	230	497	515	81	257	1,001	2,477	227	368	58	71	34	7,415
1979	513	379	151	364	419	81	217	801	2,173	106	347	76	57	40	6,174
1986	369	108	153	148	174	46	76	345	995	50	149	---	86	---	3,089

	CA	CT	FL	IL	MA	MD	MI	NJ	NY	OH	PA	RI	TX	WI	USA
1966	4.1	6.4	0.4	8.6	7.2	0.7	2.6	13.2	42.3	2.4	7.	01.2	0.2	0.6	25,154
1967	4.1	7.1	0.4	8.3	6.8	0.8	3.2	12.2	43.9	2.4	6.	00.8	0.2	0.5	26,565
1968	3.7	7.2	0.5	9.0	7.3	0.6	2.9	13.4	41.3	2.9	6.	41.0	0.3	0.5	23,593
1969	3.5	6.5	0.7	7.7	6.8	0.5	3.2	13.1	43.8	3.0	6.	31.3	0.2	0.5	23,617
1970	3.6	7.3	0.5	7.5	6.8	0.6	3.3	13.5	43.3	2.5	5.	51.6	0.2	0.5	24,973
1971	3.7	7.9	0.5	8.3	8.2	0.8	2.6	13.7	41.6	2.7	5.	11.6	0.1	0.4	22,137
1972	3.9	7.0	0.9	8.6	7.7	0.9	2.7	12.1	44.0	2.5	4.	51.6	0.2	0.5	21,427
1973	3.3	5.8	0.9	8.3	6.2	0.6	2.8	15.1	46.1	1.8	4.	11.5	0.2	0.6	22,151
1974	5.0	5.5	1.3	7.7	6.2	1.0	3.2	15.3	43.0	1.8	4.	80.9	0.3	0.5	15,884
1975	4.4	6.7	1.6	7.2	7.3	0.7	2.6	12.6	41.5	1.9	5.	40.8	0.3	0.9	11,552
1976	5.8	6.1	2.1	6.6	6.0	0.8	2.4	13.2	41.5	2.4	5.	20.9	0.8	0.6	8,380
1976q	6.3	7.6	2.9	7.8	5.6	0.6	3.2	14.5	37.6	1.5	5.	60.9	0.5	1.2	2,035
1977	6.5	7.4	3.1	8.1	5.2	1.4	3.8	12.1	37.6	2.6	5.	31.3	0.9	0.6	7,510
1978	7.9	6.5	3.1	6.7	6.9	1.1	3.5	13.5	33.4	3.1	5.	00.8	1.0	0.5	7,415
1979	8.3	6.1	2.4	5.9	6.8	1.3	3.5	13.0	35.2	1.7	5.	61.2	0.9	0.6	6,174
1986	11.9	3.5	5.0	4.8	5.6	1.5	2.5	11.2	32.2	1.6	4.	8NA	2.8	NA	3,089

TABLE 1.13
ITALIAN PERCENTAGE OF TOTAL IMMIGRANTS NATURALIZING: 1966-1986

Year	Total Naturalization	Italian Naturalization	Percent
1966	103,059	10,981	10.7
1967	104,902	10,572	10.1
1968	102,727	9,379	9.1
1969	98,709	8,773	8.9
1970	110,399	7,892	7.1
1971	108,407	7,637	7.0
1972	116,215	8,375	7.2
1973	120,740	8,902	7.4
1974	131,655	8,898	6.8
1975	141,537	8,798	6.2
1976	142,504	8,696	6.1
1976q	48,218	2,173	4.5
1977	159,873	7,891	4.9
1978	173,535	8,180	4.7
1979	164,150	7,296	4.4
1980	157,938	5,410	3.4
1981	166,317	4,287	2.6
1982	173,688	4,078	2.3
1983	178,948	3,685	2.1
1984	197,023	3,576	1.8
1985	244,717	3,816	1.6
1986	280,623	3,110	1.1

TABLE 1.14
NATURALIZED ITALIAN IMMIGRANTS BY SEX: 1966-1985

Year	Total	Males	Percentage	Females	Percentage	Males over Females	Unrep.
1966	10,981	5,625	51.2	5,356	48.8	2.4	0
1967	10,572	5,107	48.3	5,465	51.7	-3.3	0
1968	9,379	4,689	50.0	4,690	50.0	0.0	0
1969	8,773	4,500	51.3	4,273	48.7	2.5	0
1970	7,892	4,043	51.2	3,849	48.8	2.4	0
1971	7,637	3,906	51.1	3,731	48.9	2.2	0
1972	8,375	4,369	52.2	4,006	47.8	4.2	0
1973	8,902	4,711	52.9	4,191	47.1	5.8	0
1974	8,898	4,792	53.9	4,106	46.1	7.7	0
1975	8,798	4,804	54.6	3,994	45.4	9.2	0
1976	8,696	4,667	53.7	4,029	46.3	7.3	0
1976q	2,173	1,209	55.6	964	44.4	8.2	0
1977	7,891	4,366	55.3	3,525	44.7	10.6	0
1978	8,180	4,433	54.2	3,747	45.8	8.3	0
1979	7,296	3,871	53.1	3,425	46.9	6.1	0
1980	5,410	2,715	50.2	2,695	49.8	0.3	0
1981	4,287	2,160	50.4	2,127	49.6	0.7	0
1982	4,078	2,136	52.4	1,942	47.6	4.7	0
1983	3,685	1,957	53.1	1,723	46.8	6.3	5
1984	3,576	1,989	55.6	1,584	44.3	11.3	3
1985	3,816	1,981	51.9	1,778	46.6	5.3	57
Total	149,295	78,030	52.3	71,200	47.7	4.5	65

TABLE 1.15
PERSONS NATURALIZED BY COUNTRY OF BIRTH WITHIN TWELVE YEARS OF ENTRY: 1966-1986

	FRANCE		GERMANY		IRELAND		ITALY		POLAND		UNITED KINGDOM	
	Total	Percent Within 12 years	Total	Percent Within 12 years	Total	Percent Within 12 years	Total	Percent Within 12 years	Total	Percent Within 12 years	Total	Percent Within 12 years
1966	1,297	83.7	13,854	82.9	3,003	86.0	10,897	90.5	5,163	75.6	6,940	78.5
1967	1,341	79.6	13,351	80.6	3,183	83.6	10,481	86.9	4,999	74.7	6,798	80.1
1968	1,327	79.4	12,830	79.0	3,003	81.6	9,286	82.4	4,626	75.3	6,610	73.4
1969	1,327	76.9	10,876	72.4	2,657	80.0	8,662	77.1	4,127	73.3	6,353	70.7
1970	1,306	77.0	10,322	69.6	2,283	74.1	7,867	75.2	3,988	74.3	6,000	67.5
1971	1,242	72.5	8,697	66.2	2,180	73.1	7,576	72.0	3,830	73.7	5,492	65.4
1972	1,005	69.1	7,122	60.8	1,776	67.4	8,366	75.8	3,547	72.2	4,758	63.1
1973	1,007	62.9	6,808	55.4	1,758	61.9	8,865	73.2	3,665	73.0	5,082	61.9
1974	959	64.5	6,002	53.2	1,598	56.6	8,840	74.0	3,630	72.0	5,495	63.4
1975	949	56.7	5,259	51.4	1,334	52.8	8,745	73.4	3,631	72.0	5,003	62.0
1976	907	58.0	5,163	45.4	1,289	47.0	8,668	71.8	3,282	67.4	5,210	58.7
1976q	259	59.1	1,286	47.7	320	50.0	2,166	73.6	908	66.1	1,482	58.9
1977	1,005	56.6	4,900	42.4	1,190	42.4	7,899	73.5	3,025	62.6	5,635	53.0
1978	1,028	51.8	4,332	39.2	1,032	41.7	8,168	75.3	3,117	63.0	5,241	48.1
1979	797	46.2	3,440	34.0	900	43.0	7,207	63.9	2,473	60.7	4,191	48.2
1980	701	44.7	2,911	29.5	671	42.8	5,371	58.9	2,044	59.4	3,806	46.3
1981	716	43.6	2,923	27.1	686	39.8	4,314	54.1	1,985	58.2	4,665	48.9
1982	814	42.3	2,787	28.2	647	36.6	4,118	50.5	2,172	60.4	4,665	46.0
1983	787	49.9	2,402	26.9	700	39.9	3,664	45.6	2,495	61.6	4,151	43.6
1984	907	44.3	2,466	26.6	660	40.3	3,574	42.1	2,157	63.1	4,079	48.0
1985	1,033	46.7	2,618	29.3	793	40.1	3,823	35.5	2,994	64.9	4,874	49.5
1986	1,022	45.3	2,490	28.0	815	36.6	3,144	31.2	3,160	65.2	4,727	49.8

TABLE 1.16

PERCENTAGE OF NATURALIZATIONS PER IMMIGRANTS
ADMITTED FROM SELECTED EUROPEAN COUNTRIES: 1966-1986

YEAR	FRANCE	GERMANY	IRELAND	ITALY	POLAND	UNITED K.
1966	41	76	93	43	55	32
1967	39	83	121	39	84	27
1968	39	81	100	39	77	23
1969	66	117	134	37	102	42
1970	53	107	146	32	111	42
1971	62	116	135	34	132	52
1972	51	104	100	39	74	47
1973	55	103	88	40	74	48
1974	59	95	102	56	90	51
1975	70	102	104	76	92	46
1976	61	88	110	103	86	46
1976q	65	76	106	106	94	49
1977	62	77	96	105	75	45
1978	56	64	87	110	62	37
1979	47	54	92	117	56	30
1980	37	44	67	98	43	25
1981	41	45	76	93	40	31
1982	41	41	68	113	37	32
1983	38	33	64	114	39	28
1984	42	37	54	114	23	29
1985	47	37	57	119	32	36
1986	41	36	44	102	37	35

TABLE 1.17

FORMER ITALIAN CITIZENS NATURALIZED BY GENERAL AND SPECIAL PROVISIONS:
1966-1986

Year	Total	General; Provision	Married to U.S. Citizens	Children of U.S. Citizens	Military	Other
1966	10,981	8,485	1,568	892	33	3
1967	10,572	8,271	1,496	760	39	6
1968	9,379	7,509	1,256	572	41	1
1969	8,773	7,071	1,088	450	161	3
1970	7,892	6,017	1,049	389	435	2
1971	7,637	5,866	1,021	346	401	3
1972	8,375	7,024	773	249	322	7
1973	8,902	7,668	688	269	272	5
1974	8,898	7,711	717	234	233	3
1975	8,798	7,804	628	220	146	0
1976	8,696	7,815	542	211	126	2
1976q	2,173	1,938	130	62	41	2
1977	7,891	7,148	441	195	105	2
1978	8,180	7,540	362	204	73	1
1979	7,296	6,768	253	190	85	0
1980	5,410	5,060	186	119	43	2
1981	4,287	4,002	183	68	33	1
1982	4,078	3,815	168	64	31	0
1983	3,685	3,443	145	59	37	1
1984	3,576	3,344	138	42	23	29
1985	3,816	3,620	105	35	23	33
1986	3,110	2,936	106	22	21	25
Total	149,295	127,919	12,937	5,630	2,703	106

Year	Total	General; Provision	Married to U.S. Citizens	Children of U.S. Citizens	Military	Other
1966	10,981	77.3	14.3	8.1	0.3	0.0
1967	10,572	78.2	14.2	7.2	0.4	0.1
1968	9,379	80.1	13.4	6.1	0.4	0.0
1969	8,773	80.6	12.4	5.1	1.8	0.0
1970	7,892	76.2	13.3	4.9	5.5	0.0
1971	7,637	76.8	13.4	4.5	5.3	0.0
1972	8,375	83.9	9.2	3.0	3.8	0.1
1973	8,902	86.1	7.7	3.0	3.1	0.1
1974	8,898	86.7	8.1	2.6	2.6	0.0
1975	8,798	88.7	7.1	2.5	1.7	0.0
1976	8,696	89.9	6.2	2.4	1.4	0.0
1976q	2,173	89.2	6.0	2.9	1.9	0.1
1977	7,891	90.6	5.6	2.5	1.3	0.0
1978	8,180	92.2	4.4	2.5	0.9	0.0
1979	7,296	92.8	3.5	2.6	1.2	0.0
1980	5,410	93.5	3.4	2.2	0.8	0.0
1981	4,287	93.4	4.3	1.6	0.8	0.0
1982	4,078	93.6	4.1	1.6	0.8	0.0
1983	3,685	93.4	3.9	1.6	1.0	0.0
1984	3,576	93.5	3.9	1.2	0.6	0.8
1985	3,816	94.9	2.8	0.9	0.6	0.9
1986	3,110	94.4	3.4	0.7	0.7	0.8
Total	149,295	85.7	8.7	3.8	1.8	0.1

TABLE 1.18

NATURALIZED ITALIAN IMMIGRANTS BY MAJOR OCCUPATION GROUP: 1966,1986

Year	Number Admitted	Profess. Technical	Managers Administr.	Sales Workers	Clerical Workers	Transport Craftsmen	Laborers	Farmers	Service	Priv. Hous No Occup.
1966	10,981	289	196	90	453	1,762	3,073	13	899	4,206
1967	10,567	262	234	97	502	1,671	2,961	6	818	4,016
1968	9,379	285	184	108	551	1,579	2,654	9	743	3,266
1969	7,963	235	219	92	526	1,492	2,431	9	834	2,125
1970	7,892	282	204	85	482	1,319	2,019	6	792	2,703
1971	7,637	286	263	91	460	1,313	1,766	9	679	2,770
1972	8,375	314	272	116	483	1,428	2,188	9	775	2,790
1973	8,902	328	244	125	484	1,568	2,544	3	738	2,868
1974	8,898	294	323	115	511	1,534	2,525	16	649	2,931
1975	8,798	271	323	127	504	1,550	2,490	15	650	2,868
1976	8,696	284	340	128	496	1,391	2,524	13	681	2,839
1977	7,891	274	363	115	425	1,206	2,114	12	712	2,670
1978	8,180	319	412	128	449	1,258	2,363	6	729	2,516
1979	7,296	263	432	132	453	984	1,832	5	641	2,554
1980	5,410	236	317	84	339	710	1,288	9	460	1,967
1981	4,287	200	285	101	294	572	949	8	402	1,476
1982	4,078	214	307	102	299	534	857	6	448	1,311
1983	3,685	173	132	177	282	509	622	21	566	1,203
1984	3,576	220	159	173	294	533	597	32	484	1,084
1985	3,816	218	206	165	297	460	686	13	537	1,234
1986	3,110	163	170	119	292	330	473	18	588	957

Year	Number Admitted	Profess. Technical	Managers Administr.	Sales Workers	Clerical Workers	Transport Craftsmen	Laborers	Farmers	Service	Priv. Hous No Occup.
1966	10,981	2.6	1.8	0.8	4.1	16.0	28.0	0.1	8.2	38.3
1967	10,567	2.5	2.2	0.9	4.8	15.8	28.0	0.1	7.7	38.0
1968	9,379	3.0	2.0	1.2	5.9	16.8	28.3	0.1	7.9	34.8
1969	7,963	3.0	2.8	1.2	6.6	18.7	30.5	0.1	10.5	26.7
1970	7,892	3.6	2.6	1.1	6.1	16.7	25.6	0.1	10.0	34.2
1971	7,637	3.7	3.4	1.2	6.0	17.2	23.1	0.1	8.9	36.3
1972	8,375	3.7	3.2	1.4	5.8	17.1	26.1	0.1	9.3	33.3
1973	8,902	3.7	2.7	1.4	5.4	17.6	28.6	0.0	8.3	32.2
1974	8,898	3.3	3.6	1.3	5.7	17.2	28.4	0.2	7.3	32.9
1975	8,798	3.1	3.7	1.4	5.7	17.6	28.3	0.2	7.4	32.6
1976	8,696	3.3	3.9	1.5	5.7	16.0	29.0	0.1	7.8	32.6
1977	7,891	3.5	4.6	1.5	5.4	15.3	26.8	0.2	9.0	33.8
1978	8,180	3.9	5.0	1.6	5.5	15.4	28.9	0.1	8.9	30.8
1979	7,296	3.6	5.9	1.8	6.2	13.5	25.1	0.1	8.8	35.0
1980	5,410	4.4	5.9	1.6	6.3	13.1	23.8	0.2	8.5	36.4
1981	4,287	4.7	6.6	2.4	6.9	13.3	22.1	0.2	9.4	34.4
1982	4,078	5.2	7.5	2.5	7.3	13.1	21.0	0.1	11.0	32.1
1983	3,685	4.7	3.6	4.8	7.7	13.8	16.9	0.6	15.4	32.6
1984	3,576	6.2	4.4	4.8	8.2	14.9	16.7	0.9	13.5	30.3
1985	3,816	5.7	5.4	4.3	7.8	12.1	18.0	0.3	14.1	32.3
1986	3,110	5.2	5.5	3.8	9.4	10.6	15.2	0.6	18.9	30.8

TABLE 1.19
ITALIAN IMMIGRANTS ADMITTED BY SELECTED CLASSES: 1966-1986

Year	Number Admitted	Temporary Visitors for Business	Temporary Visitors for Pleasure	Transit Aliens	Treaty Traders and Investors	Students	Temporary Workers & Trainees & Spouses
1966	95,428	9,124	61,910	11,511	449	477	396
1967	105,545	10,187	70,431	15,345	504	524	573
1968	131,250	11,542	88,465	16,439	656	641	1,391
1969	154,618	13,231	103,823	13,739	644	701	445
1970	161,324	14,276	103,743	15,266	783	715	584
1971	151,414	14,824	103,400	13,965	878	779	697
1972	178,005	14,714	107,088	15,876	918	739	586
1973	179,166	17,572	97,367	16,546	999	652	971
1974	184,428	19,963	99,331	16,108	1,227	764	502
1975	170,628	18,352	91,787	16,103	1,258	704	477
1976	185,730	21,686	101,249	16,777	1,427	688	438
1976q	71,624	6,344	38,747	3,864	663	340	N.A.
1977	182,666	25,005	98,371	15,131	1,621	831	629
1978	220,016	27,099	126,927	17,028	1,957	1,127	504
1979	120,674	21,497	79,352	12,739	1,638	1,025	368
1980	N.A.	N.A.	N.A.	N.A.	N.A.	N.A.	N.A.
1981	264,234	37,420	188,829	13,535	2,478	2,241	1,151
1982	270,383	39,993	194,778	11,757	2,871	2,393	1,069
1983	222,813	44,504	151,538	11,770	1,986	2,512	967
1984	256,026	52,040	174,689	12,031	2,988	2,487	1,350
1985	258,693	62,033	166,441	11,482	3,054	3,148	1,453
1986	294,061	70,935	193,331	10,401	3,363	3,585	1,689
Total	3,858,726	552,341	2,441,597	287,413	32,362	27,073	16,240

Year	Number Admitted	Temporary Visitors for Business	Temporary Visitors for Pleasure	Transit Aliens	Treaty Traders and Investors	Students	Temporary Workers & Trainees & Spouses
1966	95,428	9.6	64.9	12.1	0.5	0.5	0.4
1967	105,545	9.7	66.7	14.5	0.5	0.5	0.5
1968	131,250	8.8	67.4	12.5	0.5	0.5	1.1
1969	154,618	8.6	67.1	8.9	0.4	0.5	0.3
1970	161,324	8.8	64.3	9.5	0.5	0.4	0.4
1971	151,414	9.8	68.3	9.2	0.6	0.5	0.5
1972	178,005	8.3	60.2	8.9	0.5	0.4	0.3
1973	179,166	9.8	54.3	9.2	0.6	0.4	0.5
1974	184,428	10.8	53.9	8.7	0.7	0.4	0.3
1975	170,628	10.8	53.8	9.4	0.7	0.4	0.3
1976	185,730	11.7	54.5	9.0	0.8	0.4	0.2
1976q	71,624	8.9	54.1	5.4	0.9	0.5	N.A.
1977	182,666	13.7	53.9	8.3	0.9	0.5	0.3
1978	220,016	12.3	57.7	7.7	0.9	0.5	0.2
1979	120,674	17.8	65.8	10.6	1.4	0.8	0.3
1980	N.A.	N.A.	N.A.	N.A.	N.A.	N.A.	N.A.
1981	264,234	14.2	71.5	5.1	0.9	0.8	0.4
1982	270,383	14.8	72.0	4.3	1.1	0.9	0.4
1983	222,813	20.0	68.0	5.3	0.9	1.1	0.4
1984	256,026	20.3	68.2	4.7	1.2	1.0	0.5
1985	258,693	24.0	64.3	4.4	1.2	1.2	0.6
1986	294,061	24.1	65.7	3.5	1.1	1.2	0.6
Total	3,858,726	14.3	63.3	7.4	0.8	0.7	0.4

APPENDIX B

Foreign Born Population in the United States from Selected European Countries

Source: *Census of Population, 1980: Foreign Born Population in the United States*. Microfiche prepared by the Bureau of the Census. Washington: The Bureau, 1985.

TABLE 2.1

FOREIGN BORN POPULATION IN THE U. S. FROM SELECTED COUNTRIES: 1930-1980

	1980	1970	1960	1940	1930	
Italy	831,922	1,008,533	1,256,999	1,427,952	1,623,580	1,790,429
France	120,215	105,385	111,582	108,547	102,930	135,592
Germany	849,384	832,965	989,815	991,321	1,237,772	1,608,814
Ireland	197,817	251,375	338,722	505,285	572,031	744,810
Poland	418,128	548,107	747,750	861,655	993,479	1,268,583
United Kingdom	669,149	686,099	833,055	846,570	1,043,072	1,402,923
Italy	46.5	56.3	70.2	79.8	90.7	100
France	88.7	77.7	82.3	80.1	75.9	100
Germany	52.8	51.8	61.5	61.6	76.9	100
Ireland	26.6	33.8	45.5	67.8	76.8	100
Poland	33.0	43.2	58.9	67.9	78.3	100
United Kingdom	47.7	48.9	59.4	60.3	74.3	100

Source: U.S. Bureau of the Census. *Historical Statistics of the United States. Colonial Times to 1970.*
Note: The terms "foreign born" and "immigrant" are used as synonyms in this appendix.

TABLE 2.2

FOREIGN BORN POPULATION BY REGION OF RESIDENCE IN THE U.S.: 1970-1980

	1980				
	U.S.	NORTHEAST	N. CENTRAL	SOUTH	WEST
France	120,215	33.5	13.3	25.4	27.9
Germany	849,384	31.8	23.0	22.9	22.3
Ireland	197,817	64.3	14.1	8.6	12.9
Italy	831,922	68.2	14.4	7.3	10.1
Poland	418,128	51.4	29.7	10.3	8.5
United K.	669,149	32.7	17.0	21.4	28.9

	1970				
	U.S.	NORTHEAST	N. CENTRAL	SOUTH	WEST
France	105,385	41.4	15.3	16.6	26.6
Germany	832,965	39.9	27.0	14.4	18.7
Ireland	251,375	69.5	14.0	6.0	10.4
Italy	1,008,533	70.1	15.0	5.3	9.6
Poland	548,107	56.5	29.9	6.4	7.2
United K.	686,099	40.2	19.2	14.9	25.8

TABLE 2.3

FOREIGN BORN POPULATION BY YEAR OF IMMIGRATION AND SEX: 1980

Year of Imm.	ITALY			FRANCE			GERMANY		
	Total	Males	Females	Total	Males	Females	Total	Males	Females
Total	831,922	406,570	425,352	120,215	44,702	75,513	835,112	321,248	513,864
Between 1975-1980	4.0	4.3	3.7	13.9	18.1	11.4	6.2	6.6	6.0
Between 1970-1974	8.1	8.8	7.4	7.2	8.4	6.5	4.4	4.2	4.5
Between 1965-1969	10.0	10.7	9.4	10.1	10.5	9.9	8.0	7.2	8.6
Between 1960-1964	8.1	8.8	7.5	13.7	13.5	13.9	12.6	11.1	13.6
1959 or earlier	69.8	67.3	72.1	55.0	49.5	58.3	68.7	71.0	67.3

Year of Imm.	IRELAND			POLAND			UNITED KINGDOM		
	Total	Males	Females	Total	Males	Females	Total	Males	Females
Total	197,817	73,013	124,804	418,128	187,414	230,714	669,149	258,155	410,994
Between 1975-1980	3.7	5.0	3.0	6.0	6.5	5.6	12.7	16.5	10.3
Between 1970-1974	3.6	4.7	3.0	5.0	5.1	4.9	7.0	7.8	6.5
Between 1965-1969	5.1	5.4	5.0	6.3	6.4	6.2	10.8	11.7	10.3
Between 1960-1964	9.4	10.5	8.8	8.2	8.6	7.8	10.7	10.1	11.1
1959 or earlier	78.1	74.5	80.3	74.5	73.4	75.5	58.8	54.1	61.8

TABLE 2.4
SEX AND AGE OF PERSONS BORN IN ITALY BY YEAR OF IMMIGRATION: 1980

	Total Immigr.	Between 1975-1980	Between 1970-1974	Between 1965-1969	Between 1960-1964	1959 or earlier	Between 1965-1980	Between 1960-1980
Total	831,922	33,109	67,344	83,492	67,515	580,462	183,945	251,460
0 to 4 years	1,708	1,708	0	0	0	0	1,708	1,708
5 to 9 years	4,467	2,298	2,169	0	0	0	4,467	4,467
10 to 14 years	11,478	2,345	6,006	3,127	0	0	11,478	11,478
15 to 19 years	20,579	2,993	7,410	7,123	3,053	0	17,526	20,579
20 to 24 years	27,688	4,310	7,167	7,788	4,970	3,453	19,265	24,235
25 to 29 years	36,787	4,595	7,899	8,498	4,907	10,888	20,992	25,899
30 to 34 years	50,927	3,767	7,818	12,178	7,689	19,475	23,763	31,452
35 to 39 years	43,818	2,509	5,317	9,882	9,159	16,951	17,708	26,867
40 to 44 years	50,887	2,009	5,332	8,874	9,999	24,473	16,415	26,414
45 to 49 years	52,689	1,944	6,001	7,593	9,099	28,052	15,538	24,637
50 to 54 years	55,180	1,378	4,912	6,370	5,357	37,163	12,660	18,017
55 to 59 years	62,375	971	3,291	4,626	4,331	49,156	8,888	13,219
60 to 64 years	43,083	625	1,390	2,540	2,809	35,719	4,555	7,364
65 years and over	370,256	1,657	2,432	4,893	6,142	355,132	8,982	15,124
Median Age	59.8	28.2	31.9	41.5	47.0	65.9	33.5	36.1

TABLE 2.5

SEX AND AGE OF PERSONS BORN IN SELECTED EUROPEAN COUNTRIES: 1980

	UNITED KINGDOM			FRANCE			GERMANY		
	Total	Males	Females	Total	Males	Females	Total	Males	Females
AGE									
Total Persons	669,149	258,155	410,994	120,215	44,702	75,513	835,112	321,248	513,864
under 5 years	5,531	2,780	2,751	1,184	591	593	7,815	3,849	3,966
5 to 9 years	11,198	5,958	5,240	1,762	925	837	12,635	6,462	6,173
10 to 14 years	18,622	9,769	8,853	2,757	1,427	1,330	19,092	9,589	9,503
15 to 19 years	27,535	13,757	13,778	5,718	3,006	2,712	33,563	16,233	17,330
20 to 24 years	30,936	14,622	16,314	9,983	4,959	5,024	47,904	21,758	26,326
25 to 29 years	35,032	15,798	19,234	9,086	4,313	4,773	47,694	21,389	26,305
30 to 34 years	48,933	19,956	28,977	10,291	4,603	5,688	80,913	34,290	46,623
35 to 39 years	52,074	18,732	33,342	9,447	3,412	6,035	62,457	19,072	43,385
40 to 44 years	53,223	17,435	35,788	10,180	3,187	6,993	69,854	20,839	49,015
45 to 49 years	43,725	15,220	28,505	10,161	3,276	6,885	58,584	19,171	39,413
50 to 54 years	49,365	16,251	33,114	11,599	3,268	8,331	69,152	20,402	48,750
55 to 59 years	57,975	19,238	38,737	9,675	2,375	7,300	61,178	21,641	39,537
60 to 64 years	38,790	15,509	23,281	3,853	1,226	2,627	31,730	12,095	19,635
65 years and over	196,210	73,130	123,080	24,519	8,134	16,385	232,541	94,638	137,903
median age	50.8	48.4	51.9	44.9	38.7	47.7	48.0	46.9	48.6

	IRELAND			ITALY			POLAND		
	Total	Males	Females	Total	Males	Females	Total	Males	Females
AGE									
Total Persons	197,817	73,013	124,804	831,922	406,570	425,352	418,128	187,414	230,714
under 5 years	355	225	130	1,708	906	802	357	180	177
5 to 9 years	792	442	350	4,467	2,439	2,028	1,107	613	494
10 to 14 years	948	519	429	11,478	5,786	5,692	2,269	1,050	1,219
15 to 19 years	1,703	950	753	20,579	10,589	9,990	4,726	2,292	2,434
20 to 24 years	3,173	1,617	1,556	27,688	14,506	13,182	10,641	4,857	5,784
25 to 29 years	5,617	2,731	2,886	36,787	19,370	17,41	14,670	6,858	7,812
30 to 34 years	9,193	3,728	5,465	50,927	27,391	23,536	16,224	7,876	8,348
35 to 39 years	13,434	4,842	8,592	43,818	23,205	20,613	13,952	6,470	7,482
40 to 44 years	15,446	6,029	9,417	50,887	26,594	24,293	16,925	8,050	8,875
45 to 49 years	14,891	5,829	9,062	52,689	28,034	24,655	17,362	8,240	9,122
50 to 54 years	15,238	6,955	8,283	55,180	28,428	26,752	30,212	13,602	16,610
55 to 59 years	13,261	6,239	7,022	62,375	31,921	30,454	45,052	22,317	22,735
60 to 64 years	10,503	4,361	6,142	43,083	21,260	21,823	30,858	17,172	13,686
65 years and over	93,263	28,546	64,717	370,256	166,141	204,115	213,773	87,837	125,936
median age	62.3	57.1	65.2	59.8	57.5	63.0	65.1	63.3	65.4

TABLE 2.6

CITIZENSHIP OF FOREIGN BORN PERSONS BY YEAR OF IMMIGRATION AND SEX: 1980

Year of Imm.	ITALY			FRANCE			GERMANY		
	Total	Males	Females	Total	Males	Females	Total	Males	Females
YEAR OF IMMMIGRATION									
NATURALIZED CITIZENS	644,152	318,394	325,758	77,010	28,365	48,645	656,321	262,631	393,690
Between 1975-1980	0.6	0.7	0.6	1.6	2.2	1.2	2.2	2.6	2.0
Between 1970-1974	2.8	3.1	2.5	2.9	3.7	2.4	2.5	2.7	2.4
Between 1965-1969	6.3	6.8	5.8	7.5	8.7	6.9	5.5	5.2	5.6
Between 1960-1964	7.1	7.9	6.4	13.8	15.4	12.9	10.6	9.4	11.3
1959 or earlier	83.1	81.5	84.6	74.1	70.0	76.6	79.2	80.0	78.7
ALIENS	187,770	88,176	99,594	43,205	16,337	26,868	178,791	58,617	120,174
Between 1975-1980	15.4	17.4	13.7	35.8	45.7	29.8	20.9	24.3	19.3
Between 1970-1974	26.2	29.7	23.2	14.9	16.6	13.9	11.2	10.9	11.3
Between 1965-1969	22.8	24.9	20.9	14.7	13.6	15.5	17.4	15.7	18.2
Between 1960-1964	11.5	11.9	11.1	13.6	10.3	15.6	20.2	18.3	21.1
1959 or earlier	24.1	16.1	31.1	20.9	13.9	25.2	30.3	30.8	30.0

Year of Imm.	IRELAND			POLAND			UNITED KINGDOM		
	Total	Males	Females	Total	Males	Females	Total	Males	Females
NATURALIZED CITIZENS	160,609	59,085	101,524	325,159	148,227	176,882	401,255	154,851	246,404
Between 1975-1980	0.6	0.9	0.5	0.5	0.5	0.5	1.3	1.6	1.1
Between 1970-1974	1.2	1.7	1.0	1.9	1.9	1.8	2.3	2.6	2.2
Between 1965-1969	3.0	3.3	2.8	4.2	4.2	4.2	6.1	7.2	5.4
Between 1960-1964	7.1	8.5	6.3	6.8	7.1	6.5	8.4	8.7	8.2
1959 or earlier	88.0	85.7	89.4	86.7	86.3	87.0	81.9	79.9	83.2
ALIENS	37,208	13,928	23,280	92,969	39,137	53,832	267,894	103,304	164,590
Between 1975-1980	17.0	22.5	13.7	25.0	28.9	22.2	29.8	38.8	24.1
Between 1970-1974	13.9	17.3	11.9	16.1	17.3	15.2	14.0	15.5	13.1
Between 1965-1969	14.3	14.2	14.4	13.6	14.7	12.9	17.9	18.3	17.6
Between 1960-1964	19.3	19.2	19.4	13.1	14.5	12.1	14.1	12.1	15.4
1959 or earlier	35.4	26.8	40.5	32.2	24.6	37.6	24.2	15.2	29.9

TABLE 2.7

MARITAL STATUS OF FOREIGN BORN PERSONS 15 YEARS AND OVER BY SEX AND AGE: 1980

	ITALY		FRANCE		GERMANY		IRELAND		POLAND		UNITED KINGDOM	
	Male	Female	Male	Female	Male	Female	Male	Female	Male	Female	Male	Female
ALL MARITAL STATUSES	397,439	416,830	41,759	72,753	301,348	494,222	71,827	123,895	185,571	228,824	239,648	394,150
15 to 44 years	121,655	109,031	23,480	31,225	133,401	208,984	19,897	28,669	36,403	40,735	100,300	147,433
Single	27.7	19.9	41.6	24.0	34.3	16.8	28.2	17.7	28.4	18.3	34.7	20.2
Married	68.6	75.0	79.9	63.6	57.8	70.3	67.0	74.0	64.9	71.5	57.0	68.6
Separated	0.9	1.2	2.5	2.7	1.6	2.6	1.4	2.3	2.1	2.5	2.3	2.5
Widowed	0.2	1.0	0.3	0.8	0.2	1.2	0.3	1.5	0.4	1.5	0.2	0.8
Divorced	2.6	2.9	5.7	8.8	6.1	9.2	3.0	4.5	4.3	6.2	5.8	7.9
45 to 64 years	109,643	103,684	10,145	25,143	73,309	147,335	23,384	30,509	61,331	62,153	66,218	123,637
Single	3.5	3.6	8.9	4.2	4.8	3.0	14.0	13.6	5.1	2.9	4.9	3.5
Married	90.8	79.7	79.0	73.5	87.1	77.3	78.6	69.8	85.7	76.4	85.0	77.2
Separated	0.9	1.4	2.8	2.2	1.2	1.6	1.2	2.1	1.5	1.8	1.9	1.7
Widowed	1.9	11.7	2.2	9.5	1.8	9.9	2.5	10.6	2.8	13.2	2.2	9.9
Divorced	2.8	3.6	7.2	10.6	5.2	8.2	3.6	4.0	4.8	5.8	6.0	7.7
65 years and over	166,141	204,115	8,134	16,385	94,638	137,903	28,546	64,717	87,837	125,936	73,130	123,080
Single	3.4	2.9	5.8	6.0	4.9	5.6	10.6	12.5	5.4	3.7	4.8	6.7
Married	74.0	30.0	72.5	29.8	75.5	34.4	65.2	27.3	72.6	29.4	74.0	31.9
Separated	0.8	0.6	0.7	0.9	0.7	0.4	0.8	1.0	1.0	0.7	0.9	0.7
Widowed	19.9	65.0	17.7	58.9	16.6	56.2	22.0	58.0	18.1	63.9	17.8	57.4
Divorced	1.9	1.5	3.4	4.4	2.3	3.3	1.4	1.2	2.9	2.4	2.5	3.2

TABLE 2.8

CHILDREN EVER BORN OF FOREIGN BORN WOMEN 15 YEARS OLD AND OVER: 1980

	ITALY	FRANCE	GERMANY	IRELAND	POLAND	UNITED K.
AVERAGE NUMBER OF CHILDREN EVER BORN PER WOMAN						
All women	2.6	1.7	1.7	2.3	2.2	1.9
Married women	2.5	1.9	1.9	2.7	2.1	2.2
Widowed, Divorced, Separated W.	3.2	2.0	1.9	2.7	2.7	2.1
AVERAGE NUMBER OF CHILDREN EVER BORN PER MOTHER						
All mothers	3.1	2.4	2.4	3.2	2.7	2.6
Married Mothers	2.8	2.4	2.4	3.2	2.4	2.6
Widowed, Divorced, Separated M.	3.5	2.5	2.4	3.2	3.1	2.6

TABLE 2.9

BIRTHPLACE OF CHILDREN UNDER 20 YEARS OF AGE FOR HOUSEHOLDS WITH FOREIGN BORN HOUSEHOLDER OR FOREIGN BORN SPOUSE: 1980

	ITALY	FRANCE	GERMANY	IRELAND	POLAND	UNITED K.
Total Households	524,149	80,543	571,484	130,076	268,850	459,238
No Children	69.3	64.2	61.9	68.2	82.0	66.9
1 Child	10.7	16.1	15.3	9.0	8.5	12.8
2 Children	11.6	13.3	14.9	9.9	6.3	13.0
3 Children	6.0	4.9	5.7	7.0	2.4	5.3
4 or more Children	2.4	1.5	2.2	5.9	0.9	2.1
Households with children	161,009	28,835	217,959	41,329	48,485	152,126
None foreign born	83.8	75.6	80.3	90.4	85.1	73.9
Foreign & US born	6.2	10.2	10.4	5.2	5.1	11.7
None U.S. born	10.0	14.2	9.3	4.4	9.8	14.4

TABLE 2.10
LABOR FORCE PARTICIPATION OF IMMIGRANTS 16 YEARS OLD AND OVER BY SEX: 1980

	ITALY			FRANCE			GERMANY		
	Total	Males	Females	Total	Males	Females	Total	Males	Females
POPULATION									
16 years and over	810,693	395,542	415,151	113,682	41,298	72,384	790,139	298,384	491,755
Total in labor force	41.8	56.2	28.1	56.9	73.6	47.4	51.7	66.4	42.8
Civilian lab. for	41.7	56.0	28.1	56.2	71.7	47.3	50.8	64.2	42.6
Employed	38.8	52.5	25.7	53.3	68.3	44.7	48.3	61.6	40.2
Unemployed	3.0	3.5	2.4	2.9	3.4	2.7	2.5	2.6	2.4
Percent of civilian lab. force	7.1	6.3	8.6	5.2	4.7	5.6	4.9	4.0	5.7
Not in labor force	58.2	43.8	71.9	43.1	26.4	52.6	48.3	33.6	57.2

	IRELAND			POLAND			UNITED KINGFOM		
	Total	Males	Females	Total	Males	Females	Total	Males	Females
LABOR FORCE PARTICIPATION	195,439	71,699	123,740	413,700	185,205	228,495	628,452	236,831	391,621
Total in labor force	40.9	58.9	30.5	41.7	56.0	30.0	50.2	66.0	40.6
Civilian lab. for	40.7	58.4	30.5	41.5	55.8	30.0	49.7	64.8	40.5
Employed	39.1	56.1	29.3	39.2	53.0	28.0	47.5	62.3	38.6
Unemployed	1.7	2.4	1.3	2.4	2.8	2.0	2.2	2.5	1.9
Percent of civilian lab. force	4.1	4.0	4.1	5.7	5.1	6.7	4.3	3.8	4.8
Not in labor force	59.1	41.1	69.5	58.3	44.0	70.0	49.8	34.0	59.4

TABLE 2.11
WORK AND UNEMPLOYEMENT OF IMMIGRANTS IN LABOR FORCE IN 1979 BY SEX: 1980

	ITALY			FRANCE			GERMANY		
	Total	Males	Females	Total	Males	Females	Total	Males	Females
Total Labor Force	357,848	231,861	125,987	69,636	32,007	37,629	443,045	209,192	233,853
Worked in 1979	98.2	98.7	97.4	98.1	98.6	97.7	98.4	99.0	97.9
Worked 50-52 weeks	59.8	65.6	49.2	58.3	65.0	52.7	62.5	71.3	54.7
Worked full-time	53.5	61.4	38.9	51.1	61.2	42.4	54.2	67.1	42.6
Worked 40-49 weeks	16.0	15.3	17.3	15.9	15.6	16.2	13.6	12.6	14.4
worked 27-39 weeks	9.0	7.8	11.2	8.0	6.2	9.6	7.3	5.1	9.2
Worked 1-26 weeks	13.4	10.0	19.7	15.8	11.8	19.3	15.1	10.1	19.6
With Unemployment	18.6	16.8	21.7	16.9	16.1	17.5	15.5	13.7	17.2
Unempl.15 or more w.	8.2	7.3	9.8	5.9	5.6	6.1	5.3	4.6	6.0
Unempl. less than 15	10.4	9.6	11.9	10.9	10.4	11.4	10.2	9.1	11.2
Average weeks of un.	16.2	15.8	16.7	13.9	13.9	14.0	13.9	13.8	14.0

	IRELAND			POLAND			UNITED K.		
	Total	Males	Females	Total	Males	Females	Total	Males	Females
Total Labor Force	84,877	44,176	40,701	183,231	109,583	73,648	343,174	165,375	177,799
Worked in 1979	98.6	98.8	98.2	98.2	98.8	97.3	98.7	99.2	98.3
Worked 50-52 weeks	62.5	70.8	55.3	65.2	69.1	59.2	62.5	71.0	54.4
Worked full-time	54.3	95.3	75.3	87.9	92.6	79.4	87.2	94.3	78.5
Worked 40-49 weeks	15.9	14.6	17.8	14.6	13.9	15.6	14.0	12.5	15.4
worked 27-39 weeks	6.9	5.3	8.7	6.8	5.8	8.4	7.6	5.4	9.6
Worked 1-26 weeks	13.3	9.2	18.2	13.4	11.2	16.8	16.0	11.1	20.6
With Unemployment	5.5	13.4	14.3	16.0	14.4	18.4	14.9	13.9	15.9
Unempl.15 or more w.	8.4	41.9	37.2	41.1	39.9	42.5	33.1	33.2	33.7
Unempl. less than 15	8.4	58.1	62.8	58.9	60.1	57.5	66.9	66.8	66.9
Average weeks of un.	15.9	16.2	15.5	16.0	15.5	16.6	13.7	13.7	13.7

TABLE 2.12

INDUSTRY OF EMPLOYED IMMIGRANTS 16 YEARS OLD AND OVER BY SEX: 1980

| | ITALY | | | FRANCE | | | GERMANY | | |
	Total	Males	Females	Total	Males	Females	Total	Males	Females
ALL INDUSTRIES	314,273	207,528	106,745	60,536	28,213	32,323	381,625	183,938	197,687
Agriculture	1.4	2.0	0.3	1.6	2.7	0.7	1.4	1.8	1.0
Mining	0.2	0.3	0.1	0.6	0.9	0.2	0.4	0.6	0.1
Construction	9.4	13.8	0.8	3.5	6.7	0.8	4.4	8.0	1.1
Manufacturing	32.4	28.7	39.6	17.7	21.9	14.0	23.8	31.0	17.0
Transportation	5.6	7.3	2.3	5.3	6.2	4.4	5.3	6.8	3.9
Trade	22.6	22.5	22.6	25.6	25.7	25.4	23.5	20.3	26.5
Finance, Insurance	4.8	4.0	6.5	6.5	5.6	7.3	6.7	4.8	8.5
Business & Repair Service	3.7	4.4	2.4	4.6	5.5	3.9	4.7	5.9	3.6
Personal Service	5.8	5.7	6.1	6.7	4.4	8.7	4.8	2.2	7.2
Entertainment Service	0.8	0.9	0.6	1.9	2.5	1.3	1.1	1.0	1.2
Professional Service	10.9	8.0	16.6	21.2	13.4	27.9	20.1	13.2	26.4
Public Administration	2.4	2.5	2.1	4.8	4.4	5.2	3.8	4.3	3.4

| | IRELAND | | | POLAND | | | UNITED KINGDOM | | |
	Total	Males	Females	Total	Males	Females	Total	Males	Females
ALL INDUSTRIES	76,395	40,200	36,195	162,007	98,079	63,928	298,645	147,573	151,072
Agriculture	0.8	1.3	0.3	0.6	0.8	0.4	1.0	1.1	0.8
Mining	0.2	0.3	0.1	0.2	0.2	0.1	0.6	1.0	0.3
Construction	8.2	14.7	1.0	4.0	6.0	0.8	4.1	7.2	1.0
Manufacturing	13.0	15.7	10.0	38.8	42.7	32.7	22.4	31.2	13.7
Transportation	10.0	15.3	4.1	3.8	4.7	2.5	5.6	7.3	4.1
Trade	17.2	15.7	19.0	19.8	19.3	20.5	19.7	15.6	23.7
Finance, Insurance	8.9	8.0	9.9	6.1	4.6	8.3	8.1	6.2	10.0
Business & Repair Service	3.8	4.4	3.2	5.1	4.7	5.8	5.4	6.4	4.3
Personal Service	5.2	2.0	8.8	4.0	2.7	6.1	4.1	2.2	5.9
Entertainment Service	1.2	1.2	1.3	0.7	0.7	0.8	1.7	1.9	1.5
Professional Service	27.2	16.6	39.0	15.0	11.7	20.1	23.8	16.6	31.0
Public Administration	4.2	4.9	3.3	1.9	1.9	1.9	3.6	3.4	3.8

TABLE 2.13
OCCUPATION OF EMPLOYED IMMIGRANTS 16 YEARS AND OVER BY SEX: 1980

	ITALY			FRANCE			GERMANY		
	Total	Males	Females	Total	Males	Females	Total	Males	Females
ALL OCCUPATIONS	314,273	207,528	106,745	60,536	28,213	32,323	381,625	183,938	197,687
Executive, Admin. & Manag.	8.0	9.9	4.2	13.7	18.1	9.8	13.6	18.0	9.5
Professional Specialty	6.1	6.4	5.6	17.2	17.6	16.9	13.4	15.7	11.3
Technical, Sales, Ad. Support	18.4	12.8	29.5	30.5	17.8	41.5	31.9	18.7	44.1
Technicians	1.6	1.8	1.2	3.2	4.0	2.5	3.4	3.7	3.0
Sales	7.5	6.3	9.8	11.7	8.9	14.2	11.9	9.5	14.2
Administrative	9.4	4.7	18.4	15.5	4.9	24.8	16.6	5.5	26.9
Services	16.3	15.5	17.9	17.9	15.7	19.8	14.1	7.4	20.4
Farming	1.6	2.3	0.2	1.5	2.7	0.4	1.2	1.7	0.8
Craft and Repair	22.0	29.5	7.4	9.4	16.1	3.5	14.0	25.3	3.4
Operators & Laborers	27.6	23.7	35.2	9.9	12.0	8.0	11.8	13.1	10.6

	IRELAND			POLAND			UNITED K.		
	Total	Males	Females	Total	Males	Females	Total	Males	Females
ALL OCCUPATIONS	76,395	40,200	36,195	162,007	98,079	63,928	298,645	147,573	151,072
Executive, Admin. & Manag.	9.5	11.9	6.8	9.2	11.5	5.7	14.8	19.9	9.9
Professional Specialty	14.5	12.6	16.5	10.8	12.2	8.8	17.2	21.4	13.1
Technical, Sales, Ad. Support	26.2	14.9	38.8	23.3	17.5	32.2	35.4	19.8	50.6
Technicians	2.1	9.8	7.1	11.4	15.6	7.8	10.1	21.5	5.8
Sales	7.5	40.4	23.4	44.5	55.8	35.1	32.9	47.4	27.3
Administrative	16.7	49.9	69.5	44.1	28.6	57.1	57.0	31.1	66.9
Services	21.7	14.4	29.7	13.5	7.8	22.3	12.3	7.3	17.2
Farming	1.2	2.1	0.3	0.7	0.9	0.4	0.8	1.1	0.5
Craft and Repair	15.4	27.7	1.7	17.4	25.8	4.6	10.7	19.4	2.2
Operators & Laborers	11.6	16.3	6.3	25.0	24.3	26.0	8.8	11.2	6.4

TABLE 2.14
CLASS OF WORKER OF EMPLOYED IMMIGRANTS 16 YEARS OLD AND OVER BY SEX: 1980

	ITALY			FRANCE			GERMANY		
	Total	Males	Females	Total	Males	Females	Total	Males	Females
ALL CLASSES OF WORKERS	314,273	207,528	106,745	60,536	28,213	32,323	381,625	183,938	197,687
Salary worker	80.6	78.2	85.1	77.9	79.7	76.3	78.3	77.7	78.8
Government employee	9.1	8.7	9.9	13.5	9.9	16.7	12.8	10.9	14.6
Self-employed	9.9	12.8	4.1	8.1	10.2	6.2	8.2	11.1	5.5
Family business	0.4	0.2	0.8	0.5	0.2	0.8	0.7	0.2	1.1

	IRELAND			POLAND			UNITED K.		
	Total	Males	Females	Total	Males	Females	Total	Males	Females
ALL CLASSES OF WORKERS	76,395	40,200	36,195	162,007	98,079	63,928	298,645	147,573	151,072
Salary worker	80.1	78.4	82.1	83.2	81.7	85.6	80.2	80.7	79.6
Government employee	14.1	14.3	13.9	7.4	6.7	8.5	12.8	10.7	14.8
Self-employed	5.3	7.3	3.2	8.9	11.4	5.0	6.5	8.4	4.6
Family business	0.4	0.0	0.8	0.5	0.2	0.9	0.6	0.2	1.0

TABLE 2.15

INCOME CHARACTERISTICS OF FOREIGN BORN POPULATION IN 1979

	ITALY	FRANCE	GERMANY	IRELAND	POLAND	UNITED K.
HOUSEHOLDS WITH:						
Head Foreign-born						
Median dol.	13,736	16,104	15,764	13,762	13,748	15,994
Mean dol.	17,453	21,397	20,864	18,000	19,003	21,099
Per Capita dol.	6,612	9,527	9,088	7,249	8,743	9,333
Head American-born						
Median dol.	21,597	25,360	23,944	24,188	21,808	23,948
Mean dol.	24,626	29,575	27,217	27,386	27,403	27,806
Per Capita dol.	7,799	9,525	8,253	7,801	9,984	8,806
FAMILIES WITH:						
Head Foreign-born						
Median dol.	17,733	21,546	20,775	20,524	19,869	21,799
Mean dol.	20,786	26,600	25,365	23,496	24,365	26,067
Per Capita dol.	6,559	8,983	8,792	6,980	8,884	9,041
Head American-born						
Median dol.	21,553	25,325	23,906	24,139	21,749	23,887
Mean dol.	24,572	29,499	27,147	27,326	27,342	27,717
Per Capita dol.	7,804	9,552	8,265	7,809	10,004	8,819
UNRELATED INDIVID.						
Median dol.	4,655	7,254	6,815	5,567	5,217	6,818
Mean dol.	7,012	10,825	9,978	8,213	8,034	10,386
MALE, 15 YEARS & OVER						
Median dol.	10,533	14,200	14,129	12,578	11,858	14,411
Percentage of full-time workers	37.4	50.3	48.5	42.4	38.7	48.1
Median Inc. full-time worker $	17,806	20,589	21,750	20,734	19,667	23,063
FEMALE, 15 YEARS & OVER						
Median dol.	4,201	6,230	5,632	4,431	4,616	5,252
Percentage of full-time workers	15.3	29.2	26.7	17.0	17.7	24.8
Median Inc. full-time worker $	9,692	11,807	11,383	11,705	11,321	11,698
PER CAPITA INCOME						
Households with head for. born $	6,808	9,526	8,738	7,405	8,918	9,114
Families with head for. born $	6,784	9,262	8,546	7,248	9,069	8,938
Persons in Group Quarters	2,434	2,978	3,167	2,736	2,344	3,066
FAMILIES						
Percent below poverty level	6.0	4.9	4.8	4.7	4.4	4.0
With householder for. born $	21,581	2,012	14,424	3,410	7,136	9,377
With own children under 20 $	11,261	1,840	14,035	2,137	2,397	7,769

TABLE 2.16
YEARS OF SCHOOL COMPLETED OF IMMIGRANTS 20 YEARS OLD AND OVER BY SEX: 1980

	ITALY			FRANCE			GERMANY		
	Total	Males	Females	Total	Males	Females	Total	Males	Females
ALL LEVELS	793,690	386,850	406,840	108,794	38,753	70,041	762,007	285,115	476,892
Elementary: 0–4 years	20.9	17.4	24.2	2.4	2.7	2.3	1.3	1.4	1.2
Elementary: 5–8 years	38.6	37.6	39.7	12.7	12.0	13.1	18.3	17.4	18.8
High School: 1–3 years	10.3	11.2	9.5	9.3	8.9	9.5	12.0	11.2	12.4
High School: 4 years	19.1	19.5	18.7	32.5	26.2	36.0	36.6	29.4	40.9
College: 1–3 years	5.7	7.0	4.4	21.1	20.3	21.5	17.4	18.4	16.7
College: 4 or more years	5.4	7.4	3.5	21.9	29.8	17.6	14.5	22.1	9.9

	IRELAND			POLAND			UNITED K.		
	Total	Males	Females	Total	Males	Females	Total	Males	Females
ALL LEVELS	194,019	70,877	123,142	409,669	183,279	226,390	606,263	225,891	380,372
Elementary: 0–4 years	3.4	3.1	3.5	14.2	10.1	17.5	1.2	1.2	1.1
Elementary: 5–8 years	31.5	29.0	33.0	32.7	31.0	34.1	12.2	11.2	12.8
High School: 1–3 years	12.5	12.2	12.7	11.6	12.2	11.1	12.3	10.8	13.2
High School: 4 years	33.5	31.2	34.8	22.7	22.4	22.9	40.6	31.7	45.8
College: 1–3 years	10.2	11.4	9.5	9.0	10.3	7.9	18.3	18.7	18.1
College: 4 or more years	8.9	13.2	6.4	9.9	14.0	6.5	15.5	26.3	9.0

TABLE 2.17
LANGUAGE USAGE OF IMMIGRANTS 5 YEARS OLD AND OVER BY SEX: 1980

	ITALY			FRANCE			GERMANY		
	Total	Males	Females	Total	Males	Females	Total	Males	Females
POPULATION 5 YEARS AND OVER	830,214	405,664	424,350	119,031	44,111	74,920	827,297	317,399	509,898
Only English spoken	18.5	21.1	16.0	32.2	34.4	30.9	42.4	47.5	39.3
Speak other language	81.5	78.9	84.1	67.8	65.6	69.1	57.6	52.5	60.7
Percent that:									
Speak English very well	39.5	41.5	37.7	64.3	62.0	69.5	71.4	71.7	71.2
Speak English well	36.0	38.3	34.0	28.1	30.1	27.0	25.2	25.3	25.1
Speak English not well	20.3	17.5	22.8	6.5	7.1	6.2	3.1	2.7	3.3
Speak English not at all	4.1	2.7	5.5	1.1	0.8	1.2	0.3	0.3	0.4

	IRELAND			POLAND			UNITED K.		
	Total	Males	Females	Total	Males	Females	Total	Males	Females
POPULATION 5 YEARS AND OVER	197,462	72,788	124,674	417,771	187,234	230,537	663,618	255,375	408,243
Only English spoken	93.1	92.6	93.3	24.0	26.6	21.9	94.8	94.4	95.0
Speak other language	6.9	7.4	6.7	76.0	73.4	78.1	5.2	5.6	5.0
Percent that:									
Speak English very well	81.7	81.6	81.8	39.7	41.3	38.4	83.9	84.0	83.9
Speak English well	14.8	15.0	14.7	38.6	39.5	38.0	12.2	12.5	12.0
Speak English not well	3.2	3.2	3.2	18.8	16.7	20.4	3.5	3.2	3.8
Speak English not at all	0.3	0.2	0.4	2.9	2.5	3.2	0.3	0.3	0.4

APPENDIX C

United States Population
of Selected Single European Ancestries.

Source: *Census of Population, 1980: General Social and Economic Characteristics. United States Summary.* Washington: The Bureau of the Census, 1983.

TABLE 3.1

GENERAL CHARACTERISTICS OF SELECTED ANCESTRY GROUPS: 1980

	ENGLISH			FRENCH			GERMAN		
	Males	Females	Total	Males	Females	Total	Males	Females	Total
AGE									
Total Persons	11,689,517	12,059,255	23,748,772	1,468,163	1,600,744	3,068,907	9,051,346	8,892,139	17,943,485
under 5 years	661,189	625,277	1,286,466	65,358	63,071	128,429	414,206	388,088	802,294
5 to 9 years	713,373	670,454	1,383,827	72,309	67,658	139,967	432,149	403,404	835,553
10 to 14 years	790,688	743,330	1,534,018	86,564	83,329	169,893	501,844	466,682	968,526
15 to 19 years	976,649	916,308	1,892,957	117,709	118,926	236,635	671,285	635,256	1,306,541
20 to 24 years	1,025,425	939,317	1,964,742	151,015	150,695	301,710	869,772	814,883	1,684,655
25 to 29 years	972,457	889,170	1,861,627	143,232	139,161	282,393	859,557	759,888	1,619,445
30 to 34 years	954,350	886,919	1,841,269	133,645	129,223	262,868	798,593	695,682	1,494,275
35 to 39 years	794,050	763,291	1,557,341	106,744	108,207	214,951	655,997	584,413	1,240,410
40 to 44 years	680,029	664,027	1,344,056	92,407	94,516	186,923	569,062	520,727	1,089,789
45 to 49 years	655,460	653,206	1,308,666	87,452	92,798	180,250	538,869	491,043	1,029,912
50 to 54 years	696,718	716,350	1,413,068	91,559	102,697	194,256	556,060	522,314	1,078,374
55 to 59 years	696,051	749,988	1,446,039	85,953	100,392	186,345	531,351	522,126	1,053,477
60 to 64 years	609,139	676,753	1,285,892	69,803	85,123	154,926	465,152	473,082	938,234
65 to 69 years	523,028	630,695	1,153,723	58,077	77,275	135,352	402,018	445,077	847,095
70 to 74 years	412,853	552,675	965,528	46,135	68,309	114,444	326,030	401,069	727,099
75 to 79 years	273,438	435,426	708,864	32,229	55,552	87,781	233,217	335,612	568,829
80 to 84 years	154,139	298,867	453,006	17,241	36,663	53,904	136,654	239,328	375,982
85 years and over	100,481	247,202	347,683	10,731	27,149	37,880	86,530	196,465	282,995
median age	33.7	37.4	35.4	33.7	37.2	35.3	34.9	37.4	36.0

	IRISH			ITALIAN			POLISH		
	Males	Females	Total	Males	Females	Total	Males	Females	Total
AGE									
Total Persons	4,942,866	5,394,487	10,337,353	3,430,899	3,452,421	6,883,320	1,847,896	1,957,844	3,805,740
under 5 years	199,573	187,256	386,829	107,199	100,583	207,782	48,803	45,074	93,877
5 to 9 years	229,220	215,827	445,047	128,699	120,538	249,237	58,184	54,119	112,303
10 to 14 years	290,289	270,980	561,269	175,173	165,507	340,680	76,937	71,989	148,926
15 to 19 years	392,799	378,324	771,123	239,514	226,287	465,801	105,685	97,322	203,007
20 to 24 years	484,077	470,148	954,225	307,859	288,798	596,657	144,448	136,809	281,257
25 to 29 years	454,395	439,577	893,972	300,457	273,309	573,766	159,410	149,689	309,099
30 to 34 years	419,772	413,410	833,182	283,470	262,998	546,468	155,181	154,709	309,890
35 to 39 years	340,381	352,761	693,142	233,071	217,313	450,384	128,419	122,858	251,277
40 to 44 years	299,572	318,425	617,997	199,434	189,990	389,424	102,654	100,752	203,406
45 to 49 years	296,032	318,965	614,997	213,941	209,445	423,386	101,839	103,066	204,905
50 to 54 years	319,750	352,140	671,890	258,531	262,076	520,607	132,343	142,557	274,900
55 to 59 years	318,012	361,377	679,389	276,776	285,751	562,527	167,407	182,965	350,372
60 to 64 years	274,645	322,493	597,138	232,937	250,547	483,484	173,791	193,555	367,346
65 to 69 years	231,810	297,464	529,274	196,927	229,374	426,301	132,485	159,267	291,752
70 to 74 years	177,253	260,283	437,536	123,264	157,503	280,767	75,894	102,730	178,624
75 to 79 years	115,900	205,045	320,945	72,989	102,945	175,934	38,683	63,608	102,291
80 to 84 years	62,443	132,783	195,226	47,323	65,394	112,717	19,572	43,161	62,733
85 years and over	36,943	97,229	134,172	33,335	44,063	77,398	16,161	33,614	49,775
median age	35.0	39.6	37.3	38.7	41.9	40.1	41.6	47.2	44.5

TABLE 3.2
PERSONS IN HOUSEHOLD AND GROUP QUARTERS FOR SELECTED ANCESTRY GROUPS

	ENGLISH	FRENCH	GERMAN	IRISH	ITALIAN	POLISH
PERSONS IN						
HOUSEHOLDS	9,603,135	1,272,564	7,795,931	4,320,542	2,960,756	1,745,432
1 person	2,143,725	283,088	1,681,842	1,020,705	589,204	418,443
2 persons	3,295,698	397,038	2,612,630	1,329,941	959,264	595,140
3 persons	1,671,004	222,758	1,329,254	728,412	530,738	291,825
4 persons	1,446,438	198,515	1,228,422	622,724	477,656	244,629
5 persons	667,001	104,374	569,959	332,017	258,029	123,420
6 or more persons	379,269	66,791	346,824	223,743	145,865	71,975
Average	2.5	2.4	2.3	2.4	2.3	2.2
PERSONS IN						
GROUP QUARTERS	561,585	82,163	479,441	300,689	121,455	83,142
Mental hospital	21,768	2,773	12,089	9,394	6,785	4,174
Home for the aged	181,252	23,775	140,533	79,276	25,006	24,458
Other institutions	69,087	7,971	32,736	25,589	14,111	6,534
Military quarters	61,908	11,382	53,239	31,815	12,525	7,055
College dormitory	183,968	26,167	193,578	112,494	51,433	28,600
Other	43,602	10,095	47,266	42,121	11,595	12,321

TABLE 3.3
NATIVITY AND PLACE OF BIRTH OF SELECTED ANCETRY GROUPS: 1980

	ENGLISH	FRENCH	GERMAN	IRISH	ITALIAN	POLISH
TOTAL PERSONS	23,748,772	3,068,907	17,943,485	10,337,353	6,883,320	3,805,740
Native	97.2	93.0	95.2	97.2	87.3	89.0
Born in State of residence	67.4	69.6	69.7	66.7	75.1	84.0
Born in different State	32.2	29.8	29.9	33.0	24.4	26.4
Northeast	16.7	38.2	19.9	30.5	67.9	54.2
North Central	25.0	23.1	49.9	25.5	15.6	34.3
South	45.1	29.2	19.3	34.7	10.0	7.8
West	12.7	9.5	10.8	9.3	6.4	3.8
Born Abroad	0.5	0.6	0.4	0.3	0.4	0.3
Foreign-Born	2.8	7.0	4.8	2.8	12.7	11.0

TABLE 3.4
RESIDENCE IN 1975 OF SELECTED ANCESTRY GROUPS

	ENGLISH	FRENCH	GERMAN	IRISH	ITALIAN	POLISH
PERSONS 5 YEARS & OVER	22,547,664	2,952,618	17,189,247	9,985,026	6,685,447	3,725,841
Same house	55.2	53.6	55.4	54.8	63.5	63.7
Different house	43.9	45.1	43.8	44.6	35.7	35.3
Same County	23.9	25.9	23.3	23.8	20.5	20.0
Different County	19.9	19.3	20.4	20.8	15.3	15.3
Same State	10.2	9.8	10.8	10.6	8.1	7.7
Armed Forces	0.1	0.1	0.1	0.1	0.1	0.1
College	1.0	1.0	1.2	1.1	0.9	0.9
Different State	9.7	9.5	9.7	10.2	7.1	7.6
Armed Forces	0.4	0.4	0.4	0.4	0.2	0.3
College	1.0	0.9	1.2	1.1	0.9	1.0
Northeast	1.5	2.9	1.7	2.8	3.9	3.1
North Central	2.1	1.8	3.7	2.3	1.1	2.4
South	4.0	3.0	2.4	3.3	1.2	1.3
West	2.0	1.7	1.9	1.8	0.9	0.8
Abroad	0.9	1.3	0.8	0.6	0.8	1.0
Armed Forces	0.1	0.2	0.2	0.1	0.1	0.1
College	0.1	0.1	0.1	0.0	0.1	0.1

TABLE 3.5

FERTILTY AND FAMILY COMPOSITION OF SELECTED ANCESTRY GROUPS: 1980

	ENGLISH	FRENCH	GERMAN	IRISH	ITALIAN	POLISH
FERTILITY						
Women 15 to 24 years	1,855,625	269,621	1,450,139	848,472	515,085	234,131
Children ever born	655,748	96,953	425,806	245,844	93,612	50,258
Per 1000 women	353	360	294	290	182	215
Women ever married	687,606	108,053	526,202	282,325	131,348	67,213
Children ever born	581,434	87,062	393,466	222,758	84,588	45,388
Per 1000 women	846	806	748	789	644	675
Women 25 to 34 years	1,776,089	268,384	1,455,570	852,987	536,307	304,398
Children ever born	2,721,418	420,565	2,104,152	1,221,088	655,709	374,401
Per 1000 women	1,532	1,567	1,446	1,432	1,223	1,230
Women ever married	1,580,712	240,337	1,288,852	732,546	443,550	251,963
Children ever born	2,677,013	415,510	2,086,291	1,207,305	649,239	370,036
Per 1000 women	1,694	1,729	1,619	1,648	1,464	1,469
Women 35 to 44 years	1,427,318	202,723	1,105,140	671,186	407,303	223,610
Children ever born	3,651,399	567,006	2,861,494	1,786,747	962,072	537,558
Per 1000 women	2,558	2,797	2,589	2,662	2,362	2,404
Women ever married	1,371,879	194,707	1,060,403	634,064	380,608	208,218
Children ever born	3,630,040	564,825	2,855,252	1,781,555	959,161	535,980
Per 1000 women	2,646	2,901	2,693	2,810	2,520	2,574
Women 15 to 44 years	5,059,032	740,728	4,010,849	2,372,645	1,458,695	762,139
Children ever born	7,028,565	1,084,524	5,391,452	3,253,679	1,711,393	962,217
Per 1000 women	1,389	1,464	1,344	1,371	1,173	1,262
Women ever married	3,640,197	543,097	2,875,457	1,648,935	955,506	527,394
Children ever born	6,888,487	1,067,397	5,335,009	3,211,618	1,692,988	951,404
Per 1000 women	1,892	1,965	1,855	1,947	1,771	1,803
HOUSEHOLD TYPE						
Total Persons	23,748,772	3,068,907	17,943,485	10,337,353	6,883,320	3,805,740
In households	23,187,187	2,986,744	17,464,044	10,036,664	6,761,865	3,722,598
Family Househ.: Male	6,245,274	812,837	5,212,294	2,667,121	1,973,836	1,101,573
Fem.	909,044	125,276	613,478	462,761	306,366	173,046
Nonfam. Househ: Male	988,825	142,076	837,381	494,327	292,234	190,514
Fem.	1,459,992	192,375	1,132,778	696,333	388,320	280,299
Spouse	5,949,066	831,544	4,629,487	2,691,209	1,770,770	1,047,097
Child	6,310,238	685,814	4,080,011	2,336,109	1,600,917	698,928
Other relatives	785,667	98,524	487,331	383,309	284,007	142,088
Nonrelatives	539,081	98,298	471,284	305,495	145,415	89,053
Persons per househ.	2.64	2.75	2.7	2.69	2.79	2.61
Persons per family	3.12	3.27	3.19	3.23	3.25	3.13
MARITAL HISTORY						
Ever Married, 15-54 years	9,633,189	1,383,168	7,753,824	4,298,684	2,751,533	1,461,817
Never wid. or div.	74.3	75.1	78.0	74.5	81.0	81.1
Widowed	2.7	2.7	2.2	3.0	2.5	2.9
Divorced	23.3	22.5	20.0	22.9	16.7	16.3
Widowed and divorced	0.3	0.3	0.2	0.4	0.2	0.2

TABLE 3.6

SCHOOL ENROLLMENT FOR SELECTED ANCESTRY GROUP: 1980

	ENGLISH	FRENCH	GERMAN	IRISH	ITALIAN	POLISH
SCHOOL ENROLLMENT						
Persons 3 years and over.	5,215,341	593,866	3,545,615	2,074,082	1,269,447	592,095
NURSERY SCHOOL	3.3	2.7	3.1	2.8	2.9	2.6
Public	32.6	37.8	33.4	30.2	31.1	31.3
Church related	31.4	22.6	29.7	30.3	27.5	28.6
Other Private	36.0	39.6	36.8	39.5	41.3	40.1
KINDERGARTEN	5.1	4.3	4.3	4.0	3.5	3.4
Public	83.3	80.2	85.0	80.5	77.8	75.7
Church related	10.5	12.6	11.4	14.1	17.8	20.1
Other Private	6.2	7.1	3.6	5.4	4.4	4.2
ELEMENTARY (1-8 YEARS)	46.3	43.4	41.8	40.3	38.4	36.6
Public	92.8	86.5	85.7	81.8	76.3	73.2
Church related	4.9	11.8	13.3	16.7	22.3	25.4
Other Private	2.3	1.7	0.8	1.5	1.4	1.4
HIGH SCHOOL (1-4 YEARS)	24.6	25.7	24.6	24.6	25.7	23.9
Public	93.5	89.9	91.4	82.6	81.1	81.6
Church related	3.7	8.0	7.4	15.1	16.5	16.0
Other Private	2.8	2.2	1.2	2.2	2.4	2.4
COLLEGE	20.7	23.9	26.2	28.3	29.5	33.5
Public	82.2	82.3	81.2	75.3	74.9	76.3
PERCENTAGE OF PERSONS ENROLLED						
3 and 4 years old	29.0	28.0	27.1	31.9	36.8	32.8
5 and 6 years old	83.7	85.6	83.6	86.3	90.7	88.5
7 to 13 years old	98.8	98.5	99.1	99.0	98.9	99.1
14 and 15 years old	97.3	97.2	98.2	97.9	98.4	98.6
16 and 17 years old	85.2	83.6	89.5	86.9	90.5	90.9
18 and 19 years old	48.0	44.5	52.1	53.2	56.2	56.8
20 and 21 years old	29.0	25.7	32.2	35.7	37.2	39.3
22 to 24 years old	15.6	13.6	15.9	17.6	18.1	19.2
25 to 34 years old	7.5	7.2	7.5	8.6	8.3	9.1

TABLE 3.7

YEARS OF SCHOOL COMPLETED OF PERSONS 25 YEARS OLD AND OVER BY ANCESTRY

		ENGLISH	FRENCH	GERMAN	IRISH	ITALIAN	POLISH
MALE, 25 AND OVER		7,522,193	975,208	6,162,090	3,346,908	2,472,455	1,413,839
Elementary:	0 to 4 years	3.3	3.7	1.4	2.6	3.9	2.4
	5 to 7 years	7.1	8.8	5.0	6.3	7.7	6.6
	8 years	7.9	9.7	10.9	8.2	8.9	10.0
High School:	1 to 3 years	14.3	15.4	12.8	14.5	16.5	15.7
	4 years	30.1	32.8	35.1	32.2	31.8	31.8
College:	1 to 3 years	15.6	14.9	15.5	16.2	14.0	14.4
	4 years	11.0	7.9	10.0	10.4	8.5	9.2
	5 or more years	10.6	6.8	9.4	9.6	8.7	9.9
High School Graduate		67.3	62.4	70.0	68.4	63.0	65.2
FEMALE, 25 AND OVER		8,164,569	1,117,065	6,183,826	3,871,952	2,550,708	1,552,531
Elementary:	0 to 4 years	2.3	3.3	1.2	1.8	5.2	3.8
	5 to 7 years	6.5	8.2	4.7	5.8	8.4	8.0
	8 years	8.3	10.5	12.1	8.9	10.7	13.0
High School:	1 to 3 years	17.3	17.8	13.9	17.3	16.8	16.3
	4 years	36.3	38.6	42.1	40.3	40.5	38.2
College:	1 to 3 years	15.6	13.2	14.5	14.3	9.9	10.9
	4 years	8.5	5.3	7.1	6.9	4.8	5.4
	5 or more years	5.2	3.2	4.3	4.6	3.7	4.5
High School Graduate		65.5	60.3	68.1	66.2	58.9	58.9

TABLE 3.8

LABOR FORCE OF SELECTED ANCESTRY GROUPS: 1980

	ENGLISH	FRENCH	GERMAN	IRISH	ITALIAN	POLISH
LABOR FORCE STATUS						
Persons 16 years and over	19,189,397	2,589,226	15,108,450	8,807,963	6,003,613	3,415,543
Labor force	11,304,268	1,574,871	9,472,220	5,277,552	3,671,551	2,040,213
Percent of pers. 16 ys. & over	58.9	60.8	62.7	59.9	61.2	59.7
Civilian labor force	58.0	59.8	61.8	59.0	60.7	59.2
Employed	54.9	56.3	58.7	55.7	57.2	55.9
Unemployed	3.1	3.5	3.0	3.3	3.4	3.3
Percent of civ. labor force	5.4	5.8	4.9	5.7	5.7	5.6
Not in labor force	41.1	39.2	37.3	40.1	38.8	40.3
Females 16 years and over	9,848,145	1,366,207	7,525,525	4,653,713	3,026,496	1,770,178
Labor force	4,410,596	637,627	3,633,917	2,186,541	1,441,756	822,880
Percent of fem. 16 ys. & over	44.8	46.7	48.3	47	47.6	46.5
Civilian labor force	44.7	46.5	48.1	46.9	47.6	46.4
Employed	42.2	43.8	45.8	44.3	44.8	43.8
Unemployed	2.5	2.7	2.3	2.6	2.8	2.6
Percent of civ. labor force	5.5	5.8	4.9	5.5	5.9	5.6
Not in labor force	55.2	53.3	51.7	53.0	52.4	53.5

TABLE 3.9

LABOR FORCE CHARACTERISTICS OF SELECTED ANCESTRY GROUPS: 1980

	English		French		German		Irish		Italian		Polish	
	Male	Female	Male	Female	Male	Female	Male	Female	Male	Female	Male	Female
16 TO 19 YEARS	793,634	744,259	96,796	98,447	551,063	526,816	323,265	311,613	196,803	186,990	87,078	80,838
Employed	43.2	37.5	47.0	43.6	47.7	45.8	43.4	42.5	43.0	45.2	45.0	45.9
Unemployed	7.1	5.7	7.5	5.7	6.8	5.3	7.4	5.7	6.8	5.2	7.4	5.6
Not in labor force	46.7	56.6	41.2	50.2	41.9	48.6	45.5	51.5	47.6	49.4	45.0	48.1
20 TO 24 YEARS	1,025,425	939,317	151,015	150,695	869,772	814,883	484,077	470,148	307,859	288,798	144,448	136,809
Employed	71.1	58.9	73.6	60.8	73.8	66.1	71.1	64.2	71.3	68.8	70.9	69.2
Unemployed	7.9	5.2	7.4	4.8	7.3	4.4	7.8	4.9	8.0	4.4	8.3	4.7
Not in labor force	16.3	35.4	12.9	33.7	13.5	28.8	15.8	30.3	17.4	26.4	16.7	25.7
25 TO 54 YEARS	4,753,064	4,572,963	655,039	666,602	3,978,138	3,574,067	2,129,902	2,195,278	1,488,904	1,415,131	789,846	773,631
Employed	87.5	57.9	87.5	56.9	90.3	60.3	87.4	58.7	89.2	57.1	89.3	60.0
Unemployed	3.8	2.7	4.3	3.0	3.6	2.6	4.2	2.9	4.1	3.1	4.2	3.2
Not in labor force	6.9	39.3	6.5	40.0	4.5	37.0	6.6	38.3	5.9	39.7	5.3	36.7
55 TO 64 YEARS	1,305,190	1,426,741	155,756	185,515	996,503	995,208	592,657	683,870	509,713	536,298	341,198	376,520
Employed	67.7	37.4	67.4	36.7	72.2	40.1	66.3	39.3	71.2	40.9	69.2	39.1
Unemployed	2.4	1.4	3.1	1.2	2.5	1.4	2.9	1.6	3.3	2.5	3.3	2.2
Not in labor force	29.9	61.2	29.4	61.6	25.2	58.4	30.8	59.1	25.5	56.7	27.4	58.7
65 YEARS AND OVER	1,463,939	2,164,865	164,413	264,948	1,187,449	1,614,551	624,349	992,804	473,838	599,279	282,795	402,380
Employed	17.9	6.7	15.1	6.3	17.7	6.9	16.5	7.0	18.0	7.5	17.8	7.9
Unemployed	0.8	0.3	0.9	0.4	0.8	0.4	0.9	0.4	1.3	0.7	1.2	0.6
Not in labor force	81.3	93.0	84.0	93.3	81.4	92.7	82.6	92.6	80.7	91.7	81.0	91.5

TABLE 3.10

CLASS OF WORKER FOR SELECTED ANCESTRY GROUP: 1980

	ENGLISH	FRENCH	GERMAN	IRISH	ITALIAN	POLISH
CLASS OF WORKER AND OCCUPATION						
Employed 16 years and ov.	10,533,050	1,458,415	8,874,549	4,902,405	3,435,377	1,908,699
Private wage and salary work.	74.0	78.0	75.2	75.6	76.6	78.9
Federal Government workers	3.6	3.2	3.1	3.8	3.3	3.4
State Government workers	5.0	4.3	4.0	4.5	3.4	3.4
Local Government workers	8.3	7.1	7.7	9.0	9.4	8.0
Self-employed workers	8.6	7.0	9.3	6.6	6.9	5.9
Unpaid family workers	0.6	0.4	0.8	0.5	0.4	0.4

TABLE 3.11

OCCUPATION OF PERSONS OF SELECTED ANCESTRY GROUPS: 1980

	ENGLISH	FRENCH	GERMAN	IRISH	ITALIAN	POLISH
Employed 16 years and ov.	10,533,050	1,458,415	8,874,549	4,902,405	3,435,377	1,908,699
Managerial and professional	24.4	19.7	23.1	24.2	23.2	23.6
Execut., Administ., Manag.	11.5	10.0	11.1	11.9	12.1	10.7
Professional Specialty occ.	12.9	9.7	11.9	12.3	11.2	12.9
Technical, Sales, Administ.	29.4	29.6	29.3	32.0	33.5	31.8
Technician and related supp	2.9	3.0	3.0	2.8	2.6	3.2
Sales Occupations	10.8	10.2	10.1	10.8	11.4	9.9
Administrative Support	15.8	16.3	16.2	18.4	19.5	18.6
Service Occupations	10.5	12.7	11.0	12.3	12.5	11.1
Private household occup.	0.4	0.4	0.4	0.3	0.2	0.3
Protective Service occ.	1.4	1.5	1.3	2.3	1.9	1.7
Other Service Occupations	8.7	10.8	9.3	9.7	10.3	9.1
Farming, forestry, fishing	3.4	2.3	5.0	2.3	1.0	1.3
Precision Prod., Craft, Repair	14.0	16.1	14.6	13.1	13.9	14.1
Operators, Fabricators, Lab.	18.2	19.5	17.0	16.1	15.9	18.1
Machine Oper., Assembl.	9.3	10.5	8.6	7.7	8.1	10.7
Transportation	4.8	5.0	4.7	4.6	3.9	3.6
Handlers, cleaners, helpers	4.1	4.0	3.8	3.8	3.9	3.7

TABLE 3.12

INDUSTRY OF SELECTED ANCESTRY GROUPS: 1980

	ENGLISH	FRENCH	GERMAN	IRISH	ITALIAN	POLISH
INDUSTRY						
Employed 16 years and ov.	10,533,050	1,458,415	8,874,549	4,902,405	3,435,377	1,908,699
Agriculture, Forestry, Fish.	5.2	4.3	6.2	3.5	1.4	1.9
Construction	6.6	7.2	6.4	6.3	6.1	4.4
Manufacturing	22.8	24.5	23.4	20.3	22.0	29.3
Nondurable goods	9.5	9.4	8.1	8.1	8.7	9.4
Durable goods	13.2	15.1	15.3	12.2	13.4	19.8
Transport., Communications	7.2	7.1	7.2	8.4	7.8	7.0
Wholesale Trade	4.4	4.3	4.7	4.5	4.7	4.7
Retail Trade	15.5	16.8	15.6	15.9	18.2	15.1
Finance, Insurance, Real Est.	6.1	5.6	5.8	7.0	7.5	6.2
Business and Repair Service	3.9	4.0	3.9	4.1	4.4	4.3
Personal, Entertainment, Recr.	3.6	4.0	3.4	3.6	4.6	3.2
Professional and Related Serv.	19.6	17.6	18.8	20.4	17.9	19.0
Health Services	6.3	6.9	6.7	7.4	6.1	7.2
Educational Services	8.9	7.2	8.2	8.5	8.0	7.6
Other Profess. & Related S.	4.4	3.5	4.0	4.5	3.8	4.2
Public Administration	5.1	4.7	4.5	6.1	5.4	4.9

TABLE 3.13

INCOME CHARACTERISTICS IN 1979 OF SELECTED ANCESTRY GROUPS

		ENGLISH	FRENCH	GERMAN	IRISH	ITALIAN	POLISH
HOUSEHOLDS							
Median	dol.	16,746	16,522	18,307	17,256	19,026	19,009
Mean	dol.	20,606	19,419	21,411	20,669	21,989	22,048
FAMILIES							
Median	dol.	19,807	19,564	21,294	20,719	21,842	22,588
Mean	dol.	23,452	22,175	24,372	23,883	24,835	25,734
UNRELATED IND. 15 YEARS AND OVER							
Median	dol.	6,629	6,195	6,954	6,556	7,016	7,008
Mean	dol.	9,582	8,659	9,538	9,180	9,678	9,690
Males 15 yrs.& ov. with income							
Median Income	dol.	12,598	12,661	13,907	12,885	14,057	14,905
Percent full-time workers		54	55	57	53	54	55
Median Income	dol.	17,594	16,974	18,191	18,169	18,940	19,776
Females 15 yrs.& ov. with inc.							
Median Income	dol.	5,180	4,940	5,387	5,291	5,409	5,585
Percent full-time workers		27.5	28.5	28.7	28.8	28.8	28.7
Median Income	dol.	10,013	9,817	10,439	10,568	10,912	11,295
Per Capita Income	dol.	8,242	7,958	9,069	8,534	9,126	9,790
Persons in Households	dol.	8,370	8,093	9,233	8,696	9,240	9,944
Pers. in group quart.	dol.	2,949	3,052	3,117	3,094	2,781	2,883
Median Income:							
No work. in family (1979)	dol.	8,594	7,530	9,474	8,506	8,623	9,398
1 worker	dol.	16,609	16,141	17,969	17,274	18,458	19,306
2 workers	dol.	22,953	22,412	23,728	23,639	24,946	26,012
3 or more workers	dol.	31,612	31,253	32,827	33,672	34,490	35,489

TABLE 3.14

INCOME TYPE IN 1979 OF SELECTED ANCESTRY GROUPS: 1980

	ENGLISH	FRENCH	GERMAN	IRISH	ITALIAN	POLISH
HOUSEHOLDS	9,603,135	1,272,564	7,795,931	4,320,542	2,960,756	1,745,432
With Earnings	78.9	80.2	81.5	79.4	80.8	78.6
Mean earnings dol.	20,972	20,271	21,694	21,452	22,572	22,862
With wage or salary	74.4	76.8	76.6	76.1	77.5	75.9
Mean wage or salary dol.	19,942	19,376	20,668	20,577	21,592	22,012
With nonfarm self-employmen	10.4	9.1	10.3	8.7	10.0	8.1
Mean non farm income dol.	13,646	13,077	12,894	13,846	14,278	14,677
With farm self-employment	4.8	2.6	6.4	3.0	0.9	1.5
Mean farm income dol.	6,039	7354	7992	5938	7204	5620
With interest, dividend, rent	42.7	37.4	50.1	41.0	47.7	53.9
Mean interest income dol.	3,747	2,704	3,032	2,730	2,752	2,784
With Social Security income	29.8	3.3	28.1	29.9	30.0	32.6
Mean Soc. Sec. inc. dol.	4,142	4,085	4,305	4,182	4,386	4,340
With Public Assistance income	6.5	7.5	4.5	6.5	5.7	5.1
Mean Publ. Ass. inc. dol.	2,291	2,428	2,410	2,372	2,629	2,558
With all other income	24.0	23.5	23.4	26.2	25.6	27.0
Mean other income dol.	4,481	3,692	3,856	4,261	3,827	3,827

TABLE 3.15

POVERTY CHARACTERITICS IN 1979 OF SELECTED ANCESTRY GROUPS

	ENGLISH	FRENCH	GERMAN	IRISH	ITALIAN	POLISH
INCOME IN 1979 BELOW POVERTY						
Families	591,705	75,430	324,907	220,225	123,102	57,204
Percent Below Poverty Level	8.3	8.0	5.6	7.0	5.4	4.5
With Children under 18 years	10.9	10.2	7.3	9.0	7.3	6.2
With Children 5 to 17 years	10.6	9.9	7.0	8.8	7.0	6.0
Female Householder, no husband	25.7	26.9	18.4	20.2	17.6	14.2
With Children under 18 ys.	36.0	38.7	24.4	28.6	25.2	20.1
With Children under 6 years	53.0	52.6	43.8	47.2	49.0	44.5
Householder 65 years and over	9.0	8.8	5.8	7.9	5.6	4.7
Unrelat. Individ. in pov.	748,382	113,643	523,961	364,061	177,019	119,359
Percent Below Poverty Level	25.1	26.1	21.3	23.9	21.3	21.0
65 years and over	29.4	31.6	24.4	28.5	24.5	23.7
Persons in poverty univ.	2,626,209	321,210	1,422,984	967,201	492,638	260,654
Percent Below Poverty Level	11.3	10.7	8.1	9.6	7.3	7.0
Related children under 18	14.7	13.6	9.9	11.6	9.4	8.5
Related children 5 to 17	14.0	12.9	9.3	11.0	9.0	8.0
60 years and over	13.6	14.4	10.3	12.8	9.0	8.9
65 years and over	15.0	15.8	11.5	14.1	9.9	10.1
INCOME IN 1979 BELOW SPEC.LEV.						
Percent of pers. in pov. univ.						
Below 75 percent of pov. l.	7.4	6.9	5.2	6.0	4.6	4.4
Below 125 percent of pov. l.	16.0	15.5	11.9	13.9	10.8	10.4
Below 150 percent of pov. l.	20.8	20.4	16.1	18.4	14.6	14.0
Below 200 percent of pov. l.	30.9	30.8	25.4	27.8	23.3	21.9

APPENDIX D

Population of Single and Multiple Italian Ancestry, Population Born in Italy and Born Abroad.

Source: *Census of Population, 1980: Unpublished Special Tabulations on the Italian Population.* Washington: The Bureau of the Census, 1987.

TABLE 4.1

**RESIDENCE, AGE AND RELATIONSHIP OF PERSONS OF ITALIAN ANCESTRY
BY TYPE OF ANCESTRY AND PLACE OF BIRTH: 1980.**

| | TOTAL | BORN IN THE U.S.A. | | SINGLE AND MULTIPLE | |
		SINGLE ANCESTRY	MULTIPLE ANCESTRY	BORN IN ITALY	BORN ABROAD
URBAN AND RURAL					
Total Persons	12,183,692	6,008,966	5,244,525	803,633	126,568
Urban	10,625,996	5,367,778	4,377,805	762,616	117,797
Rural	1,557,696	641,188	866,720	41,017	8,771
Farm	57,983	22,741	33,021	1,838	383
AGE					
Total Persons	12,183,692	6,008,966	5,244,525	803,633	126,568
under 5	922,333	206,063	713,240	1,135	1,895
5 to 9	942,595	244,355	691,249	3,613	3,378
10 to 14	1,095,240	327,816	751,585	10,231	5,608
15 to 19	1,246,582	442,238	775,587	18,945	9,812
20 to 24	1,254,511	564,693	650,603	25,996	13,219
25 to 29	1,090,676	533,908	510,336	35,362	11,070
30 to 34	955,845	494,006	403,513	48,459	9,867
35 to 44	1,252,262	738,949	403,922	91,779	17,612
45 to 54	1,140,470	830,287	189,864	104,948	15,371
55 to 59	627,834	497,458	62,623	60,441	7,312
60 to 64	524,551	437,543	39,552	41,870	5,586
65 to 74	749,223	554,814	39,254	140,674	14,481
75 to 84	301,485	122,063	10,996	159,286	9,140
85 over	80,085	14,773	2,201	60,894	2,217
median	27.9	37.6	18.0	60.1	39.8
HOUSEHOLD TYPE AND RELATIONSHIP					
In Household	11,954,137	5,904,366	5,138,251	788,536	122,984
Family Householder	3,043,694	1,930,625	747,123	326,479	39,467
Non-family Householder: Male	432,804	255,179	137,523	32,883	7,219
Female	517,414	304,820	125,818	77,662	9,114
Spouse	2,505,165	1,540,294	720,354	211,949	32,568
Other Relatives	5,175,863	1,735,491	3,276,136	133,769	30,467
Nonrelatives	279,197	137,957	131,297	5,794	4,149

TABLE 4.2

DEMOGRAPHIC CHARACTERISTICS OF PERSONS OF ITALIAN ANCESTRY BY TYPE OF ANCESTRY AND PLACE OF BIRTH: 1980.

	TOTAL	BORN IN THE U.S.A. SINGLE ANCESTRY	MULTIPLE ANCESTRY	SINGLE AND MULTIPLE BORN IN ITALY	BORN ABROAD
PERSONS IN HOUSEHOLDS					
HOUSEHOLDS	3,993,912	2,490,624	1,010,464	437,024	55,800
1 person	784,126	474,037	189,712	105,989	14,388
2 persons	1,253,767	798,824	288,217	149,281	17,445
3 persons	730,447	461,520	195,605	64,118	9,204
4 persons	675,754	413,716	194,139	59,826	8,073
5 persons	353,416	218,975	93,406	36,626	4,409
6 persons	196,402	123,552	49,385	21,184	2,281
TYPE OF GROUP QUARTERS					
Persons in Group Quarters	229,555	104,600	106,274	15,097	3,584
Inmate of Mental Hospital	8,434	5,656	1,618	1,051	109
Inmate of Home for Aged	26,697	13,633	1,594	10,732	738
Inmate of Other Institution	20,952	13,114	6,676	903	259
In Military Quarters	26,778	12,093	13,972	275	438
In College Dormitory	127,876	50,132	75,397	699	1,648
Other in Group Quarters	18,818	9,972	7,017	1,437	392
MARITAL STATUS					
Male, 15 years and over	4,538,422	2,602,795	1,494,696	385,202	55,729
Single	1,507,431	688,091	763,808	40,619	14,913
Now married, except separated	2,682,639	1,703,267	646,528	297,724	35,120
Separated	60,851	38,058	18,391	3,316	1,086
Widowed	95,816	53,467	5,607	34,703	2,039
Divorced	191,685	119,912	60,635	8,840	2,298
Female, 15 years and over	4,685,102	2,627,937	1,593,755	403,452	59,958
Sinlge	1,293,148	573,112	678,900	29,617	11,519
Now married, except separated	2,578,114	1,579,096	747,073	218,515	33,430
Separated	87,538	49,953	32,457	3,789	1,339
Widowed	463,378	276,598	34,552	142,164	10,064
Divorced	262,924	149,178	100,773	9,367	3,606
FERTILITY					
Women 15 to 44 years	2,883,771	1,340,904	1,408,335	104,237	30,295
Children ever born	2,923,790	1,513,249	1,194,313	182,153	34,075
Per 1000 women	1,014	1,129	848	1,747	1,125

TABLE 4.3

**NATIVITY AND LANGUAGE OF PERSONS OF ITALIAN ANCESTRY
BY TYPE OF ANCESTRY AND PLACE OF BIRTH: 1980.**

	TOTAL	BORN IN THE U.S.A. SINGLE ANCESTRY	MULTIPLE ANCESTRY	SINGLE AND MULTIPLE BORN IN ITALY	BORN ABROAD
NATIVITY					
Total Persons	12,183,692	6,008,966	5,244,525	803,633	126,568
Native	11,253,491	6,008,966	5,244,525	0	0
Born in State of residence	8,491,246	4,516,105	3,975,141	0	0
Born in different State	2,703,416	1,466,420	1,236,996	0	0
Born abroad	58,829	26,441	32,388	0	0
Foreign Born	930,201	0	0	803,633	126,568
LANGUAGE SPOKEN AT HOME					
Persons 5 to 17 years	2,773,014	816,111	1,918,655	24,169	14,079
Speak only English at home	2,602,720	728,274	1,866,787	1,715	5,944
Speak a language other than E.	170,286	87,023	51,868	22,454	8,941
Italian lang. spoken at home	123,422	80,279	17,181	22,174	3,788
Speak English very well	117,875	76,826	16,591	20,829	3,629
Speak English not well	5,547	3,453	590	1,345	159
Other lang. spoken at home	46,864	7,558	34,687	280	4,339
Speak English very well	43,734	6,924	32,602	265	3,943
Speak English not well	3,130	634	2,085	15	396
Persons 18 and over	8,488,345	4,986,792	2,612,630	778,329	110,594
Speak only English at home	6,951,998	4,253,297	2,514,956	142,567	41,178
Speak a language other than E.	1,536,347	733,495	97,674	635,762	69,416
Italian lang. spoken at home	1,375,724	691,692	34,143	626,237	23,652
Speak English very well	1,179,092	657,673	32,587	468,274	20,558
Speak English not well	196,632	34,019	1,556	157,963	3,094
Other lang. spoken at home	160,623	41,803	63,531	9,525	45,764
Speak English very well	145,312	38,857	60,022	7,585	38,848
Speak English not well	15,311	2,946	3,509	1,940	6,916
MEANS OF TRANSPORTATION TO WORK					
Workers 16 and over	5,324,280	3,049,101	1,923,081	292,291	59,807
Car, truck, or van	4,396,126	2,516,965	1,617,800	215,927	45,434
Drive alone	3,434,503	1,982,215	1,255,420	161,875	34,993
Carpool	961,623	534,750	362,380	54,052	10,441
Public transportation	478,766	294,912	130,178	45,706	7,970
Walked only	311,413	165,027	117,915	24,220	4,251
Other means	69,450	33,470	32,334	2,549	1,097
Worked at home	68,525	38,727	24,854	3,889	1,055

TABLE 4.4

EDUCATION, RESIDENCE IN 1975, OF PERSONS OF ITALIAN ANCESTRY BY TYPE OF ANCESTRY AND PLACE OF BIRTH: 1980.

| | TOTAL | BORN IN THE U.S.A. | | SINGLE AND MULTIPLE | |
		SINGLE ANCESTRY	MULTIPLE ANCESTRY	BORN IN ITALY	BORN ABROAD
SCHOOL ENROLLMENT					
Persons 3 years and over enrolled	3,723,285	1,216,681	2,438,805	41,285	26,514
Nursery school	167,286	36,179	130,433	155	519
Public	48,045	11,253	36,531	28	233
Private	119,241	24,926	93,902	127	286
Kindergarten & Elementary (1-8 years)	1,844,209	515,061	1,307,635	13,308	8,205
Public	1,460,253	393,711	1,049,910	10,140	6,492
Private	383,956	121,350	257,725	3,168	1,713
High School (1 to 4 years)	927,635	309,080	598,205	13,456	6,894
Public	773,310	250,630	505,968	11,098	5,614
Private	154,325	58,450	92,237	2,358	1,280
College	784,155	356,361	402,532	14,366	10,896
YEARS OF SCHOOL COMPLETED					
Persons 25 years and over	6,722,431	4,223,801	1,662,261	743,713	92,656
Elementary (0 to 8 years)	1,199,874	648,415	66,689	458,405	26,365
High School: 1 to 3 years	1,008,837	752,000	170,249	75,227	11,361
4 or more years	2,507,599	1,669,397	676,656	134,931	26,615
College: 1 to 3 years	967,183	555,969	360,437	36,849	13,928
4 or more years	1,038,938	598,020	388,230	38,301	14,387
Percent High School Graduates	67.1	66.8	85.7	28.2	59.3
RESIDENCE IN 1975					
Persons 5 years and over	11,256,132	5,818,104	4,516,932	796,604	124,492
Same house	6,517,068	3,636,872	2,253,191	565,775	61,230
Different house in U. S.	4,655,823	2,163,505	2,239,999	203,178	49,141
Same County	2,606,440	1,219,713	1,222,259	135,169	29,299
Different County	2,049,383	943,792	1,017,740	68,009	19,842
Same State	1,063,858	497,992	515,677	40,306	9,883
Different State	985,525	445,800	502,063	27,703	9,959
Abroad	83,241	17,727	23,742	27,651	14,121

TABLE 4.5

LABOR FORCE, CLASS OF WORKER, AND OCCUPAT. OF PERSONS OF ITALIAN ANCESTRY BY TYPE OF ANCESTRY AND PLACE OF BIRTH: 1980.

| | TOTAL | BORN IN THE U.S.A. | | SINGLE AND MULTIPLE | |
		SINGLE ANCESTRY	MULTIPLE ANCESTRY	BORN IN ITALY	BORN ABROAD
LABOR FORCE STATUS					
Persons 16 years and over	8,980,308	5,152,842	2,928,038	785,403	114,025
Labor force	5,815,941	3,310,631	2,112,455	327,133	65,722
Percent of persons 16 years and over	64.8	64.2	72.1	41.7	57.6
Civilian labor force	5,755,125	3,282,438	2,081,474	326,337	64,876
Employed	5,403,858	3,100,622	1,938,841	303,228	61,167
Unemployed	351,267	181,816	142,633	23,109	3,709
Percent of civilian labor force	6.1	5.5	6.9	7.1	5.7
Not in labor force	3,164,367	1,842,211	815,583	458,270	48,303
Females, 16 years and over	4,565,892	2,590,606	1,514,159	401,885	59,242
Labor force	2,404,690	1,316,217	949,205	112,143	27,125
Percent of females 16 years and over	52.7	50.8	62.7	27.9	45.8
Civilian labor force	2,399,188	1,314,103	945,984	112,063	27,038
Employed	2,254,344	1,239,972	886,639	102,422	25,311
Unemployed	144,844	74,131	59,345	9,641	1,727
Percent of civilian labor force	6.0	5.6	6.3	8.6	6.4
Not in labor force	2,161,202	1,274,389	564,954	289,742	32,117
CLASS OF WORKER AND OCCUPATION					
Employed 16 years and ov.	5,403,858	3,100,622	1,938,841	303,228	61,167
Private wage and salary work.	4,210,092	2,360,160	1,556,161	244,295	49,476
Federal Government workers	172,858	108,276	57,348	5,544	1,690
State Government workers	194,269	110,753	75,613	5,927	1,976
Local Government workers	484,579	306,693	158,479	15,934	3,473
Self-employed workers	323,159	203,824	84,703	30,196	4,436
Unpaid family workers	18,901	10,826	6,538	1,332	205
Employed 16 years and over	5,403,858	3,100,622	1,938,841	303,228	61,167
Managerial and professional	1,266,556	750,007	459,879	41,882	14,788
Execut., Administ., Managerial	624,838	386,959	206,739	23,908	7,232
Professional Specialty occupations	641,718	363,048	253,140	17,974	7,556
Technical, Sales, Administrative	1,859,253	1,085,872	699,782	55,150	18,449
Technician and related support	158,386	82,444	69,291	4,646	2,005
Sales Occupations	622,783	365,386	228,598	22,535	6,264
Administrative Support	1,078,084	629,042	401,893	27,969	19,180
Service Occupations	692,875	373,699	260,919	49,473	8,784
Private household occupations	11,090	4,953	4,941	719	477
Protective Service occupations	102,243	63,586	35,543	2,569	545
Other Service Occupations	579,542	305,160	220,435	46,185	7,762
Farming, forestry, fishing	56,336	29,046	21,864	4,923	503
Precision Prod., Craft, Repair	699,207	404,589	217,654	67,315	9,649
Operators, Fabricators, Laborers	829,631	457,409	278,743	84,485	8,994
Machine Oper., Assembl.	401,031	219,172	119,165	57,450	5,244
Transportation	203,526	124,039	69,021	8,890	1,576
Handlers, cleaners, helpers	225,074	114,198	90,557	18,145	2,174

TABLE 4.6

INDUSTRY, LABOR FORCE PARTICIPATION IN 1979 OF PERSONS OF ITALIAN ANCESTRY BY TYPE OF ANCESTRY AND PLACE OF BIRTH: 1980.

| | TOTAL | BORN IN THE U.S.A. | | SINGLE AND MULTIPLE | |
		SINGLE ANCESTRY	MULTIPLE ANCESTRY	BORN IN ITALY	BORN ABROAD
INDUSTRY					
Employed 16 years and over	5,403,858	3,100,622	1,938,841	303,228	61,167
Agriculture, Forestry, Fish.	82,137	42,156	34,498	4,792	691
Construction	311,918	177,968	101,759	28,787	3,404
Manufacturing	1,127,878	650,932	364,405	98,942	13,599
Nondurable goods	425,541	245,620	125,874	48,439	5,608
Durable goods	702,337	405,312	238,531	50,503	7,991
Transportation	254,719	159,751	80,333	11,598	3,037
Communications and Pub. Util.	151,688	90,531	54,942	5,225	990
Wholesale Trade	248,181	149,529	86,737	9,340	2,575
Retail Trade	1,039,968	560,652	408,477	59,141	11,698
Finance, Insurance, Real Est.	399,780	240,658	140,040	14,511	4,571
Business and Repair Service	247,782	138,161	94,990	11,163	3,468
Personal, Entertainment, Recr.	242,287	136,093	81,825	20,285	4,084
Professional and Related Serv.	1,013,408	576,556	393,301	32,438	11,113
Health Services	356,510	194,750	145,944	11,431	4,385
Educational Services	442,563	259,282	164,872	14,083	4,326
Other Profess. & Related S.	214,335	122,524	82,485	6,924	2,402
Public Administration	284,112	177,635	97,534	7,006	1,937
LABOR FORCE STATUS IN 1979					
Persons 16 ys./lab.f. 1979	6,333,395	3,562,703	2,354,481	345,068	71,143
Worked in 1979	6,237,671	3,510,434	2,318,408	338,983	69,846
50 to 52 weeks	3,778,810	2,268,385	1,263,656	206,675	40,094
40 to 49 weeks	823,247	446,315	310,216	55,344	11,372
1 to 39 weeks	1,635,614	795,734	744,536	76,964	18,380
35 or more hours per week	4,785,584	2,768,638	1,685,298	276,702	54,946
50 to 52 weeks	3,311,287	2,004,706	1,086,313	171,398	48,870
With unemployment in 1979	1,171,172	585,309	507,864	63,820	14,179
Unemployed 15 or more wks.	423,847	227,283	163,238	28,264	5,062
WORKERS IN FAMILY IN 1979					
Families	3,043,694	1,930,625	747,123	326,479	39,467
No Workers	338,747	211,930	33,911	86,506	6,400
1 worker	1,010,918	639,581	249,666	108,304	13,367
2 or more workers	1694029	1079114	463546	131669	19700

TABLE 4.7

INCOME CHARACTERISTICS OF PERSONS OF ITALIAN ANCESTRY
BY TYPE OF ANCESTRY AND PLACE OF BIRTH: 1980.

| | TOTAL | BORN IN THE U.S.A. | | SINGLE AND MULTIPLE | |
		SINGLE ANCESTRY	MULTIPLE ANCESTRY	BORN IN ITALY	BORN ABROAD
INCOME IN 1979					
HOUSEHOLDS	3,993,912	2,490,624	1,010,464	437,024	55,800
Less than $5,000	384,327	225,666	72,602	77,764	8,295
$5,000 to $7,499	264,805	156,192	51,272	52,363	4,978
$7,500 to $9,999	267,696	160,809	61,051	41,255	4,581
$10,000 to $14,999	568,004	347,369	148,507	63,347	8,781
$15,000 to $19,999	582,935	356,394	164,659	54,854	7,028
$20,000 to $24,999	555,361	345,067	157,199	46,883	6,212
$25,000 to $34,999	746,937	478,308	204,508	55,947	8,174
$35,000 to $49,999	419,279	280,164	104,322	30,032	4,761
$50,000 or more	204,568	140,655	46,344	14,579	2,990
Median Dol.	19,362	19,984	20,227	13,720	15,900
Mean Dol.	22,146	22,809	22,694	17,400	19,873
FAMILIES	3,043,694	1,930,625	747,123	326,479	39,467
Less than $5,000	141,672	82,162	37,181	19,740	2,589
$5,000 to $7,499	147,216	85,820	27,319	31,411	2,666
$7,500 to $9,999	169,660	101,558	33,851	31,315	2,936
$10,000 to $14,999	395,618	245,677	90,016	53,736	6,189
$15,000 to $19,999	460,969	285,651	120,060	49,872	5,386
$20,000 to $24,999	478,746	300,360	128,850	44,060	5,476
$25,000 to $34,999	675,612	437,641	176,883	53,723	7,365
$35,000 to $49,999	387,223	261,992	92,093	28,931	4,207
$50,000 or more	186,978	129,764	40,870	13,691	2,653
Median Dol.	21,960	22,737	22,528	17,711	19,970
Mean Dol.	24,841	25,529	24,900	20,829	23,273
UNRELATED INDIVID. 15 YS.	1,381,557	763,151	476,842	118,705	22,859
Less than $2,000	191,412	93,096	84,781	9,569	3,966
$2,000 to $2,999	97,281	48,883	36,126	10,781	1,491
$3,000 to $4,999	233,864	127,455	58,341	43,720	4,348
$5,000 to $7,999	221,324	122,551	69,288	25,542	3,943
$8,000 to $9,999	117,162	66,363	41,264	7,677	1,858
$10,000 to $14,999	234,389	134,028	86,434	10,610	3,317
$15,000 to $24,999	212,315	125,263	76,643	7,752	2,657
$25,000 to $49,999	63,556	39,021	21,019	2,497	1,019
$50,000 or more	10,254	6,491	2,946	557	260
Median Dol.	7,179	7,745	7,562	4,784	5,747
Mean Dol.	9,607	10,130	9,546	7,747	8,854
Per Capita Income Dol.	7,371	9,251	5,048	8,205	9,077
MEAN FAMILY INCOME BY WORKER					
No Workers Dol.	10,241	10,659	8,839	9,798	9,816
1 Worker Dol.	21,281	21,755	20,785	19,521	22,125
2 or more workers Dol.	29,886	30,728	28,203	28,962	29,541

TABLE 4.8

POVERTY CHARACTERISTICS OF PERSONS OF ITALIAN ANCESTRY BY TYPE OF ANCESTRY AND PLACE OF BIRTH: 1980.

	TOTAL	BORN IN THE U.S.A. SINGLE ANCESTRY	MULTIPLE ANCESTRY	SINGLE AND MULTIPLE BORN IN ITALY	BORN ABROAD
POVERTY STATUS IN 1979					
ALL INCOME LEVEL IN 1979					
Families	3,043,694	1,930,625	747,123	326,479	39,467
With Children under 18 years	1,562,272	920,994	498,331	123,728	19,219
With Children 5 to 17 years	1,239,800	755,747	362,978	105,883	15,192
Female Householder, no husband	337,678	204,842	94,203	33,778	4,855
With Children under 18 ys.	187,071	102,429	74,628	7,472	2,542
With Children under 6 years	57,803	27,985	27,532	1,546	740
Householder 65 years and over	446,424	278,935	19,137	139,025	9,327
Unrelated Individuals in poverty universe	1,227,168	701,065	387,599	117,731	20,773
65 years and over	276,616	162,682	15,228	91,458	7,248
Persons in poverty universe	11,951,890	5,907,475	5,131,212	789,928	123,275
Related children under 18	3,654,934	1,006,233	2,608,119	25,068	15,514
Related children 5 to 17	2,739,170	802,168	1,899,415	23,940	13,647
60 years and over	1,627,298	1,115,189	90,741	390,698	30,670
65 years and over	1,105,336	679,906	51,349	348,969	25,112
INCOME IN 1979 BELOW POVERTY					
Families	173,600	100,447	49,226	20,826	3,101
Percent Below Poverty Level	5.7	5.2	6.6	6.4	7.9
With Children under 18 years	120,847	66,128	42,948	9,817	1,954
With Children 5 to 17 years	91,521	51,707	29,954	8,428	1,432
Female Householder, no husband	69,813	38,227	26,764	3,829	993
With Children under 18 years	60,518	32,110	25,565	2,043	800
With Children under 6 years	29,494	13,922	14,682	578	312
Householder 65 years and over	24,922	14,245	1,071	8,950	656
Unrelated Individuals in poverty	259,669	143,247	80,393	26,995	9,034
Percent Below Poverty Level	21.2	20.4	20.7	22.9	43.5
65 years and over	67,420	36,910	3,190	25,238	2,082
Persons in poverty universe	869,130	414,004	371,214	71,388	12,524
Percent Below Poverty Level	7.3	7.0	7.2	9.0	10.2
Related children under 18	298,899	93,805	200,035	3,203	1,856
Related children 5 to 17	214,043	70,821	138,635	3,023	1,564
60 years and over	145,375	91,337	7,204	43,074	3,760
65 years and over	109,561	61,605	4,832	39,886	3,238

APPENDIX E

Population of Italian Ancestry in Selected States of the United States

Source: *Census of Population, 1980: Unpublished Special Tabulations on the Italian Population.* Washington: The Bureau of the Census, 1987.

TABLE 5.1
RESIDENCE, AGE, AND RELATIONSHIP OF PERSONS OF TOTAL ITALIAN ANCESTRY IN THE U.S. AND SELECTED STATES: 1980

	CA	CT	FL	IL	MA	MI	NJ	NY	OH	PA	RI	USA
URBAN AND RURAL												
Total Persons	1,144,102	561,542	461,757	640,304	749,583	344,402	1,315,632	2,811,911	520,171	1,205,823	185,080	12,183,692
Urban	1,047,863	478,020	418,935	586,887	665,254	287,422	1,202,142	2,562,068	439,618	985,802	167,127	10,625,996
Rural	96,239	83,522	42,822	53,417	84,329	56,980	113,490	249,843	80,553	220,021	17,953	1,557,696
Farm	11,759	737	787	3,767	492	1,407	2,465	4,876	2,159	2,959	47	57,983
AGE												
Total Persons	1,144,102	561,542	461,757	640,304	749,583	344,402	1,315,632	2,811,911	520,171	1,205,823	185,080	12,183,692
under 5 years	84,283	36,923	28,386	53,388	51,124	30,050	90,649	186,458	46,612	93,778	11,514	922,333
5 to 9 years	81,476	41,402	31,000	53,025	57,632	30,564	97,439	199,696	45,913	93,768	12,760	942,595
10 to 14 years	96,913	51,273	35,771	59,148	71,620	33,599	118,318	243,762	49,993	108,608	16,596	1,095,240
15 to 19 years	111,567	55,698	42,732	67,044	80,544	38,636	128,735	275,186	56,646	126,510	19,129	1,246,582
20 to 24 years	122,536	53,265	44,702	66,246	77,250	38,075	122,093	262,490	56,970	123,984	18,230	1,254,511
25 to 29 years	113,420	46,921	37,925	57,305	64,173	32,302	106,685	229,214	47,684	103,389	14,790	1,090,676
30 to 34 years	101,063	43,768	34,026	50,085	56,875	25,028	101,080	205,597	40,565	85,049	13,071	955,845
35 to 44 years	124,810	59,800	45,818	66,634	75,676	34,083	141,229	290,173	50,168	114,216	18,494	1,252,262
45 to 54 years	100,226	56,156	41,058	57,427	69,101	29,802	138,925	301,809	44,285	119,069	18,425	1,140,470
55 to 59 years	56,215	30,618	25,924	30,437	39,303	15,697	76,266	165,391	25,265	68,220	11,237	627,834
60 to 64 years	45,283	27,215	26,867	24,705	34,728	11,662	62,445	140,511	19,204	55,551	10,469	524,551
65 to 74 years	67,733	38,407	47,782	36,789	47,637	15,546	88,725	202,306	24,045	76,643	13,748	749,223
75 to 84 years	29,985	15,639	16,378	14,216	18,397	7,264	34,397	86,216	10,169	29,432	5,191	301,485
85 years and over	8,592	4,457	3,388	3,855	5,523	2,094	8,646	23,102	2,652	7,606	1,426	80,085
median age	28.3	29.5	31.5	26.9	27.9	25.2	29.7	30.2	25.4	27.7	29.8	27.9

TABLE 5.1 (Cont'd)

RESIDENCE, AGE, AND RELATIONSHIP OF PERSONS OF TOTAL ITALIAN ANCESTRY IN THE U.S. AND SELECTED STATES: 1980

	CA	CT	FL	IL	MA	MI	NJ	NY	OH	PA	RI	USA
Female	570,868	285,298	228,143	321,216	380,530	171,350	669,504	1,430,722	261,031	610,621	94,910	6,129,736
under 5 years	41,404	18,252	13,706	25,710	24,720	14,607	44,944	90,748	22,520	45,435	5,314	449,355
5 to 9 years	39,825	20,394	15,087	25,886	28,361	14,529	47,676	96,682	22,430	45,699	6,316	459,074
10 to 14 years	47,471	25,002	17,670	28,711	35,368	16,497	57,859	118,873	24,251	53,111	8,036	536,205
15 to 19 years	55,842	27,144	21,239	33,339	40,155	19,120	63,636	136,892	27,936	62,684	9,405	616,655
20 to 24 years	60,604	26,851	22,134	32,831	38,856	18,947	61,766	132,725	28,713	62,847	9,195	627,058
25 to 29 years	56,219	23,670	18,740	27,978	32,395	15,642	53,447	114,287	23,988	51,258	7,467	542,043
30 to 34 years	49,583	22,275	16,695	24,969	28,277	12,651	51,525	103,377	19,924	42,988	6,753	476,497
35 to 44 years	60,381	29,550	22,145	33,147	38,294	16,987	71,113	146,114	25,004	57,686	9,554	621,518
45 to 54 years	49,408	28,696	20,500	28,917	35,138	15,143	70,759	153,317	22,819	61,218	9,631	574,827
55 to 59 years	28,304	15,640	13,458	15,232	20,224	8,019	38,771	84,390	13,020	35,170	5,795	320,617
60 to 64 years	22,670	14,644	13,861	12,897	17,984	5,910	32,688	74,585	9,876	29,118	5,655	272,405
65 to 74 years	36,916	21,017	23,260	20,884	26,309	8,378	49,331	113,236	13,400	42,815	7,862	410,989
75 to 84 years	17,065	9,483	7,803	8,546	11,424	3,847	20,908	51,839	5,718	16,639	3,113	176,518
85 years and over	5,176	2,680	1,845	2,169	3,025	1,073	5,081	13,657	1,432	3,953	814	45,975
median age	28.6	30.3	31.6	27.5	28.5	25.6	30.5	31.2	26.0	28.5	31.3	28.5
HOUSEHOLD TYPE AND RELATIONSHIP												
In Household	1,125,642	551,342	455,181	630,270	733,669	338,188	1,302,434	2,770,432	511,042	1,181,031	181,583	11,954,137
Family Householder	282,395	144,177	129,345	156,089	183,750	81,001	338,989	723,591	124,299	300,782	48,192	3,043,694
Non-family Householder: Male	66,843	15,791	21,924	21,624	23,009	11,733	33,272	84,434	16,701	33,317	5,303	432,804
Female	65,651	22,394	22,262	26,176	32,007	11,702	48,934	124,637	19,008	47,228	7,998	517,414
Spouse	227,030	119,701	103,450	131,017	147,694	69,444	280,822	587,299	105,993	245,851	39,003	2,505,165
Other Relatives	431,695	239,674	162,563	284,342	332,183	156,280	582,145	1,206,891	234,837	534,672	78,374	5,175,863
Nonrelatives	52,028	9,605	15,637	11,022	15,026	8,028	18,272	43,580	10,204	19,181	2,713	279,197
Persons per household	2.71	3.02	2.62	3.09	3.07	3.24	3.09	2.97	3.19	3.10	2.95	2.99
Persons per family	3.33	3.49	3.06	3.66	3.61	3.79	3.55	3.48	3.74	3.59	3.44	3.52

TABLE 5.2
SELECTED DEMOGRAPHIC CHARACTERISTICS OF PERSONS OF ITALIAN ANCESTRY IN THE U.S. BY STATES: 1980

	CA	CT	FL	IL	MA	MI	NJ	NY	OH	PA	RI	USA
PERSONS IN HOUSEHOLDS												
HOUSEHOLDS	414,889	182,362	173,531	203,889	238,766	104,436	421,195	932,662	160,008	381,327	61,493	3,993,912
1 person	101,181	32,432	34,278	40,413	45,710	18,784	71,986	184,030	30,085	69,984	11,784	784,126
2 persons	144,349	57,550	71,391	62,008	71,854	31,478	126,666	277,574	48,097	116,369	19,579	1,253,767
3 persons	69,958	34,113	29,211	37,030	43,439	18,986	79,729	167,985	29,980	74,476	11,713	730,447
4 persons	59,289	33,057	22,185	34,498	41,066	18,580	76,930	163,020	28,581	65,311	10,518	675,754
5 persons	27,206	16,903	10,865	18,983	22,184	10,337	42,641	89,440	14,589	34,996	5,175	353,416
6 persons	12,906	8,307	5,601	10,957	14,513	6,271	23,243	50,613	8,674	20,191	2,724	196,402
TYPE OF GROUP QUARTERS												
Persons in Group Quarters	18,460	10,200	6,576	10,034	15,914	6,214	13,198	41,479	9,129	24,792	3,497	229,555
Inmate of Mental Hospital	660	373	225	179	505	223	989	2,754	318	1,110	14	8,434
Inmate of Home for Aged	3,014	2,134	449	1,550	2,056	794	2,205	7,676	1,012	1,692	308	26,697
Inmate of Other Institution	2,337	1,005	1,235	490	852	722	1,791	4,453	813	2,259	49	20,952
In Military Quarters	4,568	332	1,315	1,009	271	109	755	805	25	98	202	26,778
In College Dormitory	5,982	5,633	2,866	5,643	11,064	4,029	6,046	21,408	6,224	17,719	2,698	127,876
Other in Group Quarters	1,899	723	486	1,163	1,166	337	1,412	4,383	737	1,914	226	18,818
MARITAL STATUS												
Male, 15 years and over	439,262	210,294	184,920	233,834	277,126	124,472	490,201	1,057,579	185,823	443,293	68,966	4,538,422
Single	150,579	68,335	49,773	78,595	99,775	43,365	156,318	346,100	62,449	147,616	22,667	1,507,431
Now married, except separated	243,427	126,804	116,928	138,497	158,053	72,283	299,974	637,266	110,060	263,812	40,980	2,682,639
Separated	7,233	2,064	2,397	1,877	3,633	1,061	7,793	15,584	1,058	6,129	815	60,851
Widowed	8,125	4,752	4,289	4,661	6,093	2,279	11,681	27,103	3,410	10,689	1,654	95,816
Divorced	29,898	8,339	11,533	10,204	9,572	5,484	14,435	31,532	8,846	15,047	2,850	191,685
Female, 15 years and over	442,168	221,650	181,680	240,909	292,081	125,717	519,025	1,124,419	191,830	466,376	75,244	4,685,102
Single	119,375	60,419	40,078	66,497	91,127	36,045	139,305	313,049	53,696	132,435	21,310	1,293,148
Now married, except separated	233,176	123,171	106,713	133,863	152,116	70,914	290,109	606,656	108,133	253,691	40,001	2,578,114
Separated	9,739	3,004	2,742	2,655	5,981	1,404	11,222	23,779	1,969	9,635	1,234	87,538
Widowed	39,900	22,707	18,006	23,827	28,804	10,268	55,794	134,166	16,199	50,051	8,395	463,378
Divorced	39,978	12,349	14,141	14,067	14,053	7,086	22,595	46,769	11,833	20,564	4,304	262,924
FERTILITY												
Women 15 to 44 years	282,629	129,490	100,953	152,264	177,977	83,347	301,487	633,395	125,565	277,463	42,374	2,883,771
Children ever born	267,937	129,065	101,451	159,554	173,850	90,041	303,084	632,929	134,733	277,462	42,221	2,923,790
Per 1000 women	948	997	1,005	1,048	977	1,080	1,005	999	1,073	1,000	996	1,014

TABLE 5.3

NATIVITY AND LANGUAGE OF PERSONS OF TOTAL ITALIAN ANCESTRY IN THE U.S. AND SELECTED STATES: 1980

	CA	CT	FL	IL	MA	MI	NJ	NY	OH	PA	RI	USA
NATIVITY												
Total Persons	1,144,102	561,542	461,757	640,304	749,583	344,402	1,315,632	2,811,911	520,171	1,205,823	185,080	12,183,692
Native	1,054,615	510,466	424,763	586,894	690,589	314,307	1,207,948	2,507,972	489,432	1,134,225	174,491	11,253,491
Born in State of residence	659,580	414,198	93,398	510,123	608,592	253,663	896,817	2,330,362	396,429	1,013,634	153,647	8,491,246
Born in different State	387,395	94,090	327,676	74,213	79,693	59,301	306,719	167,428	91,208	117,123	20,373	2,703,416
Born abroad	7,640	2,178	3,689	2,558	2,304	1,343	4,412	10,182	1,795	3,468	471	58,829
Foreign Born	89,487	51,076	36,994	53,410	58,994	30,095	107,684	303,939	30,739	71,598	10,589	930,201
LANGUAGE SPOKEN AT HOME												
Persons 5 to 17 years	243,452	126,713	91,840	153,042	176,558	86,939	295,080	609,533	129,592	275,328	40,655	2,773,014
Speak only English at home	228,862	117,118	86,996	142,538	165,774	82,302	274,334	553,839	124,291	263,598	38,671	2,602,720
Speak a language other than English	14,590	9,595	4,844	10,504	10,784	4,637	20,746	55,697	5,301	11,730	1,984	170,286
Italian language spoken at home	7,210	7,964	2,128	8,327	8,505	3,655	16,698	46,350	3,684	8,546	1,519	123,422
Speak English very well	6,870	7,646	1,990	7,976	8,131	3,516	15,859	44,228	3,530	8,236	1,436	117,875
Speak English not well	340	318	138	351	374	139	839	2,122	154	310	83	5,547
Other language spoken at home	7,380	1,631	2,716	2,177	2,279	982	4,048	9,347	1,617	3,184	465	46,864
Speak English very well	6,911	1,549	2,491	2,054	2,084	883	3,850	8,824	1,482	2,992	404	43,734
Speak English not well	469	82	225	123	195	99	198	523	135	192	61	3,130
Persons 18 and over	816,367	397,906	341,531	433,874	521,901	227,413	929,903	2,015,920	343,967	836,717	132,911	8,488,345
Speak only English at home	673,554	314,795	277,857	356,844	423,492	183,609	751,788	1,532,276	294,876	704,187	106,657	6,951,998
Speak a language other than English	142,813	83,111	63,674	77,030	98,409	43,804	178,115	483,644	49,091	132,530	26,254	1,536,347
Italian language spoken at home	112,289	78,655	50,228	70,085	91,885	40,843	166,658	453,601	45,069	124,826	25,041	1,375,724
Speak English very well	99,142	66,613	45,768	58,648	78,686	34,853	140,806	379,671	39,234	108,578	22,057	1,179,092
Speak English not well	13,147	12,042	4,460	11,737	13,199	5,990	25,852	73,930	5,835	16,248	2,984	196,632
Other language spoken at home	30,524	4,456	13,446	6,945	6,524	2,961	11,457	30,043	4,022	7,704	1,213	160,623
Speak English very well	27,820	4,018	12,041	6,247	5,952	2,658	10,113	26,475	3,691	6,966	1,128	145,312
Speak English not well	2,704	438	1,405	698	572	303	1,344	3,568	331	738	85	15,311
MEANS OF TRANSPORTATION												
Workers 16 and over	533,906	264,756	194,522	289,379	340,148	138,103	582,484	1,180,281	216,692	491,185	81,973	5,324,280
Car, truck, or van	465,237	239,675	177,615	237,527	276,253	127,607	501,971	823,792	196,135	399,786	72,586	4,396,126
Drive alone	384,318	189,454	141,437	188,680	212,787	104,124	398,716	624,589	160,896	301,713	56,491	3,434,503
Carpool	80,919	50,221	36,178	48,847	63,466	23,483	103,255	199,203	35,239	98,073	16,095	961,623
Public transportation	23,343	9,580	2,346	30,529	32,319	2,538	39,963	248,900	7,855	41,860	3,459	478,766
Walked only	21,159	10,922	6,641	16,029	25,136	5,461	29,680	83,948	9,063	39,209	4,508	311,413
Other means	15,224	2,207	5,847	2,092	3,012	936	4,578	10,450	1,387	3,222	622	69,450
Worked at home	8,943	2,372	2,073	3,202	3,428	1,561	6,292	13,155	2,252	7,108	798	68,525

TABLE 5.4

EDUCATION, RESIDENCE IN 1975 OF PERSONS OF TOTAL ITALIAN ANCESTRY IN THE U.S. AND SELECTED STATES: 1980

	CA	CT	FL	IL	MA	MI	NJ	NY	OH	PA	RI	USA
SCHOOL ENROLLMENT												
Persons 3 years old and over enrolled	350,583	168,119	122,265	200,403	241,954	116,985	384,272	809,018	169,879	357,882	55,440	3,723,285
Nursery school	18,868	8,227	5,971	9,590	9,590	5,152	18,689	30,861	7,691	13,328	2,152	167,286
Public	5,601	2,362	1,260	3,624	3,187	2,367	5,049	8,875	1,916	3,668	605	48,045
Private	13,267	5,865	4,711	5,946	6,403	2,785	13,640	21,986	5,775	9,660	1,547	119,241
Kindergarten & Elementary (1-8 years)	161,198	83,990	61,354	101,415	117,294	57,878	194,673	401,471	87,201	181,833	26,529	1,844,209
Public	131,738	70,735	49,207	76,821	103,153	48,696	157,578	312,182	63,885	126,623	21,220	1,460,253
Private	29,460	13,255	12,147	24,594	14,141	9,182	37,095	89,289	23,316	55,210	5,309	383,956
High School (1 to 4 years)	82,186	43,850	29,489	51,159	61,196	29,191	101,445	210,809	42,915	93,210	13,979	927,635
Public	71,692	36,676	25,410	40,284	53,251	25,391	85,801	173,879	35,371	71,598	11,702	773,310
Private	10,494	7,174	4,079	10,875	7,945	3,800	15,644	36,930	7,544	21,612	2,277	154,325
College	88,331	32,052	25,451	38,259	53,874	24,764	69,465	165,877	32,072	69,511	12,780	784,155
YEARS OF SCHOOL COMPLETED												
Persons 25 years and over	647,327	322,981	279,166	341,453	411,413	173,478	758,398	1,644,319	264,037	659,175	106,851	6,722,431
Elementary (0 to 8 years)	78,638	70,110	48,949	65,242	70,683	28,465	157,077	358,941	35,936	128,279	22,387	1,199,874
High School: 1 to 3 years	75,493	47,405	45,290	50,291	62,033	25,544	119,972	277,299	43,003	109,715	23,745	1,008,837
4 or more years	226,755	115,711	103,884	126,475	158,684	66,664	286,536	604,596	110,171	271,504	34,650	2,507,599
College: 1 to 3 years	146,326	42,444	43,927	49,365	57,258	26,922	83,572	197,208	35,704	65,570	12,223	967,183
4 or more years	120,115	47,311	37,116	50,080	62,755	25,883	111,241	206,275	39,223	84,107	13,846	1,038,938
Percent High School Graduates	76.2	63.6	66.2	66.2	67.7	68.9	63.5	61.3	70.1	63.9	56.8	67.1
RESIDENCE IN 1975												
Persons 5 years and over	1,069,303	523,846	434,105	581,821	695,648	312,935	1,226,544	2,625,396	470,101	1,114,429	172,623	11,256,132
Same house	499,093	335,625	169,775	327,121	457,420	176,855	804,405	1,773,436	266,105	735,919	114,238	6,517,068
Different house in United States	557,484	185,186	258,568	251,703	234,754	134,046	416,303	836,856	201,749	374,792	57,847	4,655,823
Same County	315,624	129,393	93,784	169,697	151,408	74,545	231,236	535,490	131,607	245,208	40,622	2,606,440
Different County	241,860	55,793	164,784	82,006	83,346	59,501	185,067	301,366	70,142	129,584	17,225	2,049,383
Same State	141,055	27,469	36,327	54,645	53,290	43,765	117,319	242,205	43,553	79,671	9,092	1,063,858
Different State	100,805	28,324	128,457	27,361	30,056	15,736	67,748	59,161	26,589	49,913	8,133	985,525
Abroad	12,726	3,035	5,762	2,997	3,474	2,034	5,836	15,104	2,247	3,718	538	83,241

TABLE 5.5
LABOR FORCE AND OCCUPATION OF PERSONS OF TOTAL ITALIAN ANCESTRY IN THE U.S. AND SELECTED STATES: 1980

	CA	CT	FL	IL	MA	MI	NJ	NY	OH	PA	RI	USA
LABOR FORCE STATUS												
Persons 16 years and over	860,662	420,378	358,178	461,282	553,819	242,690	982,441	2,127,067	366,138	885,780	140,154	8,980,308
Labor force	579,705	283,979	209,474	314,521	367,607	158,249	637,936	1,295,876	241,138	544,333	91,964	5,815,941
Percent of persons 16 years	67.4	67.6	58.5	68.2	66.4	65.2	64.9	60.9	65.9	61.5	65.6	64.8
Civilian labor force	570,142	283,023	205,786	312,898	366,719	157,850	636,204	1,293,604	240,560	543,673	91,561	5,755,125
Employed	538,907	270,028	195,942	295,392	347,793	142,452	595,807	1,210,401	222,673	503,679	84,414	5,403,858
Unemployed	31,235	12,995	9,844	17,506	18,926	15,398	40,397	83,203	17,887	39,994	7,147	351,267
Percent of civilian labor force	5.5	4.6	4.8	5.6	5.2	9.8	6.3	6.4	7.4	7.4	7.8	6.1
Not in labor force	280,957	136,399	148,704	146,761	186,212	84,441	344,505	831,191	124,983	341,447	48,190	3,164,367
Females 16 years and over	431,922	215,997	177,542	234,241	284,720	122,046	506,038	1,097,491	186,238	454,516	73,366	4,565,892
Labor force	242,373	122,313	86,823	130,384	159,348	63,556	264,814	530,441	98,575	221,402	40,930	2,404,690
Percent of females 16 years and over	56.1	56.6	48.9	55.7	56.0	52.1	52.3	48.3	52.9	48.7	55.8	52.7
Civilian labor force	241,542	122,276	86,353	130,185	159,222	63,515	264,640	530,329	98,515	221,348	40,906	2,399,188
Employed	228,323	116,806	81,685	124,070	152,072	58,273	245,996	495,587	92,087	206,204	37,626	2,254,344
Unemployed	13,219	5,470	4,668	6,115	7,150	5,242	18,644	34,742	6,428	15,144	3,280	144,844
Percent of civilian labor force	5.5	4.5	5.4	4.7	4.5	8.3	7.0	6.6	6.5	6.8	8.0	6.0
Not in labor force	189,549	93,684	90,719	103,857	125,372	58,490	241,224	567,050	87,663	233,114	32,436	2,161,202
CLASS OF WORKER AND OCCUPATION												
Employed 16 years and over	538,907	270,028	195,942	295,392	347,793	142,452	595,807	1,210,401	222,673	503,679	84,414	5,403,858
Private wage and salary workers	412,464	216,150	153,865	242,708	270,773	116,346	465,032	934,981	181,310	395,602	65,077	4,210,092
Federal Government workers	15,635	5,650	5,256	5,551	10,714	2,452	17,249	36,680	4,662	17,361	2,263	172,858
State Government workers	16,546	9,529	4,892	7,518	13,851	4,876	17,727	41,867	6,287	15,067	5,415	194,269
Local Government workers	45,304	22,600	15,708	23,605	33,474	11,084	61,795	130,097	18,455	41,157	6,826	484,579
Self-employed workers	46,432	15,320	15,060	15,065	18,143	7,229	32,329	63,621	11,223	32,507	4,539	323,159
Unpaid family workers	2,526	779	1,161	945	838	465	1,675	3,155	736	1,985	294	18,901

TABLE 5.5 (Cont'd)
LABOR FORCE AND OCCUPATION OF PERSONS OF TOTAL ITALIAN ANCESTRY IN THE U.S. AND SELECTED STATES: 1980

	CA	CT	FL	IL	MA	MI	NJ	NY	OH	PA	RI	USA
OCCUPATIONS												
Employed 16 years and over	538,907	270,028	195,942	295,392	347,793	142,452	595,807	1,210,401	222,673	503,679	84,414	5,403,858
Managerial and Professional	138,662	60,439	45,486	64,034	79,971	32,111	139,857	263,196	50,367	105,309	17,292	1,266,556
Execut., Administ., Managerial	72,500	29,287	24,662	34,044	37,052	14,842	72,354	131,474	24,488	48,003	8,319	624,838
Professional Specialty occupations	66,162	31,152	20,824	29,990	42,919	17,269	67,503	131,722	25,879	57,306	8,973	641,718
Technical, Sales, Administrative	193,444	89,163	69,180	103,794	115,167	46,057	210,376	439,226	70,872	160,809	26,811	1,859,253
Technician and related support	16,146	7,500	5,754	7,494	10,726	4,579	15,968	31,147	6,617	14,805	2,167	158,386
Sales Occupations	72,007	28,488	28,195	35,783	35,048	16,403	65,374	132,144	26,241	53,061	8,952	622,783
Administrative Support	105,291	53,175	35,231	60,517	69,393	25,075	129,034	275,935	38,014	92,943	15,692	1,078,084
Service Occupations	65,841	32,585	30,653	36,541	49,410	20,324	69,184	154,643	29,252	66,023	11,500	692,875
Private household occupations	1,428	533	548	482	749	366	898	2,228	376	860	143	11,090
Protective Service occupations	8,788	4,477	4,240	5,714	7,212	1,776	12,890	29,058	3,329	7,994	1,528	102,243
Other Service Occupations	55,625	27,575	25,865	30,345	41,449	18,182	55,396	123,357	25,547	57,169	9,829	579,542
Farming, forestry, fishing	11,564	2,026	2,908	1,678	2,652	969	4,679	9,637	1,668	3,553	636	56,336
Precision Prod., Craft, Repair	66,910	37,944	27,942	38,937	43,116	19,182	77,714	155,008	28,053	69,166	12,368	699,207
Operators, Fabricators, Laborers	62,486	47,871	19,773	50,408	57,477	23,809	93,997	188,691	42,461	98,819	15,807	829,631
Machine Oper., Assembl.	24,186	29,090	7,045	22,298	31,482	13,295	44,892	89,658	22,391	51,250	9,733	401,031
Transportation	18,936	9,084	5,544	12,987	11,412	5,234	24,490	48,555	8,801	21,539	2,614	203,526
Handlers, cleaners, helpers	19,364	9,697	7,184	15,123	14,583	5,280	24,615	50,478	11,269	26,030	3,460	225,074

TABLE 5.6
INDUSTRY, LABOR FORCE IN 1979 OF PERSONS OF TOTAL ITALIAN ANCESTRY IN THE U.S. AND SELECTED STATES: 1980

	CA	CT	FL	IL	MA	MI	NJ	NY	OH	PA	RI	USA
INDUSTRY												
Employed 16 years and over	538,907	270,028	195,942	295,392	347,793	142,452	595,807	1,210,401	222,673	503,679	84,414	5,403,858
Agriculture, Forestry, Fishing	13,798	2,236	3,533	2,987	2,757	1,630	4,847	8,963	2,681	8,188	676	82,137
Construction	32,540	15,552	17,568	16,901	18,971	6,948	34,350	62,714	11,074	27,667	4,119	311,918
Manufacturing	92,070	76,953	21,097	68,303	82,984	38,371	135,292	235,840	60,082	129,344	24,505	1,127,878
Nondurable goods	27,682	19,625	7,293	23,433	29,146	6,834	70,785	107,466	15,811	50,151	5,265	425,541
Durable goods	64,388	57,328	13,804	44,870	53,838	31,537	64,507	128,374	44,271	79,193	19,240	702,337
Transportation	23,261	9,072	8,761	16,224	13,639	4,054	32,451	75,976	7,700	20,962	2,145	254,719
Communications and Public Utilities	15,658	6,730	5,799	7,983	7,454	3,267	16,687	42,618	5,220	10,864	1,311	151,688
Wholesale Trade	26,911	10,225	8,197	15,807	14,185	6,206	30,331	55,292	10,126	20,528	3,408	248,181
Retail Trade	109,935	48,460	47,952	60,352	63,924	30,346	106,923	217,337	46,712	94,111	15,369	1,039,968
Finance, Insurance, Real Estate	43,756	19,657	16,590	21,760	22,629	7,690	43,843	113,327	11,980	29,897	5,041	399,780
Business and Repair Service	29,214	10,846	10,357	13,426	14,180	5,364	31,515	59,449	7,905	18,834	2,697	247,782
Personal, Entertainment, Recreational	28,426	9,691	14,891	11,346	13,848	5,738	24,261	49,319	9,471	21,226	3,260	242,287
Professional and Related Services	98,429	49,384	32,046	46,863	73,112	27,868	102,146	225,131	41,267	97,061	16,490	1,013,408
Health Services	33,013	18,508	12,671	16,481	26,959	10,604	31,012	76,818	15,884	38,002	6,312	356,510
Educational Services	41,342	21,896	12,141	20,005	32,459	11,896	49,272	98,160	17,434	41,337	7,211	442,563
Other Profess. & Related Services	24,074	8,980	7,234	10,377	13,694	5,368	21,862	50,153	7,949	17,722	2,967	214,335
Public Administration	24,909	11,222	9,151	13,443	20,110	4,970	33,161	64,435	8,455	24,997	5,393	284,112
LABOUR FORCE STATUS IN 1979												
Persons 16 ys. in Labor Force in 1979	626,452	305,773	229,696	340,592	398,955	174,860	682,771	1,396,164	265,601	597,526	99,955	6,333,395
Worked in 1979	618,964	301,991	226,504	336,493	393,968	171,969	671,737	1,368,188	261,838	585,657	98,685	6,237,671
50 to 52 weeks	364,782	190,699	131,235	205,845	241,578	96,983	420,368	861,800	155,625	351,782	58,205	3,778,810
40 to 49 weeks	94,099	38,824	33,225	47,248	48,946	25,356	85,644	169,642	34,472	72,510	13,208	823,247
1 to 39 weeks	160,083	72,468	62,044	83,400	103,444	49,630	165,725	336,746	71,741	161,365	27,272	1,635,614
35 or more hours per week	467,696	229,221	176,966	255,639	288,739	129,409	521,174	1,057,894	199,031	453,306	72,167	4,785,584
50 to 52 weeks	317,841	165,366	117,352	179,658	205,742	84,432	370,185	754,281	135,719	309,451	48,988	3,311,287
With unemployment in 1979	118,182	48,812	45,570	57,944	65,538	37,949	128,716	261,367	49,599	114,844	19,150	1,171,172
Unemployed 15 or more weeks	37,742	16,433	14,211	18,614	23,676	13,818	55,273	111,660	16,134	46,053	7,484	423,847
Mean weeks of unemployment	13	14	13	13	14	14	16	16	13	16	15	14
WORKERS IN FAMILY IN 1979												
Families	282,395	144,177	129,345	156,089	183,750	81,001	338,989	723,591	124,299	300,782	48,192	3,043,694
No Workers	33,520	14,548	28,469	13,180	19,363	8,709	35,040	92,327	10,981	36,164	5,740	338,747
1 worker	93,744	42,504	40,366	50,386	56,908	26,833	110,894	253,501	43,227	106,470	14,671	1,010,918
2 or more workers	155,131	87,125	60,510	92,523	107,479	45,459	193,055	377,763	70,091	158,148	27,781	1,694,029

TABLE 5.7

INCOME CHARACTERISTICS OF PERSONS OF TOTAL ITALIAN ANCESTRY IN THE U.S. AND SELECTED STATES: 1980

		CA	CT	FL	IL	MA	MI	NJ	NY	OH	PA	RI	USA
INCOME IN 1979													
HOUSEHOLDS		414,889	182,362	173,531	203,889	238,766	104,436	421,195	932,662	160,008	381,327	61,493	3,993,912
Less than $5,000		39,689	15,521	18,994	15,415	26,484	8,364	35,346	100,843	13,772	39,454	7,544	384,327
$5,000 to $7,499		26,732	10,709	15,245	10,421	16,697	5,928	24,986	66,265	9,318	27,259	5,013	264,805
$7,500 to $9,999		27,662	11,556	16,482	10,948	16,301	5,963	24,827	61,800	10,206	27,954	4,988	267,696
$10,000 to $14,999		58,169	24,649	32,331	24,239	33,395	11,967	54,780	130,483	21,660	57,487	9,572	568,004
$15,000 to $19,999		54,038	28,271	26,608	26,793	35,894	13,702	59,825	134,678	24,809	60,726	9,639	582,935
$20,000 to $24,999		53,012	26,794	21,120	29,624	33,847	14,395	58,562	130,394	24,300	54,661	8,522	555,361
$25,000 to $34,999		76,913	36,377	23,662	45,343	43,557	21,915	86,187	171,710	32,436	67,327	9,655	746,937
$35,000 to $49,999		48,770	19,743	12,111	27,564	23,097	14,861	51,660	95,615	16,517	32,272	4,574	419,279
$50,000 or more		29,904	8,742	6,978	13,542	9,494	7,341	25,022	40,874	6,990	14,187	1,986	204,568
Median	Dol.	20,095	20,080	15,611	22,122	18,626	22,060	20,841	18,916	20,045	18,091	16,801	19,362
Mean	Dol.	23,782	22,528	19,095	24,939	20,894	24,984	23,527	21,340	22,194	20,500	19,362	22,146
FAMILIES		282,395	144,177	129,345	156,089	183,750	81,001	338,989	723,591	124,299	300,782	48,192	3,043,694
Less than $5,000		13,457	5,480	7,446	5,658	9,609	3,292	13,489	36,305	5,034	14,743	2,794	141,672
$5,000 to $7,499		12,853	6,120	9,590	4,887	9,998	3,478	14,120	37,770	5,000	15,607	2,991	147,216
$7,500 to $9,999		15,190	7,125	11,232	5,967	10,460	3,693	16,499	41,494	6,348	18,756	3,362	169,660
$10,000 to $14,999		33,786	17,435	24,139	14,975	23,951	8,231	40,078	96,017	14,579	43,303	7,432	395,618
$15,000 to $19,999		36,336	23,346	21,238	20,061	29,442	10,160	49,629	109,820	19,719	51,882	8,384	460,969
$20,000 to $24,999		39,493	24,085	18,010	24,936	29,939	11,918	52,169	116,175	21,436	49,436	7,884	478,746
$25,000 to $34,999		63,057	33,745	20,664	41,159	10,024	19,757	80,369	159,149	29,900	62,937	9,155	675,612
$35,000 to $49,999		42,252	18,645	10,917	25,868	21,566	13,537	48,948	89,423	15,694	30,915	4,326	387,223
$50,000 or more		25,971	8,194	6,109	12,578	8,761	6,935	23,691	37,438	6,589	13,203	1,864	186,978
Median	Dol.	23,598	22,380	17,595	25,307	21,258	24,882	23,273	21,564	22,468	20,547	19,478	21,960
Mean	Dol.	27,375	25,072	21,236	28,068	23,512	27,755	26,059	23,964	24,863	22,941	21,900	24,841

TABLE 5.7 (Cont'd)
INCOME CHARACTERISTICS OF PERSONS OF TOTAL ITALIAN ANCESTRY IN THE U.S. AND SELECTED STATES: 1980

	CA	CT	FL	IL	MA	MI	NJ	NY	OH	PA	RI	USA
Unrelated Individuals, 15 years....	193,053	53,790	63,411	65,788	81,573	35,295	107,174	275,919	52,067	117,489	18,808	1,381,557
Less than $2,000	19,504	7,287	8,359	7,520	12,817	4,498	11,209	36,371	7,875	22,500	2,891	191,412
$2,000 to $2,999	8,616	3,599	4,198	4,615	6,126	2,755	6,912	18,587	4,200	10,353	1,909	97,281
$3,000 to $4,999	28,822	9,102	10,513	9,311	16,379	5,771	18,944	55,129	8,479	21,643	4,405	233,864
$5,000 to $7,999	31,472	8,094	12,013	9,548	11,977	5,000	17,161	43,568	7,395	18,090	3,258	221,324
$8,000 to $9,999	17,505	5,164	6,581	5,533	7,020	2,730	8,930	20,894	4,318	9,233	1,562	117,162
$10,000 to $14,999	36,633	9,979	10,938	12,241	13,565	5,373	19,814	43,801	9,176	17,434	2,405	234,389
$15,000 to $24,999	35,450	8,351	7,913	12,585	10,782	6,846	17,896	42,530	8,511	14,287	1,845	212,315
$25,000 to $49,999	12,697	1,901	2,246	3,867	2,605	2,089	5,578	13,149	1,837	3,365	414	63,556
$50,000 or more	2,354	313	650	568	302	233	730	1,890	276	584	119	10,254
Median Dol.	8,893	7,511	7,133	8,633	6,238	7,762	7,877	6,764	7,121	5,598	5,161	7,179
Mean Dol.	11,357	9,446	9,159	10,929	8,418	10,508	10,143	9,479	9,259	8,029	7,580	9,607
Per Capita Income Dol.	8,753	7,479	7,200	8,092	6,782	7,766	7,618	7,128	7,028	6,618	6,586	7,371
Per Capita Income, Noninstitutional Persons Dol.	8,782	7,508	7,220	8,114	6,805	7,795	7,640	7,155	7,048	6,638	6,595	7,395
Mean Family Income By Worker												
No Workers Dol.	12,774	10,036	12,498	10,680	8,628	10,259	9,927	9,388	9,394	9,177	8,801	10,241
1 Worker Dol.	24,096	20,933	19,749	23,405	19,089	24,126	22,215	20,311	21,581	19,737	18,005	21,281
2 or more workers Dol.	32,511	29,601	26,340	33,085	28,535	33,249	31,194	29,977	29,311	28,245	2,664	29,886

TABLE 5.8
POVERTY CHARACTERISTICS OF PERSONS OF TOTAL ITALIAN ANCESTRY IN THE U.S. AND SELECTED STATES: 1980

	CA	CT	FL	IL	MA	MI	NJ	NY	OH	PA	RI	USA
ALL INCOME LEVEL IN 1979												
Families	282,395	144,177	129,345	156,089	183,750	81,001	338,989	723,591	124,299	300,782	48,192	3,043,694
With Children under 18 years	140,903	71,394	55,024	82,402	93,966	44,810	169,001	356,562	68,036	151,251	23,335	1,562,272
With Children 5 to 17 years	109,838	57,979	44,358	64,888	76,115	35,272	136,853	290,536	53,040	119,921	18,830	1,239,800
Female Householder, no husband	34,027	16,129	12,169	15,937	23,432	8,197	37,192	83,735	12,813	34,005	6,698	337,678
With Children under 18 ys.	21,663	8,346	7,529	8,547	12,785	5,140	18,121	40,537	7,376	16,897	3,648	187,071
With Children under 6 years	6,884	2,417	2,115	2,496	3,766	1,793	4,995	11,774	2,343	5,161	1,068	57,803
Householder 65 years and over	40,140	22,911	30,228	20,799	28,473	10,402	51,808	118,725	15,079	46,837	8,152	446,424
Unrelat. Individ. in pov.	182,534	47,847	59,236	59,142	70,251	31,160	100,373	253,724	45,825	99,707	15,908	1,227,168
65 years and over	30,591	13,158	13,290	13,937	17,876	5,858	29,223	76,347	8,742	27,125	4,943	276,616
Persons in poverty univ.	1,123,654	551,399	454,594	630,590	733,878	337,885	1,302,329	2,771,505	510,954	1,181,012	181,477	11,951,890
Related children under 18	321,135	162,327	118,207	204,774	225,851	115,939	383,173	789,687	174,589	365,432	51,627	3,654,934
Related children 5 to 17	238,059	125,623	90,189	151,681	175,012	86,133	292,943	604,069	128,233	272,254	40,222	2,739,170
60 years and over	148,732	83,758	93,877	78,156	104,197	35,840	191,548	443,398	55,097	167,143	30,538	1,627,298
65 years and over	103,666	56,695	67,069	53,611	69,639	24,272	129,374	303,693	36,004	111,887	20,092	1,105,336
INCOME IN 1979 BELOW POVERTY LEVEL												
Families	15,897	6,572	8,586	6,644	12,166	4,071	16,121	44,707	6,147	18,037	3,379	173,600
Percent Below Poverty Level	5.6	4.6	6.6	4.3	6.6	5.0	4.8	6.2	4.9	6.0	7.0	5.7
With Children under 18 years	10,867	4,544	4,703	4,649	8,853	3,016	10,879	30,462	4,470	12,600	2,563	120,847
With Children 5 to 17 years	8,014	3,499	3,613	3,420	6,801	2,271	8,454	23,895	3,317	9,742	1,973	91,521
Female Householder, no husband	6,408	2,951	2,240	2,653	5,692	1,805	6,535	17,707	2,700	7,491	1,693	69,813
With Children under 18 ys.	6,592	2,618	1,862	2,291	4,984	1,623	5,504	14,859	2,369	6,372	1,527	60,518
With Children under 6 years	2,980	1,292	841	1,192	2,331	897	2,509	6,790	1,234	2,764	726	29,494
Householder 65 years and over	2,047	1,082	2,004	926	1,744	496	2,556	7,079	773	2,453	391	24,922
Unrelat. Individ. in pov.	31,937	8,939	13,648	10,665	14,662	6,341	19,121	56,136	10,128	25,534	4,380	259,669
Percent Below Poverty Level	17.5	18.7	23.0	18.0	20.9	20.3	19.0	22.1	22.1	25.6	27.5	21.2
65 years and over	5,030	3,222	3,394	2,897	3,999	1,358	7,452	19,230	2,124	7,408	1,651	67,420
Persons in poverty univ.	83,715	31,424	40,212	34,472	58,520	21,309	74,194	211,244	33,302	92,204	15,949	869,130
Percent Below Poverty Level	7.5	5.7	8.8	5.5	8	6.3	5.7	7.6	6.5	7.8	8.8	7.3
Related children under 18	24,509	11,114	10,742	11,703	22,803	8,000	26,207	72,470	12,259	33,711	5,940	298,899
Related children 5 to 17	17,036	8,079	7,767	8,221	17,086	5,516	19,425	53,675	8,388	24,395	4,439	214,043
60 years and over	11,391	6,703	8,642	5,958	9,299	2,953	15,693	41,776	4,639	15,700	3,071	145,375
65 years and over	8,556	5,187	6,512	4,560	6,964	2,123	11,918	31,508	3,423	11,511	2,349	109,561

APPENDIX F

Population of Italian Ancestry by Education

Source: *Census of Population, 1980: Unpublished Special Tabulations on the Italian Population.* Washington: The Bureau of the Census, 1987.

TABLE 6.1
RESIDENCE, AGE, AND RELATIONSHIP OF PERSONS OF TOTAL ITALIAN ANCESTRY IN THE UNITED STATES BY EDUCATION: 1980

	Less Than 12 Years of School			High School Graduates			College Graduates			All Persons		
	Male	Female	Total	Male	Female	Total	Male	Female	Total	Male	Female	Total
Urban and Rural												
Total Persons	3,074,355	3,102,692	6,177,047	2,246,652	2,579,880	4,826,532	732,949	447,164	1,180,113	6,053,956	6,129,736	12,183,692
Urban	2,644,264	2,700,379	5,344,643	1,970,233	2,273,640	4,243,873	644,891	392,589	1,037,480	5,259,388	5,366,608	10,625,996
Rural	430,091	402,313	832,404	276,419	306,240	582,659	88,058	54,575	142,633	794,568	763,128	1,557,696
Farm	16,273	14,394	30,667	10,633	11,743	22,376	2,840	2,100	4,940	29,746	28,237	57,983
Age												
Total Persons	3,074,355	3,102,692	6,177,047	2,246,652	2,579,880	4,826,532	732,949	447,164	1,180,113	6,053,956	6,129,736	12,183,692
under 5 years	472,978	449,355	922,333	0	0	0	0	0	0	472,978	449,355	922,333
5 to 9 years	483,521	459,074	942,595	0	0	0	0	0	0	483,521	459,074	942,595
10 to 14 years	559,035	536,205	1,095,240	0	0	0	0	0	0	559,035	536,205	1,095,240
15 to 19 years	454,696	420,674	875,370	175,184	195,929	371,113	47	52	99	629,927	616,655	1,246,582
20 to 24 years	73,943	58,855	132,798	480,681	499,956	980,637	72,829	68,247	141,076	627,453	627,058	1,254,511
25 to 29 years	52,037	47,409	99,446	334,833	368,417	703,250	161,763	126,217	287,980	548,633	542,043	1,090,676
30 to 34 years	48,602	50,757	99,359	269,954	329,111	599,065	160,792	96,629	257,421	479,348	476,497	955,845
35 to 44 years	115,871	115,963	231,834	354,718	425,320	780,038	160,155	80,235	240,390	630,744	621,518	1,252,262
45 to 54 years	187,939	184,102	372,041	283,148	352,386	635,534	94,556	38,339	132,895	565,643	574,827	1,140,470
55 to 59 years	128,483	134,565	263,048	142,952	173,070	316,022	35,782	12,982	48,764	307,217	320,617	627,834
60 to 64 years	132,492	153,732	286,224	100,053	110,086	210,139	19,601	8,587	28,188	252,146	272,405	524,551
65 to 74 years	232,908	301,625	534,533	83,740	97,485	181,225	21,586	11,879	33,465	338,234	410,989	749,223
75 to 84 years	102,129	150,112	252,241	17,728	23,166	40,894	5,110	3,240	8,350	124,967	176,518	301,485
85 years and over	29,721	40,264	69,985	3,661	4,954	8,615	728	757	1,485	34,110	45,975	80,085
median age	15.2	16.3	15.7	32.5	33.4	33.0	34.1	31.5	33.1	27.3	28.4	27.9
Household Type and Relationship												
In Household	3,046,291	3,081,281	6,127,572	2,153,134	2,506,151	4,659,285	725,547	441,733	1,167,280	5,924,972	6,029,165	11,954,137
Family Householder	817,947	157,043	974,990	1,309,446	235,741	1,545,187	484,343	39,174	523,517	2,611,736	431,958	3,043,694
Non-family Householder: Male	102,376	0	102,376	217,417	0	217,417	113,011	0	113,011	432,804	0	432,804
Female	0	226,459	226,459	0	216,128	216,128	0	74,827	74,827	0	517,414	517,414
Spouse	31,595	673,957	705,552	42,801	1,489,742	1,532,543	20,998	246,072	267,070	95,394	2,409,771	2,505,165
Other Relatives	2,061,136	1,989,837	4,050,973	505,943	480,064	986,007	80,026	58,857	138,883	2,647,105	2,528,758	5,175,863
Nonrelatives	33,237	33,985	67,222	77,527	84,476	162,003	27,169	22,803	49,972	137,933	141,264	279,197

TABLE 6.2

SELECTED DEMOGRAPHIC CHARACTERISTICS OF PERSONS OF TOTAL ITALIAN ANCESTRY IN THE UNITED STATES BY EDUCATION

	Less Than 12 Years of School			High School Graduates			College Graduates			All Persons		
	Male	Female	Total	Male	Female	Total	Male	Female	Total	Male	Female	Total
PERSONS IN HOUSEHOLDS												
HOUSEHOLDS	920,323	383,502	1,303,825	1,526,863	451,869	1,978,732	597,354	114,001	711,355	3,044,540	949,372	3,993,912
1 person	88,984	218,992	307,976	153,896	178,607	332,503	84,835	58,812	143,647	327,715	456,411	784,126
2 persons	384,050	90,967	475,017	440,338	134,892	575,230	169,021	34,499	203,520	993,409	260,358	1,253,767
3 persons	178,966	40,270	219,236	313,842	76,411	390,253	108,875	12,083	120,958	601,683	128,764	730,447
4 persons	137,932	18,712	156,644	342,029	38,821	380,850	132,628	5,632	138,260	612,589	63,165	675,754
5 persons	78,669	8,806	87,475	181,373	15,399	196,772	67,188	1,981	69,169	327,230	26,186	353,416
6 persons	51,722	5,755	57,477	95,385	7,739	103,124	34,807	994	35,801	181,914	14,488	196,402
TYPE OF GROUP QUARTERS												
Persons in Group Quarters	28,064	21,411	49,475	93,518	73,729	167,247	7,402	5,431	12,833	128,984	100,571	229,555
Inmate of Mental Hospital	3,004	2,167	5,171	1,767	1,184	2,951	220	92	312	4,991	3,443	8,434
Inmate of Home for Aged	7,005	12,872	19,877	1,913	3,972	5,885	402	533	935	9,320	17,377	26,697
Inmate of Other Institution	9,749	3,683	13,432	6,034	936	6,970	438	112	550	16,221	4,731	20,952
In Military Quarters	4,864	277	5,141	18,486	1,928	20,414	1,053	170	1,223	24,403	2,375	26,778
In College Dormitory	341	232	573	61,363	61,333	122,696	3,077	1,530	4,607	64,781	63,095	127,876
Other in Group Quarters	3,101	2,180	5,281	3,955	4,376	8,331	2,212	2,994	5,206	9,268	9,550	18,818
MARITAL STATUS												
Persons, 15 years and over	1,558,821	1,658,058	3,216,879	2,246,652	2,579,880	4,826,532	732,949	447,164	1,180,113	4,538,422	4,685,102	9,223,524
Single	578,647	499,616	1,078,263	745,308	658,325	1,403,633	183,476	135,207	318,683	1,507,431	1,293,148	2,800,579
Now married, except separated	843,905	728,695	1,572,600	1,338,826	1,581,087	2,919,913	499,908	268,332	768,240	2,682,639	2,578,114	5,260,753
Separated	18,871	28,663	47,534	31,822	52,056	83,878	10,158	6,819	16,977	60,851	87,538	148,389
Widowed	67,652	335,164	402,816	23,062	117,697	140,759	5,102	10,517	15,619	95,816	463,378	559,194
Divorced	49,746	65,920	115,666	107,634	170,715	278,349	34,305	26,289	60,594	191,685	262,924	454,609
FERTILITY												
Women 15 to 44 years	0	693,658	693,658	0	1,818,733	1,818,733	0	371,380	371,380	0	2,883,771	2,883,771
Children ever born	0	572,806	572,806	0	2,062,010	2,062,010	0	288,974	288,974	0	2,923,790	2,923,790
Per 1000 women	0	826	826	0	1,134	1,134	0	778	778	0	1,014	1,014

TABLE 6.3
NATIVITY AND LANGUAGE OF PERSONS OF TOTAL ITALIAN ANCESTRY IN THE UNITED STATES BY EDUCATION: 1980

	Less Than 12 Years of School			High School Graduates			College Graduates			All Persons		
	Male	Female	Total	Male	Female	Total	Male	Female	Total	Male	Female	Total
NATIVITY												
Total Persons	3,074,355	3,102,692	6,177,047	2,246,652	2,579,880	4,826,532	732,949	447,164	1,180,113	6,053,956	6,129,736	12,183,692
Native	2,783,077	2,767,146	5,550,223	2,120,401	2,458,611	4,579,012	696,186	428,070	1,124,256	5,599,664	5,653,827	11,253,491
Born in State of residence	2,254,276	2,231,219	4,485,495	1,535,283	1,786,755	3,322,038	418,015	265,698	683,713	4,207,574	4,283,672	8,491,246
Born in different State	512,359	520,653	1,033,012	574,881	661,588	1,236,469	274,023	159,912	433,935	1,361,263	1,342,153	2,703,416
Born abroad	16,442	15,274	31,716	10,237	10,268	20,505	4,148	2,460	6,608	30,827	28,002	58,829
Foreign Born	291,278	335,546	626,824	125,251	121,269	247,520	36,763	19,094	55,857	454,292	475,909	930,201
LANGUAGE SPOKEN AT HOME												
Persons 5 to 17 years	1,411,488	1,348,683	2,760,171	5,195	7,635	12,830	6	7	13	1,416,689	1,356,325	2,773,014
Speak only English at home	1,328,208	1,263,141	2,591,349	4,577	6,781	11,358	6	7	13	1,332,791	1,269,929	2,602,720
Speak a language other than English	83,280	85,534	168,814	618	854	1,472	0	0	0	83,898	86,388	170,286
Italian language spoken at home	61,479	60,966	122,445	442	535	977	0	0	0	61,921	61,501	123,422
Speak English very well	58,686	58,230	116,916	442	517	959	0	0	0	59,128	58,747	117,875
Speak English not well	2,793	2,736	5,529	0	18	18	0	0	0	2,793	2,754	5,547
Other language spoken at home	21,801	24,568	46,369	176	319	495	0	0	0	21,977	24,887	46,864
Speak English very well	20,367	22,933	43,300	147	287	434	0	0	0	20,514	23,220	43,734
Speak English not well	1,434	1,635	3,069	29	32	61	0	0	0	1,463	1,667	3,130
Persons 18 and over	1,189,889	1,304,654	2,494,543	2,241,457	2,572,245	4,813,702	732,943	447,157	1,180,100	4,164,289	4,324,056	8,488,345
Speak only English at home	821,947	814,404	1,636,351	1,984,584	2,271,649	4,256,233	657,312	402,102	1,059,414	3,463,843	3,488,155	6,951,998
Speak a language other than English	367,942	490,250	858,192	256,873	300,596	557,469	75,631	45,055	120,686	700,446	835,901	1,536,347
Italian language spoken at home	349,328	466,668	815,996	216,355	254,651	471,006	56,453	32,269	88,722	622,136	753,588	1,375,724
Speak English very well	286,636	365,680	652,316	203,588	238,396	441,984	54,231	30,561	84,792	544,455	634,637	1,179,092
Speak English not well	62,692	100,988	163,680	12,767	16,255	29,022	2,222	1,708	3,930	77,681	118,951	196,632
Other language spoken at home	18,614	23,582	42,196	40,518	45,945	86,463	19,178	12,786	31,964	78,310	82,313	160,623
Speak English very well	15,432	19,224	34,656	37,778	42,512	80,290	18,275	12,091	30,366	71,485	73,827	145,312
Speak English not well	3,182	4,358	7,540	2,740	3,433	6,173	903	695	1,598	6,825	8,486	15,311
MEANS OF TRANSPORTATION												
Workers 16 and over	709,065	425,558	1,134,623	1,764,532	1,448,512	3,213,044	657,453	319,160	976,613	3,131,050	2,193,230	5,324,280
Car, truck, or van	581,145	302,483	883,628	1,525,967	1,171,682	2,697,649	551,203	263,646	814,849	2,658,315	1,737,811	4,396,126
Drive alone	457,450	190,703	648,153	1,230,984	898,393	2,129,377	448,973	208,000	656,973	2,137,407	1,297,096	3,434,503
Carpool	123,695	111,780	235,475	294,983	273,289	568,272	102,230	55,646	157,876	520,908	440,715	961,623
Public transportation	55,515	61,013	116,528	111,703	156,762	268,465	62,755	31,018	93,773	229,973	248,793	478,766
Walked only	50,639	51,653	102,292	80,392	88,989	169,381	23,557	16,183	39,740	154,588	156,825	311,413
Other means	13,293	4,175	17,468	29,378	10,409	39,787	9,665	2,530	12,195	52,336	17,114	69,450
Worked at home	8,473	6,234	14,707	17,092	20,670	37,762	10,273	5,783	16,056	35,838	32,687	68,525

TABLE 6.4
EDUCATION, RESIDENCE IN 1975 OF PERSONS OF TOTAL ITALIAN ANCESTRY IN THE UNITED STATES BY EDUCATION: 1980

	Less Than 12 Years of School			High School Graduates			College Graduates			All Persons		
	Male	Female	Total	Male	Female	Total	Male	Female	Total	Male	Female	Total
School Enrollment												
Persons 3 years old and over enrolled	1,505,347	1,433,783	2,939,130	330,602	321,409	652,011	77,349	54,795	132,144	1,913,298	1,809,987	3,723,285
Nursery school	86,880	80,406	167,286	0	0	0	0	0	0	86,880	80,406	167,286
Public	25,302	22,743	48,045	0	0	0	0	0	0	25,302	22,743	48,045
Private	61,578	57,663	119,241	0	0	0	0	0	0	61,578	57,663	119,241
Kindergarten& Elementary (1-8 years)	948,581	895,628	1,844,209	0	0	0	0	0	0	948,581	895,628	1,844,209
Public	756,874	703,379	1,460,253	0	0	0	0	0	0	756,874	703,379	1,460,253
Private	191,707	192,249	383,956	0	0	0	0	0	0	191,707	192,249	383,956
High School (1 to 4 years)	469,886	457,749	927,635	0	0	0	0	0	0	469,886	457,749	927,635
Public	392,372	380,938	773,310	0	0	0	0	0	0	392,372	380,938	773,310
Private	77,514	76,811	154,325	0	0	0	0	0	0	77,514	76,811	154,325
College	0	0	0	330,602	321,409	652,011	77,349	54,795	132,144	407,951	376,204	784,155
Years of School Completed												
Persons 25 years and over	1,030,182	1,178,529	2,208,711	1,590,787	1,883,995	3,474,782	660,073	378,865	1,038,938	3,281,042	3,441,389	6,722,431
Elementary (0 to 8 years)	544,535	655,339	1,199,874	0	0	0	0	0	0	544,535	655,339	1,199,874
High School: 1 to 3 years	485,647	523,190	1,008,837	0	0	0	0	0	0	485,647	523,190	1,008,837
4 or more years	0	0	0	1,060,467	1,447,132	2,507,599	0	0	0	1,060,467	1,447,132	2,507,599
College: 1 to 3 years	0	0	0	530,320	436,863	967,183	0	0	0	530,320	436,863	967,183
4 or more years	0	0	0	0	0	0	660,073	378,865	1,038,938	660,073	378,865	1,038,938
Percent High School Graduates	0	0	0	100.0	100.0	100.0	100.0	100.0	100.0	68.6	65.8	67.1
Residence in 1975 *												
Persons 5 years and over	2,598,730	2,646,929	5,245,659	2,247,020	2,582,863	4,829,883	732,644	447,946	1,180,590	5,578,394	5,677,738	11,256,132
Same house	1,681,306	1,742,555	3,423,861	1,196,696	1,412,221	2,608,917	309,102	175,188	484,290	3,187,104	3,329,964	6,517,068
Different house in United States	900,128	886,410	1,786,538	1,031,090	1,156,422	2,187,512	414,146	267,627	681,773	2,345,364	2,310,459	4,655,823
Same County	538,994	540,392	1,079,386	568,643	652,746	1,221,389	183,883	121,782	305,665	1,291,520	1,314,920	2,606,440
Different County	361,134	346,018	707,152	462,447	503,676	966,123	230,263	145,845	376,108	1,053,844	995,539	2,049,383
Same State	185,949	178,969	364,918	241,464	276,989	518,453	106,511	73,976	180,487	533,924	529,934	1,063,858
Different State	175,185	167,049	342,234	220,983	226,687	447,670	123,752	71,869	195,621	519,920	465,605	985,525
Abroad	17,296	17,964	35,260	19,234	14,220	33,454	9,396	5,131	14,527	45,926	37,315	83,241

* Data on residence in 1975 are based on approximately one-half of the full census sample. Therefore, figures in tabulations involving residence in 1975 may differ from tabulations based on the full sample. For example, the number of persons 5 years old and over derived from residence in 1975 tabulations may not agree with other tabulations by age. (This applies also to Tables 4.4, 5.4, 6.12, 6.20, 6.28, 6.36).

TABLE 6.5

LABOR FORCE AND OCCUPATION OF PERSONS OF TOTAL ITALIAN ANCESTRY IN THE UNITED STATES BY EDUCATION: 1980

	Less Than 12 Years of School			High School Graduates			College Graduates			All Persons		
	Male	Female	Total	Male	Female	Total	Male	Female	Total	Male	Female	Total
Labor Force Status												
Persons 16 years and over	1,434,931	1,538,928	2,973,859	2,246,536	2,579,800	4,826,336	732,949	447,164	1,180,113	4,414,416	4,565,892	8,980,308
Labor force	814,533	495,537	1,310,070	1,916,946	1,571,953	3,488,899	679,772	337,200	1,016,972	3,411,251	2,404,690	5,815,941
Percent of persons 16 years	56.8	32.2	44.1	85.3	60.9	72.3	92.7	75.4	86.2	77.3	52.7	64.8
Civilian labor force	808,081	495,151	1,303,232	1,878,317	1,567,715	3,446,032	669,539	336,322	1,005,861	3,355,937	2,399,188	5,755,125
Employed	730,104	443,635	1,173,739	1,764,431	1,484,286	3,248,717	654,979	326,423	981,402	3,149,514	2,254,344	5,403,858
Unemployed	77,977	51,516	129,493	113,886	83,429	197,315	14,560	9,899	24,459	206,423	144,844	351,267
Percent of civ. labor force	9.6	10.4	9.9	6.1	5.3	5.7	2.2	2.9	2.4	6.2	6.0	6.1
Not in labor force	620,398	1,043,391	1,663,789	329,590	1,007,847	1,337,437	53,177	109,964	163,141	1,003,165	2,161,202	3,164,367
Class of Worker and Occupation												
Employed 16 years and ov.	730,104	443,635	1,173,739	1,764,431	1,484,286	3,248,717	654,979	326,423	981,402	3,149,514	2,254,344	5,403,858
Private wage and salary work.	581,956	388,619	970,575	1,396,487	1,229,780	2,626,267	431,283	181,967	613,250	2,409,726	1,800,366	4,210,092
Federal Government workers	17,114	5,167	22,281	67,660	42,386	110,046	31,214	9,317	40,531	115,988	56,870	172,858
State Government workers	12,485	8,664	21,149	44,944	60,032	104,976	41,789	26,355	68,144	99,218	95,051	194,269
Local Government workers	47,044	25,436	72,480	118,353	104,782	223,135	91,704	97,260	188,964	257,101	227,478	484,579
Self-employed workers	69,301	13,084	82,385	133,846	38,498	172,344	58,330	10,100	68,430	261,477	61,682	323,159
Unpaid family workers	2,204	2,665	4,869	3,141	8,808	11,949	659	1,424	2,083	6,004	12,897	18,901
Employed 16 years and over	730,104	443,635	1,173,739	1,764,431	1,484,286	3,248,717	654,979	326,423	981,402	3,149,514	2,254,344	5,403,858
Managerial and Professional	53,765	20,212	73,977	312,648	214,131	526,779	438,786	227,014	665,800	805,199	461,357	1,266,556
Execut., Administ., Manag.	44,924	13,436	58,360	224,386	114,918	339,304	185,906	41,268	227,174	455,216	169,622	624,838
Professional Specialty occupations	8,841	6,776	15,617	88,262	99,213	187,475	252,880	185,746	438,626	349,983	291,735	641,718
Technical, Sales, Administrative	104,798	168,753	273,551	440,416	926,786	1,367,202	137,392	81,108	218,500	682,606	1,176,647	1,859,253
Technician and related support	5,325	3,242	8,567	66,043	44,262	110,305	24,621	14,893	39,514	95,989	62,397	158,386
Sales Occupations	56,577	80,965	137,542	200,939	191,669	392,608	72,966	19,667	92,633	330,482	292,301	622,783
Administrative Support	42,896	84,546	127,442	173,434	690,855	864,289	39,805	46,548	86,353	256,135	821,949	1,078,084
Service Occupations	128,185	123,261	251,446	189,400	215,668	405,068	24,162	12,199	36,361	341,747	351,128	692,875
Private household occupations	348	5,285	5,633	428	4,662	5,090	75	292	367	851	10,239	11,090
Protective Service occupations	14,171	2,913	17,084	65,663	6,698	72,361	11,920	878	12,798	91,754	10,489	102,243
Other Service Occupations	113,666	115,063	228,729	123,309	204,308	327,617	12,167	11,029	23,196	249,142	330,400	579,542
Farming, forestry, fishing	18,306	2,323	20,629	25,944	5,297	31,241	3,874	592	4,466	48,124	8,212	56,336
Precision Prod., Craft, Repair	187,696	19,095	206,791	430,419	26,596	457,015	33,107	2,294	35,401	651,222	47,985	699,207
Operators, Fabricators, Laborers	237,354	109,991	347,345	365,604	95,808	461,412	17,658	3,216	20,874	620,616	209,015	829,631
Machine Oper., Assembl.	85,650	87,283	172,933	151,798	67,332	219,130	6,791	2,177	8,968	244,239	156,792	401,031
Transportation	71,132	3,798	74,930	113,954	8,571	122,525	5,657	414	6,071	190,743	12,783	203,526
Handlers, cleaners, helpers	80,572	18,910	99,482	99,852	19,905	119,757	5,210	625	5,835	185,634	39,440	225,074

TABLE 6.6
INDUSTRY, LABOR FORCE IN 1979 OF PERSONS OF TOTAL ITALIAN ANCESTRY IN THE UNITED STATES BY EDUCATION: 1980

	LESS THAN 12 YEARS OF SCHOOL			HIGH SCHOOL GRADUATES			COLLEGE GRADUATES			ALL PERSONS		
	Male	Female	Total	Male	Female	Total	Male	Female	Total	Male	Female	Total
INDUSTRY												
Employed 16 years and over	730,104	443,635	1,173,739	1,764,431	1,484,286	3,248,717	654,979	326,423	981,402	3,149,514	2,254,344	5,403,858
Agriculture, Forestry, Fishing	20,046	2,980	23,026	37,087	10,719	47,806	9,495	1,810	11,305	66,628	15,509	82,137
Construction	87,207	3,316	90,523	175,505	20,170	195,675	23,739	1,981	25,720	286,451	25,467	311,918
Manufacturing	184,311	120,113	304,424	449,726	225,765	675,491	125,549	22,414	147,963	759,586	368,292	1,127,878
Nondurable goods	66,550	69,002	135,552	135,866	98,218	234,084	43,741	12,164	55,905	246,157	179,384	425,541
Durable goods	117,761	51,111	168,872	313,860	127,547	441,407	81,808	10,250	92,058	513,429	188,908	702,337
Transportation	55,218	5,705	60,923	134,011	37,903	171,914	17,421	4,461	21,882	206,650	48,069	254,719
Communications and Public Utilities	17,252	3,902	21,154	72,206	37,651	109,857	16,140	4,537	20,677	105,598	46,090	151,688
Wholesale Trade	36,044	11,256	47,300	109,567	54,337	163,904	31,278	5,699	36,977	176,889	71,292	248,181
Retail Trade	169,636	154,065	323,701	313,798	321,225	635,023	56,211	25,033	81,244	539,645	500,323	1,039,968
Finance, Insurance, Real Estate	20,094	20,546	40,640	90,752	191,092	281,844	56,371	20,925	77,296	167,217	232,563	399,780
Business and Repair Service	37,481	11,658	49,139	94,508	60,453	154,961	31,315	12,367	43,682	163,304	84,478	247,782
Personal, Entertainment, Recreational	39,746	34,482	74,228	69,551	78,396	147,947	13,464	6,648	20,112	122,761	119,526	242,287
Professional and Related Services	40,136	65,796	105,932	111,211	372,418	483,629	219,098	204,749	423,847	370,445	642,963	1,013,408
Health Services	12,954	31,783	44,737	33,449	184,994	218,443	49,040	44,290	93,330	95,443	261,067	356,510
Educational Services	17,774	22,386	40,160	45,676	112,635	158,311	107,431	136,661	244,092	170,881	271,682	442,563
Other Profess. & Related Services	9,408	11,627	21,035	32,086	74,789	106,875	62,627	23,798	86,425	104,121	110,214	214,335
Public Administration	22,933	9,816	32,749	106,509	74,157	180,666	54,898	15,799	70,697	184,340	99,772	284,112
LABOUR FORCE STATUS IN 1979												
Persons 16 ys. in Labor Force in 1979	896,758	568,247	1,465,005	2,040,826	1,768,541	3,809,367	696,353	362,670	1,059,023	3,633,937	2,699,458	6,333,395
Worked in 1979	875,786	547,452	1,423,238	2,020,097	1,741,607	3,761,704	693,033	359,696	1,052,729	3,588,916	2,648,755	6,237,671
50 to 52 weeks	487,219	225,995	713,214	1,396,011	977,405	2,373,416	524,097	168,083	692,180	2,407,327	1,371,483	3,778,810
40 to 49 weeks	114,389	78,710	193,099	235,759	230,652	466,411	83,837	79,900	163,737	433,985	389,262	823,247
1 to 39 weeks	274,178	242,747	516,925	388,327	533,550	921,877	85,099	111,713	196,812	747,604	888,010	1,635,614
35 or more hours per week	662,782	285,389	948,171	1,788,674	1,152,566	2,941,240	633,733	262,440	896,173	3,085,189	1,700,395	4,785,584
50 to 52 weeks	433,397	156,688	590,085	1,313,527	765,419	2,078,946	501,349	140,907	642,256	2,248,273	1,063,014	3,311,287
With unemployment in 1979	200,209	140,511	340,720	370,177	329,562	699,739	70,371	60,342	130,713	640,757	530,415	1,171,172
Unemployed 15 or more weeks	89,304	56,547	145,851	135,334	103,365	238,699	22,995	16,302	39,297	247,633	176,214	423,847
WORKERS IN FAMILY IN 1979												
Families	817,947	157,043	974,990	1,309,446	235,741	1,545,187	484,343	39,174	523,517	2,611,736	431,958	3,043,694
No Workers	186,362	42,930	229,292	65,275	29,662	94,937	12,239	2,279	14,518	263,876	74,871	338,747
1 worker	256,336	63,802	320,138	417,143	104,947	522,090	154,004	14,686	168,690	827,483	183,435	1,010,918
2 or more workers	375,249	50,311	425,560	827,028	101,132	928,160	318,100	22,209	340,309	1,520,377	173,652	1,694,029

TABLE 6.7
INCOME CHARACTERISTICS OF PERSONS OF TOTAL ITALIAN ANCESTRY IN THE UNITED STATES BY EDUCATION: 1980

	Less Than 12 Years of School			High School Graduates			College Graduates			All Persons		
	Male	Female	Total	Male	Female	Total	Male	Female	Total	Male	Female	Total
INCOME IN 1979												
HOUSEHOLDS	920,323	383,502	1,303,825	1,526,863	451,869	1,978,732	597,354	114,001	711,355	3,044,540	949,372	3,993,912
Less than $5,000	75,034	150,963	225,997	55,863	76,467	132,330	15,830	10,170	26,000	146,727	237,600	384,327
$5,000 to $7,499	82,144	64,116	146,260	51,031	49,223	100,254	11,413	6,878	18,291	144,588	120,217	264,805
$7,500 to $9,999	86,874	41,707	128,581	64,275	52,359	116,634	13,999	8,482	22,481	165,148	102,548	267,696
$10,000 to $14,999	160,802	49,517	210,319	189,859	100,909	290,768	43,778	23,139	66,917	394,439	173,565	568,004
$15,000 to $19,999	143,552	28,983	172,535	254,466	65,299	319,765	68,912	21,723	90,635	466,930	116,005	582,935
$20,000 to $24,999	121,336	18,689	140,025	273,483	39,952	313,435	86,839	15,062	101,901	481,658	73,703	555,361
$25,000 to $34,999	146,295	17,684	163,979	368,539	41,502	410,041	156,922	15,995	172,917	671,756	75,181	746,937
$35,000 to $49,999	75,331	8,455	83,786	191,325	18,270	209,595	117,595	8,303	125,898	384,251	35,028	419,279
$50,000 or more	28,955	3,388	32,343	78,022	7,888	85,910	82,066	4,249	86,315	189,043	15,525	204,568
Median Dol.	16,791	6,590	13,592	22,414	12,053	20,472	28,246	16,732	26,703	22,122	10,413	19,362
Mean Dol.	19,605	9,992	16,738	24,818	14,849	22,551	32,979	19,909	29,251	24,464	13,458	22,146
FAMILIES	817,947	157,043	974,990	1,309,446	235,741	1,545,187	484,343	39,174	523,517	2,611,736	431,958	3,043,694
Less than $5,000	43,518	27,226	70,744	30,029	32,944	62,973	5,857	2,098	7,955	79,404	62,268	141,672
$5,000 to $7,499	65,700	19,853	85,553	33,013	22,040	55,053	4,972	1,638	6,610	103,685	43,531	147,216
$7,500 to $9,999	74,596	17,813	92,409	45,170	23,127	68,297	6,966	1,988	8,954	126,732	42,928	169,660
$10,000 to $14,999	144,482	28,941	173,423	145,557	46,596	192,153	25,115	4,927	30,042	315,154	80,464	395,618
$15,000 to $19,999	132,514	22,074	154,588	214,619	36,151	250,770	49,239	6,372	55,611	396,372	64,597	460,969
$20,000 to $24,999	114,67	15,753	130,432	246,103	25,648	271,751	71,136	5,427	76,563	431,918	46,828	478,746
$25,000 to $34,999	141,638	15,214	156,852	342,405	29,712	372,117	138,408	8,235	146,643	622,451	53,161	675,612
$35,000 to $49,999	73,229	7,376	80,605	180,217	13,579	193,796	107,333	5,489	112,822	360,779	26,444	387,223
$50,000 or more	27,591	2,793	30,384	72,333	5,944	78,277	75,317	3,000	78,317	175,241	11,737	186,978
Median Dol.	17,897	12,196	17,114	23,641	14,182	22,637	30,377	22,169	30,184	23,294	14,179	21,960
Mean Dol.	20,631	15,131	19,777	26,048	17,128	24,657	35,483	26,176	32,671	25,680	17,169	24,841

TABLE 6.7 (Cont'd)
INCOME CHARACTERISTICS OF PERSONS OF TOTAL ITALIAN ANCESTRY IN THE UNITED STATES BY EDUCATION: 1980

	Less Than 12 Years of School			High School Graduates			College Graduates			All Persons		
	Male	Female	Total	Male	Female	Total	Male	Female	Total	Male	Female	Total
UNRELATED INDIVIDUALS, 15 YEARS....	132,987	252,735	385,722	378,748	368,241	746,989	146,522	102,324	248,846	658,257	723,300	1,381,557
Less than $2,000	14,403	27,860	42,263	56,446	74,788	131,234	10,156	7,759	17,915	81,005	110,407	191,412
$2,000 to $2,999	8,016	26,569	34,585	26,890	28,059	54,949	4,206	3,541	7,747	39,112	58,169	97,281
$3,000 to $4,999	27,439	92,862	120,301	42,527	51,084	93,611	10,192	9,760	19,952	80,158	153,706	233,864
$5,000 to $7,999	26,696	55,040	81,736	54,614	57,785	112,399	15,152	12,037	27,189	96,462	124,862	221,324
$8,000 to $9,999	12,831	19,322	32,153	28,485	37,953	66,438	9,251	9,320	18,571	50,567	66,595	117,162
$10,000 to $14,999	20,609	21,173	41,782	66,563	72,497	139,060	26,892	26,655	53,547	114,064	120,325	234,389
$15,000 to $24,999	17,923	8,000	25,923	77,101	39,321	116,422	42,819	27,151	69,970	137,843	74,472	212,315
$25,000 to $49,999	4,255	1,590	5,845	22,903	5,985	28,888	23,077	5,746	28,823	50,235	13,321	63,556
$50,000 or more	815	319	1,134	3,219	769	3,988	4,777	355	5,132	8,811	1,443	10,254
Median Dol.	6,725	4,458	4,929	8,591	6,542	7,501	14,438	11,615	13,086	9,281	5,946	7,179
Mean Dol.	9,047	5,661	6,898	10,727	7,697	9,393	17,012	12,207	14,567	11,604	7,830	9,607
Per Capita Income Dol.	4,566	1,738	3,146	15,053	5,641	7,008	24,083	9,738	18,647	10,821	3,964	7,371
MEAN FAMILY INCOME BY WORKER												
No Workers Dol.	10,030	7,117	9,485	12,493	7,037	10,788	19,173	15,549	18,604	11,063	7,342	10,241
1 Worker Dol.	18,045	14,159	17,271	21,751	13,192	20,031	34,014	19,633	32,762	22,885	14,044	21,281
2 or more workers Dol.	27,663	23,202	27,135	29,286	24,173	28,729	36,822	31,593	36,480	30,462	24,841	29,886

TABLE 6.8
POVERTY CHARACTERISTICS OF PERSONS OF TOTAL ITALIAN ANCESTRY IN THE UNITED STATES BY EDUCATION: 1980

	LESS THAN 12 YEARS OF SCHOOL			HIGH SCHOOL GRADUATES			COLLEGE GRADUATES			ALL PERSONS		
	Male	Female	Total	Male	Female	Total	Male	Female	Total	Male	Female	Total
ALL INCOME LEVEL IN 1979												
Families	817,947	157,043	974,990	1,309,446	235,741	1,545,187	484,343	39,174	523,517	2,611,736	431,958	3,043,694
With Children under 18 years	279,384	57,107	336,491	761,034	143,539	904,573	301,497	19,711	321,208	1,341,915	220,357	1,562,272
With Children 5 to 17 years	242,624	47,962	290,586	588,268	121,263	709,531	223,971	15,712	239,683	1,054,863	184,937	1,239,800
Female Householder, no husband	0	130,996	130,996	0	184,093	184,093	0	22,589	22,589	0	337,678	337,678
With Children under 18 ys.	0	50,828	50,828	0	122,238	122,238	0	14,005	14,005	0	187,071	187,071
With Children under 6 years	0	17,317	17,317	0	36,710	36,710	0	3,776	3,776	0	57,803	57,803
Householder 65 years and over	267,221	60,113	327,334	81,891	13,791	95,682	21,514	1,894	23,408	370,626	75,798	446,424
Unrelat. Individ. in pov.	127,956	252,317	380,273	298,899	304,980	603,879	142,392	100,624	243,016	569,247	657,921	1,227,168
65 years and over	50,366	163,958	214,324	12,985	39,915	52,900	3,449	5,943	9,392	66,800	209,816	276,616
Persons in poverty univ.	3,038,634	3,073,154	6,111,788	2,157,089	2,510,527	4,667,616	727,759	444,727	1,172,486	5,923,482	6,028,408	11,951,890
Related children under 18	1,865,672	1,778,349	3,644,021	4,554	6,346	10,900	6	7	13	1,870,232	1,784,702	3,654,934
Related children 5 to 17	1,396,089	1,332,168	2,728,257	4,554	6,346	10,900	6	7	13	1,400,649	1,338,521	2,739,170
60 years and over	489,400	632,149	1,121,549	203,317	231,904	435,221	46,632	23,896	70,528	739,349	887,949	1,627,298
65 years and over	357,776	479,234	837,010	103,682	122,211	225,893	27,085	15,348	42,433	488,543	616,793	1,105,336
INCOME IN 1979 BELOW POVERTY												
Families	48,951	31,448	80,399	42,600	40,445	83,045	7,708	2,448	10,156	99,259	74,341	173,600
Percent Below Poverty Level	6.0	20.0	8.2	3.3	17.2	5.4	1.6	6.2	1.9	3.8	17.2	5.7
With Children under 18 years	22,944	23,941	46,885	30,097	36,646	66,743	5,190	2,029	7,219	58,231	62,616	120,847
With Children 5 to 17 years	18,309	18,654	36,963	21,411	27,954	49,365	3,666	1,527	5,193	43,386	48,135	91,521
Female Householder, no husband	0	29,302	29,302	0	38,310	38,310	0	2,201	2,201	0	69,813	69,813
With Children under 18 ys.	0	23,171	23,171	0	35,421	35,421	0	1,926	1,926	0	60,518	60,518
With Children under 6 years	0	11,132	11,132	0	17,425	17,425	0	937	937	0	29,494	29,494
Householder 65 years and over	15,791	4,370	20,161	3,493	655	4,148	568	45	613	19,852	5,070	24,922
Unrelat. Individ. in pov.	28,082	82,620	110,702	49,503	68,243	117,746	16,926	14,295	31,221	94,511	165,158	259,669
Percent Below Poverty Level	21.9	32.7	29.1	16.6	22.4	19.4	11.9	14.2	12.8	16.6	25.1	21.2
65 years and over	9,337	46,987	56,324	1,707	7,859	9,566	424	1,106	1,530	11,468	55,952	67,420
Persons in poverty univ.	241,662	311,310	552,972	104,879	164,034	268,913	25,931	21,314	47,245	372,472	496,658	869,130
Percent Below Poverty Level	8.0	10.1	9.0	4.9	6.5	5.8	3.6	4.8	4.0	6.3	8.2	7.3
Related children under 18	152,193	146,073	298,266	298	335	633	0	0	0	152,491	146,408	298,899
Related children 5 to 17	108,349	105,061	213,410	298	335	633	0	0	0	108,647	105,396	214,043
60 years and over	35,091	80,087	115,178	9,228	17,603	26,831	1,440	1,926	3,366	45,759	99,616	145,375
65 years and over	26,729	63,526	90,255	5,559	11,265	16,824	1,036	1,446	2,482	33,324	76,237	109,561

TABLE 6.9
RESIDENCE, AGE, AND RELATIONSHIP OF PERSONS OF SINGLE ITALIAN ANCESTRY IN THE UNITED STATES BY EDUCATION: 1980

	Less Than 12 Years of School			High School Graduates			College Graduates			All Persons		
	Male	Female	Total	Male	Female	Total	Male	Female	Total	Male	Female	Total
URBAN AND RURAL												
Total Persons	1,527,170	1,611,318	3,138,488	1,439,812	1,593,643	3,033,455	463,917	247,460	711,377	3,430,899	3,452,421	6,883,320
Urban	1,374,135	1,473,292	2,847,427	1,283,890	1,433,860	2,717,750	411,479	220,296	631,775	3,069,504	3,127,448	6,196,952
Rural	153,035	138,026	291,061	155,922	159,783	315,705	52,438	27,164	79,602	361,395	324,973	686,368
Farm	6,062	4,890	10,952	5,501	5,851	11,352	1,579	822	2,401	13,142	11,563	24,705
AGE												
Total Persons	1,527,170	1,611,318	3,138,488	1,439,812	1,593,643	3,033,455	463,917	247,460	711,377	3,430,899	3,452,419	6,883,320
under 5 years	107,199	100,583	207,782	0	0	0	0	0	0	107,199	100,583	207,782
5 to 9 years	128,699	120,538	249,237	0	0	0	0	0	0	128,699	120,538	249,237
10 to 14 years	175,173	165,507	340,680	0	0	0	0	0	0	175,173	165,505	340,680
15 to 19 years	163,248	147,348	310,596	76,236	78,929	155,165	30	10	40	239,514	226,287	465,801
20 to 24 years	38,506	29,177	67,683	232,164	228,015	460,179	37,189	31,606	68,795	307,859	288,798	596,657
25 to 29 years	30,408	26,788	57,196	181,742	184,325	366,067	88,307	62,196	150,503	300,457	273,309	573,766
30 to 34 years	33,113	32,646	65,759	159,704	181,151	340,855	90,653	49,201	139,854	283,470	262,998	546,468
35 to 44 years	88,590	85,376	173,966	241,023	275,386	516,409	102,892	46,541	149,433	432,505	407,303	839,808
45 to 54 years	165,924	159,993	325,917	233,481	284,047	517,528	73,067	27,481	100,548	472,472	471,521	943,993
55 to 59 years	118,962	124,559	243,521	127,658	151,041	278,699	30,156	10,151	40,307	276,776	285,751	562,527
60 to 64 years	125,253	145,280	270,533	90,678	98,436	189,114	17,006	6,831	23,837	232,937	250,547	483,484
65 to 74 years	223,799	289,383	513,182	77,028	87,423	164,451	19,364	10,071	29,435	320,191	386,877	707,068
75 to 84 years	99,143	145,111	244,254	16,607	20,499	37,106	4,562	2,729	7,291	120,312	168,339	288,651
85 years and over	29,153	39,029	68,182	3,491	4,391	7,882	691	643	1,334	33,335	44,063	77,398
median age	44.9	51.1	48	37.7	39.2	38.8	36.3	33	34.9	39	42.1	40.5
HOUSEHOLD TYPE AND RELATIONSHIP												
In Household	1,506,504	1,592,673	3,099,177	1,394,801	1,563,757	2,958,558	459,985	244,145	704,130	3,361,290	3,400,575	6,761,865
Family Householder	724,646	131,894	856,540	930,437	152,831	1,083,268	318,753	21,641	340,394	1,973,836	306,366	2,280,202
Non-family Householder: Male	88,078	0	88,078	137,328	0	137,328	66,828	0	66,828	292,234	0	292,234
Female	0	209,708	209,708	0	140,339	140,339	0	38,273	38,273	0	388,320	388,320
Spouse	27,906	577,166	605,072	30,275	982,428	1,012,703	12,890	140,105	152,995	71,071	1,699,699	1,770,770
Other Relatives	647,757	657,015	1,304,772	252,076	248,216	500,292	46,685	33,175	79,860	946,518	938,406	1,884,924
Nonrelatives	18,117	16,890	35,007	44,685	39,943	84,628	14,829	10,951	25,780	77,631	67,784	145,415

TABLE 6.10
SELECTED DEMOGRAPHIC CHARACTERISTICS OF PERSONS OF SINGLE ITALIAN ANCESTRY IN THE UNITED STATES BY EDUCATION

	Less Than 12 Years of School			High School Graduates			College Graduates			All Persons		
	Male	Female	Total	Male	Female	Total	Male	Female	Total	Male	Female	Total
PERSONS IN HOUSEHOLDS												
HOUSEHOLDS	812,724	341,602	1,154,326	1,067,765	293,170	1,360,935	385,581	59,914	445,495	2,266,070	694,686	2,960,756
1 person	78,548	204,209	282,757	101,827	122,311	224,138	51,318	30,991	82,309	231,693	357,511	589,204
2 persons	353,695	79,864	433,559	315,317	84,949	400,266	108,031	17,408	125,439	777,043	182,221	959,264
3 persons	156,130	32,102	188,232	218,982	47,007	265,989	69,949	6,568	76,517	445,061	85,677	530,738
4 persons	115,808	14,197	130,005	234,061	24,275	258,336	86,168	3,147	89,315	436,037	41,619	477,656
5 persons	65,869	6,785	72,654	128,628	9,847	138,475	45,725	1,175	46,900	240,222	17,807	258,029
6 persons	42,674	4,445	47,119	68,950	4,781	73,731	24,390	625	25,015	136,014	9,851	145,865
TYPE OF GROUP QUARTERS												
Persons in Group Quarters	20,666	18,645	39,311	45,011	29,886	74,897	3,932	3,315	7,247	69,609	51,846	121,455
Inmate of Mental Hospital	2,500	1,872	4,372	1,277	900	2,177	155	81	236	3,932	2,853	6,785
Inmate of Home for Aged	6,717	12,202	18,919	1,734	3,535	5,269	335	483	818	8,786	16,220	25,006
Inmate of Other Institution	6,482	2,763	9,245	3,801	653	4,454	318	94	412	10,601	3,510	14,111
In Military Quarters	2,495	114	2,609	8,707	740	9,447	412	57	469	11,614	911	12,525
In College Dormitory	176	79	255	27,174	21,910	49,084	1,426	668	2,094	28,776	22,657	51,433
Other in Group Quarters	2,296	1,615	3,911	2,318	2,148	4,466	1,286	1,932	3,218	5,900	5,695	11,595
MARITAL STATUS												
Persons, 15 years and over	1,116,099	1,224,690	2,340,789	1,439,812	1,593,643	3,033,455	463,917	247,460	711,377	3,019,828	3,065,793	6,085,621
Single	251,695	213,944	465,639	380,139	324,000	704,139	104,275	70,281	174,556	736,109	608,225	1,344,334
Now married, except separated	746,024	623,026	1,369,050	948,412	1,041,455	1,989,867	327,426	152,164	479,590	2,021,862	1,816,645	3,838,507
Separated	14,629	20,765	35,394	20,718	29,967	50,685	6,668	3,682	10,350	42,015	54,414	96,429
Widowed	64,937	318,688	383,625	20,490	99,811	120,301	4,297	8,113	12,410	89,724	426,612	516,336
Divorced	38,814	48,267	87,081	70,053	98,410	168,463	21,251	13,220	34,471	130,118	159,897	290,015
FERTILITY												
Women 15 to 44 years	0	321,335	321,335	0	947,806	947,806	0	189,554	189,554	0	1,458,695	1,458,695
Children ever born	0	369,474	369,474	0	1,184,525	1,184,525	0	157,394	157,394	0	1,711,393	1,711,393
Per 1000 women	0	1,150	1,150	0	1,250	1,250	0	830	830	0	1,173	1,173

TABLE 6.11
NATIVITY AND LANGUAGE OF PERSONS OF SINGLE ITALIAN ANCESTRY IN THE UNITED STATES BY EDUCATION: 1980

	Less Than 12 Years of School			High School Graduates			College Graduates			All Persons		
	Male	Female	Total	Male	Female	Total	Male	Female	Total	Male	Female	Total
NATIVITY												
Total Persons	1,527,170	1,611,318	3,138,488	1,439,812	1,593,643	3,033,455	463,917	247,460	711,377	3,430,899	3,452,421	6,883,320
Native	1,245,517	1,285,893	2,531,410	1,325,677	1,487,406	2,813,083	432,563	231,910	664,473	3,003,757	3,005,209	6,008,966
Born in State of residence	994,169	1,021,081	2,015,250	971,512	1,107,779	2,079,291	269,546	152,018	421,564	2,235,227	2,280,878	4,516,105
Born in different State	244,824	258,495	503,319	348,699	374,764	723,463	160,675	78,963	239,638	754,198	712,222	1,466,420
Born abroad	6,524	6,317	12,841	5,466	4,863	10,329	2,342	929	3,271	14,332	12,109	26,441
Foreign Born	281,653	325,425	607,078	114,135	106,237	220,372	31,354	15,550	46,904	427,142	447,212	874,354
LANGUAGE SPOKEN AT HOME												
Persons 5 to 17 years	433,652	407,106	840,758	2,426	3,549	5,975	6	0	6	436,084	410,655	846,739
Speak only English at home	376,681	349,848	726,529	2,016	2,980	4,996	6	0	6	378,703	352,828	731,531
Speak a language other than English	56,971	57,258	114,229	410	569	979	0	0	0	57,381	57,827	115,208
Italian language spoken at home	52,525	52,218	104,743	360	486	846	0	0	0	52,885	52,704	105,589
Speak English very well	50,050	49,779	99,829	360	472	832	0	0	0	50,410	50,251	100,661
Speak English not well	2,475	2,439	4,914	0	14	14	0	0	0	2,475	2,453	4,928
Other language spoken at home	4,446	5,040	9,486	50	83	133	0	0	0	4,496	5,123	9,619
Speak English very well	4,064	4,623	8,687	44	65	109	0	0	0	4,108	4,688	8,796
Speak English not well	382	417	799	6	18	24	0	0	0	388	435	823
Persons 18 and over	986,319	1,103,629	2,089,948	1,437,386	1,590,094	3,027,480	463,911	247,460	711,371	2,887,616	2,941,183	5,828,799
Speak only English at home	629,658	627,187	1,256,845	1,214,555	1,332,121	2,546,676	402,593	213,189	615,782	2,246,806	2,172,497	4,419,303
Speak a language other than English	356,661	476,442	833,103	222,831	257,973	480,804	61,318	34,271	95,589	640,810	768,686	1,409,496
Italian language spoken at home	345,312	461,790	807,102	205,491	240,395	445,886	52,687	29,274	81,961	603,490	731,459	1,334,949
Speak English very well	283,017	361,300	644,317	193,239	224,805	418,044	50,569	27,621	78,190	526,825	613,726	1,140,551
Speak English not well	62,295	100,490	162,785	12,252	15,590	27,842	2,118	1,653	3,771	76,665	117,733	194,398
Other language spoken at home	11,349	14,652	26,001	17,340	17,578	34,918	8,631	4,997	13,628	37,320	37,227	74,547
Speak English very well	9,044	11,405	20,449	15,953	15,903	31,856	8,179	4,677	12,856	33,176	31,985	65,161
Speak English not well	2,305	3,247	5,552	1,387	1,675	3,062	452	320	772	4,144	5,242	9,386
MEANS OF TRANSPORTATION												
Workers 16 and over	521,879	293,876	815,755	1,122,414	851,148	1,973,562	411,986	170,744	582,730	2,056,279	1,315,768	3,372,047
Car, truck, or van	429,292	199,623	628,915	967,890	673,703	1,641,593	344,826	140,428	485,254	1,742,008	1,013,754	2,755,762
Drive alone	345,121	124,157	469,278	787,748	512,211	1,299,959	281,761	110,671	392,432	1,414,630	747,039	2,161,669
Carpool	84,171	75,466	159,637	180,142	161,492	341,634	63,065	29,757	92,822	327,378	266,715	594,093
Public transportation	46,417	50,142	96,559	81,742	107,986	189,728	41,242	17,375	58,617	169,401	175,503	344,904
Walked only	32,951	37,066	70,017	46,400	52,253	98,653	14,112	8,952	23,064	93,463	98,271	191,734
Other means	6,671	2,502	9,173	15,389	5,467	20,856	5,299	1,203	6,502	27,359	9,172	36,531
Worked at home	6,548	4,543	11,091	10,993	11,739	22,732	6,507	2,786	9,293	24,048	19,068	43,116

TABLE 6.12
EDUCATION, RESIDENCE IN 1975 OF PERSONS OF SINGLE ITALIAN ANCESTRY IN THE UNITED STATES BY EDUCATION: 1980

	Less Than 12 Years of School			High School Graduates			College Graduates			All Persons		
	Male	Female	Total	Male	Female	Total	Male	Female	Total	Male	Female	Total
School Enrollment												
Persons 3 years old and over enrolled	461,264	433,126	894,390	163,005	141,851	304,856	42,517	27,684	70,201	666,786	602,661	1,269,447
Nursery school	18,701	17,775	36,476	0	0	0	0	0	0	18,701	17,775	36,476
Public	5,824	5,532	11,356	0	0	0	0	0	0	5,824	5,532	11,356
Private	12,877	12,243	25,120	0	0	0	0	0	0	12,877	12,243	25,120
Kindergarten& Elementary (1-8 years)	275,849	256,151	532,000	0	0	0	0	0	0	275,849	256,151	532,000
Public	213,107	193,513	406,620	0	0	0	0	0	0	213,107	193,513	406,620
Private	62,742	62,638	125,380	0	0	0	0	0	0	62,742	62,638	125,380
High School (1 to 4 years)	166,714	159,200	325,914	0	0	0	0	0	0	166,714	159,200	325,914
Public	136,045	128,341	264,386	0	0	0	0	0	0	136,045	128,341	264,386
Private	30,669	30,859	61,528	0	0	0	0	0	0	30,669	30,859	61,528
College	0	0	0	163,005	141,851	304,856	42,517	27,684	70,201	205,522	169,535	375,057
Years of School Completed												
Persons 25 years and over	914,345	1,048,165	1,962,510	1,131,412	1,286,699	2,418,111	426,698	215,844	642,542	2,472,455	2,550,708	5,023,163
Elementary (0 to 8 years)	507,329	620,471	1,127,800	0	0	0	0	0	0	507,329	620,471	1,127,800
High School: 1 to 3 years	407,016	427,694	834,710	0	0	0	0	0	0	407,016	427,694	834,710
4 or more years	0	0	0	785,379	1,034,161	1,819,540	0	0	0	785,379	1,034,161	1,819,540
College: 1 to 3 years	0	0	0	346,033	252,538	598,571	0	0	0	346,033	252,538	598,571
4 or more years	0	0	0	0	0	0	426,698	215,844	642,542	426,698	215,844	642,542
Percent High School Graduates	0	0	0	100	100	100	100	100	100	63	58.9	60.9
Residence in 1975												
Persons 5 years and over	1,423,810	1,513,212	2,937,022	1,439,781	1,595,047	3,034,828	465,168	248,429	713,597	3,328,759	3,356,688	6,685,447
Same house	1,004,798	1,095,120	2,099,918	830,759	978,381	1,809,140	221,214	112,861	334,075	2,056,771	2,186,362	4,243,133
Different house in United States	407,381	406,047	813,428	597,679	608,481	1,206,160	237,826	132,585	370,411	1,242,886	1,147,113	2,389,999
Same County	253,393	257,529	510,922	335,540	350,526	686,066	109,042	63,515	172,557	697,975	671,570	1,369,545
Different County	153,988	148,518	302,506	262,139	257,955	520,094	128,784	69,070	197,854	544,911	475,543	1,020,454
Same State	84,345	81,494	165,839	138,100	143,083	281,183	60,671	35,292	95,963	283,116	259,869	542,985
Different State	69,643	67,024	136,667	124,039	114,872	238,911	68,113	33,778	101,891	261,795	215,674	477,469
Abroad	11,631	12,045	23,676	11,343	8,185	19,528	6,128	2,983	9,111	29,102	23,213	52,315

TABLE 6.13
LABOR FORCE AND OCCUPATION OF PERSONS OF SINGLE ITALIAN ANCESTRY IN THE UNITED STATES BY EDUCATION: 1980

	Less Than 12 Years of School			High School Graduates			College Graduates			All Persons		
	Male	Female	Total	Male	Female	Total	Male	Female	Total	Male	Female	Total
Labor Force Status												
Persons 16 years and over	1,073,441	1,185,441	2,258,882	1,439,759	1,593,595	3,033,354	463,917	247,460	711,377	2,977,117	3,026,496	6,003,613
Labor force	592,626	340,395	933,021	1,211,349	921,011	2,132,360	425,820	180,350	606,170	2,229,795	1,441,756	3,671,551
Percent of persons 16 years	55.2	28.7	41.3	84.1	57.8	70.3	91.8	72.9	85.2	74.9	47.6	61.2
Civilian labor force	589,323	340,219	929,542	1,192,690	919,297	2,111,987	420,711	180,014	600,725	2,202,724	1,439,530	3,642,254
Employed	540,437	307,766	848,203	1,128,367	872,446	2,000,813	411,705	174,656	586,361	2,080,509	1,354,868	3,435,377
Unemployed	48,886	32,453	81,339	64,323	46,851	111,174	9,006	5,358	14,364	122,215	84,662	206,877
Percent of civ. labor force	8.3	9.5	8.8	5.4	5.1	5.3	2.1	3.0	2.4	5.5	5.9	5.7
Not in labor force	480,815	845,046	1,325,861	228,410	672,584	900,994	38,097	67,110	105,207	747,322	1,584,740	2,332,062
Class of Worker and Occupation												
Employed 16 years and ov.	540,437	307,766	848,203	1,128,367	872,446	2,000,813	411,705	174,656	586,361	2,080,509	1,354,868	3,435,377
Private wage and salary work.	416,105	265,230	681,335	873,098	715,697	1,588,795	265,498	94,401	359,899	1,554,701	1,075,328	2,630,029
Federal Government workers	14,479	3,704	18,183	47,167	25,190	72,357	19,406	4,730	24,136	81,052	33,624	114,676
State Government workers	9,926	6,455	16,381	28,330	33,858	62,188	25,608	13,407	39,015	63,864	53,720	117,584
Local Government workers	38,872	19,835	58,707	80,742	68,319	149,061	60,556	56,075	116,631	180,170	144,229	324,399
Self-employed workers	59,638	10,497	70,135	97,075	23,701	120,776	40,275	5,248	45,523	196,988	39,446	236,434
Unpaid family workers	1,417	2,045	3,462	1,955	5,681	7,636	362	795	1,157	3,734	8,521	12,255
Employed 16 years and over	540,437	307,766	848,203	1,128,367	872,446	2,000,813	411,705	174,656	586,361	2,080,509	1,354,868	3,435,377
Managerial and Professional	44,882	14,022	58,904	212,876	120,910	333,786	282,011	123,759	405,770	539,769	258,691	798,460
Execut., Administ., Manag.	38,182	9,733	47,915	156,909	68,454	225,363	119,485	21,737	141,222	314,576	99,924	414,500
Professional Specialty occupations	6,700	4,289	10,989	55,967	52,456	108,423	162,526	102,022	264,548	225,193	158,767	383,960
Technical, Sales, Administrative	76,764	106,755	183,519	288,925	553,163	842,088	82,903	41,752	124,655	448,592	701,670	1,150,262
Technician and related support	3,693	2,188	5,881	39,630	21,761	61,391	13,601	7,099	20,700	56,924	31,048	87,972
Sales Occupations	40,602	47,536	88,138	135,700	111,988	247,688	45,073	10,320	55,393	221,375	169,844	391,219
Administrative Support	32,469	57,031	89,500	113,595	419,414	533,009	24,229	24,333	48,562	170,293	500,778	671,071
Service Occupations	88,280	78,223	166,503	120,896	120,243	241,139	14,263	5,904	20,167	223,439	204,370	427,809
Private household occupations	204	2,954	3,158	269	2,345	2,614	15	130	145	488	5,429	5,917
Protective Service occupations	11,401	2,162	13,563	41,607	3,830	45,437	6,986	443	7,429	59,994	6,435	66,429
Other Service Occupations	76,675	73,107	149,782	79,020	114,068	193,088	7,262	5,331	12,593	162,957	192,506	355,463
Farming, forestry, fishing	12,924	1,166	14,090	15,492	2,277	17,769	2,130	238	2,368	30,546	3,681	34,227
Precision Prod., Craft, Repair	148,742	16,072	164,814	274,990	16,357	291,347	20,143	1,231	21,374	443,875	33,660	477,535
Operators, Fabricators, Laborers	168,845	91,528	260,373	215,188	59,496	274,684	10,255	1,772	12,027	394,288	152,796	547,084
Machine Oper., Assembl.	65,699	74,901	140,600	90,383	43,604	133,987	4,005	1,134	5,139	160,087	119,639	279,726
Transportation	53,563	2,457	56,020	69,811	4,478	74,289	3,262	267	3,529	126,636	7,202	133,838
Handlers, cleaners, helpers	49,583	14,170	63,753	54,994	11,414	66,408	2,988	371	3,359	107,565	25,955	133,520

TABLE 6.14
INDUSTRY, LABOR FORCE IN 1979 OF PERSONS OF SINGLE ITALIAN ANCESTRY IN THE UNITED STATES BY EDUCATION: 1980

	Less Than 12 Years of School			High School Graduates			College Graduates			All Persons		
	Male	Female	Total	Male	Female	Total	Male	Female	Total	Male	Female	Total
INDUSTRY												
Employed 16 years and over	540,437	307,766	848,203	1,128,367	872,446	2,000,813	411,705	174,656	586,361	2,080,509	1,354,868	3,435,377
Agriculture, Forestry, Fishing	13,521	1,609	15,130	21,118	5,183	26,301	4,987	823	5,810	39,626	7,615	47,241
Construction	68,111	2,368	70,479	110,802	11,705	122,507	14,850	966	15,816	193,763	15,039	208,802
Manufacturing	143,327	100,128	243,455	283,109	140,648	423,757	78,823	11,422	90,245	505,259	252,198	757,457
Nondurable goods	52,328	60,077	112,405	87,598	63,548	151,146	27,596	6,360	33,956	167,522	129,985	297,507
Durable goods	90,999	40,051	131,050	195,511	77,100	272,611	51,227	5,062	56,289	337,737	122,213	459,950
Transportation	44,727	3,827	48,554	89,950	21,732	111,682	10,267	2,367	12,634	144,944	27,926	172,870
Communications and Public Utilities	13,743	2,827	16,570	46,039	21,689	67,728	9,650	2,272	11,922	69,432	26,788	96,220
Wholesale Trade	27,399	7,775	35,174	70,276	32,606	102,882	19,051	3,129	22,180	116,726	43,510	160,236
Retail Trade	106,323	90,287	196,610	198,023	183,574	381,597	35,225	12,671	47,896	339,571	286,532	626,103
Finance, Insurance, Real Estate	16,370	14,438	30,808	64,544	115,658	180,202	35,554	10,817	46,371	116,468	140,913	257,381
Business and Repair Service	26,593	7,563	34,156	57,473	34,614	92,087	18,659	6,149	24,808	102,725	48,326	151,051
Personal, Entertainment, Recreational	31,019	22,838	53,857	47,350	45,756	93,106	8,250	3,301	11,551	86,619	71,895	158,514
Professional and Related Services	30,457	46,678	77,135	68,899	213,065	281,964	142,167	112,662	254,829	241,523	372,405	613,928
Health Services	9,338	21,468	30,806	20,613	100,653	121,266	33,491	22,615	56,106	63,442	144,736	208,178
Educational Services	14,370	17,656	32,026	27,346	68,755	96,101	69,269	77,940	147,209	110,985	164,351	275,336
Other Profess. & Related Services	6,749	7,554	14,303	20,940	43,657	64,597	39,407	12,107	51,514	67,096	63,318	130,414
Public Administration	18,847	7,428	26,275	70,784	46,216	117,000	34,222	8,077	42,299	123,853	61,721	185,574
LABOUR FORCE STATUS IN 1979												
Persons 16 ys. in Labor Force in 1979	639,518	380,150	1,019,668	1,276,582	1,018,473	2,295,055	435,634	193,625	629,259	2,351,734	1,592,248	3,943,982
Worked in 1979	626,667	367,430	994,097	1,263,437	1,002,225	2,265,662	433,423	191,870	625,293	2,323,527	1,561,525	3,885,052
50 to 52 weeks	389,655	174,230	563,885	917,070	593,467	1,510,537	331,384	90,036	421,420	1,638,109	857,733	2,495,842
40 to 49 weeks	83,458	58,435	141,893	138,062	130,185	268,247	53,500	43,974	97,474	275,020	232,594	507,614
1 to 39 weeks	153,554	134,765	288,319	208,305	278,573	486,878	48,539	57,860	106,399	410,398	471,198	881,596
35 or more hours per week	515,976	217,073	733,049	1,136,684	668,462	1,805,146	396,444	138,639	535,083	2,049,104	1,024,174	3,073,278
50 to 52 weeks	356,164	125,986	482,150	869,328	464,405	1,333,733	316,820	74,879	391,699	1,542,312	665,270	2,207,582
With unemployment in 1979	125,433	87,501	212,934	201,666	171,791	373,457	39,936	29,701	69,637	367,035	288,993	656,028
Unemployed 15 or more weeks	58,453	38,574	97,027	78,521	59,591	138,112	13,812	9,229	23,041	150,786	107,394	258,180
WORKERS IN FAMILY IN 1979												
Families	724,646	131,894	856,540	930,437	152,831	1,083,268	318,753	21,641	340,394	1,973,836	306,366	2,280,202
No Workers	177,730	35,294	213,024	58,101	19,842	77,943	10,578	1,512	12,090	246,409	56,648	303,057
1 worker	226,326	53,432	279,758	299,261	63,671	362,932	104,679	8,086	112,765	630,266	125,189	755,455
2 or more workers	320,590	43,168	363,758	573,075	69,318	642,393	203,496	12,043	215,539	1,097,161	124,529	1,221,690

TABLE 6.15

INCOME CHARACTERISTICS OF PERSONS OF SINGLE ITALIAN ANCESTRY IN THE UNITED STATES BY EDUCATION: 1980

Income in 1979	Less Than 12 Years of School			High School Graduates			College Graduates			All Persons		
Households	812,724	341,602	1,154,326	1,067,765	293,170	1,360,935	385,581	59,914	445,495	2,266,070	694,686	2,960,756
Less than $5,000	67,216	136,007	203,223	39,276	51,123	90,399	9,865	5,566	15,431	116,357	192,696	309,053
$5,000 to $7,499	75,560	57,201	132,761	36,147	32,130	68,277	7,261	3,619	10,880	118,968	92,950	211,918
$7,500 to $9,999	78,576	36,780	115,356	43,879	32,833	76,712	8,495	4,256	12,751	130,950	73,869	204,819
$10,000 to $14,999	142,028	43,293	185,321	129,718	63,251	192,969	26,352	11,244	37,596	298,098	117,788	415,886
$15,000 to $19,999	124,305	25,320	149,625	170,434	42,253	212,687	41,993	10,986	52,979	336,732	78,559	415,291
$20,000 to $24,999	104,851	16,663	121,514	186,004	25,917	211,921	53,806	8,125	61,931	344,661	50,705	395,366
$25,000 to $34,999	127,709	15,612	143,321	259,103	27,699	286,802	100,090	8,674	108,764	486,902	51,985	538,887
$35,000 to $49,999	66,789	7,619	74,408	142,419	12,465	154,884	78,682	4,810	83,492	287,890	24,894	312,784
$50,000 or more	25,690	3,107	28,797	60,785	5,499	66,284	59,037	2,634	61,671	145,512	11,240	156,752
Median (Dol.)	16,604	6,521	13,395	22,806	12,093	20,930	29,148	17,180	27,867	21,914	9,588	19,026
Mean (Dol.)	19,492	9,972	16,638	25,356	15,008	23,065	34,095	20,619	30,349	24,327	12,940	21,989
Families	724,646	131,894	856,540	930,437	152,831	1,083,268	318,753	21,641	340,394	1,973,836	306,366	2,280,202
Less than $5,000	38,743	18,888	57,631	22,009	18,827	40,836	3,986	1,062	5,048	64,738	38,777	103,515
$5,000 to $7,499	60,767	15,988	76,755	24,512	13,433	37,945	3,396	937	4,333	88,675	30,358	119,033
$7,500 to $9,999	67,928	14,997	82,925	32,072	14,055	46,127	4,602	1,077	5,679	104,602	30,129	134,731
$10,000 to $14,999	128,543	25,118	153,661	102,080	29,211	131,291	15,768	2,336	18,104	246,391	56,665	303,056
$15,000 to $19,999	115,299	19,431	134,730	145,955	24,423	170,378	30,362	3,327	33,689	291,616	47,181	338,797
$20,000 to $24,999	99,666	14,289	113,955	168,464	17,600	186,064	44,389	3,111	47,500	312,519	35,000	347,519
$25,000 to $34,999	124,096	13,780	137,876	242,867	21,212	264,079	88,989	4,595	93,584	455,952	39,587	495,539
$35,000 to $49,999	65,071	6,810	71,881	135,700	9,805	145,505	72,505	3,311	75,816	273,276	19,926	293,202
$50,000 or more	24,533	2,593	27,126	56,778	4,265	61,043	54,756	1,885	56,641	136,067	8,743	144,810
Median (Dol.)	17,712	13,098	17,126	24,007	15,168	23,092	31,038	23,242	30,967	23,054	14,758	21,842
Mean (Dol.)	20,529	15,921	19,860	26,527	18,021	25,221	36,482	27,175	33,497	25,485	17,726	24,835

TABLE 6.15 (Cont'd)
INCOME CHARACTERISTICS OF PERSONS OF SINGLE ITALIAN ANCESTRY IN THE UNITED STATES BY EDUCATION: 1980

	Less Than 12 Years of School			High School Graduates			College Graduates			All Persons		
Unrelated Individuals, 15 years....	107,558	224,909	332,467	220,212	205,080	425,292	84,781	51,881	136,662	412,551	481,870	894,421
Less than $2,000	10,051	21,356	31,407	30,163	33,316	63,479	5,521	4,158	9,679	45,735	58,830	104,565
$2,000 to $2,999	6,172	23,701	29,873	13,268	13,475	26,743	2,185	1,786	3,971	21,625	38,962	60,587
$3,000 to $4,999	23,715	86,046	109,761	23,017	30,413	53,430	5,566	5,255	10,821	52,298	121,714	174,012
$5,000 to $7,999	22,301	49,612	71,913	30,482	33,819	64,301	8,532	5,640	14,172	61,315	89,071	150,386
$8,000 to $9,999	10,238	17,035	27,273	16,550	21,733	38,283	4,976	4,449	9,425	31,764	43,217	74,981
$10,000 to $14,999	16,480	18,443	34,923	40,414	43,118	83,532	15,068	12,789	27,857	71,962	74,350	146,312
$15,000 to $24,999	14,547	7,072	21,619	48,588	24,648	73,236	25,349	14,090	39,439	88,484	45,810	134,294
$25,000 to $49,999	3,349	1,353	4,702	15,389	4,015	19,404	14,519	3,473	17,992	33,257	8,841	42,098
$50,000 or more	705	291	996	2,341	543	2,884	3,065	241	3,306	6,111	1,075	7,186
Median Dol.	6,723	4,476	4,912	9,565	7,227	8,245	15,110	11,833	13,637	9,593	5,722	7,016
Mean Dol.	9,092	5,698	6,872	11,503	8,311	10,118	17,783	12,556	15,167	11,955	7,738	9,678
Per Capita Income Dol.	7,757	2,823	5,224	16,101	5,688	10,630	25,280	9,904	19,931	13,628	4,653	9,126
MEAN FAMILY INCOME BY WORKER												
No Workers Dol.	10,020	7,669	9,630	12,390	7,738	11,206	19,144	14,255	18,533	10,971	7,869	8,623
1 Worker Dol.	18,087	14,955	17,489	22,031	14,105	20,641	34,697	20,941	33,711	22,718	14,909	18,458
2 or more workers Dol.	28,078	23,864	27,578	30,309	24,562	29,689	38,302	32,983	38,005	31,140	25,134	27,786

TABLE 6.16

POVERTY CHARACTERISTICS OF PERSONS OF SINGLE ITALIAN ANCESTRY IN THE UNITED STATES BY EDUCATION: 1980

	Less Than 12 Years of School			High School Graduates			College Graduates			All Persons		
	Male	Female	Total	Male	Female	Total	Male	Female	Total	Male	Female	Total
ALL INCOME LEVEL IN 1979												
Families	724,646	131,894	856,540	930,437	152,831	1,083,268	318,753	21,641	340,394	1,973,836	306,366	2,280,202
With Children under 18 years	223,933	38,608	262,541	505,948	82,158	588,106	193,265	10,198	203,463	923,146	130,964	1,054,110
With Children 5 to 17 years	199,270	33,428	232,698	407,736	71,127	478,863	149,574	8,300	157,874	756,580	112,855	869,435
Female Householder, no husband	0	109,425	109,425	0	118,787	118,787	0	13,036	13,036	0	241,248	241,248
With Children under 18 ys.	0	34,186	34,186	0	69,572	69,572	0	7,178	7,178	0	110,936	110,936
With Children under 6 years	0	9,959	9,959	0	18,149	18,149	0	1,688	1,688	0	29,796	29,796
Householder 65 years and over	258,113	57,961	316,074	75,803	12,395	88,198	19,406	1,665	21,071	353,322	72,021	425,343
Unrelat. Individ. in pov.	104,980	224,762	329,742	184,331	182,430	366,761	82,943	51,156	134,099	372,254	458,348	830,602
65 years and over	48,166	156,857	205,023	11,745	35,108	46,853	3,023	4,814	7,837	62,934	196,779	259,713
Persons in poverty univ.	1,505,289	1,590,837	3,096,126	1,397,119	1,565,905	2,963,024	461,271	246,077	707,348	3,363,679	3,402,819	6,766,498
Related children under 18	533,087	500,123	1,033,210	2,065	2,853	4,918	6	0	6	535,158	502,976	1,038,134
Related children 5 to 17	426,917	400,536	827,453	2,065	2,853	4,918	6	0	6	428,988	403,389	832,377
60 years and over	469,713	605,842	1,075,555	186,039	207,290	393,329	41,277	19,763	61,040	697,029	832,895	1,529,924
65 years and over	345,311	461,342	806,653	95,741	109,200	204,941	24,311	12,964	37,275	465,363	583,506	1,048,869
INCOME IN 1979 BELOW POVERTY												
Families	42,128	21,389	63,517	30,117	23,016	53,133	5,207	1,245	6,452	77,452	45,650	123,102
Percent Below Poverty Level	5.8	16.2	7.4	3.2	15.1	4.9	1.6	5.8	1.9	3.9	14.9	5.4
With Children under 18 years	17,854	14,493	32,347	20,069	20,125	40,194	3,371	1,019	4,390	41,294	35,637	76,931
With Children 5 to 17 years	14,752	11,841	26,593	14,981	16,054	31,035	2,527	760	3,287	32,260	28,655	60,915
Female Householder, no husband	0	19,684	19,684	0	21,717	21,717	0	1,111	1,111	0	42,512	42,512
With Children under 18 ys.	0	14,037	14,037	0	19,483	19,483	0	959	959	0	34,479	34,479
With Children under 6 years	0	5,842	5,842	0	8,321	8,321	0	441	441	0	14,604	14,604
Householder 65 years and over	15,189	4,110	19,299	3,253	587	3,840	532	38	570	18,974	4,735	23,709
Unrelat. Individ. in pov.	21,467	70,614	92,081	29,506	38,574	68,080	9,304	7,554	16,858	60,277	116,742	177,019
Percent Below Poverty Level	20.4	31.4	27.9	16.0	21.1	18.6	11.2	14.8	12.6	16.2	25.5	21.3
65 years and over	8,856	44,943	53,799	1,605	7,001	8,606	414	928	1,342	10,875	52,872	63,747
Persons in poverty univ.	121,864	179,520	301,384	67,282	97,165	164,447	15,284	11,523	26,807	204,430	288,208	492,638
Percent Below Poverty Level	8.1	11.3	9.7	4.8	6.2	5.5	3.3	4.7	3.8	6.1	8.5	7.3
Related children under 18	50,333	47,196	97,529	170	159	329	0	0	0	50,503	47,355	97,858
Related children 5 to 17	38,008	36,242	74,250	170	159	329	0	0	0	38,178	36,401	74,579
60 years and over	33,466	76,437	109,903	8,605	15,899	24,504	1,324	1,647	2,971	43,395	93,983	137,378
65 years and over	25,578	60,857	86,435	5,204	10,160	15,364	985	1,235	2,220	31,767	72,252	104,019

TABLE 6.17
RESIDENCE, AGE, AND RELATIONSHIP OF PERSONS OF SINGLE ITALIAN ANCESTRY BORN IN THE U.S. BY EDUCATION: 1980

	Less Than 12 Years of School			High School Graduates			College Graduates			All Persons		
	Male	Female	Total	Male	Female	Total	Male	Female	Total	Male	Female	Total
URBAN AND RURAL												
Total Persons	1,245,517	1,285,893	2,531,410	1,325,677	1,487,406	2,813,083	432,563	231,910	664,473	3,003,757	3,005,209	6,008,966
Urban	1,107,291	1,162,530	2,269,821	1,176,244	1,333,677	2,509,921	382,334	205,702	588,036	2,665,869	2,701,909	5,367,778
Rural	138,226	123,363	261,589	149,433	153,729	303,162	50,229	26,208	76,437	337,888	303,300	641,188
Farm	5,370	4,144	9,514	5,335	5,618	10,953	1,481	793	2,274	12,186	10,555	22,741
AGE												
Total Persons	1,245,517	1,285,893	2,531,410	1,325,677	1,487,406	2,813,083	432,563	231,910	664,473	3,003,757	3,005,209	6,008,966
under 5 years	106,206	99,857	206,063	0	0	0	0	0	0	106,206	99,857	206,063
5 to 9 years	126,097	118,258	244,355	0	0	0	0	0	0	126,097	118,258	244,355
10 to 14 years	168,659	159,157	327,816	0	0	0	0	0	0	168,659	159,157	327,816
15 to 19 years	154,259	138,987	293,246	73,177	75,775	148,952	30	10	40	227,466	214,772	442,238
20 to 24 years	34,155	25,360	59,515	221,163	217,602	438,765	35,818	30,595	66,413	291,136	273,557	564,693
25 to 29 years	24,591	20,729	45,320	170,432	174,198	344,630	84,405	59,553	143,958	279,428	254,480	533,908
30 to 34 years	23,639	22,412	46,051	146,356	169,551	315,907	85,228	46,820	132,048	255,223	238,783	494,006
35 to 44 years	60,611	55,961	116,572	221,786	259,307	481,093	97,240	44,044	141,284	379,637	359,312	738,949
45 to 54 years	129,036	124,368	253,404	216,077	267,611	483,688	67,904	25,291	93,195	413,017	417,270	830,287
55 to 59 years	99,683	104,148	203,831	116,871	140,883	257,754	27,104	8,769	35,873	243,658	253,800	497,458
60 to 64 years	109,769	128,321	238,090	85,029	92,599	177,628	15,629	6,196	21,825	210,427	227,116	437,543
65 to 74 years	168,905	219,362	388,267	65,309	76,177	141,486	16,336	8,725	25,061	250,550	304,264	554,814
75 to 84 years	36,195	60,749	96,944	8,692	12,082	20,774	2,673	1,672	4,345	47,560	74,503	122,063
85 years and over	3,712	8,224	11,936	785	1,621	2,406	196	235	431	4,693	10,080	14,773
median age	31.9	45.2	38.7	37.1	38.8	38.3	35.9	32.8	34.6	35.6	37.0	36.3
HOUSEHOLD TYPE AND RELATIONSHIP												
In Household	1,229,319	1,274,739	2,504,058	1,282,581	1,459,482	2,742,063	429,160	229,085	658,245	2,941,060	2,963,306	5,904,366
Family Householder	522,169	99,310	621,479	848,190	143,730	991,920	297,016	20,210	317,226	1,667,375	263,250	1,930,625
Non-family Householder: Male	63,888	0	63,888	128,432	0	128,432	62,859	0	62,859	255,179	0	255,179
Female	0	140,514	140,514	0	128,323	128,323	0	35,983	35,983	0	304,820	304,820
Spouse	21,286	431,506	452,792	27,687	916,854	944,541	11,794	131,167	142,961	60,767	1,479,527	1,540,294
Other Relatives	605,575	587,982	1,193,557	235,498	231,724	467,222	43,577	31,135	74,712	884,650	850,841	1,735,491
Nonrelatives	16,401	15,427	31,828	42,774	38,851	81,625	13,914	10,590	24,504	73,089	64,868	137,957

TABLE 6.18
SELECTED DEMOGRAPHIC CHARACTERISTICS OF PERSONS OF SINGLE ITALIAN ANCESTRY BORN IN THE U.S. BY EDUCATION

	LESS THAN 12 YEARS OF SCHOOL			HIGH SCHOOL GRADUATES			COLLEGE GRADUATES			ALL PERSONS		
	Male	Female	Total	Male	Female	Total	Male	Female	Total	Male	Female	Total
PERSONS IN HOUSEHOLDS												
HOUSEHOLDS												
1 person	586,057	239,824	825,881	976,622	272,053	1,248,675	359,875	56,193	416,068	1,922,554	568,070	2,490,624
2 persons	55,516	136,321	191,837	94,244	110,881	205,125	48,107	28,968	77,075	197,867	276,170	474,037
3 persons	256,699	59,030	315,729	287,498	79,700	367,198	99,445	16,452	115,897	643,642	155,182	798,824
4 persons	119,645	24,734	144,379	201,478	44,394	245,872	65,106	6,163	71,269	386,229	75,291	461,520
5 persons	81,591	11,114	92,705	213,737	23,175	236,912	81,177	2,922	84,099	376,505	37,211	413,716
5 persons	43,551	5,192	48,743	116,761	9,306	126,067	43,037	1,128	44,165	203,349	15,626	218,975
6 persons	29,055	3,433	32,488	62,904	4,597	67,501	23,003	560	23,563	114,962	8,590	123,552
TYPE OF GROUP QUARTERS												
Persons in Group Quarters	16,198	11,154	27,352	43,096	27,924	71,020	3,403	2,825	6,228	62,697	41,903	104,600
Inmate of Mental Hospital	2,118	1,363	3,481	1,133	819	1,952	148	75	223	3,399	2,257	5,656
Inmate of Home for Aged	3,442	6,059	9,501	1,254	2,415	3,669	177	286	463	4,873	8,760	13,633
Inmate of Other Institution	6,076	2,474	8,550	3,655	556	4,211	284	69	353	10,015	3,099	13,114
In Military Quarters	2,442	107	2,549	8,392	690	9,082	405	57	462	11,239	854	12,093
In College Dormitory	163	75	238	26,469	21,513	47,982	1,276	636	1,912	27,908	22,224	50,132
Other in Group Quarters	1,957	1,076	3,033	2,193	1,931	4,124	1,113	1,702	2,815	5,263	4,709	9,972
MARITAL STATUS												
Persons, 15 years and over	844,555	908,621	1,753,176	1,325,677	1,487,406	2,813,083	432,563	231,910	664,473	2,602,795	2,627,937	5,230,732
Single	229,742	196,383	426,125	359,917	309,614	669,531	98,432	67,115	165,547	688,091	573,112	1,261,203
Now married, except separated	535,152	464,856	1,000,008	863,794	971,845	1,835,639	304,321	142,395	446,716	1,703,267	1,579,096	3,282,363
Separated	12,357	17,967	30,324	19,448	28,535	47,983	6,253	3,451	9,704	38,058	49,953	88,011
Widowed	33,699	186,941	220,640	16,253	83,228	99,481	3,515	6,429	9,944	53,467	276,598	330,065
Divorced	33,605	42,474	76,079	66,265	94,184	160,449	20,042	12,520	32,562	119,912	149,178	269,090
FERTILITY												
Women 15 to 44 years	0	263,449	263,449	0	896,433	896,433	0	181,022	181,022	0	1,340,904	1,340,904
Children ever born	0	255,258	255,258	0	1,109,068	1,109,068	0	148,923	148,923	0	1,513,249	1,513,249
Per 1000 women	0	969	969	0	1,237	1,237	0	823	823	0	1,129	1,129

TABLE 6.19
NATIVITY AND LANGUAGE OF PERSONS OF SINGLE ITALIAN ANCESTRY BORN IN THE U.S. BY EDUCATION: 1980

	LESS THAN 12 YEARS OF SCHOOL			HIGH SCHOOL GRADUATES			COLLEGE GRADUATES			ALL PERSONS		
	Male	Female	Total	Male	Female	Total	Male	Female	Total	Male	Female	Total
NATIVITY												
Total Persons	1,245,517	1,285,893	2,531,410	1,325,677	1,487,406	2,813,083	432,563	231,910	664,473	3,003,757	3,005,209	6,008,966
Native	1,245,517	1,285,893	2,531,410	1,325,677	1,487,406	2,813,083	432,563	231,910	664,473	3,003,757	3,005,209	6,008,966
Born in State of residence	994,169	1,021,081	2,015,250	971,512	1,107,779	2,079,291	269,546	152,018	421,564	2,235,227	2,280,878	4,516,105
Born in different State	244,824	258,495	503,319	348,699	374,764	723,463	160,675	78,963	239,638	754,198	712,222	1,466,420
Born abroad	6,524	6,317	12,841	5,466	4,863	10,329	2,342	929	3,271	14,332	12,109	26,441
Foreign Born												
LANGUAGE SPOKEN AT HOME												
Persons 5 to 17 years	418,172	392,354	810,526	2,276	3,303	5,579	6	0	6	420,454	395,657	816,111
Speak only English at home	374,971	348,339	723,310	2,010	2,948	4,958	6	0	6	376,987	351,287	728,274
Speak a language other than English	43,201	43,201	86,402	266	355	621	0	0	0	43,467	43,556	87,023
Italian language spoken at home	39,772	39,962	79,734	243	302	545	0	0	0	40,015	40,264	80,279
Speak English very well	38,097	38,184	76,281	243	302	545	0	0	0	38,340	38,486	76,826
Speak English not well	1,675	1,778	3,453	0	0	0	0	0	0	1,675	1,778	3,453
Other language spoken at home	3,429	4,053	7,482	23	53	76	0	0	0	3,452	4,106	7,558
Speak English very well	3,130	3,735	6,865	17	42	59	0	0	0	3,147	3,777	6,924
Speak English not well	299	318	617	6	11	17	0	0	0	305	329	634
Persons 18 and over	721,139	793,682	1,514,821	1,323,401	1,484,103	2,807,504	432,557	231,910	664,467	2,477,097	2,509,695	4,986,792
Speak only English at home	577,052	581,536	1,158,588	1,185,435	1,307,308	2,492,743	392,695	209,271	601,966	2,155,182	2,098,115	4,253,297
Speak a language other than English	144,087	212,146	356,233	137,966	176,795	314,761	39,862	22,639	62,501	321,915	411,580	733,495
Italian language spoken at home	139,590	206,601	346,191	126,871	165,631	292,502	33,880	19,119	52,999	300,341	391,351	691,692
Speak English very well	131,628	194,723	326,351	121,403	158,724	280,127	32,662	18,533	51,195	285,693	371,980	657,673
Speak English not well	7,962	11,878	19,840	5,468	6,907	12,375	1,218	586	1,804	14,648	19,371	34,019
Other language spoken at home	4,497	5,545	10,042	11,095	11,164	22,259	5,982	3,520	9,502	21,574	20,229	41,803
Speak English very well	4,037	5,036	9,073	10,443	10,323	20,766	5,697	3,321	9,018	20,177	18,680	38,857
Speak English not well	460	509	969	652	841	1,493	285	199	484	1,397	1,549	2,946
MEANS OF TRANSPORTATION												
Workers 16 and over	413,200	235,693	648,893	1,042,190	807,994	1,850,184	387,521	162,503	550,024	1,842,911	1,206,190	3,049,101
Car, truck, or van	344,219	167,034	511,253	900,873	644,145	1,545,018	326,122	134,572	460,694	1,571,214	945,751	2,516,965
Drive alone	277,599	107,139	384,738	733,099	491,267	1,224,366	266,802	106,309	373,111	1,277,500	704,715	1,982,215
Carpool	66,620	59,895	126,515	167,774	152,878	320,652	59,320	28,263	87,583	293,714	241,036	534,750
Public transportation	31,810	36,508	68,318	73,445	99,326	172,771	37,783	16,040	53,823	143,038	151,874	294,912
Walked only	26,109	26,576	52,685	42,903	48,422	91,325	12,809	8,208	21,017	81,821	83,206	165,027
Other means	5,727	2,015	7,742	14,605	5,098	19,703	4,938	1,087	6,025	25,270	8,200	33,470
Worked at home	5,335	3,560	8,895	10,364	11,003	21,367	5,869	2,596	8,465	21,568	17,159	38,727

TABLE 6.20
EDUCATION, RESIDENCE IN 1975 OF PERSONS OF SINGLE ITALIAN ANCESTRY BORN IN THE U.S. BY EDUCATION: 1980

	LESS THAN 12 YEARS OF SCHOOL			HIGH SCHOOL GRADUATES			COLLEGE GRADUATES			ALL PERSONS		
	Male	Female	Total	Male	Female	Total	Male	Female	Total	Male	Female	Total
SCHOOL ENROLLMENT												
Persons 3 years old and over enrolled	443,942	416,378	860,320	154,729	135,749	290,478	39,770	26,113	65,883	638,441	578,240	1,216,681
Nursery school	18,539	17,640	36,179	0	0	0	0	0	0	18,539	17,640	36,179
Public	5,781	5,472	11,253	0	0	0	0	0	0	5,781	5,472	11,253
Private	12,758	12,168	24,926	0	0	0	0	0	0	12,758	12,168	24,926
Kindergarten& Elementary (1-8 years)	266,998	248,063	515,061	0	0	0	0	0	0	266,998	248,063	515,061
Public	206,277	187,434	393,711	0	0	0	0	0	0	206,277	187,434	393,711
Private	60,721	60,629	121,350	0	0	0	0	0	0	60,721	60,629	121,350
High School (1 to 4 years)	158,405	150,675	309,080	0	0	0	0	0	0	158,405	150,675	309,080
Public	129,131	121,499	250,630	0	0	0	0	0	0	129,131	121,499	250,630
Private	29,274	29,176	58,450	0	0	0	0	0	0	29,274	29,176	58,450
College	0	0	0	154,729	135,749	290,478	39,770	26,113	65,883	194,499	161,862	356,361
YEARS OF SCHOOL COMPLETED												
Persons 25 years and over	656,141	744,274	1,400,415	1,031,337	1,194,029	2,225,366	396,715	201,305	598,020	2,084,193	2,139,608	4,223,801
Elementary (0 to 8 years)	292,240	356,175	648,415	0	0	0	0	0	0	292,240	356,175	648,415
High School: 1 to 3 years	363,901	388,099	752,000	0	0	0	0	0	0	363,901	388,099	752,000
4 or more years	0	0	0	711,112	958,285	1,669,397	0	0	0	711,112	958,285	1,669,397
College: 1 to 3 years	0	0	0	320,225	235,744	555,969	0	0	0	320,225	235,744	555,969
4 or more years	0	0	0	0	0	0	396,715	201,305	598,020	396,715	201,305	598,020
Percent High School Graduates				100.0	100.0	100.0	100.0	100.0	100.0	68.5	65.2	66.8
RESIDENCE IN 1975												
Persons 5 years and over	1,144,868	1,190,986	2,335,854	1,327,930	1,487,982	2,815,912	433,824	232,514	666,338	2,906,622	2,911,482	5,818,104
Same house	800,823	853,553	1,654,376	762,658	909,918	1,672,576	205,345	104,575	309,920	1,768,826	1,868,046	3,636,872
Different house in United States	341,814	335,411	677,225	559,712	574,614	1,134,326	225,335	126,619	351,954	1,126,861	1,036,644	2,163,505
Same County	207,821	208,888	416,709	311,573	328,724	640,297	102,481	60,226	162,707	621,875	597,838	1,219,713
Different County	133,993	126,523	260,516	248,139	245,890	494,029	122,854	66,393	189,247	504,986	438,806	943,792
Same State	72,164	67,872	140,036	129,872	136,477	266,349	57,653	33,954	91,607	259,689	238,303	497,992
Different State	61,829	58,651	120,480	118,267	109,413	227,680	65,201	32,439	97,640	245,297	200,503	445,800
Abroad	2,231	2,022	4,253	5,560	3,450	9,010	3,144	1,320	4,464	10,935	6,792	17,727

TABLE 6.21
LABOR FORCE AND OCCUPATION OF PERSONS OF SINGLE ITALIAN ANCESTRY BORN IN THE U.S. BY EDUCATION: 1980

	LESS THAN 12 YEARS OF SCHOOL			HIGH SCHOOL GRADUATES			COLLEGE GRADUATES			ALL PERSONS		
	Male	Female	Total	Male	Female	Total	Male	Female	Total	Male	Female	Total
LABOR FORCE STATUS												
Persons 16 years and over	804,049	871,331	1,675,380	1,325,624	1,487,365	2,812,989	432,563	231,910	664,473	2,562,236	2,590,606	5,152,842
Labor force	469,582	271,211	740,793	1,124,516	873,459	1,997,975	400,316	171,547	571,863	1,994,414	1,316,217	3,310,631
Percent of persons 16 years	58.4	31.1	44.2	84.8	58.7	71.0	92.5	74.0	86.1	77.8	50.8	64.2
Civilian labor force	466,379	271,063	737,442	1,106,555	871,817	1,978,372	395,401	171,223	566,624	1,968,335	1,314,103	3,282,438
Employed	426,963	246,047	673,010	1,046,680	827,733	1,874,413	387,007	166,192	553,199	1,860,650	1,239,972	3,100,622
Unemployed	39,416	25,016	64,432	59,875	44,084	103,959	8,394	5,031	13,425	107,685	74,131	181,816
Percent of civ. labor force	8.5	9.2	8.7	5.4	5.1	5.3	2.1	2.9	2.4	5.5	5.6	5.5
Not in labor force	334,467	600,120	934,587	201,108	613,906	815,014	32,247	60,363	92,610	567,822	1,274,389	1,842,211
CLASS OF WORKER AND OCCUPATION												
Employed 16 years and ov.	426,963	246,047	673,010	1,046,680	827,733	1,874,413	387,007	166,192	553,199	1,860,650	1,239,972	3,100,622
Private wage and salary work.	326,367	210,468	536,835	807,364	678,113	1,485,477	248,616	89,232	337,848	1,382,347	977,813	2,360,160
Federal Government workers	12,928	3,278	16,206	45,009	24,222	69,231	18,389	4,450	22,839	76,326	31,950	108,276
State Government workers	8,750	5,537	14,287	27,152	32,635	59,787	23,997	12,682	36,679	59,899	50,854	110,753
Local Government workers	33,693	17,310	51,003	77,643	65,654	143,297	58,192	54,201	112,393	169,528	137,165	306,693
Self-employed workers	44,099	7,936	52,035	87,605	21,800	109,405	37,494	4,890	42,384	169,198	34,626	203,824
Unpaid family workers	1,126	1,518	2,644	1,817	5,309	7,126	319	737	1,056	3,262	7,564	10,826
Employed 16 years and over	426,963	246,047	673,010	1,046,680	827,733	1,874,413	387,007	166,192	553,199	1,860,650	1,239,972	3,100,622
Managerial and Professional	37,439	12,165	49,604	199,608	116,034	315,642	266,001	118,760	384,761	503,048	246,959	750,007
Execut., Administ., Manag.	31,609	8,552	40,161	146,841	65,534	212,375	113,706	20,717	134,423	292,156	94,803	386,959
Professional Specialty occupations	5,830	3,613	9,443	52,767	50,500	103,267	152,295	98,043	250,338	210,892	152,156	363,048
Technical, Sales, Administrative	67,492	97,067	164,559	273,844	529,787	803,631	78,338	39,344	117,682	419,674	666,198	1,085,872
Technician and related support	3,122	1,972	5,094	37,222	21,025	58,247	12,472	6,631	19,103	52,816	29,628	82,444
Sales Occupations	35,279	42,544	77,823	128,781	105,803	234,584	43,210	9,769	52,979	207,270	158,116	365,386
Administrative Support	20,091	52,551	72,642	107,841	402,959	510,800	22,656	22,944	45,600	150,588	478,454	629,042
Service Occupations	66,893	65,166	132,059	109,960	113,103	223,063	13,115	5,462	18,577	189,968	183,731	373,699
Private household occupations	148	2,322	2,470	235	2,128	2,363	15	105	120	398	4,555	4,953
Protective Service occupations	10,265	1,995	12,260	40,493	3,659	44,152	6,751	423	7,174	57,509	6,077	63,586
Other Service Occupations	56,480	60,849	117,329	69,232	107,316	176,548	6,349	4,934	11,283	132,061	173,099	305,160
Farming, forestry, fishing	9,327	984	10,311	14,369	2,180	16,549	1,954	232	2,186	25,650	3,396	29,046
Precision Prod., Craft, Repair	110,886	10,212	121,098	249,940	14,171	264,111	18,337	1,043	19,380	379,163	25,426	404,589
Operators, Fabricators, Laborers	134,926	60,453	195,379	198,959	52,458	251,417	9,262	1,351	10,613	343,147	114,262	457,409
Machine Oper., Assembl.	48,588	47,390	95,978	81,482	37,428	118,910	3,476	808	4,284	133,546	85,626	219,172
Transportation	47,739	2,068	49,807	66,568	4,388	70,956	3,033	243	3,276	117,340	6,699	124,039
Handlers, cleaners, helpers	38,599	10,995	49,594	50,909	10,642	61,551	2,753	300	3,053	92,261	21,937	114,198

TABLE 6.22
INDUSTRY, LABOR FORCE IN 1979 OF PERSONS OF SINGLE ITALIAN ANCESTRY BORN IN THE U.S. BY EDUCATION: 1980

	Less Than 12 Years of School			High School Graduates			College Graduates			All Persons		
	Male	Female	Total	Male	Female	Total	Male	Female	Total	Male	Female	Total
INDUSTRY												
Employed 16 years and over	426,963	246,047	673,010	1,046,680	827,733	1,874,413	387,007	166,192	553,199	1,860,650	1,239,972	3,100,622
Agriculture, Forestry, Fishing	10,510	1,387	11,897	19,831	5,034	24,865	4,593	801	5,394	34,934	7,222	42,156
Construction	48,906	1,999	50,905	101,236	11,211	112,447	13,690	926	14,616	163,832	14,136	177,968
Manufacturing	109,532	67,700	177,232	259,471	129,928	389,399	73,788	10,513	84,301	442,791	208,141	650,932
Nondurable goods	39,318	36,706	76,024	80,422	57,366	137,788	25,993	5,815	31,808	145,733	99,887	245,620
Durable goods	70,214	30,994	101,208	179,049	72,562	251,611	47,795	4,698	52,493	297,058	108,254	405,312
Transportation	39,186	3,436	42,622	84,857	20,670	105,527	9,389	2,213	11,602	133,432	26,319	159,751
Communications and Public Utilities	11,746	2,584	14,330	43,867	20,973	64,840	9,167	2,194	11,361	64,780	25,751	90,531
Wholesale Trade	23,833	6,597	30,430	66,862	31,163	98,025	18,085	2,989	21,074	108,780	40,749	149,529
Retail Trade	83,827	77,818	161,645	180,907	173,200	354,107	33,035	11,865	44,900	297,769	262,883	560,652
Finance, Insurance, Real Estate	13,037	13,112	26,149	60,804	109,921	170,725	33,678	10,106	43,784	107,519	133,139	240,658
Business and Repair Service	21,804	6,463	28,267	53,300	33,181	86,481	17,547	5,866	23,413	92,651	45,510	138,161
Personal, Entertainment, Recreational	22,090	18,337	40,427	42,225	42,711	84,936	7,635	3,095	10,730	71,950	64,143	136,093
Professional and Related Services	25,412	39,895	65,307	64,889	204,919	269,808	133,531	107,910	241,441	223,832	352,724	576,556
Health Services	7,800	18,134	25,934	19,325	97,016	116,341	30,823	21,652	52,475	57,948	136,802	194,750
Educational Services	11,943	15,116	27,059	25,855	65,925	91,780	65,761	74,682	140,443	103,559	155,723	259,282
Other Profess. & Related Services	5,669	6,645	12,314	19,709	41,978	61,687	36,947	11,576	48,523	62,325	60,199	122,524
Public Administration	17,080	6,719	23,799	68,431	44,822	113,253	32,869	7,714	40,583	118,380	59,255	177,635
LABOUR FORCE STATUS IN 1979												
Persons 16 ys. in Labor Force in 1979	510,178	305,926	816,104	1,186,482	966,789	2,153,271	409,189	184,139	593,328	2,105,849	1,456,854	3,562,703
Worked in 1979	499,576	295,389	794,965	1,174,184	951,571	2,125,755	407,138	182,576	589,714	2,080,898	1,429,536	3,510,434
50 to 52 weeks	310,990	141,132	452,122	853,967	564,532	1,418,499	312,406	85,358	397,764	1,477,363	791,022	2,268,385
40 to 49 weeks	61,926	44,505	106,431	125,955	122,383	248,338	49,501	42,045	91,546	237,382	208,933	446,315
1 to 39 weeks	126,660	109,752	236,412	194,262	264,656	458,918	45,231	55,173	100,404	366,153	429,581	795,734
35 or more hours per week	406,214	167,398	573,612	1,056,327	633,865	1,690,192	372,978	131,856	504,834	1,835,519	933,119	2,768,638
50 to 52 weeks	283,728	100,360	384,088	809,633	441,246	1,250,879	298,835	70,904	369,739	1,392,196	612,510	2,004,706
With unemployment in 1979	100,485	68,643	169,128	187,610	162,823	350,433	37,441	28,307	65,748	325,536	259,773	585,309
Unemployed 15 or more weeks	47,155	29,580	76,735	72,858	56,080	128,938	12,926	8,684	21,610	132,939	94,344	227,283
WORKERS IN FAMILY IN 1979												
Families	522,169	99,310	621,479	848,190	143,730	991,920	297,016	20,210	317,226	1,667,375	263,250	1,930,625
No Workers	110,479	26,392	136,871	47,272	18,046	65,318	8,371	1,370	9,741	166,122	45,808	211,930
1 worker	166,213	39,093	205,306	270,325	59,773	330,098	96,727	7,450	104,177	533,265	106,316	639,581
2 or more workers	245,477	33,825	279,302	530,593	65,911	596,504	191,918	11,390	203,308	967,988	111,126	1,079,114

TABLE 6.23
INCOME CHARACTERISTICS OF PERSONS OF SINGLE ITALIAN ANCESTRY BORN IN THE U.S. BY EDUCATION: 1980

Income in 1979	Less Than 12 Years of School			High School Graduates			College Graduates			All Persons		
HOUSEHOLDS	586,057	239,824	825,881	976,622	272,053	1,248,675	359,875	56,193	416,068	1,922,554	568,070	2,490,624
Less than $5,000	43,747	89,299	133,046	34,102	44,839	78,941	8,777	4,902	13,679	86,626	139,040	225,666
$5,000 to $7,499	46,616	39,776	86,392	30,870	29,294	60,164	6,354	3,282	9,636	83,840	72,352	156,192
$7,500 to $9,999	52,634	27,281	79,915	38,809	30,434	69,243	7,614	4,037	11,651	99,057	61,752	160,809
$10,000 to $14,999	103,047	33,123	136,170	116,891	59,534	176,425	24,146	10,628	34,774	244,084	103,285	347,369
$15,000 to $19,999	91,979	19,225	111,204	155,618	40,090	195,708	39,083	10,399	49,482	286,680	69,714	356,394
$20,000 to $24,999	78,577	12,563	91,140	171,150	24,637	195,787	50,492	7,648	58,140	300,219	44,848	345,067
$25,000 to $34,999	97,864	11,163	109,027	240,498	26,276	266,774	94,214	8,293	102,507	432,576	45,732	478,308
$35,000 to $49,999	51,622	5,321	56,943	132,615	11,809	144,424	74,252	4,545	78,797	258,489	21,675	280,164
$50,000 or more	19,971	2,073	22,044	56,069	5,140	61,209	54,943	2,459	57,402	130,983	9,672	140,655
Median (Dol.)	17,372	6,924	14,171	23,035	12,296	21,120	29,282	17,298	27,992	22,681	10,527	19,984
Mean (Dol.)	20,234	10,225	17,296	25,552	15,199	23,247	34,160	20,751	30,460	25,098	13,614	22,479
FAMILIES	522,169	99,310	621,479	848,190	143,730	991,920	297,016	20,210	317,226	1,667,375	263,250	1,930,625
Less than $5,000	25,698	15,468	41,166	18,781	17,792	36,573	3,444	979	4,423	47,923	34,239	82,162
$5,000 to $7,499	36,981	12,358	49,339	20,377	12,458	32,835	2,777	869	3,646	60,135	25,685	85,820
$7,500 to $9,999	44,696	11,124	55,820	27,791	13,018	40,809	3,935	994	4,929	76,422	25,136	101,558
$10,000 to $14,999	92,043	19,080	111,123	90,762	27,444	118,206	14,228	2,120	16,348	197,033	48,644	245,677
$15,000 to $19,999	84,475	14,530	99,005	132,447	23,064	155,511	28,049	3,086	31,135	244,971	40,680	285,651
$20,000 to $24,999	74,289	10,558	84,847	154,410	16,670	171,080	41,525	2,908	44,433	270,224	30,136	300,360
$25,000 to $34,999	94,801	9,828	104,629	224,921	19,996	244,917	83,706	4,389	88,095	403,428	34,213	437,641
$35,000 to $49,999	50,174	4,662	54,836	126,330	9,261	135,591	68,464	3,101	71,565	244,968	17,024	261,992
$50,000 or more	19,012	1,702	20,714	52,371	4,027	56,398	50,888	1,764	52,652	122,271	7,493	129,764
Median (Dol.)	18,551	12,677	17,691	24,260	15,232	23,274	31,166	23,447	31,096	23,834	14,083	22,737
Mean (Dol.)	21,255	15,385	20,342	26,765	18,036	25,401	36,563	27,275	33,633	26,296	17,715	25,126

TABLE 6.23 (Cont'd)
INCOME CHARACTERISTICS OF PERSONS OF SINGLE ITALIAN ANCESTRY BORN IN THE U.S. BY EDUCATION: 1980

	Less Than 12 Years of School			High School Graduates			College Graduates			All Persons		
Unrelated Individuals, 15 years....	81,295	153,753	235,048	208,260	191,308	399,568	79,567	48,968	128,535	369,122	394,029	763,151
Less than $2,000	8,404	15,662	24,066	28,561	31,730	60,291	4,980	3,759	8,739	41,945	51,151	93,096
$2,000 to $2,999	4,451	15,647	20,098	12,704	12,392	25,096	2,029	1,660	3,689	19,184	29,699	48,883
$3,000 to $4,999	15,259	54,360	69,619	21,368	26,605	47,973	5,082	4,781	9,863	41,709	85,746	127,455
$5,000 to $7,999	15,773	33,852	49,625	28,551	31,247	59,798	7,896	5,232	13,128	52,220	70,331	122,551
$8,000 to $9,999	8,030	13,040	21,070	15,779	20,519	36,298	4,762	4,233	8,995	28,571	37,792	66,363
$10,000 to $14,999	13,714	14,379	28,093	38,385	41,055	79,440	14,182	12,313	26,495	66,281	67,747	134,028
$15,000 to $24,999	12,281	5,610	17,891	46,309	23,492	69,801	24,089	13,482	37,571	82,679	42,584	125,263
$25,000 to $49,999	2,784	987	3,771	14,481	3,827	18,308	13,659	3,283	16,942	30,924	8,097	39,021
$50,000 or more	599	216	815	2,122	441	2,563	2,888	225	3,113	5,609	882	6,491
Median Dol.	7,307	4,610	5,226	9,615	7,381	8,365	15,182	11,971	13,747	10,070	6,494	8,457
Mean Dol.	9,560	5,914	7,286	11,480	8,365	10,183	17,880	12,659	16,177	12,817	8,307	10,489
Per Capita Income Dol.	7,239	2,577	4,871	16,174	5,735	10,654	25,361	9,991	19,997	13,792	4,712	9,251
Mean Family Income By Worker												
No Workers Dol.	10,357	7,342	9,776	12,688	7,538	11,265	19,780	14,247	19,002	11,495	7,626	10,659
1 Worker Dol.	18,091	14,174	17,345	22,197	13,946	20,703	34,748	21,178	33,778	23,194	14,537	21,755
2 or more workers Dol.	28,303	23,060	27,668	30,346	24,620	29,713	38,209	32,830	37,908	31,387	24,987	30,728

TABLE 6.24

POVERTY CHARACTERISTICS OF PERSONS OF SINGLE ITALIAN ANCESTRY BORN IN THE U.S. BY EDUCATION: 1980

	Less Than 12 Years of School			High School Graduates			College Graduates			All Persons		
	Male	Female	Total	Male	Female	Total	Male	Female	Total	Male	Female	Total
ALL INCOME LEVEL IN 1979												
Families	522,169	99,310	621,479	848,190	143,730	991,920	297,016	20,210	317,226	1,667,375	263,250	1,930,625
With Children under 18 years	155,051	32,666	187,717	462,961	78,440	541,401	182,246	9,630	191,876	800,258	120,736	920,994
With Children 5 to 17 years	137,222	28,079	165,301	373,469	68,008	441,477	141,152	7,817	148,969	651,843	103,904	755,747
Female Householder, no husband	0	81,369	81,369	0	111,448	111,448	0	12,025	12,025	0	204,842	204,842
With Children under 18 ys.	0	29,160	29,160	0	66,533	66,533	0	6,736	6,736	0	102,429	102,429
With Children under 6 years	0	9,019	9,019	0	17,373	17,373	0	1,593	1,593	0	27,985	27,985
Householder 65 years and over	157,903	35,030	192,933	59,327	9,864	69,191	15,421	1,390	16,811	232,651	46,284	278,935
Unrelat. Individ. in pov.	78,783	153,617	232,400	173,399	169,105	342,504	77,886	48,275	126,161	330,068	370,997	701,065
65 years and over	27,690	92,673	120,363	8,684	27,456	36,140	2,310	3,869	6,179	38,684	123,998	162,682
Persons in poverty univ.	1,227,813	1,272,415	2,500,228	1,284,774	1,461,413	2,746,187	430,273	230,787	661,060	2,942,860	2,964,615	5,907,475
Related children under 18	516,776	484,849	1,001,625	1,955	2,647	4,602	6	0	6	518,737	487,496	1,006,233
Related children 5 to 17	411,589	385,971	797,560	1,955	2,647	4,602	6	0	6	413,550	388,618	802,168
60 years and over	314,713	410,425	725,138	158,601	180,256	338,857	34,655	16,539	51,194	507,969	607,220	1,115,189
65 years and over	205,724	282,841	488,565	73,931	87,981	161,912	19,054	10,375	29,429	298,709	381,197	679,906
INCOME IN 1979 BELOW POVERTY												
Families	28,991	17,959	46,950	26,052	21,758	47,810	4,539	1,148	5,687	59,582	40,865	100,447
Percent Below Poverty Level	5.6	18.1	7.6	3.1	15.1	4.8	1.5	5.7	1.8	3.6	15.5	5.2
With Children under 18 years	12,359	12,995	25,354	17,640	19,175	36,815	3,003	956	3,959	33,002	33,126	66,128
With Children 5 to 17 years	9,926	10,491	20,417	13,068	15,282	28,350	2,224	716	2,940	25,218	26,489	51,707
Female Householder, no husband	0	16,592	16,592	0	20,616	20,616	0	1,019	1,019	0	38,227	38,227
With Children under 18 ys.	0	12,616	12,616	0	18,593	18,593	0	901	901	0	32,110	32,110
With Children under 6 years	0	5,532	5,532	0	7,968	7,968	0	422	422	0	13,922	13,922
Householder 65 years and over	8,855	2,370	11,225	2,169	447	2,616	382	22	404	11,406	2,839	14,245
Unrelat. Individ. in pov.	16,416	48,627	65,043	27,562	35,202	62,764	8,504	6,936	15,440	52,482	90,765	143,247
Percent Below Poverty Level	20.8	31.7	28.0	15.9	20.8	18.3	10.9	14.4	12.2	15.9	24.5	20.4
65 years and over	4,732	25,288	30,020	1,056	4,862	5,918	282	690	972	6,070	30,840	36,910
Persons in poverty univ.	100,158	140,522	240,680	60,486	88,757	149,243	13,749	10,332	24,081	174,393	239,611	414,004
Percent Below Poverty Level	8.2	11.0	9.6	4.7	6.1	5.4	3.2	4.5	3.6	5.9	8.1	7.0
Related children under 18	48,261	45,243	93,504	159	142	301	0	0	0	48,420	45,385	93,805
Related children 5 to 17	36,092	34,428	70,520	159	142	301	0	0	0	36,251	34,570	70,821
60 years and over	21,402	48,717	70,119	6,581	12,401	18,982	981	1,255	2,236	28,964	62,373	91,337
65 years and over	14,430	34,955	49,385	3,471	7,178	10,649	691	880	1,571	18,592	43,013	61,605

TABLE 6.25
RESIDENCE, AGE, AND RELATIONSHIP OF PERSONS OF MULTIPLE ITALIAN ANCESTRY BORN IN THE U.S. BY EDUCATION: 1980

	Less Than 12 Years of School			High School Graduates			College Graduates			All Persons		
	Male	Female	Total	Male	Female	Total	Male	Female	Total	Male	Female	Total
URBAN AND RURAL												
Total Persons	1,537,560	1,481,253	3,018,813	794,724	971,205	1,765,929	263,623	196,160	459,783	2,595,907	2,648,618	5,244,525
Urban	1,261,338	1,218,075	2,479,413	675,070	826,001	1,501,071	228,304	169,017	397,321	2,164,712	2,213,093	4,377,805
Rural	276,222	263,178	539,400	119,654	145,204	264,858	35,319	27,143	62,462	431,195	435,525	866,720
Farm	10,179	9,454	19,633	5,075	5,799	10,874	1,252	1,262	2,514	16,506	16,515	33,021
AGE												
Total Persons	1,537,560	1,481,253	3,018,813	794,724	971,205	1,765,929	263,623	196,160	459,783	2,595,907	2,648,618	5,244,525
under 5 years	365,024	348,216	713,240	0	0	0	0	0	0	365,024	348,216	713,240
5 to 9 years	353,702	337,547	691,249	0	0	0	0	0	0	353,702	337,547	691,249
10 to 14 years	382,485	369,100	751,585	0	0	0	0	0	0	382,485	369,100	751,585
15 to 19 years	289,681	271,773	561,454	98,091	115,983	214,074	17	42	59	387,789	387,798	775,587
20 to 24 years	35,021	29,326	64,347	245,656	269,106	514,762	35,168	36,326	71,494	315,845	334,758	650,603
25 to 29 years	21,282	20,362	41,644	151,060	181,926	332,986	72,464	63,242	135,706	244,806	265,530	510,336
30 to 34 years	15,117	17,730	32,847	108,715	146,021	254,736	69,133	46,797	115,930	192,965	210,548	403,513
35 to 44 years	26,558	29,763	56,321	111,767	147,156	258,923	55,896	32,782	88,678	194,221	209,701	403,922
45 to 54 years	21,291	23,145	44,436	48,246	66,223	114,469	20,618	10,341	30,959	90,155	99,709	189,864
55 to 59 years	9,152	9,445	18,597	14,840	21,157	35,997	5,358	2,671	8,029	29,350	33,273	62,623
60 to 64 years	7,023	8,113	15,136	9,041	11,247	20,288	2,472	1,656	4,128	18,536	21,016	39,552
65 to 74 years	8,317	11,439	19,756	6,265	9,466	15,731	2,023	1,744	3,767	16,605	22,649	39,254
75 to 84 years	2,498	4,224	6,722	933	2,428	3,361	447	466	913	3,878	7,118	10,996
85 years and over	409	1,070	1,479	110	492	602	27	93	120	546	1,655	2,201
median age	10.7	10.7	10.7	26.8	27.8	27.3	31.7	29.9	31.0	17.5	18.5	18.0
HOUSEHOLD TYPE AND RELATIONSHIP												
In Household	1,530,339	1,478,639	3,008,978	746,989	927,940	1,674,929	260,261	194,083	454,344	2,537,589	2,600,662	5,138,251
Family Householder	89,969	24,409	114,378	372,361	81,231	453,592	162,040	17,113	179,153	624,370	122,753	747,123
Non-family Householder: Male	13,778	0	13,778	78,510	0	78,510	45,235	0	45,235	137,523	0	137,523
Female	0	15,690	15,690	0	74,090	74,090	0	36,038	36,038	0	125,818	125,818
Spouse	3,587	93,941	97,528	12,046	498,896	510,942	7,983	103,901	111,884	23,616	696,738	720,354
Other Relatives	1,408,167	1,327,731	2,735,898	251,933	229,825	481,758	33,033	25,447	58,480	1,693,133	1,583,003	3,276,136
Nonrelatives	14,838	16,868	31,706	32,139	43,898	76,037	11,970	11,584	23,554	58,947	72,350	131,297

TABLE 6.26

SELECTED DEMOGRAPHIC CHARACTERISTICS OF PERSONS OF MULTIPLE ITALIAN ANCESTRY BORN IN THE U.S.

	Less Than 12 Years of School			High School Graduates			College Graduates			All Persons		
	Male	Female	Total	Male	Female	Total	Male	Female	Total	Male	Female	Total
PERSONS IN HOUSEHOLDS												
HOUSEHOLDS	103,747	40,099	143,846	450,871	155,321	606,192	207,275	53,151	260,426	761,893	248,571	1,010,464
1 person	9,973	13,751	23,724	50,910	54,788	105,698	32,851	27,439	60,290	93,734	95,978	189,712
2 persons	29,074	10,745	39,819	122,716	49,148	171,864	59,780	16,754	76,534	211,570	76,647	288,217
3 persons	22,058	7,988	30,046	93,235	28,818	122,053	38,093	5,413	43,506	153,386	42,219	195,605
4 persons	21,417	4,355	25,772	106,201	14,262	120,463	45,496	2,408	47,904	173,114	21,025	194,139
5 persons	12,417	1,982	14,399	51,868	5,435	57,303	20,929	775	21,704	85,214	8,192	93,406
6 persons	8,808	1,278	10,086	25,941	2,870	28,811	10,126	362	10,488	44,875	4,510	49,385
TYPE OF GROUP QUARTERS												
Persons in Group Quarters	7,221	2,614	9,835	47,735	43,265	91,000	3,362	2,077	5,439	58,318	47,956	106,274
Inmate of Mental Hospital	504	276	780	484	278	762	65	11	76	1,053	565	1,618
Inmate of Home for Aged	266	612	878	171	437	608	58	50	108	495	1,099	1,594
Inmate of Other Institution	3,210	896	4,106	2,155	283	2,438	114	18	132	5,479	1,197	6,676
In Military Quarters	2,301	156	2,457	9,607	1,163	10,770	632	113	745	12,540	1,432	13,972
In College Dormitory	154	138	292	33,704	38,954	72,658	1,591	856	2,447	35,449	39,948	75,397
Other in Group Quarters	786	536	1,322	1,614	2,150	3,764	902	1,029	1,931	3,302	3,715	7,017
MARITAL STATUS												
Persons, 15 years and over	436,349	426,390	862,739	794,724	971,205	1,765,929	263,623	196,160	459,783	1,494,696	1,593,755	3,088,451
Single	324,654	283,784	608,438	361,151	330,927	692,078	78,003	64,189	142,192	763,808	678,900	1,442,708
Now married, except separated	94,448	102,571	197,019	383,242	530,559	913,801	168,838	113,943	282,781	646,528	747,073	1,393,601
Separated	4,175	7,728	11,903	10,890	21,655	32,545	3,326	3,074	6,400	18,391	32,457	50,848
Widowed	2,420	15,164	17,584	2,427	17,111	19,538	760	2,277	3,037	5,607	34,552	40,159
Divorced	10,652	17,143	27,795	37,014	70,953	107,967	12,969	12,677	25,646	60,635	100,773	161,408
FERTILITY												
Women 15 to 44 years	0	368,954	368,954	0	860,192	860,192	0	179,189	179,189	0	1,408,335	1,408,335
Children ever born	0	199,537	199,537	0	865,603	865,603	0	129,173	129,173	0	1,194,313	1,194,313
Per 1000 women	0	541	541	0	1,006	1,006	0	721	721	0	848	848

TABLE 6.27
NATIVITY AND LANGUAGE OF PERSONS OF MULTIPLE ITALIAN ANCESTRY BORN IN THE U.S. BY EDUCATION: 1980

	Less Than 12 Years of School			High School Graduates			College Graduates			All Persons		
	Male	Female	Total	Male	Female	Total	Male	Female	Total	Male	Female	Total
NATIVITY												
Total Persons	1,537,560	1,481,253	3,018,813	794,724	971,205	1,765,929	263,623	196,160	459,783	2,595,907	2,648,618	5,244,525
Native	1,537,560	1,481,253	3,018,813	794,724	971,205	1,765,929	263,623	196,160	459,783	2,595,907	2,648,618	5,244,525
Born in State of residence	1,260,107	1,210,138	2,470,245	563,771	678,976	1,242,747	148,469	113,680	262,149	1,972,347	2,002,794	3,975,141
Born in different State	267,535	262,158	529,693	226,182	286,824	513,006	113,348	80,949	194,297	607,065	629,931	1,236,996
Foreign Born	9,918	8,957	18,875	4,771	5,405	10,176	1,806	1,531	3,337	16,495	15,893	32,388
LANGUAGE SPOKEN AT HOME												
Persons 5 to 17 years	974,044	937,859	1,911,903	2,725	4,020	6,745	0	7	7	976,769	941,886	1,918,655
Speak only English at home	949,313	911,157	1,860,470	2,550	3,760	6,310	0	7	7	951,863	914,924	1,866,787
Speak a language other than English	24,731	26,702	51,433	175	260	435	0	0	0	24,906	26,962	51,868
Italian language spoken at home	8,644	8,410	17,054	82	45	127	0	0	0	8,726	8,455	17,181
Speak English very well	8,340	8,124	16,464	82	45	127	0	0	0	8,422	8,169	16,591
Speak English not well	304	286	590	0	0	0	0	0	0	304	286	590
Other language spoken at home	16,087	18,292	34,379	93	215	308	0	0	0	16,180	18,507	34,687
Speak English very well	15,155	17,173	32,328	70	204	274	0	0	0	15,225	17,377	32,602
Speak English not well	932	1,119	2,051	23	11	34	0	0	0	955	1,130	2,085
Persons 18 and over	198,492	195,178	393,670	791,999	967,185	1,759,184	263,623	196,153	459,776	1,254,114	1,358,516	2,612,630
Speak only English at home	190,587	185,402	375,989	765,025	933,302	1,698,327	252,925	187,715	440,640	1,208,537	1,306,419	2,514,956
Speak a language other than English	7,905	9,776	17,681	26,974	33,883	60,857	10,698	8,438	19,136	45,577	52,097	97,674
Italian language spoken at home	2,818	3,518	6,336	9,415	12,487	21,902	3,223	2,682	5,905	15,456	18,687	34,143
Speak English very well	2,666	3,312	5,978	8,940	11,914	20,854	3,128	2,627	5,755	14,734	17,853	32,587
Speak English not well	152	206	358	475	573	1,048	95	55	150	722	834	1,556
Other language spoken at home	5,087	6,258	11,345	17,559	21,396	38,955	7,475	5,756	13,231	30,121	33,410	63,531
Speak English very well	4,801	5,830	10,631	16,563	20,192	36,755	7,137	5,499	12,636	28,501	31,521	60,022
Speak English not well	286	428	714	996	1,204	2,200	338	257	595	1,620	1,889	3,509
MEANS OF TRANSPORTATION												
Workers 16 and over	184,050	129,720	313,770	632,983	589,336	1,222,319	240,894	146,098	386,992	1,057,927	865,154	1,923,081
Car, truck, or van	149,432	101,570	251,002	550,795	491,767	1,042,562	202,736	121,500	324,236	902,963	714,837	1,617,800
Drive alone	110,432	65,742	176,174	437,405	381,508	818,913	164,285	96,048	260,333	712,122	543,298	1,255,420
Carpool	39,000	35,828	74,828	113,390	110,259	223,649	38,451	25,452	63,903	190,841	171,539	362,380
Public transportation	8,687	10,515	19,202	29,020	47,606	76,626	21,000	13,350	34,350	58,707	71,471	130,178
Walked only	17,517	14,346	31,863	33,459	36,312	69,771	9,242	7,039	16,281	60,218	57,697	117,915
Other means	6,531	1,673	8,204	13,734	4,853	18,587	4,246	1,297	5,543	24,511	7,823	32,334
Worked at home	1,883	1,616	3,499	5,975	8,798	14,773	3,670	2,912	6,582	11,528	13,326	24,854

TABLE 6.28
EDUCATION, RESIDENCE IN 1975 OF PERSONS OF MULTIPLE ITALIAN ANCESTRY BORN IN THE U.S. BY EDUCATION: 1980

	LESS THAN 12 YEARS OF SCHOOL			HIGH SCHOOL GRADUATES			COLLEGE GRADUATES			ALL PERSONS		
	Male	Female	Total	Male	Female	Total	Male	Female	Total	Male	Female	Total
SCHOOL ENROLLMENT												
Persons 3 years old and over enrolled	1,039,848	996,425	2,036,273	165,012	176,852	341,864	34,014	26,654	60,668	1,238,874	1,199,931	2,438,805
Nursery school	67,961	62,472	130,433	0	0	0	0	0	0	67,961	62,472	130,433
Public	19,387	17,144	36,531	0	0	0	0	0	0	19,387	17,144	36,531
Private	48,574	45,328	93,902	0	0	0	0	0	0	48,574	45,328	93,902
Kindergarten & Elementary (1-8 years)	670,479	637,156	1,307,635	0	0	0	0	0	0	670,479	637,156	1,307,635
Public	541,911	507,999	1,049,910	0	0	0	0	0	0	541,911	507,999	1,049,910
Private	128,568	129,157	257,725	0	0	0	0	0	0	128,568	129,157	257,725
High School (1 to 4 years)	301,408	296,797	598,205	0	0	0	0	0	0	301,408	296,797	598,205
Public	254,875	251,093	505,968	0	0	0	0	0	0	254,875	251,093	505,968
Private	46,533	45,704	92,237	0	0	0	0	0	0	46,533	45,704	92,237
College	0	0	0	165,012	176,852	341,864	34,014	26,654	60,668	199,026	203,506	402,532
YEARS OF SCHOOL COMPLETED												
Persons 25 years and over	111,647	125,291	236,938	450,977	586,116	1,037,093	228,438	159,792	388,230	791,062	871,199	1,662,261
Elementary (0 to 8 years)	34,677	32,012	66,689	0	0	0	0	0	0	34,677	32,012	66,689
High School: 1 to 3 years	76,970	93,279	170,249	0	0	0	0	0	0	76,970	93,279	170,249
4 or more years	0	0	0	270,674	405,982	676,656	0	0	0	270,674	405,982	676,656
College: 1 to 3 years	0	0	0	180,303	180,134	360,437	0	0	0	180,303	180,134	360,437
4 or more years	0	0	0	0	0	0	228,438	159,792	388,230	228,438	159,792	388,230
Percent High School Graduates			0	100.0	100.0	100.0	100.0	100.0	100.0	85.9	85.6	40.7
RESIDENCE IN 1975												
Persons 5 years and over	1,166,397	1,124,644	2,291,041	795,055	972,478	1,767,533	262,102	196,256	458,358	2,223,554	2,293,378	4,516,932
Same house	672,897	642,993	1,315,890	361,624	427,894	789,518	86,330	61,453	147,783	1,120,851	1,132,340	2,253,191
Different house in United States	489,084	476,897	965,981	427,149	540,455	967,604	173,170	133,244	306,414	1,089,403	1,150,596	2,239,999
Same County	283,344	280,703	564,047	229,467	298,051	527,518	73,325	57,369	130,694	586,136	636,123	1,222,259
Different County	205,740	196,194	401,934	197,682	242,404	440,086	99,845	75,875	175,720	503,267	514,473	1,017,740
Same State	100,965	96,865	197,830	102,136	132,366	234,502	45,122	38,223	83,345	248,223	267,454	515,677
Different State	104,775	99,329	204,104	95,546	110,038	205,584	54,723	37,652	92,375	255,044	247,019	502,063
Abroad	4,416	4,754	9,170	6,282	4,129	10,411	2,602	1,559	4,161	13,300	10,442	23,742

TABLE 6.29
LABOR FORCE AND OCCUPATION OF PERSONS OF MULTIPLE ITALIAN ANCESTRY BORN IN THE U.S. BY EDUCATION: 1980

	Less Than 12 Years of School			High School Graduates			College Graduates			All Persons		
	Male	Female	Total	Male	Female	Total	Male	Female	Total	Male	Female	Total
Labor Force Status												
Persons 16 years and over	355,595	346,826	702,421	794,661	971,173	1,765,834	263,623	196,160	459,783	1,413,879	1,514,159	2,928,038
Labor force	218,409	152,861	371,270	695,664	642,079	1,337,743	249,177	154,265	403,442	1,163,250	949,205	2,112,455
Percent of persons 16 years	61.4	44.1	52.9	87.5	66.1	75.8	94.5	78.6	87.7	82.3	62.7	72.1
Civilian labor force	215,337	152,658	367,995	676,025	639,603	1,315,628	244,128	153,723	397,851	1,135,490	945,984	2,081,474
Employed	186,518	133,781	320,299	627,017	603,533	1,230,550	238,667	149,325	387,992	1,052,202	886,639	1,938,841
Unemployed	28,819	18,877	47,696	49,008	36,070	85,078	5,461	4,398	9,859	83,288	59,345	142,633
Percent of civ. labor force	13.4	12.4	13.0	7.2	5.6	6.5	2.2	2.9	2.5	7.3	6.3	6.9
Not in labor force	137,186	193,965	331,151	98,997	329,094	428,091	14,446	41,895	56,341	250,629	564,954	815,583
Class of Worker and Occupation												
Employed 16 years and ov.	186,518	133,781	320,299	627,017	603,533	1,230,550	238,667	149,325	387,992	1,052,202	886,639	1,938,841
Private wage and salary work.	163,120	121,604	284,724	515,723	507,274	1,022,997	162,393	86,047	248,440	841,236	714,925	1,556,161
Federal Government workers	2,604	1,434	4,038	20,288	16,912	37,200	11,614	4,496	16,110	34,506	22,842	57,348
State Government workers	2,525	2,161	4,686	16,484	25,853	42,337	15,903	12,687	28,590	34,912	40,701	75,613
Local Government workers	8,062	5,503	13,565	37,365	35,947	73,312	30,829	40,773	71,602	76,256	82,223	158,479
Self-employed workers	9,425	2,484	11,909	35,988	14,466	50,454	17,632	4,708	22,340	63,045	21,658	84,703
Unpaid family workers	782	595	1,377	1,169	3,081	4,250	297	614	911	2,248	4,290	6,538
Employed 16 years and over	186,518	133,781	320,299	627,017	603,533	1,230,550	238,667	149,325	387,992	1,052,202	886,639	1,938,841
Managerial and Professional	8,626	6,038	14,664	98,268	91,669	189,937	153,600	101,678	255,278	260,494	199,385	459,879
Execut., Administ., Manag.	6,557	3,616	10,173	66,459	45,696	112,155	65,262	19,149	84,411	138,278	68,461	206,739
Professional Specialty occupations	2,069	2,422	4,491	31,809	45,973	77,782	88,338	82,529	170,867	122,216	130,924	253,140
Technical, Sales, Administrative	27,670	61,285	88,955	149,364	369,139	518,503	53,661	38,663	92,324	230,695	469,087	699,782
Technician and related support	1,584	1,011	2,595	26,050	22,219	48,269	10,775	7,652	18,427	38,409	30,882	69,291
Sales Occupations	15,787	33,115	48,902	64,312	78,693	143,005	27,509	9,182	36,691	107,608	120,990	228,598
Administrative Support	10,299	27,159	37,458	59,002	268,227	327,229	15,377	21,829	37,206	84,678	317,215	401,893
Service Occupations	39,191	44,433	83,624	67,383	93,970	161,353	9,761	6,181	15,942	116,335	144,584	260,919
Private household occupations	136	2,244	2,380	121	2,226	2,347	60	154	214	317	4,624	4,941
Protective Service occupations	2,717	751	3,468	23,910	2,818	26,728	4,912	435	5,347	31,539	4,004	35,543
Other Service Occupations	36,338	41,438	77,776	43,352	88,926	132,278	4,789	5,592	10,381	84,479	135,956	220,435
Farming, forestry, fishing	5,307	1,152	6,459	10,340	2,988	13,328	1,723	354	2,077	17,370	4,494	21,864
Precision Prod., Craft, Repair	38,045	2,938	40,983	153,023	9,981	163,004	12,618	1,049	13,667	203,686	13,968	217,654
Operators, Fabricators, Laborers	67,679	17,935	85,614	148,639	35,786	184,425	7,304	1,400	8,704	223,622	55,121	278,743
Machine Oper., Assembl.	19,550	11,938	31,488	60,571	23,352	83,923	2,744	1,010	3,754	82,865	36,300	119,165
Transportation	17,393	1,333	18,726	43,741	4,052	47,793	2,355	147	2,502	63,489	5,532	69,021
Handlers, cleaners, helpers	30,736	4,664	35,400	44,327	8,382	52,709	2,205	243	2,448	77,268	13,289	90,557

TABLE 6.30
INDUSTRY, LABOR FORCE IN 1979 OF PERSONS OF MULTIPLE ITALIAN ANCESTRY BORN IN THE U.S. BY EDUCATION: 1980

	Less Than 12 Years of School			High School Graduates			College Graduates			All Persons		
	Male	Female	Total	Male	Female	Total	Male	Female	Total	Male	Female	Total
Industry												
Employed 16 years and over	186,518	133,781	320,299	627,017	603,533	1,230,550	238,667	149,325	387,992	1,052,202	886,639	1,938,841
Agriculture, Forestry, Fishing	6,450	1,361	7,811	15,808	5,483	21,291	4,409	987	5,396	26,667	7,831	34,498
Construction	18,793	942	19,735	63,963	8,376	72,339	8,681	1,004	9,685	91,437	10,322	101,759
Manufacturing	40,089	19,485	59,574	164,211	83,932	248,143	45,887	10,801	56,688	250,187	114,218	364,405
Nondurable goods	13,933	8,614	22,547	47,555	34,181	81,736	15,873	5,718	21,591	77,361	48,513	125,874
Durable goods	26,156	10,871	37,027	116,656	49,751	166,407	30,014	5,083	35,097	172,826	65,705	238,531
Transportation	10,326	1,853	12,179	43,378	15,798	59,176	6,965	2,013	8,978	60,669	19,664	80,333
Communications and Public Utilities	3,468	1,061	4,529	25,914	15,822	41,736	6,433	2,244	8,677	35,815	19,127	54,942
Wholesale Trade	8,532	3,426	11,958	38,857	21,373	60,230	12,037	2,512	14,549	59,426	27,311	86,737
Retail Trade	62,551	63,175	125,726	113,947	136,019	249,966	20,627	12,158	32,785	197,125	211,352	408,477
Finance, Insurance, Real Estate	3,590	5,983	9,573	25,756	74,424	100,180	20,378	9,909	30,287	49,724	90,316	140,040
Business and Repair Service	10,689	4,023	14,712	36,374	25,368	61,742	12,436	6,100	18,536	59,499	35,491	94,990
Personal, Entertainment, Recreational	8,512	11,345	19,857	21,664	31,922	53,586	5,113	3,269	8,382	35,289	46,536	81,825
Professional and Related Services	9,454	18,769	28,223	41,662	157,430	199,092	75,260	90,726	165,986	126,376	266,925	393,301
Health Services	3,517	10,152	13,669	12,592	83,502	96,094	14,903	21,278	36,181	31,012	114,932	145,944
Educational Services	3,345	4,610	7,955	18,147	43,257	61,404	37,562	57,951	95,513	59,054	105,818	164,872
Other Profess. & Related Services	2,592	4,007	6,599	10,923	30,671	41,594	22,795	11,497	34,292	36,310	46,175	82,485
Public Administration	4,064	2,358	6,422	35,483	27,586	63,069	20,441	7,602	28,043	59,988	37,546	97,534
Labour Force Status in 1979												
Persons 16 ys. in Labor Force in 1979	253,502	185,453	438,955	753,647	739,836	1,493,483	255,804	166,239	422,043	1,262,953	1,091,528	2,354,481
Worked in 1979	245,538	177,461	422,999	746,188	729,392	1,475,580	254,743	165,086	419,829	1,246,469	1,071,939	2,318,408
50 to 52 weeks	95,657	50,742	146,399	472,278	379,027	851,305	189,172	76,780	265,952	757,107	506,549	1,263,656
40 to 49 weeks	30,280	19,876	50,156	96,102	98,959	195,061	29,684	35,315	64,999	156,066	154,150	310,216
1 to 39 weeks	119,601	106,843	226,444	177,808	251,406	429,214	35,887	52,991	88,878	333,296	411,240	744,536
35 or more hours per week	143,939	66,764	210,703	642,780	477,139	1,119,919	232,921	121,755	354,676	1,019,640	665,658	1,685,298
50 to 52 weeks	75,496	29,903	105,399	437,954	296,935	734,889	181,120	64,905	246,025	694,570	391,743	1,086,313
With unemployment in 1979	73,899	52,431	126,330	166,053	155,506	321,559	29,850	30,125	59,975	269,802	238,062	507,864
Unemployed 15 or more weeks	30,502	17,743	48,245	56,046	43,055	99,101	8,960	6,932	15,892	95,508	67,730	163,238
Workers in Family in 1979												
Families	89,969	24,409	114,378	372,361	81,231	453,592	162,040	17,113	179,153	624,370	122,753	747,123
No Workers	7,875	7,449	15,324	6,776	9,553	16,329	1,524	734	2,258	16,175	17,736	33,911
1 worker	28,974	10,037	39,011	115,790	40,454	156,244	47,979	6,432	54,411	192,743	56,923	249,666
2 or more workers	53,120	6,923	60,043	249,795	31,224	281,019	112,537	9,947	122,484	415,452	48,094	463,546

TABLE 6.31
INCOME CHARACTERISTICS OF PERSONS OF MULTIPLE ITALIAN ANCESTRY BORN IN THE U.S. BY EDUCATION: 1980

INCOME IN 1979		Less Than 12 Years of School			High School Graduates			College Graduates			All Persons		
HOUSEHOLDS		103,747	40,099	143,846	450,871	155,321	606,192	207,275	53,151	260,426	761,893	248,571	1,010,464
Less than $5,000		7,429	14,264	21,693	16,029	24,663	40,692	5,726	4,491	10,217	29,184	43,418	72,602
$5,000 to $7,499		6,242	6,620	12,862	14,519	16,665	31,184	4,028	3,198	7,226	24,789	26,483	51,272
$7,500 to $9,999		7,875	4,736	12,611	19,849	19,065	38,914	5,397	4,129	9,526	33,121	27,930	61,051
$10,000 to $14,999		18,016	5,935	23,951	58,899	36,969	95,868	16,913	11,775	28,688	93,828	54,679	148,507
$15,000 to $19,999		18,779	3,518	22,297	82,787	22,564	105,351	26,429	10,582	37,011	127,995	36,664	164,659
$20,000 to $24,999		15,957	1,938	17,895	86,230	13,822	100,052	32,504	6,748	39,252	134,691	22,508	157,199
$25,000 to $34,999		18,087	2,008	20,095	107,683	13,562	121,245	55,953	7,215	63,168	181,723	22,785	204,508
$35,000 to $49,999		8,220	812	9,032	48,063	5,684	53,747	38,095	3,448	41,543	94,378	9,944	104,322
$50,000 or more		3,142	268	3,410	16,812	2,327	19,139	22,230	1,565	23,795	42,184	4,160	46,344
Median	Dol.	18,166	7,185	15,181	21,732	12,014	19,577	26,861	16,263	24,783	22,674	12,419	20,227
Mean	Dol.	20,486	10,172	17,578	23,577	14,574	21,446	30,863	19,127	27,385	24,879	14,908	22,426
FAMILIES		89,969	24,409	114,378	372,361	81,231	453,592	162,040	17,113	179,153	624,370	122,753	747,123
Less than $5,000		4,564	8,186	12,750	7,807	13,870	21,677	1,748	1,006	2,754	14,119	23,062	37,181
$5,000 to $7,499		4,665	3,754	8,419	8,318	8,372	16,690	1,535	675	2,210	14,518	12,801	27,319
$7,500 to $9,999		6,316	2,743	9,059	12,759	8,868	21,627	2,310	855	3,165	21,385	12,466	33,851
$10,000 to $14,999		15,274	3,663	18,937	42,497	17,042	59,539	8,977	2,563	11,540	66,748	23,268	90,016
$15,000 to $19,999		16,791	2,554	19,345	67,663	11,526	79,189	18,538	2,988	21,526	102,992	17,068	120,060
$20,000 to $24,999		14,494	1,387	15,881	76,537	7,900	84,437	26,297	2,235	28,532	117,328	11,522	128,850
$25,000 to $34,999		17,054	1,387	18,441	97,874	8,353	106,227	48,655	3,560	52,215	163,583	13,300	176,883
$35,000 to $49,999		7,876	548	8,424	43,764	3,677	47,441	34,095	2,133	36,228	85,735	6,358	92,093
$50,000 or more		2,935	187	3,122	15,142	1,623	16,765	19,885	1,098	20,983	37,962	2,908	40,870
Median	Dol.	19,173	7,741	17,074	22,849	12,445	21,662	29,056	20,935	28,801	23,939	12,804	22,528
Mean	Dol.	21,440	10,890	19,190	24,864	15,468	23,339	33,478	25,014	31,127	26,296	15,798	24,571

TABLE 6.31 (Cont'd)
INCOME CHARACTERISTICS OF PERSONS OF MULTIPLE ITALIAN ANCESTRY BORN IN THE U.S. BY EDUCATION: 1980

	Less Than 12 Years of School			High School Graduates			College Graduates			All Persons		
UNRELATED INDIVIDUALS, 15 YEARS....	24,548	26,515	51,063	155,574	160,255	315,829	60,330	49,620	109,950	240,452	236,390	476,842
Less than $2,000	4,188	6,238	10,426	25,571	40,797	66,368	4,465	3,522	7,987	34,224	50,557	84,781
$2,000 to $2,999	1,821	2,742	4,563	13,480	14,416	27,896	1,970	1,697	3,667	17,271	18,855	36,126
$3,000 to $4,999	3,515	6,464	9,979	19,168	20,215	39,383	4,540	4,439	8,979	27,223	31,118	58,341
$5,000 to $7,999	4,238	5,181	9,419	23,576	23,559	47,135	6,437	6,297	12,734	34,251	35,037	69,288
$8,000 to $9,999	2,519	2,196	4,715	11,718	15,882	27,600	4,177	4,772	8,949	18,414	22,850	41,264
$10,000 to $14,999	3,980	2,563	6,543	25,690	28,956	54,646	11,568	13,677	25,245	41,238	45,196	86,434
$15,000 to $24,999	3,296	876	4,172	28,115	14,275	42,390	17,192	12,889	30,081	48,603	28,040	76,643
$25,000 to $49,999	881	227	1,108	7,392	1,935	9,327	8,360	2,224	10,584	16,633	4,386	21,019
$50,000 or more	110	28	138	864	220	1,084	1,621	103	1,724	2,595	351	2,946
Median Dol.	6,771	4,237	5,179	7,385	5,586	6,545	13,588	11,449	12,507	8,788	6,513	7,562
Mean Dol.	8,902	5,350	7,277	9,671	6,915	8,641	15,922	11,852	14,350	11,428	8,223	9,811
Per Capita Income Dol.	1,385	555	978	13,173	5,564	8,988	21,942	9,520	16,642	7,081	3,056	5,048
MEAN FAMILY INCOME BY WORKER												
No Workers Dol.	10,082	4,551	7,393	13,220	5,571	8,745	19,873	18,222	19,336	12,319	5,666	8,839
1 Worker Dol.	17,637	9,872	15,639	21,031	11,753	18,629	32,363	18,002	30,665	23,342	12,127	20,785
2 or more workers Dol.	25,199	19,188	24,506	26,956	23,308	26,551	34,138	30,049	33,806	28,677	24,109	28,203

TABLE 6.32

POVERTY CHARACTERISTICS OF PERSONS OF MULTIPLE ITALIAN ANCESTRY BORN IN THE U.S. BY EDUCATION: 1980

	Less Than 12 Years of School			High School Graduates			College Graduates			All Persons		
	Male	Female	Total	Male	Female	Total	Male	Female	Total	Male	Female	Total
ALL INCOME LEVEL IN 1979												
Families	89,969	24,409	114,378	372,361	81,231	453,592	162,040	17,113	179,153	624,370	122,753	747,123
With Children under 18 years	53,836	18,143	71,979	250,967	60,238	311,205	105,911	9,236	115,147	410,714	87,617	498,331
With Children 5 to 17 years	42,025	14,237	56,262	177,638	49,213	226,851	72,666	7,199	79,865	292,329	70,649	362,978
Female Householder, no husband	0	20,960	20,960	0	63,992	63,992	0	9,251	9,251	0	94,203	94,203
With Children under 18 ys.	0	16,313	16,313	0	51,716	51,716	0	6,599	6,599	0	74,628	74,628
With Children under 6 years	0	7,237	7,237	0	18,262	18,262	0	2,033	2,033	0	27,532	27,532
Householder 65 years and over	8,134	1,958	10,092	5,624	1,311	6,935	1,898	212	2,110	15,656	3,481	19,137
Unrelat. Individ. in pov.	22,174	26,266	48,440	112,263	120,138	232,401	58,107	48,651	106,758	192,544	195,055	387,599
65 years and over	1,923	6,360	8,283	1,067	4,451	5,518	356	1,071	1,427	3,346	11,882	15,228
Persons in poverty univ.	1,523,897	1,472,347	2,996,244	748,603	930,090	1,678,693	261,163	195,112	456,275	2,533,663	2,597,549	5,131,212
Related children under 18	1,328,164	1,274,032	2,602,196	2,457	3,459	5,916	0	7	7	1,330,621	1,277,498	2,608,119
Related children 5 to 17	965,498	927,994	1,893,492	2,457	3,459	5,916	0	7	7	967,955	931,460	1,899,415
60 years and over	18,054	24,299	42,353	16,249	23,305	39,554	4,931	3,903	8,834	39,234	51,507	90,741
65 years and over	11,048	16,223	27,271	7,246	12,105	19,351	2,473	2,254	4,727	20,767	30,582	51,349
INCOME IN 1979 BELOW POVERTY												
Families	6,538	9,861	16,399	12,180	17,104	29,284	2,372	1,171	3,543	21,090	28,136	49,226
Percent Below Poverty Level	7.3	40.4	14.3	3.3	21.2	6.5	1.5	6.8	2.0	3.4	22.9	6.6
With Children under 18 years	4,900	9,283	14,183	9,803	16,231	26,034	1,753	978	2,731	16,456	26,492	42,948
With Children 5 to 17 years	3,411	6,675	10,086	6,310	11,709	18,019	1,111	738	1,849	10,832	19,122	29,954
Female Householder, no husband	0	9,425	9,425	0	16,281	16,281	0	1,058	1,058	0	26,764	26,764
With Children under 18 ys.	0	8,969	8,969	0	15,661	15,661	0	935	935	0	25,565	25,565
With Children under 6 years	0	5,210	5,210	0	8,979	8,979	0	493	493	0	14,682	14,682
Householder 65 years and over	534	220	754	211	68	279	31	7	38	776	295	1,071
Unrelat. Individ. in pov.	6,432	11,478	17,910	19,410	29,068	48,478	7,423	6,582	14,005	33,265	47,128	80,393
Percent Below Poverty Level	29.0	43.7	37.0	17.3	24.2	20.9	12.8	13.5	13.1	17.3	24.2	20.7
65 years and over	438	1,779	2,217	73	731	804	10	159	169	521	2,669	3,190
Persons in poverty univ.	118,772	130,386	249,158	36,672	65,562	102,234	10,310	9,512	19,822	165,754	205,460	371,214
Percent Below Poverty Level	7.8	8.9	8.3	4.9	7.0	6.1	3.9	4.9	4.3	6.5	7.9	7.2
Related children under 18	101,369	98,369	199,738	121	176	297	0	0	0	101,490	98,545	200,035
Related children 5 to 17	69,934	68,404	138,338	121	176	297	0	0	0	70,055	68,580	138,635
60 years and over	1,484	3,303	4,787	563	1,504	2,067	105	245	350	2,152	5,052	7,204
65 years and over	1,022	2,346	3,368	297	936	1,233	46	185	231	1,365	3,467	4,832

TABLE 6.33
RESIDENCE, AGE, AND RELATIONSHIP OF PERSONS OF TOTAL ITALIAN ANCESTRY BORN IN ITALY BY EDUCATION: 1980

	LESS THAN 12 YEARS OF SCHOOL			HIGH SCHOOL GRADUATES			COLLEGE GRADUATES			ALL PERSONS		
	Male	Female	Total	Male	Female	Total	Male	Female	Total	Male	Female	Total
URBAN AND RURAL												
Total Persons	264,748	305,209	569,957	101,298	92,323	193,621	27,006	13,049	40,055	393,052	410,581	803,633
Urban	250,935	291,647	542,582	95,535	87,167	182,702	25,110	12,222	37,332	371,580	391,036	762,616
Rural	13,813	13,562	27,375	5,763	5,156	10,919	1,896	827	2,723	21,472	19,545	41,017
Farm	644	721	1,365	165	189	354	90	29	119	899	939	1,838
AGE												
Total Persons	264,748	305,209	569,957	101,298	92,323	193,621	27,006	13,049	40,055	393,052	410,581	803,633
under 5 years	670	465	1,135	0	0	0	0	0	0	670	465	1,135
5 to 9 years	1,954	1,659	3,613	0	0	0	0	0	0	1,954	1,659	3,613
10 to 14 years	5,226	5,005	10,231	0	0	0	0	0	0	5,226	5,005	10,231
15 to 19 years	7,256	6,780	14,036	2,459	2,450	4,909	0	0	0	9,715	9,230	18,945
20 to 24 years	3,943	3,367	7,310	8,642	8,290	16,932	1,062	692	1,754	13,647	12,349	25,996
25 to 29 years	5,410	5,867	11,277	9,953	8,788	18,741	3,267	2,077	5,344	18,630	16,732	35,362
30 to 34 years	9,041	9,838	18,879	12,176	10,598	22,774	4,845	1,961	6,806	26,062	22,397	48,459
35 to 44 years	26,695	27,934	54,629	17,000	13,571	30,571	4,555	2,024	6,579	48,250	43,529	91,779
45 to 54 years	35,236	33,638	68,874	15,532	14,297	29,829	4,349	1,896	6,245	55,117	49,831	104,948
55 to 59 years	18,322	19,145	37,467	9,888	9,102	18,990	2,756	1,228	3,984	30,966	29,475	60,441
60 to 64 years	14,442	15,712	30,154	5,035	4,902	9,937	1,180	599	1,779	20,657	21,213	41,870
65 to 74 years	51,187	65,091	116,278	10,600	9,850	20,450	2,778	1,168	3,946	64,565	76,109	140,674
75 to 84 years	60,540	80,767	141,307	7,411	7,814	15,225	1,735	1,019	2,754	69,686	89,600	159,286
85 years and over	24,826	29,941	54,767	2,602	2,661	5,263	479	385	864	27,907	32,987	60,894
median age	65.8	68.6	67.4	45.3	46.7	46.0	44.4	43.8	44.3	57.8	63.4	60.1
HOUSEHOLD TYPE AND RELATIONSHIP												
In Household	260,573	298,129	558,702	100,024	90,666	190,690	26,565	12,579	39,144	387,162	401,374	788,536
Family Householder	193,102	30,769	223,871	74,519	7,933	82,452	18,934	1,222	20,156	286,555	39,924	326,479
Non-family Householder: Male	22,552	0	22,552	7,137	0	7,137	3,194	0	3,194	32,883	0	32,883
Female	0	65,335	65,335	0	10,456	10,456	0	1,871	1,871	0	77,662	77,662
Spouse	6,203	137,672	143,875	2,342	57,302	59,644	898	7,532	8,430	9,443	202,506	211,949
Other Relatives	37,240	63,174	100,414	14,651	14,219	28,870	2,776	1,709	4,485	54,667	79,102	133,769
Nonrelatives	1,476	1,179	2,655	1,375	756	2,131	763	245	1,008	3,614	2,180	5,794

TABLE 6.34
SELECTED DEMOGRAPHIC CHARACTERISTICS OF PERSONS OF TOTAL ITALIAN ANCESTRY BORN IN ITALY BY EDUCATION

	Less Than 12 Years of School			High School Graduates			College Graduates			All Persons		
	Male	Female	Total	Male	Female	Total	Male	Female	Total	Male	Female	Total
PERSONS IN HOUSEHOLDS												
HOUSEHOLDS	215,654	96,104	311,758	81,656	18,389	100,045	22,128	3,093	25,221	319,438	117,586	437,024
1 person	21,535	64,106	85,641	6,146	9,982	16,128	2,556	1,664	4,220	30,237	75,752	105,989
2 persons	91,862	19,628	111,490	24,769	4,643	29,412	7,546	833	8,379	124,177	25,104	149,281
3 persons	34,814	6,938	41,752	15,671	2,127	17,798	4,251	317	4,568	54,736	9,382	64,118
4 persons	32,767	2,950	35,717	18,623	993	19,616	4,314	179	4,493	55,704	4,122	59,826
5 persons	21,523	1,499	23,022	10,885	465	11,350	2,219	35	2,254	34,627	1,999	36,626
6 persons	13,153	983	14,136	5,562	179	5,741	1,242	65	1,307	19,957	1,227	21,184
TYPE OF GROUP QUARTERS												
Persons in Group Quarters	4,175	7,080	11,255	1,274	1,657	2,931	441	470	911	5,890	9,207	15,097
Inmate of Mental Hospital	358	500	858	113	75	188	5	5	10	476	580	1,056
Inmate of Home for Aged	3,119	5,792	8,911	410	1,068	1,478	158	185	343	3,687	7,045	10,732
Inmate of Other Institution	365	287	652	113	79	192	34	25	59	512	391	903
In Military Quarters	40	7	47	200	21	221	7	7	14	247	35	282
In College Dormitory	0	7	7	228	578	806	32	114	146	260	699	959
Other in Group Quarters	286	494	780	88	186	274	155	228	383	529	908	1,437
MARITAL STATUS												
Persons, 15 years and over	256,898	298,080	554,978	101,298	92,323	193,621	27,006	13,049	40,055	385,202	403,452	788,654
Single	19,062	15,353	34,415	16,651	11,717	28,368	4,906	2,547	7,453	40,619	29,617	70,236
Now married, except separated	200,935	149,541	350,476	76,725	60,790	137,515	20,064	8,184	28,248	297,724	218,515	516,239
Separated	2,004	2,495	4,499	969	1,099	2,068	343	195	538	3,316	3,789	7,105
Widowed	30,091	125,514	155,605	3,894	15,135	19,029	718	1,515	2,233	34,703	142,164	176,867
Divorced	4,806	5,177	9,983	3,059	3,582	6,641	975	608	1,583	8,840	9,367	18,207
FERTILITY												
Women 15 to 44 years	0	53,786	53,786	0	43,697	43,697	0	6,754	6,754	0	104,237	104,237
Children ever born	0	108,792	108,792	0	66,152	66,152	0	7,209	7,209	0	182,153	182,153
Per 1000 women	0	2,023	2,023	0	1,514	1,514	0	1,067	1,067	0	1,747	1,747

TABLE 6.35

NATIVITY AND LANGUAGE OF PERSONS OF TOTAL ITALIAN ANCESTRY BORN IN ITALY BY EDUCATION: 1980

	LESS THAN 12 YEARS OF SCHOOL			HIGH SCHOOL GRADUATES			COLLEGE GRADUATES			ALL PERSONS		
	Male	Female	Total	Male	Female	Total	Male	Female	Total	Male	Female	Total
NATIVITY												
Total Persons	264,748	305,209	569,957	101,298	92,323	193,621	27,006	13,049	40,055	393,052	410,581	803,633
Native												
Born in State of residence												
Born in different State												
Born abroad												
Foreign Born	264,748	305,209	569,957	101,298	92,323	193,621	27,006	13,049	40,055	393,052	410,581	803,633
LANGUAGE SPOKEN AT HOME												
Persons 5 to 17 years	12,259	11,605	23,864	122	183	305	0	0	0	12,381	11,788	24,169
Speak only English at home	859	826	1,685	6	24	30	0	0	0	865	850	1,715
Speak a language other than English	11,400	10,779	22,179	116	159	275	0	0	0	11,516	10,938	22,454
Italian language spoken at home	11,251	10,655	21,906	109	159	268	0	0	0	11,360	10,814	22,174
Speak English very well	10,520	10,046	20,566	109	154	263	0	0	0	10,629	10,200	20,829
Speak English not well	731	609	1,340	0	5	5	0	0	0	731	614	1,345
Other language spoken at home	149	124	273	7	0	7	0	0	0	156	124	280
Speak English very well	149	109	258	7	0	7	0	0	0	156	109	265
Speak English not well	0	15	15	0	0	0	0	0	0	0	15	15
Persons 18 and over	251,819	293,139	544,958	101,176	92,140	193,316	27,006	13,049	40,055	380,001	398,328	778,329
Speak only English at home	47,605	40,125	87,730	24,156	19,327	43,483	8,306	3,048	11,354	80,067	62,500	142,567
Speak a language other than English	204,214	253,014	457,228	77,020	72,813	149,833	18,700	10,001	28,701	299,934	335,828	635,762
Italian language spoken at home	201,467	249,903	451,370	75,462	71,509	146,971	18,174	9,722	27,896	295,103	331,134	626,237
Speak English very well	147,858	162,534	310,392	68,860	63,066	131,926	17,275	8,681	25,956	233,993	234,281	468,274
Speak English not well	53,609	87,369	140,978	6,602	8,443	15,045	899	1,041	1,940	61,110	96,853	157,963
Other language spoken at home	2,747	3,111	5,858	1,558	1,304	2,862	526	279	805	4,831	4,694	9,525
Speak English very well	1,972	2,248	4,220	1,439	1,181	2,620	484	261	745	3,895	3,690	7,585
Speak English not well	775	863	1,638	119	123	242	42	18	60	936	1,004	1,940
MEANS OF TRANSPORTATION												
Workers 16 and over	102,651	54,339	156,990	70,962	36,464	107,426	21,006	6,869	27,875	194,619	97,672	292,291
Car, truck, or van	80,444	30,331	110,775	59,432	24,792	84,224	16,069	4,859	20,928	155,945	59,982	215,927
Drive alone	63,811	15,605	79,416	48,395	17,550	65,945	12,925	3,589	16,514	125,131	36,744	161,875
Carpool	16,633	14,726	31,359	11,037	7,242	18,279	3,144	1,270	4,414	30,814	23,238	54,052
Public transportation	13,820	12,854	26,674	7,441	7,495	14,936	2,975	1,121	4,096	24,236	21,470	45,706
Walked only	6,428	9,841	16,269	2,955	3,265	6,220	1,099	632	1,731	10,482	13,738	24,220
Other means	832	424	1,256	615	297	912	288	93	381	1,735	814	2,549
Worked at home	1,127	889	2,016	519	615	1,134	575	164	739	2,221	1,668	3,889

TABLE 6.36
EDUCATION, RESIDENCE IN 1975 OF PERSONS OF TOTAL ITALIAN ANCESTRY BORN IN ITALY BY EDUCATION: 1980

	LESS THAN 12 YEARS OF SCHOOL			HIGH SCHOOL GRADUATES			COLLEGE GRADUATES			ALL PERSONS		
	Male	Female	Total	Male	Female	Total	Male	Female	Total	Male	Female	Total
SCHOOL ENROLLMENT												
Persons 3 years old and over enrolled	13,710	13,209	26,919	6,405	4,668	11,073	2,100	1,193	3,293	22,215	19,070	41,285
Nursery school	98	57	155	0	0	0	0	0	0	98	57	155
Public	12	16	28	0	0	0	0	0	0	12	16	28
Private	86	41	127	0	0	0	0	0	0	86	41	127
Kindergarten& Elementary (1-8 years)	7,010	6,298	13,308	0	0	0	0	0	0	7,010	6,298	13,308
Public	5,365	4,775	10,140	0	0	0	0	0	0	5,365	4,775	10,140
Private	1,645	1,523	3,168	0	0	0	0	0	0	1,645	1,523	3,168
High School (1 to 4 years)	6,602	6,854	13,456	0	0	0	0	0	0	6,602	6,854	13,456
Public	5,527	5,571	11,098	0	0	0	0	0	0	5,527	5,571	11,098
Private	1,075	1,283	2,358	0	0	0	0	0	0	1,075	1,283	2,358
College	0	0	0	6,405	4,668	11,073	2,100	1,193	3,293	8,505	5,861	14,366
YEARS OF SCHOOL COMPLETED												
Persons 25 years and over	245,699	287,933	533,632	90,197	81,583	171,780	25,944	12,357	38,301	361,840	381,873	743,713
Elementary (0 to 8 years)	206,175	252,230	458,405	0	0	0	0	0	0	206,175	252,230	458,405
High School: 1 to 3 years	39,524	35,703	75,227	0	0	0	0	0	0	39,524	35,703	75,227
4 or more years	0	0	0	67,536	67,395	134,931	0	0	0	67,536	67,395	134,931
College: 1 to 3 years	0	0	0	22,661	14,188	36,849	0	0	0	22,661	14,188	36,849
4 or more years	0	0	0	0	0	0	25,944	12,357	38,301	25,944	12,357	38,301
Percent High School Graduates				100.0	100.0	100.0	100.0	100.0	100.0	32.1	24.6	28.2
RESIDENCE IN 1975												
Persons 5 years and over	262,089	302,551	564,640	99,099	92,523	191,622	27,067	13,275	40,342	388,255	408,349	796,604
Same house	193,224	228,338	421,562	62,155	60,682	122,837	14,152	7,224	21,376	269,531	296,244	565,775
Different house in United States	60,772	65,564	126,336	32,779	28,497	61,276	10,732	4,834	15,566	104,283	98,895	203,178
Same County	42,394	45,031	87,425	20,932	18,438	39,370	5,651	2,723	8,374	68,977	66,192	135,169
Different County	18,378	20,533	38,911	11,847	10,059	21,906	5,081	2,111	7,192	35,306	32,703	68,009
Same State	11,313	12,792	24,105	7,117	5,502	12,619	2,543	1,039	3,582	20,973	19,333	40,306
Different State	7,065	7,741	14,806	4,730	4,557	9,287	2,538	1,072	3,610	14,333	13,370	27,703
Abroad	8,093	8,649	16,742	4,165	3,344	7,509	2,183	1,217	3,400	14,441	13,210	27,651

TABLE 6.37
LABOR FORCE AND OCCUPATION OF PERSONS OF TOTAL ITALIAN ANCESTRY BORN IN ITALY BY EDUCATION: 1980

	Less Than 12 Years of School			High School Graduates			College Graduates			All Persons		
	Male	Female	Total	Male	Female	Total	Male	Female	Total	Male	Female	Total
Labor Force Status												
Persons 16 years and over	255,214	296,520	551,734	101,298	92,316	193,614	27,006	13,049	40,055	383,518	401,885	785,403
Labor force	116,069	64,685	180,754	76,986	40,138	117,124	21,935	7,320	29,255	214,990	112,143	327,133
Percent of persons 16 years	45.5	21.8	32.8	76.0	43.5	60.5	81.2	56.1	73.0	56.1	27.9	41.7
Civilian labor force	115,993	64,657	180,650	76,517	40,091	116,608	21,764	7,315	29,079	214,274	112,063	326,337
Employed	107,182	57,649	164,831	72,418	37,721	110,139	21,206	7,052	28,258	200,806	102,422	303,228
Unemployed	8,811	7,008	15,819	4,099	2,370	6,469	558	263	821	13,468	9,641	23,109
Percent of civ. labor force	7.6	10.8	8.8	5.4	5.9	5.5	2.6	3.6	2.8	6.3	8.6	7.1
Not in labor force	139,145	231,835	370,980	24,312	52,178	76,490	5,071	5,729	10,800	168,528	289,742	458,270
Class of Worker and Occupation												
Employed 16 years and ov.	107,182	57,649	164,831	72,418	37,721	110,139	21,206	7,052	28,258	200,806	102,422	303,228
Private wage and salary work.	84,676	51,216	135,892	58,089	31,851	89,940	14,311	4,152	18,463	157,076	87,219	244,295
Federal Government workers	1,450	386	1,836	1,778	787	2,565	899	244	1,143	4,127	1,417	5,544
State Government workers	1,117	847	1,964	1,040	968	2,008	1,355	600	1,955	3,512	2,415	5,927
Local Government workers	4,827	2,321	7,148	2,769	2,178	4,947	2,122	1,717	3,839	9,718	6,216	15,934
Self-employed workers	14,840	2,374	17,214	8,615	1,606	10,221	2,476	285	2,761	25,931	4,265	30,196
Unpaid family workers	272	505	777	127	331	458	43	54	97	442	890	1,332
Employed 16 years and over	107,182	57,649	164,831	72,418	37,721	110,139	21,206	7,052	28,258	200,806	102,422	303,228
Managerial and Professional	6,931	1,614	8,545	11,441	3,822	15,263	13,770	4,304	18,074	32,142	9,740	41,882
Execut., Administ., Manag.	6,161	1,031	7,192	8,673	2,288	10,961	4,884	871	5,755	19,718	4,190	23,908
Professional Specialty occupations	770	583	1,353	2,768	1,534	4,302	8,886	3,433	12,319	12,424	5,550	17,974
Technical, Sales, Administrative	8,525	8,551	17,076	12,938	19,406	32,344	3,881	1,849	5,730	25,344	29,806	55,150
Technician and related support	523	169	692	1,982	659	2,641	954	359	1,313	3,459	1,187	4,646
Sales Occupations	4,931	4,460	9,391	6,011	5,160	11,171	1,565	408	1,973	12,507	10,028	22,535
Administrative Support	3,071	3,922	6,993	4,945	13,587	18,532	1,362	1,082	2,444	9,378	18,591	27,969
Service Occupations	20,254	11,908	32,162	9,902	6,036	15,938	1,014	359	1,373	31,170	18,303	49,473
Private household occupations	43	527	570	13	116	129	20	20	56	663	719	1,382
Protective Service occupations	1,055	161	1,216	980	144	1,124	209	20	229	2,244	325	2,569
Other Service Occupations	19,156	11,220	30,376	8,909	5,776	14,685	805	319	1,124	28,870	17,315	46,185
Farming, forestry, fishing	3,475	156	3,631	1,054	78	1,132	154	6	160	4,683	240	4,923
Precision Prod., Craft, Repair	35,756	5,583	41,339	22,425	1,907	24,332	1,500	144	1,644	59,681	7,634	67,315
Operators, Fabricators, Laborers	32,241	29,837	62,078	14,658	6,472	21,130	887	390	1,277	47,786	36,699	84,485
Machine Oper., Assembl.	16,366	26,526	42,892	8,041	5,726	13,767	496	295	791	24,903	32,547	57,450
Transportation	5,391	347	5,738	2,844	83	2,927	201	24	225	8,436	454	8,890
Handlers, cleaners, helpers	10,484	2,964	13,448	3,773	663	4,436	190	71	261	14,447	3,698	18,145

TABLE 6.38
INDUSTRY, LABOR FORCE IN 1979 OF PERSONS OF TOTAL ITALIAN ANCESTRY BORN IN ITALY BY EDUCATION: 1980

	Less Than 12 Years of School			High School Graduates			College Graduates			All Persons		
	Male	Female	Total	Male	Female	Total	Male	Female	Total	Male	Female	Total
INDUSTRY												
Employed 16 years and over	107,182	57,649	164,831	72,418	37,721	110,139	21,206	7,052	28,258	200,806	102,422	303,228
Agriculture, Forestry, Fishing	2,910	189	3,099	1,193	129	1,322	349	22	371	4,452	340	4,792
Construction	18,366	338	18,704	8,639	427	9,066	977	40	1,017	27,982	805	28,787
Manufacturing	32,333	30,969	63,302	21,216	9,376	30,592	4,279	769	5,048	57,828	41,114	98,942
Nondurable goods	12,403	22,398	34,801	6,409	5,455	11,864	1,305	469	1,774	20,117	28,322	48,439
Durable goods	19,930	8,571	28,501	14,807	3,921	18,728	2,974	300	3,274	37,711	12,792	50,503
Transportation	5,131	350	5,481	4,371	846	5,217	767	133	900	10,269	1,329	11,598
Communications and Public Utilities	1,886	210	2,096	2,014	614	2,628	439	62	501	4,339	886	5,225
Wholesale Trade	3,328	1,099	4,427	2,861	1,195	4,056	752	105	857	6,941	2,399	9,340
Retail Trade	21,099	11,392	32,491	15,344	8,797	24,141	1,895	614	2,509	38,338	20,803	59,141
Finance, Insurance, Real Estate	3,057	1,176	4,233	3,279	4,825	8,104	1,561	613	2,174	7,897	6,614	14,511
Business and Repair Service	4,317	1,011	5,328	3,502	1,159	4,661	952	222	1,174	8,771	2,392	11,163
Personal, Entertainment, Recreational	8,417	4,038	12,455	4,592	2,554	7,146	508	176	684	13,517	6,768	20,285
Professional and Related Services	4,697	6,212	10,909	3,386	6,628	10,014	7,528	3,987	11,515	15,611	16,827	32,438
Health Services	1,442	3,059	4,501	1,076	2,938	4,014	2,197	719	2,916	4,715	6,716	11,431
Educational Services	2,275	2,337	4,612	1,279	2,288	3,567	3,081	2,823	5,904	6,635	7,448	14,083
Other Profess. & Related Services	980	816	1,796	1,031	1,402	2,433	2,250	445	2,695	4,261	2,663	6,924
Public Administration	1,641	665	2,306	2,021	1,171	3,192	1,199	309	1,508	4,861	2,145	7,006
LABOUR FORCE STATUS IN 1979												
Persons 16 ys. in Labor Force in 1979	121,924	69,337	191,261	79,551	43,729	123,280	22,706	7,821	30,527	224,181	120,887	345,068
Worked in 1979	119,811	67,322	187,133	78,820	42,786	121,606	22,577	7,667	30,244	221,208	117,775	338,983
50 to 52 weeks	74,650	30,925	105,575	56,420	24,630	81,050	16,240	3,810	20,050	147,310	59,365	206,675
40 to 49 weeks	20,289	13,069	33,358	10,479	6,357	16,836	3,479	1,671	5,150	34,247	21,097	55,344
1 to 39 weeks	24,872	23,328	48,200	11,921	11,799	23,720	2,858	2,186	5,044	39,651	37,313	76,964
35 or more hours per week	103,864	46,544	150,408	71,297	29,223	100,520	20,224	5,550	25,774	195,385	81,317	276,702
50 to 52 weeks	68,810	24,004	92,814	53,503	19,712	73,215	2,132	3,237	5,369	124,445	46,953	171,398
With unemployment in 1979	23,362	17,682	41,044	12,066	7,548	19,614	2,132	1,030	3,162	37,560	26,260	63,820
Unemployed 15 or more weeks	10,649	8,417	19,066	4,916	3,123	8,039	748	411	1,159	16,313	11,951	28,264
	16.3	17.3	16.7	15.2	15.3	15.2	13.8	16.2	14.6	15.8	16.7	16.2
WORKERS IN FAMILY IN 1979												
Families	193,102	30,769	223,871	74,519	7,933	82,452	18,934	1,222	20,156	286,555	39,924	326,479
No Workers	64,246	8,460	72,706	10,064	1,615	11,679	1,990	131	2,121	76,300	10,206	86,506
1 worker	57,298	13,520	70,818	26,602	3,421	30,023	6,928	535	7,463	90,828	17,476	108,304
2 or more workers	71,558	8,789	80,347	37,853	2,897	40,750	10,016	556	10,572	119,427	12,242	131,669

TABLE 6.39

INCOME CHARACTERISTICS OF PERSONS OF TOTAL ITALIAN ANCESTRY BORN IN ITALY BY EDUCATION: 1980

	LESS THAN 12 YEARS OF SCHOOL			HIGH SCHOOL GRADUATES			COLLEGE GRADUATES			ALL PERSONS		
INCOME IN 1979												
HOUSEHOLDS	215,654	96,104	311,758	81,656	18,389	100,045	22,128	3,093	25,221	319,438	117,586	437,024
Less than $5,000	22,219	44,197	66,416	4,408	5,503	9,911	909	528	1,437	27,536	50,228	77,764
$5,000 to $7,499	27,661	16,405	44,066	4,715	2,543	7,258	782	257	1,039	33,158	19,205	52,363
$7,500 to $9,999	24,623	8,964	33,587	4,594	2,127	6,721	763	184	947	29,980	11,275	41,255
$10,000 to $14,999	36,976	9,590	46,566	11,271	3,168	14,439	1,856	486	2,342	50,103	13,244	63,347
$15,000 to $19,999	30,867	5,676	36,543	13,368	1,876	15,244	2,535	532	3,067	46,770	8,084	54,854
$20,000 to $24,999	25,062	3,881	28,943	13,543	1,100	14,643	2,914	383	3,297	41,519	5,364	46,883
$25,000 to $34,999	28,235	4,222	32,457	16,820	1,217	18,037	5,113	340	5,453	50,168	5,779	55,947
$35,000 to $49,999	14,479	2,197	16,676	8,719	543	9,262	3,867	227	4,094	27,065	2,967	30,032
$50,000 or more	5,532	972	6,504	4,218	312	4,530	3,389	156	3,545	13,139	1,440	14,579
Median Dol.	14,429	5,587	11,268	20,797	8,850	18,835	27,138	15,743	25,883	17,025	6,115	13,720
Mean Dol.	17,610	9,376	15,014	23,356	12,447	21,113	32,633	18,817	28,777	19,913	9,847	17,205
FAMILIES	193,102	30,769	223,871	74,519	7,933	82,452	18,934	1,222	20,156	286,555	39,924	326,479
Less than $5,000	12,350	3,168	15,518	2,812	883	3,695	455	72	527	15,617	4,123	19,740
$5,000 to $7,499	22,863	3,344	26,207	3,783	840	4,623	548	33	581	27,194	4,217	31,411
$7,500 to $9,999	22,109	3,668	25,777	3,936	916	4,852	594	92	686	26,639	4,676	31,315
$10,000 to $14,999	34,719	5,785	40,504	10,171	1,540	11,711	1,351	170	1,521	46,241	7,495	53,736
$15,000 to $19,999	29,500	4,583	34,083	12,303	1,237	13,540	2,030	219	2,249	43,833	6,039	49,872
$20,000 to $24,999	24,216	3,530	27,746	12,841	782	13,623	2,524	167	2,691	39,581	4,479	44,060
$25,000 to $34,999	27,769	3,788	31,557	16,286	1,048	17,334	4,654	178	4,832	48,709	5,014	53,723
$35,000 to $49,999	14,236	2,056	16,292	8,414	471	8,885	3,561	193	3,754	26,211	2,720	28,931
$50,000 or more	5,340	847	6,187	3,973	216	4,189	3,217	98	3,315	12,530	1,161	13,691
Median Dol.	15,707	14,474	15,576	21,463	14,214	21,030	28,686	20,679	28,573	18,147	14,634	17,711
Mean Dol.	18,681	17,654	18,607	24,111	17,859	23,279	34,636	24,993	31,419	20,955	17,869	20,578

TABLE 6.39 (Cont'd)
INCOME CHARACTERISTICS OF PERSONS OF TOTAL ITALIAN ANCESTRY BORN IN ITALY BY EDUCATION: 1980

	Less Than 12 Years of School			High School Graduates			College Graduates			All Persons		
Unrelated Individuals, 15 years....	24,345	66,986	91,331	9,150	11,647	20,797	4,201	2,376	6,577	37,696	81,009	118,705
Less than $2,000	1,455	5,262	6,717	920	1,219	2,139	382	331	713	2,757	6,812	9,569
$2,000 to $2,999	1,606	7,596	9,202	430	920	1,350	143	86	229	2,179	8,602	10,781
$3,000 to $4,999	8,042	30,084	38,126	1,417	3,363	4,780	422	392	814	9,881	33,839	43,720
$5,000 to $7,999	6,061	14,837	20,898	1,521	2,246	3,767	542	335	877	8,124	17,418	25,542
$8,000 to $9,999	2,013	3,713	5,726	602	1,044	1,646	172	133	305	2,787	4,890	7,677
$10,000 to $14,999	2,516	3,759	6,275	1,549	1,711	3,260	685	390	1,075	4,750	5,860	10,610
$15,000 to $24,999	2,069	1,344	3,413	1,854	912	2,766	1,056	517	1,573	4,979	2,773	7,752
$25,000 to $49,999	483	327	810	687	149	836	675	176	851	1,845	652	2,497
$50,000 or more	100	64	164	170	83	253	124	16	140	394	163	557
Median Dol.	5,410	4,240	4,560	8,935	5,400	6,696	12,839	8,846	11,630	5,816	4,483	4,784
Mean Dol.	7,593	5,208	6,450	12,252	7,482	10,098	16,025	11,157	14,995	10,216	6,328	7,563
Per Capita Income Dol.	10,165	3,812	6,763	15,437	4,932	10,428	23,369	8,718	18,596	12,431	4,220	8,205
Mean Family Income By Worker												
No Workers Dol.	9,465	8,700	9,376	11,254	10,237	11,113	17,026	17,039	17,027	9,898	9,050	9,798
1 Worker Dol.	18,082	17,127	17,900	20,603	16,851	20,175	33,309	18,943	32,279	19,982	17,129	19,521
2 or more workers Dol.	27,435	27,083	27,396	29,994	23,298	29,518	39,054	32,689	38,719	29,221	26,442	28,962

TABLE 6.40

POVERTY CHARACTERISTICS OF PERSONS OF TOTAL ITALIAN ANCESTRY BORN IN ITALY BY EDUCATION: 1980

	Less Than 12 Years of School			High School Graduates			College Graduates			All Persons		
	Male	Female	Total	Male	Female	Total	Male	Female	Total	Male	Female	Total
ALL INCOME LEVEL IN 1979												
Families	193,102	30,769	223,871	74,519	7,933	82,452	18,934	1,222	20,156	286,555	39,924	326,479
With Children under 18 years	66,180	5,480	71,660	39,080	3,086	42,166	9,448	454	9,902	114,708	9,020	123,728
With Children 5 to 17 years	59,667	4,956	64,623	31,087	2,622	33,709	7,143	408	7,551	97,897	7,986	105,883
Female Householder, no husband	0	26,484	26,484	0	6,405	6,405	0	889	889	0	33,778	33,778
With Children under 18 ys.	0	4,605	4,605	0	2,495	2,495	0	372	372	0	7,472	7,472
With Children under 6 years	0	820	820	0	649	649	0	77	77	0	1,546	1,546
Householder 65 years and over	95,522	21,912	117,434	15,262	2,373	17,635	3,683	273	3,956	114,467	24,558	139,025
Unrelat. Individ. in pov.	24,298	66,979	91,277	8,600	11,398	19,998	4,112	2,344	6,456	37,010	80,721	117,731
65 years and over	19,338	60,925	80,263	2,737	6,907	9,644	667	884	1,551	22,742	68,716	91,458
Persons in poverty univ.	260,843	298,594	559,437	100,112	90,852	190,964	26,720	12,807	39,527	387,675	402,253	789,928
Related children under 18	12,850	11,954	24,804	110	154	264	0	0	0	12,960	12,108	25,068
Related children 5 to 17	12,180	11,496	23,676	110	154	264	0	0	0	12,290	11,650	23,940
60 years and over	147,403	185,112	332,515	25,163	24,054	49,217	6,005	2,961	8,966	178,571	212,127	390,698
65 years and over	133,020	169,443	302,463	20,140	19,167	39,307	4,837	2,362	7,199	157,997	190,972	348,969
INCOME IN 1979 BELOW POVERTY												
Families	12,437	3,143	15,580	3,524	1,080	4,604	564	78	642	16,525	4,301	20,826
Percent Below Poverty Level	6.4	10.2	7.0	4.7	13.6	5.6	3.0	6.4	3.2	5.8	10.8	6.4
With Children under 18 years	5,244	1,306	6,550	2,085	822	2,907	303	57	360	7,632	2,185	9,817
With Children 5 to 17 years	4,624	1,189	5,813	1,647	674	2,321	256	38	294	6,527	1,901	8,428
Female Householder, no husband	0	2,824	2,824	0	932	932	0	73	73	0	3,829	3,829
With Children under 18 ys.	0	1,229	1,229	0	762	762	0	52	52	0	2,043	2,043
With Children under 6 years	0	251	251	0	308	308	0	19	19	0	578	578
Householder 65 years and over	6,008	1,672	7,680	992	133	1,125	136	9	145	7,136	1,814	8,950
Unrelat. Individ. in pov.	4,656	20,662	25,318	353	195	548	637	492	1,129	5,646	21,349	26,995
Percent Below Poverty Level	19.2	30.8	27.7	4.1	1.7	2.7	15.5	21.0	17.5	15.3	26.4	22.9
65 years and over	3,862	18,677	22,539	463	1,912	2,375	113	211	324	4,438	20,800	25,238
Persons in poverty univ.	20,075	36,264	56,339	5,621	7,246	12,867	1,251	931	2,182	26,947	44,441	71,388
Percent Below Poverty Level	7.7	12.1	10.1	5.6	8.0	6.7	4.7	7.3	5.5	7.0	11.0	9.0
Related children under 18	1,664	1,511	3,175	11	17	28	0	0	0	1,675	1,528	3,203
Related children 5 to 17	1,575	1,420	2,995	11	17	28	0	0	0	1,586	1,437	3,023
60 years and over	11,324	26,184	37,508	1,809	3,119	4,928	292	346	638	13,425	29,649	43,074
65 years and over	10,508	24,566	35,074	1,555	2,692	4,247	256	309	565	12,319	27,567	39,886

12.95